One Way and Another

By the same author

Winnicott
On Kissing, Tickling and Being Bored
On Flirtation
Terrors and Experts
Monogamy
The Beast in the Nursery
Darwin's Worms
Promises, Promises
Houdini's Box
Equals
Going Sane
Intimacies (with Leo Bersani)
Side Effects
On Kindness (with Barbara Taylor)
The Concise Dictionary of Dress (with Judith Clark)
On Balance
Missing Out

EDITOR OF

Charles Lamb: Selected Prose
Walter Pater: The Renaissance
Edmund Burke: A Philosophical Enquiry
The Electrified Tightrope: Selected Psychoanalytic
Papers of Michael Eigen
Richard Howard: Selected Poems
(with Hugh Haughton)
John Clare in Context (with Hugh Haughton)
The Book of Interruptions (with David Hillman)
General Editor of the new Penguin Modern
Classics Freud translations

One Way and Another
New and Selected Essays

ADAM PHILLIPS

HAMISH HAMILTON
an imprint of
PENGUIN BOOKS

HAMISH HAMILTON

Published by the Penguin Group
Penguin Books Ltd, 80 Strand, London WC2R ORL, England
Penguin Group (USA) Inc., 375 Hudson Street, New York, New York 10014, USA
Penguin Group (Canada), 90 Eglinton Avenue East, Suite 700, Toronto, Ontario, Canada M4P 2Y3
(a division of Pearson Penguin Canada Inc.)
Penguin Ireland, 25 St Stephen's Green, Dublin 2, Ireland (a division of Penguin Books Ltd)
Penguin Group (Australia), 707 Collins Street, Melbourne, Victoria 3008, Australia
(a division of Pearson Australia Group Pty Ltd)
Penguin Books India Pvt Ltd, 11 Community Centre, Panchsheel Park, New Delhi – 110 017, India
Penguin Group (NZ), 67 Apollo Drive, Rosedale, Auckland 0632, New Zealand
(a division of Pearson New Zealand Ltd)
Penguin Books (South Africa) (Pty) Ltd, Block D, Rosebank Office Park,
181 Jan Smuts Avenue, Parktown North, Gauteng 2193, South Africa

Penguin Books Ltd, Registered Offices: 80 Strand, London WC2R ORL, England

www.penguin.com

First published 2013
001

Copyright © Adam Phillips, 2013
Introduction copyright © John Banville, 2013

The moral right of the authors has been asserted

'With God On Our Side', Words and Music by Bob Dylan © 1963. Reproduced by
Permission of Special Rider Music, London W1F 9LD

Set in 12/14.75pt Bembo Book MT Std
Typeset by Jouve (UK), Milton Keynes
Printed in Great Britain by Clays Ltd, St Ives plc

A CIP catalogue record for this book is available from the British Library

ISBN: 978-0-241-14580-7

www.greenpenguin.co.uk

For Mia, Marianne and Seth

i migliori fabbri

I would not pay overmuch attention to these theories, beyond using them for all they are worth.

James Joyce, Letter to Harriet
Shaw Weaver, 21 May 1926

The surprising fact, C, is observed;
But if A were true, C would be a matter of course.
Hence, there is reason to suspect that A is true.

C. S. Peirce, *Collected Papers*, Vol. V

She fingered his thick hair. 'Don't make me into something I'm not.'
'Why,' he said. 'I'm always making myself into something I'm not.'

M K Ahn, 'Long and Oval'

They told exactly the same story only it was different, very different.

Gertrude Stein, *The Autobiography of Alice B. Toklas*

Contents

Introduction

Adam Phillips is that rarest of phenomena, a trained clinician who is also a sublime writer. He is a psychoanalyst with a special interest in the treatment of children; as a writer his interests appear limitless. Comparisons, if not entirely odious, are certainly inadequate, yet it is hard to resist suggesting that the literary figure Phillips most resembles, in his irrepressible curiosity and breadth of reference, is Sir Thomas Browne. Phillips insists that psychoanalysis and psychoanalytic writing are a kind of poetry, and the ingenious machinery that is his own work harks back to the Metaphysical poets from whom Browne took so many conceits of style and topic.

One Way and Another, a selection from Phillips's numerous earlier books along with a generous handful of pieces published in periodicals but not collected in book form, gives a broad overview of his thinking, especially in regard to the present state of psychoanalysis. In these essays he treats of his discipline not so much in terms of therapy – although he writes always with the authority and insight of a practitioner – but as a strategy for dealing with life, with other people, and with our worldly predicament as creatures who pay an enormous price for the privilege of being able to think, to choose, to remember and to forget.

In the final piece here, 'Coda: Up to a Point' – which one might suggest, perhaps heretically, as a good place for the reader to start – Adam Phillips points to the interesting fact that psychoanalysts, including Freud, the daddy of them all, rarely describe their written work as essays: 'they tend to write lectures or papers or chapters, or what are called, perhaps optimistically, contributions'. Typically, out of this small observation he elaborates an intricate meditation on what it is to make an essay – that is, to test or attempt – without the illusory expectation of making an end. He points out that Freud's *Three Essays on the Theory of Sexuality* in part explore, hermeneutically, what it might be that would constitute an ending, and concludes, following Freud, that 'The desire for completion is the nearest we are ever going to get to completion.'

From the start, the question of ending has preoccupied psychoanalysis, presenting to psychoanalysts and patients alike a worry that will not go away. Phillips devotes to the topic an absorbing and stimulating essay, with the endearing title 'Talking Nonsense and Knowing When to Stop'. In it, he adapts Paul Valéry's pronouncement on the poem and suggests that 'an analysis is never finished, it is only abandoned'. The calm good sense on display here is as exemplary as it is welcome. Psychoanalytic theory, Phillips points out, 'is a more or less coherent, plausible and persuasive account of guess-work', and psychoanalysis proceeds in part by allowing the patient – a word Phillips is never entirely comfortable with – the freedom to utter a great deal of what, on the face of it, may sound like, may even be, gibberish. Here, again, Phillips turns to the poets, and ends with Wallace Stevens's beautiful and consoling line from *Notes Toward a Supreme Fiction*: 'Life's nonsense pierces us with strange relation.'

Phillips's prose is poetic in the best sense; it is muscular, resonant, and thrums with a dark music that is all its own. He eschews metaphor and tropes in general in favour of directness and clarity, so that alongside the Metaphysical bent there is his debt to the great essayists of the eighteenth and early nineteenth century – Doctor Johnson makes a happy appearance when his definition of the essay as 'a loose sally of the mind . . . not a regular and orderly composition' is adduced, with the trace of a rueful smile, as a handy description of a psychoanalytic session.

Psychoanalytic writing, Phillips shrewdly remarks, 'has been tyrannized by the wish to get something right at the cost of saying something interesting and useful'. His own work is blessedly free of such tyranny. He identifies the best and most desirable characteristics of the essay form as 'genial scepticism, hospitable curiosity, the sociability of knowledge', qualities that are on display on every page of this collection. He ends the list, 'of course', with 'inspired dogmatism'. The glory of *One Way and Another* is that it is never dogmatic, and never less than inspired.

Phillips is an unregenerate Freudian, and will have no truck with the blustering dismissals of the founding father that have become fashionable, inside and outside of professional psychoanalytic circles, since the Freudian heyday in the two or three decades after the Second World War. His attitude towards the 'Viennese quack', as Vladimir Nabokov gleefully had it, is sensible and judicious. He has a deep reverence for him – no Oedipal drive here – not as a scientist, but as a deviser of scenarios, as a fabulist of genius. He suggests, in a footnote, that 'it is more illuminating to read psychoanalysts as poets – mostly, of course, poor ones – rather than failed or aspiring scientists . . .' Continuing this theme elsewhere he writes:

> Freud sometimes calls what happens in the gap we call forgetting, 'dream-work'; and at other times, though he does not use this phrase, 'art-work'. The making of a dream, like the making of a work of art, in his account, is essentially a process of reworking . . . And these reworkings, these phantasmal constructions, are akin to that protracted unconscious free-floating attention that Freud prescribed for the analyst. What the analyst does from outside, the dreamer and the artist do from inside: a sustained, forgetful self-listening.

In this context Phillips pays due attention to Freud's own bemused acknowledgement that his case histories frequently read more like short stories than medical reports. Freud, especially in the early part of his career, devoted much jealous energy to the attempt at validating psychoanalysis as scientifically based. Phillips prefers to think of the analyst's work, and the patient's, not only as a poetic endeavour but also as a kind of ongoing shared narrative the end purpose of which is not so much curative as normative. '[T]he aim of psychoanalysis,' he writes, 'is not to cure people but to show them that there is nothing wrong with them.' Freud would surely have approved of this formula, echoing as it does Freud himself who, when one of his women patients asked him if he would be able to cure her, gently replied that all he could do would be to restore her to ordinary human unhappiness. ' "Cure",' Phillips writes, with dry wit, 'is the psychoanalytic word for the happy ending.' The implication here, of course, is that not only is there no happy ending, there is no ending at all, save for the obvious and terrible one awaiting every one of us.

The range of these essays is breathtaking, from the first, 'On Tickling', to the last, 'Psychoanalysis; or, Is It Worth It?' – the latter reverts to the ticklish topic of ending, with the insistence that 'psychoanalysts . . . are interested . . . not in cures but in new ways of living' – with considerations along the way of such subjects as 'Clutter', which takes in the painter Francis Bacon's studio and parental despair over their teenage children's bedrooms, and 'Arbus's Freaks', who Phillips wonderfully suggests are 'a bit like Jews, born members of the aristocracy of trauma'.

One of the most significant, and certainly one of the most substantial, essays here, 'The Dream Horizon', goes to the very heart of the psychoanalytic project. Phillips begins by observing that if we did not dream, very many things in life would be different, for instance 'the way we describe prophecy, reality, scepticism, memory, desire, identity, irrationality and hope . . .' The dream is always stranger than we know, more potent, more subversive, and carries in its limitless depths a greater load of information about ourselves than we care to acknowledge. And yet 'dreams show us . . . that there is somewhere else, somewhere beyond our sovereignty though, which each individual is nevertheless the sovereign reporter of . . . Paradoxically . . . in our dreams we are at once most obscurely and most essentially ourselves.'

From the psychoanalytical point of view, the dream is not quite 'the royal road to the unconscious' that Freud claimed it to be. There is the question of what it is that constitutes a dream, or, rather, what it is that remains of the dream after it has been dreamed. 'Our dreams,' Phillips writes, 'will only ever be apparently available in language . . . by the time you are providing your account the dream is no longer there, and the listener is never in a position to compare the account with its object.' This is an obvious and yet a profoundly disturbing state of affairs, for the analyst more than the analysand. All descriptions of dreams are partial, necessarily, and are radically edited. The patient on the couch is at one remove from his dream, but the doctor is at a far greater distance from it. Phillips quotes a passage from a book by the art critic Michael Baxandall – is there *anything* Phillips has not read? – which points out that commentators such as Vasari wrote in the assumption that their readers would not be familiar with the pictures being discussed, would probably never even have seen them, and therefore 'his celebrated and strange descriptions are often calculated to evoke the character of works not known to the reader . . .' When it comes to describing our dreams, Phillips remarks, we are all Vasaris. What is it, then, that the psychoanalyst 'interprets'? Not the dream, in fact – in fact! – but the dreamer's 'strange description' of it. So that Freud's seminal work should more properly have been called *The Interpretation of the Interpretations of Dreams*.

From this and numerous other interventions we see not just how fearless Phillips is in probing the assumptions and claims of psychoanalysis, but how subversive he can be. In the essay 'Bombs Away', for instance, he examines the testaments of a number of psychotherapists, such as Melanie Klein and D. W. Winnicott, and relates a funny, absurd and unsettling incident during the Blitz when at a meeting of the British Psychoanalytical Society, with bombs falling all round, Winnicott stood up and said: 'I should like to point out there is an air-raid going on,' and sat down. The person reporting the occasion observed: 'No notice was taken and the meeting went on as before.' This, according to Phillips, 'is a formulation of the problem; how could you make the war real for the psychoanalysts of the British Society, get them to notice it, or pay attention to it, so that the meeting is interrupted?' In other words, was it an instance of the mind-doctors' sangfroid, or of their blinkered indifference?

Here Phillips identifies an essential dichotomy in psychoanalysis: is the analyst in need of analysing, and if so, who is there who can take on the task? And further, what, in the end, is the end of psychoanalysis? Phillips can be bleak in his conclusions – 'Analysis may be more of a search for dreams than of a search for insight' – yet he never really doubts the value of his chosen discipline, in its essays as well as in its achievements. Like Freud's book on slips and mistakes, psychoanalysis 'reveals with scientific sobriety the slapstick of everyday life' and thereby both aids in and seeks to meliorate 'Man's preposterous project' of escaping from himself, his obsessions and traumas, his intolerable desires.

On Tickling

We have pushed a process into a goal.

D. H. Lawrence, *Aaron's Rod*

If you tickle us do we not laugh? asks Shylock, defining himself as human as he begins to 'feed' his revenge. And what is more ordinary in the child's life than his hunger for revenge and, indeed, the experience of being tickled? From a psychoanalytic point of view it is curious that this common, perhaps universal, experience has never been thought about; and not surprising that once we look at it we can see so much.

An absolute of calculation and innocence, the adult's tickling of the child is an obviously acceptable form of sensuous excitement between parents and children in the family. An initiation, perhaps, into a kind of ecstasy. The child who will be able to feed himself, the child who will masturbate, will never, of course, be able to tickle himself. It is the pleasure he cannot reproduce in the absence of the other. 'From the fact that a child can hardly tickle itself,' Darwin wrote in his *Expression of the Emotions in Man and Animals*, 'or in a much less degree than when tickled by another person, it seems that the precise point to be touched must not be known.' An enigmatic conclusion, which though manifestly untrue – children know exactly, like adults, where they are ticklish – alerts us to the fact that these 'precise points' are a kind of useless knowledge to the child, that they matter only as shared knowledge. They require the enacted recognition of another person.

Helpless with pleasure, and usually inviting this helplessness, the child in the ordinary, affectionate, perverse scenario of being tickled, is wholly exploitable. Particular adults know where the child is ticklish – it is, of course, only too easy to find out – but it is always idiosyncratic, a piece of personal history, and rarely what Freud called one of the 'predestined erotogenic zones'. Through tickling, the child will be initiated in a distinctive way into the helplessness and disarray of a certain primitive kind of pleasure, dependent on the adult to hold and not to exploit the experience. And this means to stop at that blurred point, so acutely felt in tickling, at which pleasure becomes pain, and the child experiences an intensely anguished confusion; because the tickling narrative, unlike the sexual narrative, has no climax. It has to stop or the real humiliation begins. The child, as the mother says, will get hysterical.

In English, the meaning of the word 'tickle' is, so to speak, almost antithetical, employing, as Freud said of the dream-work, 'the same means of representation for expressing contraries'. The *Oxford English Dictionary* cites, among nineteen definitions of the word, the following: 'In unstable equilibrium, easily upset or overthrown, insecure, tottering, crazy . . . nicely poised.' Other definitions describe a range of experience from excessive credulity to incontinence. The word speaks of the precarious, and so of the erotic. To tickle is, above all, to seduce, often by amusement. But of the two references to tickling in Freud (both in the *Three Essays*), it is used as virtually synonymous with stroking: included, quite accurately and unobtrusively, as part of the child's ordinary sensuous life. Describing the characteristics of an erotogenic zone, Freud writes:

> It is part of the skin or mucous membrane in which stimuli of a certain sort evoke a feeling of pleasure possessing a particular quality. There can be no doubt that the stimuli which produce the pleasure are governed by special conditions, though we do not know what those are. A rhythmic character must play a part among them and the analogy of tickling is forced upon our notice. It seems less certain whether the character of the pleas-

urable feeling evoked by the stimulus should be described as a 'specific' one – a 'specific' quality in which the sexual factor would precisely lie. Psychology is still so much in the dark in questions of pleasure and unpleasure that the most cautious assumption is the one most to be recommended.

Freud is certain here only of what he does not know. But in the light of this, which provokes the most careful questions, what is the most cautious assumption we can make about these specific pleasures called tickling and being tickled? In the elaborate repertoire of intrusions, what is the quality – that is to say, the fantasy – of the experience? Certainly there is no immediate, pressing biological need in this intent, often frenetic contact that so quickly reinstates a distance, only equally quickly to create another invitation. Is the tickling scene, at its most reassuring, not a unique representation of the overdisplacement of desire, and, at its most unsettling, a paradigm of the perverse contract? Does it not highlight, this delightful game, the impossibility of satisfaction and of reunion, with its continual re-enactment of the irresistible attraction and the inevitable repulsion of the object, in which the final satisfaction is frustration?

A girl of eight who keeps 'losing her stories' in the session because she has too much to say, who cannot keep still for a moment, suddenly interrupts herself by saying to me, 'I can only think of you when I don't think of you.' This same, endlessly elusive child – elusiveness, which is the inverse of obsessionality – ends a session telling me, 'When we play monsters, and Mummy catches me, she never kills me, she only tickles me!'

'We can cause laughing by tickling the skin,' Darwin noted of the only sensuous contact that makes one laugh. An extraordinary fact condensing so much of psychoanalytic interest, but one of which so little is spoken. Perhaps in the cumulative trauma that is development we have had the experience but deferred the meaning.

On Being Bored

I

Life, friends, is boring. We must not say so.

John Berryman, 'Dream Song 14'

Children are not oracles, but they ask with persistent regularity the great existential question, 'What shall we do?' Every adult remembers, among many other things, the great ennui of childhood, and every child's life is punctuated by spells of boredom: that state of suspended anticipation in which things are started and nothing begins, the mood of diffuse restlessness which contains that most absurd and paradoxical wish, the wish for a desire.

As psychoanalysis has brought to our attention the passionate intensity of the child's internal world, it has tended to equate significance with intensity and so has rarely found a place, in theory, for all those less vehement, vaguer, often more subtle feelings and moods that much of our lives consist of. It is part of Winnicott's contribution to have alerted us to the importance, in childhood, of states of relative quiescence, of moods that could never figure, for example, in Melanie Klein's gothic melodrama of emotional development. Although there are several references in the psychoanalytic literature to the project of the boring patient, and fewer to the seemingly common adult fear of being boring, very little has been written about the child's ordinary experience of being bored, a mood that by definition seems to preclude elaborate description. As any child will tell us, it's just having nothing to do. But moods, of course, are points of view.

Clinically one comes across children unable to be bored, and more often, children unable to be anything else. In any discussion of waiting, at least in relation to the child, it makes sense to speak of boredom because the bored child is waiting, unconsciously, for an experience of anticipation. In ordinary states of boredom the child returns to the possibility of his own desire. That boredom is actually a precarious process in which the child is, as it were, both waiting for something and looking for something, in which hope is being secretly negotiated; and in this sense boredom is akin to free-floating attention. In the muffled, sometimes irritable, confusion of boredom the child is reaching to a recurrent sense of emptiness out of which his real desire can crystallize. But to begin with, of course, the child needs the adult to hold, and hold to, the experience – that is, to recognize it as such, rather than to sabotage it by distraction. The child's boredom starts as a regular crisis in the child's developing capacity to be alone in the presence of the mother. In other words, the capacity to be bored can be a developmental achievement for the child.

Experiencing a frustrating pause in his usually mobile attention and absorption, the bored child quickly becomes preoccupied by his lack of preoccupation. Not exactly waiting for someone else, he is, as it were, waiting for himself. Neither hopeless nor expectant, neither intent nor resigned, the child is in a dull helplessness of possibility and dismay. In simple terms the child always has two concurrent, overlapping projects: the project of self-sufficiency in which use of, and need for, the other is interpreted, by the child, as a concession; and a project of mutuality that owns up to, and can even enjoy, a dependence. In the banal crisis of boredom, the conflict between the two projects is once again renewed. Is it not, indeed, revealing what the child's boredom evokes in the adults? Heard as a demand, sometimes as an accusation of failure or disappointment, it is rarely agreed to, simply acknowledged. How often, in fact, the child's boredom is met by that most perplexing form of disapproval, the adult's wish to distract him – as though the adults have decided that the child's life must be, or be seen to be, endlessly interesting. It is one of the most oppressive demands of adults that the child should be interested, rather than take time to find what interests him. Boredom is integral to the process of taking one's time.

While the child's boredom is often recognized as an incapacity, it is usually denied as an opportunity. A precociously articulate eleven-year-old boy was referred to me because, in his mother's words, he was 'more miserable than he realized', and had no friends because of his 'misleading self-presentation'. For several weeks, while we got to know each other, he chatted fluently in a quite happy, slightly dissociated way about his vast array of interests and occupations. The only significant negative transference occurred when he mentioned, in passing, that he might sometimes be too busy to come and see me. He was mostly in a state of what I can only describe as blank exuberance about how full his life was. As he was terrified of his own self-doubt, I asked him very few questions, and they were always tactful. But at one point, more direct than I intended to be, I asked him if he was ever bored. He was surprised by the question and replied, with a gloominess I hadn't seen before in this relentlessly cheerful child, 'I'm not allowed to be bored.' I asked him what would happen if he allowed himself to be bored, and he paused for the first time, I think, in the treatment, and said, 'I wouldn't know what I was looking forward to,' and was, momentarily, quite panic-stricken by this thought. This led us, over the next year, into a discussion of what in one language would be called this boy's false self. Being good, in terms of the maternal demand, was having lots of interests; interests, that is, of a respectable, unembarrassing sort, nothing that could make him feel awkward and strong. In the course of the treatment he gradually developed in himself a new capacity, the capacity to be bored. I once suggested to him that being good was a way of stopping people knowing him, to which he agreed but added, 'When I'm bored I don't know myself!'

If the bored child cannot sufficiently hold the mood, or use the adult as an unimpinging auxiliary ego, there is a premature flight from uncertainty, the familiar orgy of promiscuous and disappointing engagements that is also, as it were, a trial action in action, a trying things out. At its worst there is what the adult will come to know, from his repertoire of displacements, as the simulation of his desire, which in the child often takes the form of a regressive fabrication of need (and culture, through education, can pre-empt the elaboration of desire by prematurely naming what we want; urges and impulses of bodily life are often too quickly identified, as language speaks on our behalf).

A boy of eight referred for – that is, described as – being 'excessively greedy and always bored', said to me in the first session, 'If I eat everything I won't have to eat any more.' This could have meant several things, but for him it meant that if he could eat everything then he would no longer need to be hungry. One magical solution, of course, to the problem of having been tantalized is to have no desire. For this boy greed was, among other things, an attack on the desiring part of the self, a wish to get to the end of his appetite and finish with it once and for all. Part of the total fantasy of greed is always the attempt to eat up one's own appetite. But for this desolate child greed was a form of self-cure for a malign boredom that continually placed him on the threshold of an emptiness, a lack, which he couldn't bear; an emptiness in which his own idiosyncratic, unconscious desire lurked as a possibility. When I asked him if he was ever lonely, he said that he was 'too bored to be lonely'.

II

Inability to tolerate empty space limits the amount of
space available.

W. R. Bion, *Cogitations*

The child is dependent not only on the mother, but also on his
desire. Both can be lost and refound. So perhaps boredom is
merely the mourning of everyday life? 'It is really only because
we know so well how to explain it,' Freud wrote of mourning,
'that this attitude does not seem to us pathological.' But the
child's boredom is a mood that seems to negate the possibility of
explanation. It is itself unexplaining, inarticulate; certainly not
pathological but nevertheless somehow unacceptable. Some of
the things Freud says in 'Mourning and Melancholia' about the
melancholic can easily be said of the bored child. 'One feels . . .
a loss . . . has occurred, but one cannot see clearly what it is that
has been lost, and it is all the more reasonable to suppose that the
patient cannot consciously perceive what he has lost either.'
What the bored child experiences himself as losing is 'something to do' at the moment in which nothing is inviting. 'The
inhibition of the melancholic seems puzzling to us,' Freud
writes, 'because we cannot see what it is that is absorbing him so
entirely.' In a sense, the bored child is absorbed by his lack of
absorption, and yet he is also preparing for something of which
he is unaware, something that will eventually occasion an easy
transition or a mild surprise of interest. 'In mourning it is the
world that has become poor and empty; in melancholia it is the
ego itself.' And in boredom, we might add, it is both. The brief
but intense boredoms of childhood are reactive to no great loss,
but are merely an interruption – after something and before something else. Like all genuine transitional states, their destination is

unclear. Certainly when bored as an adult one cannot, in Freud's words from 'Mourning and Melancholia', 'hide the weakness of one's own nature'. But what, we might ask, following Freud's approach in this extraordinary paper, is the work that boredom performs for the child?

Winnicott, who often refers to instinctual life as a 'complication', provides a way of looking at boredom in his paper 'The Observation of Infants in a Set Situation' (1941), particularly with his notion of the period of hesitation, a state of preconscious surmise. In the set situation of Winnicott's consultation he asks 'the mother to sit opposite me with the angle of the table coming between me and her, she sits down with the baby on her knee. As a routine I place a right-angled shining tongue-depressor at the edge of the table and I invite the mother to place the child in such a way that, if the child should wish to handle the spatula, it is possible.' This sets the scene for the three stages of the infant's behaviour that are to become for Winnicott a paradigm of the analytic process. The spatula, like the 'good' interpretation, and even the analyst himself, is that which the patient is ready to use, that makes sense to him to use; and the setting is one in which the child 'only becomes able to find his desire again in so far as his testing of the environment affords satisfactory results'. The bored child is waiting, without the conscious representation of an object, to find his desire again. Once again he does not know what he is looking forward to. This is Winnicott's description of part of the process:

Stage 1. The baby puts his hand to the spatula, but at this moment discovers unexpectedly that the situation must be given thought. He is in a fix. Either with his hand resting on the spatula and his body quite still he looks at me and his mother with big eyes, and watches and waits, or, in certain cases, he withdraws interest completely and buries his face in the front of his mother's blouse. It is usually possible to manage the situation so that active reassurance is not given, and it is very interesting to watch the gradual and spontaneous return of the child's interest in the spatula.

Stage 2. All the time, in 'the period of hesitation' (as I call it), the baby holds his body still (but not rigid). Gradually he becomes brave enough to let his feelings develop, and then the picture changes quite quickly. The moment at which this first phase changes into the second is evident, for the child's acceptance of the reality of desire for the spatula is heralded by a change in the inside of the mouth, which becomes flabby, while the tongue looks thick and soft, and saliva flows copiously. Before long he puts the spatula into his mouth and is chewing it with his gums, or seems to be copying father smoking a pipe. The change in the baby's behaviour is a striking feature. Instead of expectancy and stillness there now develops self-confidence, and there is free bodily movement, the latter related to manipulation of the spatula.

I have frequently made the experiment of trying to get the spatula to the infant's mouth during the stage of hesitation. Whether the hesitation corresponds to my normal or differs from it in degree or quality, I find that it is impossible during this stage to get the spatula to the child's mouth apart from the exercise of brutal strength. In certain cases where the inhibition is acute any effort on my part that results in the spatula being moved towards the child produces screaming, mental distress, or actual colic.

The baby now seems to feel that the spatula is in his possession, perhaps in his power, certainly available for the purposes of self-expression.

Clearly, for the bored child nothing is 'available for the purposes of self-expression'. Instead of 'expectancy and stillness' there is a dreary agitation; instead of 'self-confidence, and . . . free bodily movement' there is a cramped restlessness. Boredom, one could say, is the set situation before there is a spatula to be found; or, perhaps, more absurdly, a set situation full of spatulas in which the child has to find one that really appeals to him. The bored child, a sprawl of absent possibilities, is looking for something to hold his attention. He is like a man who walks as quickly as possible through a gallery until a picture actually arrests his attention, until he is stopped – and at that point, we might add, the transference has taken. For the child to be allowed to have what Winnicott calls 'the full course of the experience' the child needs the use of an environment that will suggest things without imposing them; not pre-empt the actuality of the child's desire by force-feeding, not distract the child by forcing the spatula into his mouth. It is a process, Winnicott is saying, that is easily violated – although I would say that in growing up one needs a certain flair for distraction – and analogous to the analytic situation, in which the analyst's interpretations offer views rather than imposing convictions. In psychoanalysis, by definition, a militant or moralistic competence is inappropriate, merely a distraction.

The shining spatula, like Winnicott's initial squiggle, is, of course, an invitation to the child, an offering. What Winnicott calls the 'environment', though not exactly asserting itself, is at least tentatively promising; hinting, as it were. Gradually gaining interest in something that has attracted his attention, the infant, in his period of hesitation, 'becomes brave enough to let his feelings develop'. The period, wonderfully observed and imagined by Winnicott, in which the infant begins to experience his desire is an intrinsically problematic, difficult time. A child described later in the paper gets asthma during the period of hesitation. 'For this child,' Winnicott writes, 'asthma was associated with the moment at which there is normally hesitation, and hesitation implies mental conflict.' One can ask then, adapting Freud's phrase, what are the individual's preconditions for desire, for letting his feelings develop? What are the situations he sets – the occasions he organizes – to make desire possible? Boredom, of course, is prehesitation, but in each period of boredom the child returns to these questions.

The ordinary boredom of childhood is the benign version of what gets acted out, or acted out of, in what Winnicott in *Deprivation and Delinquency* calls the 'antisocial tendency'. But as adults boredom returns us to the scene of inquiry, to the poverty of our curiosity, and the simple question, what does one want to do with one's time? What is a brief malaise for the child becomes for the adult a kind of muted risk. After all, who can wait for nothing?

III

CLOV: Do you believe in the life to come?
HAMM: Mine was always that.

Samuel Beckett, *Endgame*

In the process of waiting for the mother, the child discovers a capacity for representation as a means of deferral. Representation – fantasy – is the medium in which he desires and waits. The child can conceive of himself as a desiring subject, in her absence, only in the space that comes between them. Optimally, with the cumulative experience of waiting for a reliable mother, the child will confidently find himself as the source of possibilities; and he will be relatively unembittered by his gradual pre-Oedipal disillusionment and loss of omnipotence. What Melanie Klein has described in 'Notes on Some Schizoid Mechanisms' as the 'paranoid-schizoid position' may be simply an account of the state of mind of an infant who has been made to wait beyond his capacity or tolerance, to the point at which desire is experienced intra-psychically as a threat to the always precarious integrity of the ego. What Klein does reveal, following Freud, is what could be called the individual's will to substitution, the need for every absence to be a presence. For the infant, in the agonies of waiting indefinitely, the good breast turns into the bad persecuting breast, but is nevertheless present as such in the infant's mind. In Klein's developmental theory, therefore, the whole notion of waiting is being rethought because, in a sense, the infant is never alone. Without sufficient attentiveness by the mother there is to an excessive degree what Laplanche in *Life and Death in Psychoanalysis* so starkly describes, in a different context, as an 'attack of the drives on the ego'; which will become, through projection, a refusal of the eventual presence of the object. It is difficult to enjoy people for whom we have waited too long. And in this familiar situation, which evokes such intensities of feeling, we wait and we try to do something other than waiting, and we often get bored – the boredom of protest that is always a screen for rage.

One can, of course, distract oneself only from what one has seen, or imagines one has seen. The defences, as Freud described them, are forms of recognition, instruments for the compromising of knowledge. We can think of boredom as a defence against waiting, which is, at one remove, an acknowledgement of the possibility of desire. And we can use as an analogy here Freud's explanation of the double-think in fetishism from his paper of 1927. After the child has been confronted with the fact that, as he understands it, the woman lacks a penis, 'we see,' Freud writes in 'Fetishism', 'that the perception has persisted, and that a very energetic action has been undertaken to maintain the disavowal'. The child 'has retained that belief but he has also given it up'; like the patient Freud mentions, he 'oscillates . . . between two assumptions'. In boredom, we can also say, there are two assumptions, two impossible options: there is something I desire, and there is nothing I desire. But which of the two assumptions, or beliefs, is disavowed is always ambiguous, and this ambiguity accounts, I think, for the curious paralysis of boredom (it is worth remembering Joyce McDougall's sense of disavowal, that it 'implies the notion of "avowal" followed by a destruction of meaning' (*Plea for a Measure of Abnormality*)). In boredom there is the lure of a possible object of desire, and the lure of the escape from desire, of its meaninglessness.

In this context what begins for the child as the object of desire becomes, for the adult, what Christopher Bollas has described in his book *The Shadow of the Object* as the 'transformational object'. Initially the mother, it is 'an object that is experientially identified by the infant with the process of the alteration of self experience'. This earliest relationship becomes the precursor of, the paradigm for, 'the person's search for an object (a person, place, event, ideology) that promises to transform the self'. At the first stage 'the mother is not yet identified as an object but is experienced as a process of transformation, and this feature remains in the trace of this object-seeking in adult life, where I believe the object is sought for its function as signifier of the process of transformation of being. Thus, in adult life, the quest is not to possess the object; it is sought in order to surrender to it as a process that alters the self.' But just as, for example, we cannot know beforehand which of the day's events from what Freud calls the 'dream-day' will be used as day-residues in the dream-work, we cannot necessarily know what will serve as a transformational object. The fact that anything *might* serve to transform a person's life has extravagant consequences for the possible shapes of a life, and, of course, for the significance attributed to therapeutic interventions. We are drawn, in fact, to ask a brash question: a madeleine or an analyst? An analysis can at least be arranged. But it cannot, alas, organize epiphanies, or guarantee those processes of transformation – those articulations – that return the future to us through the past. Of our own past, Proust writes in *Swann's Way* (1913), 'It is a labour in vain to attempt to recapture it: all the efforts of our intellect must prove futile. The past is hidden somewhere outside the realm, beyond the reach of intellect, in some material object (in the sensation which that material object will give us) which we do not suspect. And as for that object, it depends on chance whether we come upon it or not before we ourselves die.' The past can also, as we know, be hidden in the transference, and so can appear to be hidden in that material object called the analyst. But can we believe that there is a royal road, so to speak, to the transformational object?

Boredom, I think, protects the individual, makes tolerable for him the impossible experience of waiting for something without knowing what it could be. So the paradox of the waiting that goes on in boredom is that the individual does not know what he was waiting for until he finds it, and that often he does not know that he is waiting. One could, in this sense, speak of the 'analytic attitude' as an attentive boredom. With his set of approximations the bored individual is clueless and mildly resentful, involved in a half-hearted, despondent search for something to do that will make a difference.

Clearly, we should speak not of boredom, but of the boredoms, because the notion itself includes a multiplicity of moods and feelings that resist analysis; and this, we can say, is integral to the function of boredom as a kind of blank condensation of psychic life. In that more ordinary, more fleeting, boredom of the child the waiting is repressed. The more common risk for the adult – less attended to, more set in his ways, than the child – is that the boredom will turn into waiting. That the individual will become 'brave enough to let his feelings develop' in the absence of an object – towards a possible object, as it were – and by doing so commit himself, or rather, entrust himself, to the inevitable elusiveness of that object. For the adult, it seems, boredom needs to be the more permanent suspended animation of desire. Adulthood, one could say, is when it begins to occur to you that you may not be leading a charmed life.

Worrying and Its Discontents

I

If I can think of it, it isn't what I want.

Randall Jarrell, 'The Sick Child'

A boy of ten was referred to me because of his general despondency at school. His teachers described him as having become, in the last few months, 'preoccupied and sad'. During an interview his mother said that he seemed to have a lot of worries but wouldn't always tell her what they were; sometimes he determinedly kept them to himself. She was genuinely bemused, and once alone with him I found something in this boy's distracted manner that distracted me. Intending to say 'What are the worries?' I in fact said to him, 'What are worries?' Quite naturally puzzled by the question, he thought for a moment, then replied triumphantly, 'Farts that don't work,' and blushed. I said, 'Yes, some farts are worth keeping.' He grinned and said, 'Treasure.'

For this boy, worrying was a way of holding on to something, a form of storage. It transpired from our conversations that worries were like gifts he kept for his mother, and he was fearful of running out of them. What better gift to give to one's mother – especially if she was unsure of herself – than a worry she could resolve and so feel fully empowered as a good mother? He told me that he frequently dreamed of 'rooms full of the heads of big game on the walls', and it was clear from his associations that he had conceived a scenario in which one day he would give his mother his complete collection of trophies, all his best worries.

With remarkable economy he was using worries both to look after his mother – giving her something, one day, to make her feel better – and to seduce the Oedipal mother of desire with irresistible invitations that were proof of his potency. He was, in short, as we both soon realized, very worried about losing his worries. If he did, he might have to use another part of his body – alluded to by the heads in the dream and how they got on the wall – to engage an object. From a psychoanalytic perspective it is the patient's need for the symptom, despite his paradoxical invitation to the analyst to help rid him of it, that radically revises any conventional notions of cure. After all, what would he be thinking about if he wasn't worrying?

The description of worries as 'farts that don't work' raises, by implication, the question of what kind of work it is imagined that farts are supposed to be doing. (It's worth noting that one of this boy's manifest symptoms was an inability to work.) If, in this boy's view, worries are farts that don't work, what is the equivalent in mental life of farts that do work? Farts are often intimations of things to come, hints or bulletins from an internal somatic process that can be beyond omnipotent control, and in most contexts they are socially inappropriate reminders of this process. So a fart that doesn't work is a portent of nothing; it does not disclose a necessary process under way. And it isn't disruptive; it produces no change in the surrounding atmosphere. It is a thwarted internal experience rather than an exchange between inner and outer. If we take the kind of biological analogy familiar in Kleinian theory from Wilfred Bion's work, we can say, as he does in *Seven Servants*, that thinking something through can be described as metabolizing or digesting emotional experience. For this boy, then, worrying could be a form of emotional constipation, an unproductive mental process that got him nowhere; and this was part of its value to him. Like all symptoms, from a psychoanalytic point of view, it was among other things an attempt to arrest the passing of time. Auden reported a well-known Icelandic proverb, 'Every man loves the smell of his own farts.' Not everyone, though, loves the smell of his own thoughts, perhaps because they reek of change.

To approach the ordinary subject of worrying, it is useful, from a developmental point of view, to remember that we are 'worried about' before we begin to worry. Being worried about is both one of the oppressions and one of the reassurances of childhood. Potentially a threat, 'I'm worried about you' continues into adult life as an accusation and a claim. But it is a crucial constituent of the infant's and child's life to be able to evoke concern and interest, to have another person available to worry about him. What we think of in psychoanalysis as a symptom is often in children a way of making someone worry and therefore of making someone think. Winnicott writes in *Deprivation and Delinquency*, for example, of the 'nuisance-value' of the symptom. The parent's worry can signify a hidden preoccupation in the child, a loss of contact through a breakdown of understanding and an excess of pain. In adolescence we see a different stage of this in the use of what can be called symptoms – but are often bemusing forms of privacy – to get out of the parents' orbit even while maintaining sufficient contact with it. Parents keep the necessary link alive through worrying. It is curious, in this light, that worrying tends almost always to be talked of pejoratively. It may be part of our terror of dependency that we never hear anyone described as a good worrier.

We were once, even if we are not now, the object of someone else's worry. And, clearly, the way one was worried about – the quality of the worry we received – will to some extent be reflected in the way one worries about oneself. In object-relations theory, worrying can cover the whole spectrum from ordinary self-care to a thwarted conversation with an unlocatable object. How one uses other people in the process of worrying – to whom one tells what, and when, or whether one keeps one's worries to oneself – will be a repetition, with variations, of earlier relationships or transactions with objects. In other words, what worries are used for – what kind of medium of exchange or currency they become in one's relationship with other people and oneself – may be as revealing as what prompts them. (The question may not be 'What are you worried about?' but 'Whom is this worry for?') What one finds preying on one's mind, or, rather, what worries are made of, may be related to what and for whom they are made. It is, of course, easy to forget that worries are imaginative creations, small epics of personal failure and anticipated catastrophe. They are, that is to say, made up. And like inverted masturbation fantasies, they are among our most intimate inventions. It is almost as though we recognize ourselves too well, are perhaps overly familiar with ourselves, as worriers. Indeed, one's own personal history of worrying – the subjects chosen, their modification over time, the people involved, the relative pain and pleasure of the experience – all this would seem to be a potentially lucid revelation of character. But Freud, of course, made us unusually suspicious of the foreground; and worries, when they are there, crowd to the front of the stage.

II

Don't worry; it may never happen.

Traditional saying

We can be both the subjects and the objects of our own worries. Worrying, like being concerned, preoccupied, or absorbed – but unlike dreaming, thinking or feeling – can be done to us, according to ordinary usage. I can say 'It worries me' and also 'I am worried about something.' I can say 'I dreamed about something' – although this, as we shall see, is different – but not, as perhaps I should, 'It dreams me.' So in relation to my worries I can be – in the language of a traditional mystification – both active and passive. I can be their victim and I can try to master them. Worries, unlike dreams, thoughts and feelings, are something to which we give agency. We can, with the irony that characterizes the defences, allow them to be beyond omnipotent control, whereas for dreams we claim authorship. We can be worried, but we can't be dreamed.

The history of the word 'worrying' is itself revealing. Deriving from the Old English 'wyrgan', meaning 'to kill by strangulation', it was originally a hunting term, describing what dogs did to their prey as they caught it. The *Oxford English Dictionary* has, among several meanings from the fourteenth to the early nineteenth century: 'To swallow greedily or to devour . . . to choke a person or animal with a mouthful of food . . . to seize by the throat with the teeth and tear or lacerate; to kill or injure by biting or shaking. Said, e.g., of dogs or wolves attacking sheep, or of hounds when they seize their prey.' Johnson's *Dictionary* of 1755 has for 'worry': 'To tear or mangle as a beast tears its prey. To harass or persecute brutally.' A worrier for Johnson is someone who persecutes others, 'one who worries or torments them'. Two things are immediately striking in all of this. First there is the original violence of the term, the way it signifies the vicious but successful outcome of pursuing an object of desire. This sense of brutal foreplay is picked up in Dryden's wonderful lines in *All for Love*: 'And then he grew familiar with her hand / Squeez'd it, and worry'd it with ravenous kisses.' Worrying, then, is devouring, a peculiarly intense, ravenous form of eating. The second striking thing is that worrying, until the nineteenth century, is something one does to somebody or something else. In other words, at a certain point in history worrying became something that people could do to themselves. Using, appropriately enough, an analogy from hunting, worrying becomes a consuming, or rather self-consuming, passion. What was once thought of as animal becomes human, indeed all too human. What was once done by the mouths of the rapacious, the desirous, is now done, often with a relentless weariness, by the minds of the troubled.

It is not until the early nineteenth century, a time of significant social transformation, that we get the psychological sense of worrying as something that goes on inside someone, what the *OED* calls 'denoting a state of mind', giving as illustration a quotation from Hazlitt's *Table Talk*: 'Small pains are . . . more within our reach: we can fret and worry ourselves about them.' Domestic agitation replaces any sense of quest in Hazlitt's essay 'On Great and Little Things'. By the 1850s we find many of Dickens's characters worrying or 'worriting'. Where once wild or not-so-wild animals had worried their prey, we find Dickens's people worrying their lives away about love and money and social status. From, perhaps, the middle of the nineteenth century people began to prey on themselves in a new kind of way. Worry begins to catch on as a description of a new state of mind. It is now impossible to imagine a life without worry. In little more than a century worrying has become what we call a fact of life, as integral to our lives, as apparently ahistorical, as any of our most familiar feelings. So in Philip Roth's 1988 fictional autobiography, *The Facts*, it is surprising to find the word made interesting again in the narrator's description of his hard-working Jewish father: 'Despite a raw emotional nature that makes him prey to intractable worry, his life has been distinguished by the power of resurgence.' The pun on 'prey' suggests the devotion of that generation of American Jews to a new god. But the narrator also implies that his father's nature and history make him subject to his own persecution in the form of relentless worrying, and also that something about his life is reflected in the quality of his worry, its intractability, its obstinate persistence. A new kind of heroic resilience is required to deal with the worries of everyday life.

Even in this most cursory bit of philology we find 'worry' as pursuit and persecution, two things that in psychoanalysis tend to be associated with desire. But 'worrying', as the word is used now, is manifestly countererotic; no one says 'I had a really erotic worry last night', or indeed thinks of himself worrying his loved one's hands with kisses. In A. S. Byatt's novel *Still Life* one of the heroines is propositioned on a French train by a Frenchman, who offers her a 'taste of Cointreau, Grand Marnier, Chartreuse' in his sleeping compartment. 'Frederica replied brightly that that would be very agreeable. This was despite a strong sense that the man was unduly anxious about the outcome of his overture: anxiety is a great destroyer of response, and Frederica had no taste for being closed in a sleeping compartment with a worried man.' The strong sense here is that worrying is a form of insulation, that in the excess of worry something in the proposition, to the young heroine's relief, is retracted. But Byatt alerts us to a distinction between anxiety and worrying that she cannot make. As in the seduction, something is implied and glossed over at the same time. The distinction we tend to make is that worry always has an object, that worrying is beyond displacement, whereas one can feel anxious without knowing what the anxiety is about.

Interestingly, 'anxious', which we may think of as a nineteenth-century medical term, is in its conventional psychological sense an older word than 'worrying'. The *OED* offers a seventeenth-century meaning of 'anxious' as 'troubled or uneasy in mind about some uncertain event; being in painful or disturbing suspense; concerned; solicitous'. 'Anxiety', of course, immediately found a place in the language of psychoanalysis, while 'worrying' still has not. It has been subsumed by, or implicitly included in, a broad range of psychoanalytic categories, from obsessionality to phobic terrors. And this despite the rather obvious point that most adults who speak English come for psychoanalytic treatment because, in their own words, they are 'worried about' something. The children I see clinically are referred because someone, quite explicitly, is worried about them. It is worth wondering, I think, given that psychoanalysis is essentially a theory of censorship, why certain words that come to mind for patients are excluded by psychoanalytic theorists; or why there need be any disparity between the language of analysts and 'patients'. Depression, for example, has been the subject of extensive psychoanalytic speculation, but not sadness; mania has been accounted for theoretically, but not the intense pleasure of erotic excitement. Despite increased psychoanalytic interest in adolescence, no one has written about crushes. It is a fact that no one worries in the Bible – the actual word does not occur – but it seems peculiar that the word cannot be found in the Index of the *Standard Edition* of Freud's work.

III

I have a life without latent content.

Alexander Portnoy

In beginning to consider the worrying of everyday life as the product of an extreme form of secondary revision – a worry, that is to say, as a stifled, indeed an overprotected, dream – it may be useful to remember the possible implications of the etymology of the word itself. After all, even spurious etymologies were once a respectable source of psychoanalytic speculation. When we worry, then, what are we trying to eat? What is there to pursue or get rid of? How does one hunt for something in oneself – or, more ominously, prey on oneself – and what would it mean to devour what one caught? We are familiar with the notion of worrying away at a problem, like a dog gnawing a bone, but is it absurd to suggest that we are doing a kind of violence to ourselves when we worry? Worrying can, for example, be an aggression, a critique turned against the self. When we lie awake at night worrying, there may be a dream we are trying not to have. Certainly people are more often starved of dreams than of worries. And the ordinary worry that projects a catastrophe into the future can easily be seen as the equivalent in consciousness of what Freud in *Beyond the Pleasure Principle* called 'punishment dreams', which 'merely replace the forbidden wish-fulfilment by the appropriate punishment for it: that is to say, they fulfil the wish of the sense of guilt which is the reaction to the repudiated impulse'. Worries, then, can be punishments for wishes, or wishes cast in persecutory form; in the familiar act of worrying we may wish to avert the catastrophe and also to precipitate it. Flirting with possibilities, we are both the hunter and the hunted. There are, one could say, elaborating Freud's phrase, those wrecked by success, and those wrecked by anticipating failure; or, rather, those apparently wrecked by the wish to fail or the fear of success. Even if worrying is a covert critique of the fantasies of success in the culture, it is clear that worrying has an equivocal relationship with the wishing that in Freud's view dominates mental life.

The unconscious, Freud writes, 'consists of wishful impulses. These instinctual impulses are co-ordinate with one another . . . and are exempt from mutual contradiction . . . There are in this system no negation, no doubt, no degrees of certainty.' Since worrying by definition implies conflict, we must infer that the unconscious doesn't, so to speak, have any worry in it. We have to imagine, according to Freud, that there is a part of ourselves that has nothing to worry about, that is exempt from this most persistent form of self-doubt. Worrying, like dreaming, is born of conflict, and therefore of censorship. It involves the compromise of representation and derives from instinctual wishes. But the dream-work that Freud described is ingenious in its transformation of the forbidden into the sufficiently acceptable. Compared with the dream, the worry is almost pure, uncooked day-residue; indeed, it is addicted to reality. There is apparently little condensation or displacement; there seems to be no question of intelligibility, although there is a noticeable intensity of feeling. Worrying, that is to say, often has the appearance, the screen, that we associate with a certain version of reality.

Compared with the extraordinary invention of the dream, the ordinary worry seems drab. As remote as possible from the forbidden, the worry, unlike the dream, is part of the routine, the predictability of everyday life. A moment's thought will tell us what, if anything, we have to worry about tomorrow. No amount of thinking will tell us what we will dream tonight. All of us may be surrealists in our dreams, but in our worries we are incorrigibly bourgeois. It may be worth considering, then, a glib Freudian paradox: that some of the most efficient forms of censorship are those that render themselves invisible. How would one begin, or bother, to think that a shopping list or a telephone directory was a product of censorship? To worry about one's health, or about one's children, about money, or being late, or losing one's job, is not in any obvious sense enigmatic or puzzling. And yet it may be one of the functions of worrying to cramp and contain – to over-organize – more imaginatively elaborate or even violent responses to such very real predicaments. As a furtive protest, worrying is an attempt at simplification. It can give a local habitation and a name to a diversity of grievance and desire. A worry, one could say, is a muted dream, an overprotection of the self. But one could feel baffled, indeed radically misrecognized, if one's ordinary worries were interpreted as a Freudian analyst might interpret a dream. There is no obvious reason, though, why our associations to any of the elements in a worry should not be revealing. It may not be the dream that is the royal road to the unconscious, but the style of interpretation it makes possible.

Nevertheless, from a psychoanalytic perspective, 'What did you dream about?' and 'What are you worried about?' are quite different kinds of questions. The answers to them confront us with our assumptions about interpretation – both what is subject to what we call interpretation and what, in the form of interpretation, we might pertinently say. Clearly, the demand, or invitation, in the answers to these questions are different. And when we answer the question 'What are you worried about?' we, in a recognizable sense, mean what we say; we have conviction about what we are referring to. But when I say that

I dreamed about a green cat last night, I am giving a true report, yet we can assume that a process of substitution, of symbolization, has been in play. We infer that work has been done on the stuff of emotional life, that there is an overnight history of transformation that opens into a vast unconscious personal history, whereas worrying seems like a reaction to and not a reworking of our experience. By binding us to the present and the future it abolishes the past that is, so to speak, behind this particular piece of worrying, that existed prior to its appearance as a preoccupation. It seals time by encapsulating a sequence. When we worry, we look forward but are not tempted to look very far back. We are dutiful in the way Orpheus should have been.

Worrying implies a future, a way of looking forward to things. It is a conscious conviction that a future exists, one in which something terrible might happen, which is of course ultimately true. So worrying is an ironic form of hope. But dreams are always set in the past, both in Freud's sense of their being the disguised fulfilment of a repressed infantile wish and in the more verifiable sense that you cannot, by definition, ask someone what he is dreaming because a dream is always a retrospective report, never the so-called thing-in-itself. And always the question 'What did you dream?' in its most straightforward sense is notoriously difficult to answer. The dream, or perhaps the dreaming subject, 'fades', as Lacan puts it, when the dreamer awakens. The dreaming subject is even more elusive – almost impossible to construct – than his or her product, the dream. 'Who is dreaming?' is clearly a less ludicrous question than 'Who is worrying?'

What people do to their dreams effortlessly – that is, forget them – people have to try to do to their worries. To remember a worry is as easy as to forget a dream. Worries are present and tend to recur, and we are manifestly present in them. They show a coherent subject in an intelligible, if unsettling, narrative; they assume a pragmatic self bent on problem-solving, not an incurably desiring subject in the disarray of not knowing what he wants. We use worries to focus and are prone to use them to simulate purpose (just as when we are intimidated by possibility). When people describe a known task – passing an exam, paying a debt, being cured of an illness – they do not seem to allude to an unlocatable lack or, more absurdly, a certain death. As an integral part of a familiar internal environment, these specific worries can be very reassuring because they pre-empt what is in actuality an unknowable future. The worst thing that could happen is more comforting than the unimaginable thing.

Worrying tacitly constitutes a self – or, at least, a narrator – by assuming the existence of one; for how could there be a worry without a worrier? It is, of course, difficult to imagine a dream without a dreamer, but also to know what the dreamer looks like. A worrier has, so to speak, a familiar face; the iconography of the dreaming self is nowhere to be found. And it is exactly in this elusive area of inquiry that worrying focuses a contemporary dilemma in psychoanalysis. In what could, broadly speaking, be called object-relations theory, we have potentially guaranteed subjects or selves in relation to potentially knowable and facilitating objects in search of personal development through intimacy. A modernized Freudian, on the other hand, can easily see the self as merely a function of representation – where else is it except in its descriptions? – in a world of comparably oblique objects. Here fantasies of growth or purpose conceal the impossibility, the unexorcizable lack, at the heart of being. Relationships, in this view, are necessarily ironized, because although they are essential to survival, the persistence of desire prefigures defeat. Desire implies a lack that no object can appease. Worrying, in this kind of arena, looks silly. It seems to lack metaphysical ambition. But from an object-relations point of view we could say that worrying prepares the self, at best in collaboration with responsive others. And we could also say that potentially, through refusing the benefit of others, worrying impoverishes the self by attacking the possibility of its imaginative modification. As a medium of exchange, then, worrying regulates intimacy, and it is often an appropriate response to ordinary demands that begin to feel excessive. But from a modernized Freudian view, worrying – as a reflex response to demand – never puts the self or the objects of its interest into question, and that is precisely its function in psychic life. It domesticates self-doubt.

If we adapt Wittgenstein's famous question 'Is belief an experience?' to the matter in hand and ask 'Is worrying an experience?' we are left more empty-handed than we may want to be. If we were anthropologists who had discovered a tribe that engaged in a pervasive activity they called worrying, how would we go about getting a sense of what they meant? I seem to know when I'm worried – I recognize the signs – but this in itself can preclude my finding out what I'm doing when I worry. The tendentious comparison with dreaming reveals, I think, how worrying sets limits to the kind of curiosity we can have about it. We can think about thinking, but perhaps we don't worry enough about worrying. If worrying is, say, a defence against dreaming, if the worry is the contrived, conscious alternative to the dream, at the opposite end of some imaginary spectrum, then there may also be something, paradoxically, that they have in common. They both incorporate reality to defeat interpretation, and they do not always succeed.

Looking at Obstacles

I

The way to solve the problem you see in life is to live in
a way that makes the problem disappear.

Ludwig Wittgenstein, *Culture and Value*

A twelve-year-old girl was referred to me for what turned out
to be an array of symptoms that she had managed to organize
into a school phobia. At the age of ten, having nursed a sense of
neglect in the family, which she perceived as two groups, the
parents and 'the girls', her two elder sisters, both leaving her
out, she asked her parents if she could go to boarding school.
This had been an unconscious test of their devotion to her; she
was dismayed to find herself, within three months of the request,
in a public school three hundred miles from home. At first timid
and pliable – the headmistress referred to her as 'sweet and
helpful' – she suddenly came to life after a year in a phobia with
which she was terrorizing herself. She was unable to walk into
the classroom; as she said, it made her feel 'too excited', and she
thought she would faint or 'screech like an owl'. When I said to
her in our first awkward meeting that owls kill at night she
thought for a moment and then said with some relish, 'In the
dark things don't get in the way.' I was reassured by this because
it made me feel that, despite all the uncertainties and refusals in
which she hoarded her rage, she knew about the fluency in herself. I thought that she no longer wanted to guard her grudges.
Unusually for a phobic child, she entered into the spirit of

psychotherapy with some vigour after a few months' stubborn impatience in which, quite sensibly, she treated me as part of the problem. The only thing that struck me as genuinely odd about her was her attitude to my holiday breaks. When I told her of the dates of my holidays or made comments to prepare her, she treated all these remarks as a kind of hiatus in the conversation; I felt quite suddenly as though I was talking in her sleep. She was oblivious but in no way puzzled. Very politely she would let me have my say, as though I was someone with an intrusive obsession who every so often needed to blurt something out about the difficulties of separation. If I got irritated and asked her if she had heard what I was saying, she was mildly bemused, but it made no difference. She would treat the sessions before the holiday as quite ordinary and would carry on the next session as though nothing had come between us. I found her absolute refusal to take me seriously as someone who went away rather endearing. I was aware that she had intrigued me with this, which, in another context, or in someone else, might have given me serious cause for concern.

And then in the session before the third holiday break she arrived with an atlas. I had told her, and had been telling her for some time, that I was going away for two weeks to America. In what sense she had heard this I had no way of knowing. But in this session she went straight to the table and traced maps of America and Britain. She then reproduced them on a piece of paper and said to me, 'While you're *there* [pointing to America], I'll be *here* [pointing to Britain] making the tea.' I said, 'That's amazing! *T* is the difference between here and there'; and she grinned and said, 'So I'll be making the difference.' A lot can be made of this, but for my purposes here I would say that she could allow herself to recognize the holiday as an obstacle only when, in fantasy, she could bring it within the range of her own omnipotence: when she was making the tea. The initial 'difference' has to be made, or rather imagined to have been made, by the subject, not by the object. So the first question is: what are the preconditions for the recognition of an obstacle? And the first assertion is: one can recognize an obstacle – which can mean construct something as an obstacle – only when it can be tolerated. Only through knowing what we think of as an obstacle can we understand our fantasies of continuity.

In an interview with a couple and their first child, who was now a toddler, the mother was describing how frantic her son made her by his clinging. She couldn't go to the toilet, or go shopping, or do anything without his hanging on to her, wound round her legs. Her description evoked in me the image of somebody running who was gradually being metamorphosed into a tree. She could 'never', she said, 'have a moment to herself'; he was always – this son who was insinuating himself up and down her body like roots – 'in the way'. And it was this familiar phrase – 'He is always in the way' – that was insistently repeated. It was not difficult to make some sense of all this in terms of the changed relationship between the couple. And it is, of course, put as schematically as this, a common family scenario with children at this developmental stage. But towards the end of the session the thought came into my mind, 'Where would she be going if her son was not in the way?' So I asked her, and she replied quite cheerfully, 'Oh, I wouldn't know where I was!' The second question then is: how are obstacles unconsciously constructed? And the second assertion is: the obstacle is used to conceal – to pack up, as it were – the unconscious desire. If the child is always in the way – and parents and children may cooperate to ensure that this is the case – then the mother can never find out where she would be going if no one was in the way (of course, one should not underestimate a person's wish to be an obstacle). So one way of describing the family situation is that the parent needs the child to cling in order to paralyse any realization – or recognition – of alternative unconscious projects. The obstacle is a way of not letting something else happen, a necessary blind spot.

In *Being and Nothingness* Sartre describes the situation of a walker confronted with an overhanging cliff face. 'For the simple traveller,' he writes, 'who passes over this road and whose free project is a pure aesthetic ordering of the landscape, the crag is not revealed either as scalable or not scalable; it is manifested only as beautiful or ugly.' If I am simply on a walk, the rock face is an obstacle; if I am a painter, it is not. But the absurd – the psychoanalytic – possibility that Sartre does not consider is that I may realize I am on a walk only when I perceive the cliff as an obstacle. That is to say, the only way to discover your projects is to notice – to make conscious – what you reckon are obstacles. So the third question would be: what kind of obstacles does one find oneself making, what is one's vocabulary of impediments? (And in clinical terms one could ask: what is the patient's – and, of course, the analyst's – personal repertoire of obstacles?) And the third assertion would be: the desire does not reveal the obstacle, the obstacle reveals the desire. And if only it was as simple as this we could say to our patients, or to ourselves, 'Tell me what your obstacles are, and I will tell you what you desire.'

There is an apocryphal story about Adler, who in his early, more psychoanalytic, days would ask the patient at the end of the first consultation, 'What would you do if you were cured?' The patient would answer, and then Adler would say, 'Well, go and do it then!'

A thirty-two-year-old man came to see me for a consultation, but very unsure whether his 'problem', as he referred to it ironically, warranted psychotherapy, or even consideration as a problem. He talked about how the problem might not be one, but without telling me for some time what it was. He was both jaunty and shy about it all and eventually told me – having made himself rather unavailable – that the problem was that he always fell for 'unavailable women'. I asked him in what sense they were unavailable, and he said that they always had partners. I said, 'Yes, so in what sense are they unavailable?' He smiled and said, 'So you mean, what's the problem?' I apologized for being harsh, though in retrospect I think I was also speaking the voice of his disowned rivalry – in psychoanalysis one exaggerates the patient's muted voices – and I replied that he might feel safer with the conviction that they were unavailable, and that we might be able to understand why he needed an obstacle to free his desire. He agreed that he found it slightly reassuring that these women he wanted had men who would protect them from him. I wondered if perhaps he wanted to be protected by a stronger man. And he replied, almost as though it was a proverb, or a piece of folklore, 'If you want to get a man, try to get a woman.'

It is impossible to imagine desire without obstacles, and wherever we find something to be an obstacle we are at the same time desiring. It is part of the fascination of the Oedipus story in particular, and perhaps of narrative in general, that we and the heroes and heroines of their fictions never know whether obstacles create desire, or desire creates obstacles. We are never quite sure which it is we are seeking, and it is difficult to imagine how to keep the story going without both. So the next question is: why do we need to think of them as inextricable? And the answer to this question would tell us something interesting about our fictions about desire. A psychoanalytic answer – or, rather, response – might be: desire without obstacles is merging or incest, and so the death of desire; and obstacles without desire are literally unthinkable, or surreal like Magritte's doors suspended in the air.

This apparently inevitable twining of obstacle and desire suggests, in the case of my male patient, another assertion: the object of unconscious desire can be represented only by the obstacles to the conscious object of desire. This man was conscious of his desire for women, and conscious of their partners as obstacles. But for him the unconscious object of desire was the obstacle, the man. The desire for the object can be used to mask the desire for the obstacle. When we unpack the obstacles in analysis – when we think of them as the way rather than as something in the way – we find them, like Pandora's box, full of the unusual and the forbidden. If I know what I want by coming up against what prevents me from having it, then there must anyway be a wish for obstacles as unconscious mnemonics of desire. The obstacle reminds me of what I want, in one part of my mind, to forget.

Symptoms, of course, are always construed by the patient as obstacles; so it is always worth wondering what the patient's imaginary unobstructed life would look like in the absence of such constraints. What are the catastrophic – or catastrophically pleasurable – scenarios that his cherished obstacles both protect him from and sustain as an anticipated possibility in an always deferred future? Rousseau writes in Book 1 of the *Confessions*:

> Countless times during my apprenticeship and since, I have gone out with the idea of buying some sweet thing. As I come to the pastry cook's I catch sight of the women behind the counter and can already imagine them laughing among themselves and making fun of the greedy youngster. Then I pass a fruiterer's and look at the ripe pears out of the corner of my eye; the scent of them tempts me. But two or three young people over there are looking at me; a man I know is standing in front of the shop; I can see a girl coming in the distance. Is she not our maidservant? My short sight is constantly deceiving me. I take everyone who passes for someone I know. I am frightened by everything and discover obstacles everywhere. As my discomfort grows my desire increases. But in the end I go home like an idiot, consumed by longing and with money enough in my pocket to satisfy it, but not having dared to buy anything.

Satisfaction for Rousseau is the death of possibility. So Rousseau needs not to master the obstacles, but to nurture them. Anticipation is the mother of invention. And in his commitment to innocence there is always the covert suggestion that nothing is forbidden, that we are not controlling ourselves, just finding ways of making what we don't do more exciting. In this almost frenzied and certainly fraught scenario we find Rousseau's wish to make a spectacle of his desire apparently controlled by the projected disapproval of others. He creates an entirely reassuring and familiar world – 'I take everyone who passes for someone I know' – policed by exciting obstacles.

And this catalogue of obstacles – the women behind the counter, the young people, the man and the maid – he supposes to be excessively interested in his desire. He has money in his pocket, but he needs these obstacles to make his ordinary desire seem, at least to himself, criminal. If it is dangerous to buy a ripe pear, only a dangerous man can do it. If his aliveness or his potency are in doubt – and how could they not be? – then the obstacles he creates have the effect of making his desire seem inordinately powerful; so powerful, in fact, so socially disruptive, that the audience he has simulated forgets everything else. He is unable to think what would happen if no one was at all interested in his desire. 'I am frightened by everything,' he writes, 'and discover obstacles everywhere.' But he is frightened by everything – that is, excited by everything – *because* he discovers obstacles everywhere; because every obstacle makes him potentially a criminal. And if Rousseau is not unconsciously a criminal he is not, in his own eyes at least, a man.

What Rousseau alerts us to here is the passion for obstacles. And this leads me to the next assertion: the first relationship is not with objects but with obstacles. Or, to put it another way, from the other end, so to speak: People fall in love at the moments in their lives when they are most terrorized by possibilities. In order to fall in love with someone they must be perceived to be an obstacle, a necessary obstacle.

II

We can analyse what people actually do; we can make no coherent sense of what they ought to do.

Ross Harrison, *Hobbes, Locke and Confusions MasterPiece*

'We can only laugh,' Freud wrote, 'when a joke has come to our help.' It is as though we need something to release, or permit, the laugh that is already inside us. It is through the joke, Freud suggests, that we are momentarily released from the obstacles we have imposed on our pleasure. It is, in fact, in *Jokes and Their Relation to the Unconscious* that Freud uses the word 'obstacle' – at least in the English translation – with the greatest frequency. And the joke is so important for Freud because it is the most ingeniously efficient way of rescuing our pleasure from the obstacles. And rescuing pleasure, in Freud's terms, is a form of remembrance. Jokes

> make possible the satisfaction of an instinct (whether lustful or hostile) in the face of an obstacle that stands in its way. They circumvent this obstacle and in that way draw pleasure from a source which the obstacle had made inaccessible . . . The repressive activity of civilisation brings it about that primary possibilities of enjoyment, which have now, however, been repudiated by the censorship in us, are lost to us. But to the human psyche all renunciation is exceedingly difficult, and so we find that tendentious jokes provide a means of undoing the renunciation and retrieving what was lost.

Jokes, like dreams, are the saboteurs of repression. Civilization makes an obstacle course of our pleasures, but jokes link us to our losses, what Freud calls our 'primary possibilities of enjoyment'. The obstacles keep us safe, but the joke endangers us with excitement. What Freud makes less explicit is that the obstacle provides us with an additional source of pleasure – the pleasure to be got from successfully circumventing the obstacle. Outwitting is the other soul of wit. So there is always an ironic sense in which the search for obstacles is also the search for pleasure. ('Failure to understand a joke,' as Proust's narrator *in Within a Budding Grove* reminds us, 'has never yet made anyone find it less amusing.') One of the aims of psychoanalytic treatment may be to enable the patient to find, or be able to tolerate, more satisfying obstacles to contend with. Poor obstacles impoverish us.

★

An obstacle is literally something that stands in the way, a 'hindrance, impediment, obstruction . . . resistance, objection' as the *Oxford English Dictionary* has it, adding a seventeenth-century usage of 'to make obstacle', meaning 'to offer opposition'. These definitions are all obviously suggestive in relation to psychoanalytic theory. In the repetition compulsion, for example, what is the obstacle, what prevents the patient from organizing a more exact repetition? Or to think of resistance as the construction of an obstacle might lead us to redescribe resistances as peculiarly inventive artefacts. (What is 'analysed' in a psychoanalysis are the obstacles to two people enjoying each other's company.) 'The real resistance,' Sándor Ferenczi and Otto Rank write in *The Development of Psychoanalysis*, 'far from disturbing the analytic work is actually a requisite and acts as a mainspring in regulating its course . . . the content of the resistance is also of importance for it almost always is a sign that the patient here too reproduces instead of remembers and in the material betrays also that which he would like by means of reproduction to withdraw from analytic elaboration.' The resistance encodes the past that, by being repeated rather than remembered, is an obstacle to the future. Like all defences it apparently forecloses the future, one thing the patient and the analyst will never know anything about. What is repressed in advance is the novelty of experience. The obstacle of repetition – resistance as repetition – creates the illusion of foresight. And psychoanalytic theory can collude with this by implying that the future is merely the past in different terms.

As George Crabb writes in his once extremely popular *English Synonymes Explained* (1818), 'the obstacle opposes itself, it is properly met in the way, and intervenes between us and our object'. And just in case we might forget that, from a psychoanalytic point of view, the fetish, after the father, is the paradigmatic obstacle, Crabb gives us as a further definition: 'In Latin *obstaculum* from *obsto* to stand in the way, signifies the thing that stands in the way between the person and the object that he has in view.' Given the emphasis on the visual here – the object in view – it is always worth considering which of the senses is being used for analogy in the construction of the obstacle. I can smell and hear round corners; if there is a wall between us I won't be able to taste you.

'The thing that stands in the way between the person and the object he has in view' is Freud's description in 'Fetishism' of the making of a fetish. 'When the fetish is instituted . . . the subject's interest comes to a halt half-way, as it were; it is as though the last impression before the uncanny and traumatic one is retained as a fetish. Thus the foot or shoe owes its preference as a fetish – or part of it – to the circumstances that the inquisitive boy peered at the woman's genital from below, from her legs up.' The terror of castration, Freud claims, and thus the loss of bodily integrity, produces a need to find obstacles to the perception that there are two sexes. The fetish sponsors the idea that there is nothing to lose. As Victor Smirnoff says in *Psychoanalysis in France* (ed. D. Widlocher and S. Lebovici), the fetishist is 'someone who is trying to secure a triple guarantee – to make good his fundamental loss, to maintain and assure continuity, and to recognise his own sexual status in relation to the fantasy of the phallic mother'. But the irony of this obstacle, the fetish, is that it is needed to stop the fetishist from seeing what he has already seen, what Smirnoff calls, 'his fundamental loss'. Like all defences it is a form of acknowledgement, a tolerable way of thinking about something unacceptable. What the boy first saw, in fantasy, as it were, was that there was no obstacle – or was the penis an obstacle? – to becoming a woman. What was absent was an obstacle to castration.

'The fetish,' Freud writes, 'is a substitute for the mother's penis,' so it provides an obstacle to the thought 'a person can lose a penis', and an obstacle to the thought 'I'm different from my mother.' 'He has retained the belief [that a woman has a penis],' Freud writes, 'but he has also given it up.' Just as it is the sign of a good theory that it can be used to support contradictory positions, it is the sign of a good fetish that it keeps incompatible ideas alive. The obstacle that is found to seeing the female genitals – a shoe in Freud's example – is a way of sustaining belief that there are two sexes and denying it at the same time. The obstacle secretly confronts the fetishist with what it protects him from. But the object of desire is unbearable without the obstacle of the fetish.

But how can one have, as Freud suggests, and indeed keeps referring to throughout his work, opposing 'currents' in mental life? In the essay on fetishism he describes two boys for whom 'it was only one current in their mental life that had not recognised their father's death; there was another current that took full account of that fact'. How can we describe the obstacles – which are fantasies – that stop these contradictory thoughts from contaminating each other? Perhaps we talk too much about dissociation without trying to describe what we put between states of mind to keep them apart. And this is a particularly interesting project because what keeps them apart – and this is the essence of the obstacle – also links them. Sometimes, in fact, what keeps things apart may be the only connection between them. In the attack on linking, the attack becomes the link.

Once we are talking of this paradox of the link that separates we are inevitably reminded of Winnicott's apparently familiar concept of the transitional object, something that comes between to make a more facilitating connection. The intermediate area of transitional phenomena, he writes, 'exists as a resting place for the individual engaged in the perpetual human task of keeping inner and outer reality separate yet interrelated'. It is with the idea of transitional phenomena that Winnicott introduces something that I think should be called 'obstacle-relations' as an addition, or perhaps an alternative, to object-relations. If the fetish is an acknowledgement through disavowal of the threat of castration, the transitional object is an acknowledgement through mediation of the dual threat of merging and absolute isolation. And this dual threat we think of as pre-Oedipal in origin. We could, in fact, describe the differences between the Oedipal and the pre-Oedipal in terms of the difference of obstacles. Winnicott, however, never makes clear the connection between the use of transitional objects and the shift from pre-Oedipal to Oedipal relationships. In 'Transitional Objects and Transitional Phenomena' he writes only that 'the object represents the infant's transition from the state of being in relation to the mother as something outside and separate'. It is an obstacle to merging and absolute loss – the two fundamental terrors construed by psychoanalysis – and so creates the space for experiencing. In the transitional space neither threat is pre-emptive or overwhelming. 'The term transitional object,' he writes, 'according to my suggestion, gives room for the process of becoming able to accept difference and similarity,' unlike the fetish, one might add, which out of the terror of difference is used to simulate sameness. In this 'process of becoming able to accept difference and similarity', difference entails the making or finding of obstacles, similarity the relinquishing or destroying of obstacles.

There are no obstacles to one's own death, but the obstacles to murder are unsurprising. The second murderer in *Richard III*, describing conscience, says to his accomplice: ' 'Tis a blushing, shamefac'd spirit that mutinies in a man's bosom. It fills a man full of obstacles.' It is to the filling and emptying of obstacles in a person's life – at its most extreme in manic-depressive states – that we should turn our attention if we wish to understand something new about the conundrum of sameness and difference. The obstacle makes the difference; so in developmental terms it is the obstacle that makes possible the object, that makes possible the idea of someone else.

A person's life, we should remember, in the terms of Freud's later work, was described as an obstacle between two quiescent states. But then Freud believed in the opposition, the antagonism, between life and death.

I was standing one day in a queue in a post office in Camberwell, and a small child in a pushchair in the queue next to me kept throwing her doll away, much to her mother's annoyance. Each time it happened the mother retrieved it, much to the child's surprise, and then it was immediately thrown away again. After about the fifth or sixth time the mother brought the doll back and said crossly to her daughter, 'If you lose that you've had it.' This struck me then as rather an interesting remark. Obviously I have no idea what the child made of it – although she did stop throwing out the doll – and I have some idea of what the mother intended. But it did occur to me that this little girl may have been trying to find out something about what came between herself and an object – what the distance or the difference was made of – and how it is removed. To throw away the doll was to impose an obstacle, and by doing so to find out something about the object. This is the kind of object that only certain obstacles can come between; and these certain obstacles seem, at least at first, to be automatically removed by the mother. If the girl had finally lost it – found an absolute obstacle to its presence – she would indeed have had it in a specific sense.

In a commentary on Simone Weil's statement that 'All human progress consists in changing constraint into an obstacle,' the philosopher Peter Winch writes: 'When I see things as obstacles I am already on the way to investigating and developing systematic ideas about their properties and interrelations; about the necessities to which they are subject' (*Simone Weil: The Just Balance*). What I am suggesting is that the child can find out what the object is – or, rather, get a version of what it might be, its properties and interrelations – only by finding or constructing obstacles to its access or availability. The search for obstacles – the need to impose them in their familiar guise of time and space – is part of the endless, baffled inquiry into the nature of the object. I know what something or someone is by finding out what comes between us.

The little girl throwing her doll away is, of course, reminiscent of Freud's description of his grandson's Fort-Da game. When the child discovers the cotton-reel, that he can pull back what he has thrown away, Freud suggests, he is on his way to mastering, by symbolic substitution, the absence imposed upon him by his mother. The child is beginning to work out what it is that is between people, which is related to what it is that comes between people. There is no thread of cotton connecting them; rather, he is hanging by the thread of his wishful desire. But the existence of that extraordinary phenomenon, the wish, always implies a prior perception of obstacles. After all, why would we need to wish if nothing were in the way?

The way we get to know what we eventually call a mother is through the obstacles to her presence. To feel hunger is to feel a growing obstacle to its gratification. In what Winnicott calls the 'moment of illusion' – the moment of desire when it is imagined that the infant fantasizes the edible mother and she actually feeds him – it is as though the object of desire emerges out of the obstacles to her presence, as out of a fog. At the beginning, perhaps, there is not a mother in mind, but an obstacle to a mother; not a mother that is absent, but an obstacle that is present. (Another way of saying this would be to ask the slightly absurd question, is the first thought the absence of mother or the presence of time?) At the so-called beginning the child enters not a world of objects, but a world of obstacles. Consciousness is of obstacles. Wherever you look, as the Chinese proverb says, there's something in the way.

The unconscious in Freud's description is, so to speak, a place without obstacles; or, rather, a world immune from the obstacles created by what he calls 'secondary-process thinking'; a world, he writes in *The Unconscious*, 'exempt from mutual contradiction . . . There are in this system, no negation, no doubt, no degrees of certainty'; the unconscious, he mentions on several occasions, is 'timeless'. So a good question to ask of a dream – indeed a question often crucial to its interpretation – is, what are the obstacles that have been removed to make this extraordinary scene possible? In the Freudian topography we are not only, in the familiar formula, half man half beast; we are also composed of two worlds: a world without the usual obstacles – the unconscious that Freud called 'the other place' – and a world that is an obstacle course, a world presided over by the ego in its desperate search for obstacles. And interpretation – the linking of these two worlds – becomes nothing more than the addition, subtraction or modification of obstacles.

John Cage said in an interview in *For the Birds* that it was through reading D. T. Suzuki on Zen Buddhism that he came to realize that 'sound no longer comprises an obstacle to silence; silence is no longer a screen with regard to sound'. Perhaps this is one way of picturing something as really bizarre, something as virtually unthinkable, as the Freudian unconscious. The unconscious as a 'seething cauldron' is easier to imagine than a place without obstacles. And without obstacles the notion of development, at least in its progressivist sense, is inconceivable. There would be nothing to master.

I wrote this essay to show that obstacles are the clue to desire, that the word is full of meaning. But I have an uneasy feeling, which we probably all remember from childhood, and which may be pertinent to the subject at hand; the feeling that comes when one endlessly repeats a word only to be left with an enigmatic obstacle as to its sense.

First Hates

I

His radical solutions were rendered vain by the
conventionality of his problems.

George Santayana, *My Host the World*

In his chapter 'Instinct' in *Psychology: The Briefer Course* (1892),
William James writes:

> The progress from brute to man is characterised by nothing so
> much as by the decrease in frequency of proper occasions for fear.
> In civilised life, in particular, it has at last become possible for large
> numbers of people to pass from the cradle to the grave without
> ever having had a pang of genuine fear. Many of us need an attack
> of mental disease to teach us the meaning of the word. Hence the
> possibility of so much blindly optimistic philosophy and religion.

James, of course, is always looking for good transitions, for the
passages that work for us. Like Freud, but for different reasons, he
is wary of the progress in civilized life. For Freud, civilization
compromises our desire; for James here, it compromises our fear.
If civilization protects us, or overprotects us, the absence of danger
can make us unrealistic. We may need an attack of mental disease
as the only available reminder of 'proper occasions for fear'. Without proper occasions we lose the meaning of an important word.
This mental disease that James recommends, partly from his own
experience, or rather the real fear that it entails, should temper
speculation, setting limits to the naive ambitions of metaphysics.

But fear, especially at its most irrational, perplexes James in an interesting way; it connects for him three of his most consistent preoccupations: blindness, optimism, and the doing of philosophy. Because, unlike Freud, he doesn't see fear and desire as inextricable, he is more openly puzzled. Even though 'a certain amount of timidity obviously adapts us to the world we live in', he writes, 'the fear paroxysm is surely altogether harmful to him who is its prey'. After considering the virtues of immobility – the insane and the terrified 'feel safer and more comfortable' in their 'statue-like, crouching immobility' – James refers at the very end of his chapter on fear to 'the strange symptom which has been described of late years by the rather absurd name of agoraphobia'. After describing the symptoms, which 'have no utility in a civilised man', he manages to make sense of this puzzling new phenomenon only by comparing it to the way in which both domestic cats and many small wild animals approach large open spaces. He writes:

> When we see this we are strongly tempted to ask whether such an odd kind of fear in us be not due to the accidental resurrection, through disease, of a sort of instinct which may in some of our more remote ancestors have had a permanent and on the whole a useful part to play.

The 'disease' returns the patient to his instinctual heritage; but this heritage is now redundant because, in actuality, there is nothing to fear. Agoraphobics, James suggests, are living in the past, the evolutionary past ('the ordinary cock-sure evolutionist', James remarks in his droll way, 'ought to have no difficulty in explaining these terrors'). The agoraphobic is, as it were, speaking a dead language. So to understand agoraphobia in James's terms, we have to recontextualize the fear, put it back in its proper place, or, rather, time. There is nothing really irrational about phobic terror; it is an accurate recognition of something, something that Darwinian evolution can supply a picture for. Fear itself cannot be wrong, even if it is difficult to find out where it fits.

A phobia nevertheless is, perhaps in both senses, an improper occasion for fear, an enforced suspension of disbelief. James's description of the agoraphobic patient 'seized with palpitation and terror at the sight of any open place or broad street which he has to cross alone' is a vivid picture of a phobia as an impossible transition. And it can be linked – as a kind of cartoon – with one of James's famous notions of truth; the agoraphobic becoming, as it were, the compulsive saboteur of some of his own truth. 'Pragmatism,' James writes in his book of that title,

> gets her general notion of truth as something essentially bound up with the way in which one moment in our experience may lead us towards other moments which it will be worth while to have been led to. Primarily, and on the common-sense level, the truth of a state of mind means this function of *a leading that is worth while*.

The agoraphobic is the figure of the compromised pragmatist. The threshold of experience between this one moment and the next is aversive. He wants to go somewhere – or, in James's more suggestive terms, be led somewhere – but he is unable to find out whether it is as worthwhile (in both senses) as he thinks. The terror, or the inability to hold the terror, pre-empts possible future states of mind, and so precludes their evaluation. A phobia, in other words, protects a person from his own curiosity.

'Agoraphobia,' Freud wrote in a letter to Wilhelm Fliess in 1887, 'seems to depend on a romance of prostitution.' Despite James's misgiving about its 'rather absurd name', and despite its being Greeked for prestigious legitimation, agoraphobia seems rather nicely named. The agora, after all, was that ancient place where words and goods and money were exchanged. Confronted with an open space, as James and Freud both agree, the agoraphobic fears that something nasty is going to be exchanged: one state of mind for another, one desire for another. But the phobia ensures a repression of opportunity, a foreclosing of the possibilities for exchange ('a projection is dangerous', the psychoanalyst André Green has written in 'Passions and Their Vicissitudes (from *On Private Madness*), 'when it prevents the simultaneous formation of an introjection'; in a phobia one is literally unable to take in what one has invented). The agoraphobic, that is to say, knows – Freud would say unconsciously – what the space is for, or what he wants to use it for. It then ceases, as though by magic, to be an open space, or what James calls a 'pluralistic universe'. It simply leads into the past, into the old world.

James and Freud use explanation in quite different ways. For James the question is not so much, is it true? as, how would my life be better if I believed it? For Freud the first question – the unconscious question, so to speak – is, what do I want? and then, what fantasies of truth do I need to legitimate it? But because for James there can never be any knowing beforehand, he cannot presume to universalize his conclusions. And this is because there is no end to them; in this sense he is a freer associationist than Freud. 'It is enough to ask of each of us,' he concludes in his great talk 'On a Certain Blindness in Human Beings' (from *Talks on Psychology and Life's Ideals*), 'that he should be faithful to his own opportunities and make the most of his own blessings, without presuming to regulate the rest of the vast field.' The risk for the phobic person, as for the psychoanalyst, is that he has already used his explanations to delimit his opportunities.

II

. . . a face which inspires fear or delight (the object of
fear or delight) is not on that account its cause, but –
one might say – its target.

Ludwig Wittgenstein, *Philosophical Investigations*

The question of where the fear belongs – or what it is worthwhile to fear – is one that occupies both the phobic person and his interpreter. Freud himself at one point, in his *Inhibitions, Symptoms and Anxiety*, speculated that childhood phobias of small animals and thunder could be 'the atrophied remainders of congenital preparation for real dangers that are so clearly developed in other animals'. If Freud and James agree here, with Darwinian common sense, that phobias are derivative forms of self-protection, that phobic terror is irrational only in so far as it has missed its target, they radically disagree about what there is to fear and where it comes from. They fill the agoraphobic space – its empty page, so to speak – in quite different ways.

James's open space, for the agoraphobic, evokes phylogenetic memory; Freud's open space evokes personal memory (and memory for Freud is always of desire and the parented past). James's open space may be full of potential predators, but in Freud's open space a person may turn into a predator. Freud wrote in 1926:

> The anxiety felt in agoraphobia (a subject that has been less thoroughly studied) seems to be the ego's fear of sexual temptation – a fear which, after all, must be connected in its origins with the fear of castration. As far as can be seen at present, the majority of phobias go back to an anxiety of this kind felt by the ego in regard to the demands of the libido.

For the agoraphobic the open space represents the setting for a possible incestuous sexual encounter punishable by castration. Because sexuality begins in incestuous fantasy, it always smacks of the forbidden. So the phobic scenario, in Freud's view, appears to invite an illicit re-enactment from the past, a place where, quite unwittingly, a memory could be cast. For the agoraphobic to go out is to give the past a future, to bring it forward, so to speak. What the phobic fears, unconsciously, is not only the replication of this truant past, but also its modification in ways that cannot be anticipated. If one loses the replica, one might lose the original. These phobic scenarios are like anti-epiphanies in which memory, rather than being released into images and atmospheres, is frozen into terror. Whereas the epiphany, in the Proustian sense, is contingent and surprising, the phobia is reliable. The phobia, which hoards the past, can be the one place in a person's life where meaning apparently never changes; but this depends upon one's never knowing what the meaning is.

Given the insistence and the mobility of the libido in Freud's account, any occasion might be a proper occasion for fear. Desire – or what we can, in a different language, call parts of the self – in so far as it is experienced as intolerable, has to be put somewhere else, projected into hiding. There it can be acknowledged in terror, but never known about. The profoundest way of recognizing something, or the only way of recognizing some things, Freud will imply, is through hiding them from oneself. And what is profound, or, rather, of interest, is not only what one has hidden but also the ways one has of hiding it. We know only, of course – as in a phobia – about the repressions that break down. So it is as though, from a psychoanalytic point of view, our unbearable self-knowledge leads a secret life; as though there is self-knowledge, but not for us. For Freud, what has to be explained is not why someone is phobic, but how anyone ever stops being anything other than phobic.

III

A 'no' from a person in analysis is quite as
ambiguous as a 'yes'.

Sigmund Freud, *Constructions in Analysis*

An acutely claustrophobic man in his early forties – although his phobia has increasingly focused on the theatre, which he has always 'loved' – remembers, in an otherwise desultory session, a childhood memory. At about age eight he goes to the oculist, and one of the tests he is made to do 'to find out about his coordination' is to look down something like a telescope and with his hands put the dog he sees into the cage that he sees. He does it successfully and with real pleasure; and the oculist, a 'benign man', says to him, 'Well, you'll never be able to join the RAF!' Understanding that he will never be able to be a pilot, he is 'shattered', 'although until that moment it had never occurred to me that I wanted to'. And then he adds, sarcastically, that as an adult he has always been really excited about travelling in aeroplanes. It is clear to both of us that this is something of an ambiguous triumph.

I remind him that his terror in the theatre – the fantasy he desperately wards off, and so 'sees' instead of the play – is that he will jump off the balcony (he had confessed to me in our first meeting, with some satisfaction, that he always sat in the circle). He thinks about this but is clearly much less impressed by it than I am. So I try to impress him by adding that the theatre is a place where you mustn't fly but must look at other people. He says he remembers reading about a play in Italy in which the actors came on stage and looked at the audience 'instead'. I say, 'So you might be wondering in the theatre, how can I get them to look at me?' He mumbles agreement and then says, slightly mocking me, I think, with one of my own words, 'You mean the actors are rivals.' I say, 'Actors seem like people who are permitted to do forbidden things, to play other parts.' And he says with some quickness in his voice, 'I've always been waiting for someone to ask me to do something I'm not allowed, but once they've invited me then it's allowed!' After this new description of the trap there is a pause in which it seems as though we are both mulling the last bit over. I'm thinking, among a lot of other things, that he has told me what he has come to analysis for; and that even if someone is an oculist it doesn't mean that he necessarily has good eyesight, good enough to be able to fly. He then says that he feels something has really happened in this session – and certainly his words no longer feel like spectators – but he adds that he knows that when he goes to the theatre next he will feel that he is going to die of anxiety; and I find myself thinking, why not agree to die and see what happens?

The childhood memory that helped us push off into the conversation is clearly very suggestive in terms of the relationship between what you can see, what you can put together, and the parts you are allowed to play. If flying had represented possibility for the eight-year-old boy, and possibility, at least from an Oedipal perspective, was inspired by the forbidden, then the theatre – or, indeed, any confined space – was the place to be. Flying would turn into falling, looking would become being seen, performance would turn into failure. The theatre was the place where he was connected, through terror, with his wish to enact forbidden versions of himself. And forbidden versions, in this context, means both those disapproved of by the parents and those outside the parents' orbit of recognition. As a child one may experience as forbidden simply the versions of oneself that turned up under the blank stare of one's parents' blind spots. The child's most puzzling and urgent projects – which can pursue him through life like Frankenstein's monster – sometimes come to life in this no man's land. One of this man's pictures of himself as an adolescent was of someone auditioning in a completely empty theatre.

Describing the way he made sketches, Bonnard wrote in his notebook: 'The practice of cropping of the visual field almost always gives something which doesn't seem true. Composition at the second degree consists of *bringing back certain elements which lie outside the rectangle*.' The phobic person is suspended between the first and the second degree of composition; he assumes, quite sensibly, that making the transition will break the frame rather than, as Bonnard intimates, making it a frame for something that seems true. He hovers in his terror, unable to make that decisive transition.

If horror, as William James wrote, is a 'vertiginous baffling of the expectation', then phobic horror is a baffling of the awareness of expectation; there is nothing but paralysis or flight.

But in thinking about phobias it's worth taking seriously the difference between a phobic situation and a phobic object like an insect. A phobic situation, broadly speaking, one can choose to avoid, but a phobic object can turn up unexpectedly. One might say, for example, that a person who imagines that his hate could turn up at any moment, like an unwanted guest – who has to live in a state of continual internal vigilance to ensure that he will always be fair – might choose an object rather than a situation. A situation phobia is a controlled temptation. And clearly the availability of, the potential for access to, the phobic object or situation is an essential factor, because it signifies access – and a person's attitude to this proximity – to otherwise repressed states of mind or versions of oneself.

A sixteen-year-old girl was referred to me for provocative behaviour in school. She would do absurd things to enrage her teachers like sitting in lessons with a shoe on her head, but as though this was quite normal. She was popular with her peers, who seemed to view her with a rather wary admiration. As we talked about this for several weeks – linking it to the life she led in her family – I began to suggest to her in bits and pieces that being provocative was one of her ways of getting to know people; that in order to find out whether she could like people she had to find the hate in them. She was playing, as it were, hunt the monster to discover what the worst version of the other person was that she was going to have to comply with. As I repeated this in different ways I noticed that occasionally she became curious; and at the point at which her curiosity was aroused she would say, quite rightly, that none of this was helping. After one rather tedious version of this interpretation she mentioned that she was terrified of spiders; indeed, she often had nightmares about them. I asked her if she hated me when I bored her, and she grinned.

It began to occur to me that she could manage a self that hated only if it was incarnated in someone else. By being provocative it was as though she was continually expelling this version of herself, but also keeping it alive and close at hand (she told me that even though spiders terrified her she never killed them; partly, I think, because she needed to know that her hate was alive and well, and also that to kill one might confirm the murderous power of her hatred). Her references to spiders were sporadic, and when I referred to them she told me categorically that this was something she was not prepared to talk about. I said that sometimes I might need to but that I would always warn her so she could put her fingers in her ears. She would then be able to regulate what she heard.

It was after establishing this ritual that I noticed that she was becoming interested in her dreams; not, I should add, in my attempted interpretations, but in the dream scenes themselves. As she said, 'You go to bed and you never know what you're going to see.' After what seemed like months of endlessly reported dreams she arrived one day for a session to tell me that she had had 'the spider dream' again, and it was clear she wanted something from me. I asked her if anything had happened recently that she had given in to and regretted having done so. Her first reaction was to say that she was always giving in to things; and it had been evident from talking to her that she was very much a parental child whose parents were always effectively saying to her, 'You mustn't get cross, because we need your help.' But then she added – as though this was an odd bit of the answer – that in school the previous day the teacher had asked the class a question and she had answered it. I wondered if secretly she had bitterly resented this, as though answering the question felt like playing his game. She replied that she had bitten her tongue at lunch. I said that I thought the dream might be a protest and that in order to get really furious she had to find a spider to let her do it. She said, 'You mean if I was a spider I could be really horrible.' I said, 'Yes, spiders are good to hate people with'; there was a pause and then she said, 'Say some more.' I said that I thought that probably every week she gave in to lots of things almost without noticing, and that if she came across a spider she was suddenly reminded of how cross she was and how much those feelings frightened her. Sometimes, when she felt really insulted, as she had yesterday with the teacher, she needed a spider so much that she had to dream one up. She listened to this intently and then said, 'So a spider's a bit like turning on a tap?', and I agreed.

IV

Ignorance of myself is something I must work at; it is something studied like a dead language.

Stanley Cavell, *The Claim of Reason*

A useful way to think about a symptom is to ask how you could teach someone to have it (what would I need to do, or who would I have to appear to be, to persuade someone that open spaces are terrifying?). For the phobic person the object or the situation that inspires the terror is beyond scepticism; he will behave as though he knows exactly what it is, however absurd this may seem to himself or other people. All his scepticism is kept for the interpreters. In a phobia a person explicitly pretends to a private language, to a secretive exemption from shared meanings. The phobia reveals virtually nothing about the object except its supposed power to frighten; it baffles inquiry. Just as, in actuality, there is no repetition, only a wish for the idea of repetition as a way of familiarizing the present, so, with the phobic object or situation, the person thinks that he knows where he is. Better the devil you know than an angel you don't.

But it is, paradoxically, the very certainty of the phobic person that robs him of his autonomy (of course Freud would say that being a person robs him of his autonomy). Before the phobic object he submits to something akin to possession, to an experience without the mobility of perspectives. A phobia, like virtually nothing else, shows the capacity of the body to be gripped by occult meaning; it is like a state of somatic conviction. 'The phobic object,' Julia Kristeva writes in *Powers of Horror*, 'is precisely avoidance of choice, it tries as long as possible to maintain the subject far from decision', or from the notion that this could be a matter for decision. It is as though the object is issuing the orders, and the body responds even in anticipation of its presence. As the victim of terror the subject is as far as possible, in his own mind, from being the one who terrorizes. But he is sustaining a relationship, even in his avoidance, constituted by terror. 'Such avoidances,' the psychoanalyst Roger Money-Kyrle remarked in his *Collected Papers*, 'are superimposed upon seekings.'

If a phobia has the effect of empowering and disempowering a person at the same time – like a kind of quotidian sublime, filling him with terror and rendering him helpless – it is also, by the same token, a way of making ordinary places and things extremely charged, like an unconscious estrangement technique. To be petrified by a pigeon is a way of making it new. The phobia is an eroticization not so much of danger as of significance. The creation towards the end of the nineteenth century of these new sexual objects – the familiar phobias became 'symptoms' in the 1870s – the discovery that a panic akin to sexual excitement was felt by certain people when confronted with birds, rodents, insects, theatres, or open spaces, could be used as evidence of the idea of an unconscious mind; or of irrational selves inhabiting respectable selves, as in Jekyll and Hyde (Stevenson's tale was published in 1886). But those who made category mistakes – pigeons, after all, are not killers – had to be categorized. The advantage of pathologizing – and, of course, self-pathologizing – is that it appears to place the participants in a structure of pre-existing knowledge and authority. The very absurdity of phobias, often even to the people who have them, could seem like a parody of the diagnostic process.

As symptoms, phobias provide a useful focus for what Donald Davidson has described in his essay 'Paradoxes of Irrationality' as 'the underlying paradox of irrationality': 'If we explain it too well,' he writes, 'we turn it into a concealed form of rationality; while if we assign incoherence too glibly, we merely compromise our ability to diagnose irrationality by withdrawing the background of rationality needed to justify any diagnosis at all.' One of the functions of a phobia is to fix such distinctions, to take the paradox out of them (phobia, ritualized as taboo, maintains a sensible universe). For the phobic person the phobia guarantees the difference – marks out a boundary – between the acceptably safe and the dangerously forbidden and exciting; and for his double, the interpreter, between the rational and the irrational (so one could ask, for example, 'What would I have to say about one of my dislikes to make you think I was phobic of it, rather than just very discriminating?' or 'Are we phobic of all the things we never do and all the places we never go, unconsciously phobic, as it were?'). The catastrophe that the phobic and his interpreter are both trying to avert is the collapse of their distinctions, the loss, or rather the mixing, of their categories. Practising the martial arts of purity and danger, what can they do for each other beyond providing mutual reassurance?

Symptoms are a way of thinking about difficult things, thinking with the sound turned off, as it were. One of the reasons, perhaps, that Freud was so intrigued by phobias – several of the great case histories are analyses of phobias – was that the making of a phobia was the model for the making of a theory. A phobia, like a psychoanalytic theory, is a story about where the wild things are. And these theories, like their phobic paradigm, organize themselves around a fantasy of the impossible, the unacceptable in its most extreme form. Because Freud refused to assign incoherence too glibly – realizing that the rational and the irrational have to double for each other – he began to describe curiosity and knowledge, including, of course, the knowledge that is psychoanalytic theory, as reactive to fear; an attempt to master the phobia – the first recognition – that by inaugurating consciousness depletes it. If terror is the object of knowledge, knowledge is counterphobic.

In order to become what Freud thinks of as a person, one has to become phobic; and one can become phobic only by believing that there is an external and an internal world that are discrete. 'What is bad, what is alien to the ego and what is external are, to begin with, identical,' Freud writes in 'Negation', his extraordinary paper of 1925. For the ego to sustain itself as good, which means in Freud's terms for the ego to sustain itself, depends upon expelling everything experienced as bad into the outside world. The assumption is that at the very beginning unpleasure is soon intolerable and spells death, and that consciousness is of unpleasure. The 'bad' – or Melanie Klein would say the 'hate' – is, pre-Oedipally, the excess of desire that threatens to destroy the ego and, slightly later, the object; and Oedipally, the forbidden incestuous desires. 'In so far as the objects which are presented to it are sources of pleasure,' Freud writes in 'Instincts and Their Vicissitudes' (1915), 'the ego takes them into itself, "introjects" them . . . and, on the other hand, it expels whatever within itself becomes a cause of unpleasure.' The first world we find outside is, in part, a repository for the terror inside us, an elsewhere for those desires and objects that bring unpleasure. And that world we make outside is the world we need to get away from. It is the place, or one of the places, where we put the objects and desires we wish did not belong to us. To be at home in the world we need to keep it inhospitable.

The ego needs a place elsewhere – which will be called outside – and another place elsewhere that Freud will call 'the repressed unconscious', which is inside. And this matches, of course, the good/bad distinction (a different way of putting it might be to say: there's no such thing as an internal world; there are just collections of words that seem to do justice to the complexity of what we feel). But in Freud's terms the ego, in this process of distributing the bad things, is depleting itself in the hopeless task of keeping itself what Freud calls a 'pure pleasure ego'. The developmental question, in Freud's view – conceived of, or rather enacted, before the individual could describe it like this – is, what is unbearable about oneself and where is one going to put it? And the consequent preoccupation becomes, once one has supposedly got rid of it, how is one going to live in a state of such impoverishment, so emptied of oneself? The phobic object becomes the promise – the (unconscious) gift returned, as it were – that has to be refused. But the refusal, of course, is a way of keeping the promise.

If, as Freud believed, one is fundamentally unable – or ill-equipped in childhood – to contain oneself, then it is part of the developmental project to find a phobia, to localize the impossible in oneself elsewhere. But of course for Freud fantasies – and the fantasy that makes a phobia – are forms of magical thinking; in the phobic fantasy you convince a part of yourself that the bad things are elsewhere only because there is really no elsewhere (or the only real elsewhere is the place you cannot put parts of yourself). Finding hate-objects may be every bit as essential as finding love-objects, but if one can tolerate some of one's 'badness' – meaning recognize it as yours – then one can take some fear out of the world. In this psychoanalytic picture the treatment is a method of retrieval; almost, one might say, of the misplaced persons in oneself. With this picture, though, psychoanalysis can become unwittingly punitive, because each person has a limit to what he can take (not to mention the fact that there is a tyrannically omniscient fantasy at work here of what constitutes a 'whole' person). In Freud's view, the ego depends upon its phobia. It is, so to speak, its first relationship, and one that is inevitably paranoid (paranoia being, as it were, a refusal to be left out).

The idea of the unconscious is, among other things, a way of describing the fact that there are things we didn't know we could say. A phobia is a conviction that bad things are unspeakable, and therefore that the unspeakable is always bad. And this makes tacit understandings for the phobic person always dangerous. If you articulate the terror for the phobic person he may be persecuted by it again, and if you don't you collude with the notion that there is something truly unbearable.

Phobias, that is to say, confront the psychoanalyst very starkly, with the dilemma of cure. The art of psychoanalysis, for both the participants, is to produce interesting redescriptions: redescriptions that the patient is free – can bear – to be interested in. Or to put it another way: the aim of psychoanalysis is not to cure people but to show them that there is nothing wrong with them.

On Success

I

I do not believe that things will turn out well, but the
idea that they might is of decisive importance.

Theodor Adorno and Max Horkheimer,
Towards a New Manifesto

John Stuart Mill's extraordinary education has become a kind of
fable of pedagogic ambition, and of the way in which parental
demand can structure a child's life. Taught exclusively by his
father, and having no contact with other children apart from his
own siblings whom he had to teach, Mill started learning Greek
when he was three, and Latin when he was eight. Between the
ages of eight and twelve he learned 'elementary geometry and
algebra thoroughly, the differential calculus and other portions
of the higher mathematics'. As well as reading at this time a
good deal of the most important classical literature, what he
refers to as his 'private' reading was mostly history, which he
also wrote (in the form of a history of Roman government).

At twelve he began learning logic – Aristotle and Hobbes –
and when he was thirteen his father gave him what he calls 'a
complete course in political economy'. His father, Mill wrote in
his *Autobiography*, 'exerted an amount of labour, care and perse-
verance rarely, if ever, employed for a similar purpose, in
endeavouring to give, according to his own conception, the
highest order of intellectual education'. 'If I have accomplished
anything,' Mill concludes without obvious misgivings, 'I owe

it, among other fortunate circumstances, to the fact that through the early training bestowed on me by my father, I started, I may fairly say, with an advantage of a quarter of a century over my contemporaries.' That is to say, by the age of fifteen he had the learning of a man in his late thirties; 'the experiment was', as Isaiah Berlin has written, 'in a sense, an appalling success'.

One's history, of course, never begins with oneself; everyone's life, in a sense, is the afterthought of unknowable previous generations. James Mill, J. S. Mill's father, acquired a formal education only because he came to the notice of what, in this context, we could call a substitute father, a patron, Sir John Stuart, who sent him to the University of Edinburgh. Mill records in his *Autobiography* that his father was 'the son of a petty tradesman and (I believe) small farmer'. (For us, of course, in this transgenerational story, the absence of significant mothers is striking.) The implication of Mill's brief account of his grandfather as a petty tradesman is that the family history is a kind of progress narrative, a success story of sorts.

And yet the ultimate success of the story seems to have depended on its breaking down: at the age of twenty Mill suffered a catastrophic disillusionment. And again it involved fathers not being good enough to get their sons where they wanted to go. But like all disillusionments, it was made from a history of illusionments; an implicit belief in belief itself. Well prepared by his father's educational project, in 1822 at the age of sixteen Mill read Dumont's *Traité de Législation* – a French translation of the work of his father's good friend Jeremy Bentham. 'The reading of this book,' Mill writes in his *Autobiography*, 'was an epoch in my life; one of the turning points in my mental history.' Reading this book, and Bentham himself, gave Mill – as what we call an adolescent – 'what might truly be called an object in life: to be a reformer of the world. My conception of my own happiness was entirely identified with this object . . . my whole reliance was placed on this.' From an accumulation of fathers living and dead (all the books he records reading are, of course, by men) he had acquired a project: to reform the world according to Bentham's Utilitarian principle of the greatest happiness for the greatest number.

Like all ideals, Mill's gave him that most paradoxical thing, a picture of the future. It was, as he says, his 'object in life'; the least flirtatious of men, he was entirely identified with it and placed his 'whole reliance' on it. And all of these, of course, would be ways in which a psychoanalyst might describe a child's relation to a parent; then in adolescence, to put it at its most reductive, parents are replaced by ideals, and sexual desire is partly usurped by moral principle and ambition. Indeed, Mill describes his new-found 'object in life' in ways that are particularly revealing from a psychoanalytic point of view. He was made happy in this project, he writes, 'through placing my happiness in something durable and distant, in which some progress might be always making, while it could never be exhausted by complete attainment'. As with belief in a god, the durability of this object depends upon its distance. Just as we only identify with what we don't understand, authority – of a person or an ideal – is constituted by unfamiliarity. The paradox that Mill presents us with – and that may be integral to fantasies of success (the attainment of ideals) – is that fantasies are reliable *because* they cannot be achieved; that both the person and his or her ideal may fear being 'exhausted by complete attainment'. That success entails a fear of success; that something will be depleted by its realization. It is as though we need to know the end of the story, but have to ensure that we don't experience it. Mill's description of placing his happiness in 'something durable and distant' suggests the way in which those beliefs we call our ideals, our fantasies of success, are hypnotic like the horizon. And there is an implicit idea of the self here as something that needs a strong belief, a commitment, to organize it and hold it together. But our success stories, in which our problems are solved and our desires gratified, may be forms of self-hypnosis. In other words, the risk – as in psychotherapy or counselling itself – is that we use our solutions as ways of pre-empting experience of the problem (listening for the answer is not listening). If I eat every time I feel hungry I may never find out what my hunger is (for). For several years Mill could successfully devote himself to his project because, as he puts it, it 'seemed enough to fill up an interesting and animated existence'. And then, as I have said, in his twentieth year he suffered a disillusionment, a breakdown, which he describes as the breaking of a spell, an awakening:

> [T]he time came when I awakened from this as from a dream. It was in the autumn of 1826. I was in a dull state of nerves, such as everybody is occasionally liable to; unsusceptible to enjoyment or pleasurable excitement; one of those moods when what is pleasure at other times becomes insipid or indifferent; the state, I should think, in which converts to Methodism usually are, when smitten by their first 'conviction of sin'. In this frame of mind it occurred to me to put the question directly to myself, 'Suppose that all your objects in life were realised; that all the changes in institutions and opinions which you are looking forward to, could be completely effected at this very instant; would this be a great joy and happiness to you?' And an irrepressible self-consciousness distinctly answered, 'No'. At this my heart sank within me; the whole foundation on which my life was constructed fell down. All my happiness was to have been found in the continual pursuit of this end. The end had ceased to charm, and how could there ever again be any interest in the means? I seemed to have nothing left to live for.

It is easy to see this as, so to speak, a traditional Oedipal crisis; Mill compares it to a Methodist's first conviction of sin against God; later in his account he reminds himself of Macbeth who, of course, killed a king. And he begins to recover from this crisis – 'a small ray of light broke in upon my gloom' – when he starts reading Marmontel's *Memoirs* and 'came to the passage which relates his father's death, the distressed position of the family, and the sudden inspiration by which he, then a mere boy, felt and made them feel that he would be everything to them – would supply the place of all that they had lost'. After reading this account of a son replacing a father, Mill describes himself as literally coming back to life: 'from this moment my burthen grew lighter. The oppression of the thought that all feeling was dead within me, was gone. I was no longer hopeless; I was not a stick or a stone.'

Clearly, one cannot psychoanalyse a writer from his text; one can only appropriate him. But it is nevertheless plausible, despite the fact that Mill does not say it, that his crisis, among other things, was a protest against the life his father had organized for him; an attempt to renegotiate it. The question Mill puts directly to himself – if all his ambitions in life were realized, would he be happy? – was a question he dared not ask of his father; his breakdown – like most breakdowns, given a sufficiently attentive environment – was also a breakthrough. And one of the many things that tend to break through in such crises are repressed questions addressed to the parents, or to the parents internalized as parts of oneself. In psychoanalytic language one can say that the children carry, often in the form of symptoms, the parents' repressed doubts about their own ideals and ambitions; this is one of the things Freud meant when he suggested that 'a child's super-ego is in fact constructed on the model not of its parents but of its parents' super-ego'. Just as every internal prohibition represents an ambition – a moral aim for the ego – so every symptom is a transgenerational task. A crisis is always also on behalf of someone else, even if that someone else is part of one-self. It is as though the generations – each subject contingently to different economic, political and historical conditions – are processing each other's ambitions. And university is, of course, for some people essentially a crisis of ambition.

John Stuart Mill's crisis was prompted, finally, by a simple imaginative act: he fast-forwarded his life and looked back at it from the position of having achieved his ambitions; he imagined that he had already become his own ideal. Having lived by the lure of an endlessly deferred future – having organized his life around the demands of a specific ambition – he made the wished-for future present and killed his aspiring self. And once, in his mind, this future had already happened, the foundation of his life was destroyed. Mill, that is to say, here does consciously what Freud says we do each night unconsciously, in our dreams: he imaginatively fulfils a wish (in psychoanalytic terms dreams are our paradigm for success). And at this point, as though it were a conscious nightmare, he awakens to his own despair; he has nothing left to live for; he has become inanimate, like a stone.

Now that he has realized that success would be a form of failure for him, what has Mill woken up to? It would be reassuring to say that he has simply rediscovered a piece of traditional wisdom: that it is better to travel hopefully than to arrive. But actually he has discovered something that seems now more psychoanalytic, and pertinent to our present subject: that sometimes, with some ambitions, you can travel hopefully *only* if you ensure you never arrive (hope is only ever false in retrospect). That in order to hope – or, as Freud would say, wish – you need an object; and these objects, these ideals that encode our fantasies of success, though they derive from past experiences, are set in the future. They are aims, targets for desire; they have to be separate from us – they have to keep their distance – in order to make a journey of it. (No one says, as perhaps they should, 'I'm aiming to be what I am already.') Ambitions, in other words, are ways of locating – or rather, ways of describing – possible futures and possible future selves. Without belief in the future, the idea of success would disappear.

So to have ambitions – and therefore fantasies (conscious and unconscious) of what it would be to succeed or fail – one needs, firstly, an object of desire, an ideal, a state of the world or of oneself sufficiently separate from oneself to aspire to. So one needs to have perceived a lack, of sorts, in oneself. Secondly, one needs a belief in Time as a promising medium to do things in; one needs to be able to suffer the pains and pleasures of anticipation and deferral. And thirdly, as Mill's example shows, one needs a tolerable relationship to satisfaction; and this involves something that Freud uniquely problematized: belief in the accuracy, the possibility, of one's desire. For Freud, as we will see, knowing what one wants can be a contradiction in terms; and this means that success and failure often double for each other.

The need for a separate object, the commitment to waiting in Time, and the relationship to satisfaction – all these ingredients of success (and failure) reveal our ambitions, from a psychoanalytic point of view, as versions of our erotic life, in which satisfaction is always conflictual. Ambitions can be described as wishes, and therefore derivatives of instinctual life. To talk about one's ambitions is to find a respectable way, an unembarrassing way, of talking about what one wants (which is not always respectable). Ambitions are more or less culturally legitimated desires. Nothing is less disreputable than the wish to get to university – or the wish for academic success. But these wishes may be ways of encoding, or disguising, more problematic desires – like, for example, the wish to consolidate, or deconstruct, a precarious sexual identity cobbled together in adolescence. So it is to the *use* of ideals, and to the relationship to satisfaction, to success – the material of any therapeutic encounter – that I want to turn now.

II

fear a too great consistency

A. R. Ammons, 'One: Many'

One of the papers in a series, 'Some Character Types Met With in Psychoanalytic Work', that Freud wrote in 1916 is entitled 'Those Wrecked by Success'. In it he uses the examples of Macbeth and Ibsen's Rosmer to explain something that defies common sense: that people can fall ill 'upon the fulfilment of a wish and put an end to all enjoyment of it'; that 'people occasionally fall ill precisely when a deeply rooted and long cherished wish has come to fulfilment'. It is not that they discover that they didn't really want what they have now succeeded in getting, but rather that having got it they now need to punish themselves with the suffering of an illness. There is, Freud intimates, nothing like success to show us that we are not quite who we think we are. In his view it is not that the wish is necessarily wrong, nor the object chosen for its gratification; but rather that, from a psychoanalytic point of view, we are always doing at least two if not three (or more) things at once.

In order to make sense of the experience that wanting is always conflictual – that people can be wrecked by success – Freud suggests that we imagine our lives as a story in which three parts of ourselves are always involved; that in doing any one thing we have at least three projects: we are satisfying a desire, we are sustaining a sense of moral well-being, and we are ensuring our survival. In this useful fiction the id is productive of desire, the super-ego is the carrier of our ethical ideals, and the ego tries to make these often conflicting demands compatible with keeping going. 'Analytic work,' Freud writes, with blithe self-confidence, 'has no difficulty in showing us that it is forces of conscience which forbid the subject to gain the long hoped for advantage from the fortunate change in reality.' The super-ego is an essentialist, and always has a fixed view of the ego; like all fixed views, it can only ultimately be sustained by intimidation. Having changed reality in pursuit of success, we realize that we are at cross-purposes with ourselves. 'For a neurosis to be generated,' Freud writes, 'there must be a conflict between a person's libidinal wishes, and the part of his personality we call the ego.' And since there is always a conflict, ambition spells self-division. Success can make people feel guilty; but guilt is also something one can hide in (from oneself).

It is easy to forget that an ambition begins as a wish, and that a wish has a history. Wanting something (like academic success) or someone connects us with the past. My success – the fulfilment of a wish – is always an echo of previous encounters with my own desire. My ambition, so to speak, as a baby to be warm and sufficiently nurtured can be linked with my ambition to get a good degree. Satisfactions can be described as both repeating and modifying earlier satisfactions: pleasures are echoes. From a psychoanalytic point of view, we are always talking of a person's relationship to his or her own wishes, a relationship that has evolved over time. Frustration and satisfaction become synonymous with, or rather precursors of, our ideas of failure and success: the child is very much alive in the young aspiring adult. 'People fall ill of a neurosis,' Freud writes, 'as a result of frustration.' The picture becomes complicated, as I have said, when frustration for one part of the self, say, the super-ego, is satisfaction for another part, the id. In this picture one kind of success can be another kind of failure. In psychotherapy one always has to remember that anyone who is failing at one thing is always succeeding at another. The therapist, or counsellor, is useful as someone who can show the patient the paradoxical nature of his acts. If I fail as a student to have a girlfriend, I succeed at keeping myself as someone who loves only in the family. If I fail my exams I successfully maintain myself as someone who is not ready for the next stage. If I can't write my essay, I can show myself to be capable of refusing a demand by a figure of authority. In this context the aim of the therapy is not so much to help people make more competent choices as to show them how many choices they are (unconsciously) making.

So if we are to think of success from a psychodynamic point of view, we have to bear in mind three things which are inevitably connected. Firstly, it can be useful to think of ourselves as multiple personalities; of our internal worlds as more like a novel than a monologue. Each character, or part of ourselves, has different projects, and different criteria of success; so some people, for example, live as though they would prefer to be morally right than sexually satisfied, or clever rather than ordinary. In these cases it is as though an internal democracy has become a meritocracy; certain internal voices become muted because a repertoire of ways of being has been turned into a set of alternatives (in actuality, one can be clever *and* ordinary). Conflict requires the forging of incompatibles. The second point that follows from this is that because our different selves have different projects, success and failure are inextricable; success for one self can feel like failure for another, and vice versa. We are always doing at least two things at once, and this can mean that the art of psychotherapy is turning what feel like contradictions—incompatibilities—into paradoxes. This does not entail ironing out the conflicts, but rather extending the repertoire of ways of describing them.

So a useful interpretation in this context might be something like: up until now you have been getting your sexual satisfaction by being morally right; there may be other ways of doing both things. Or, if you could be clever *and* ordinary, what would your life look like? These forms of redescription are revisions of the past. And this leads me to the third point, which is that these internal selves and their relationship have a history; that we have grown up in particular families in particular cultures, in sexed and gendered bodies, and subject, of course, to the multiple contingencies – economic, political, psychological – of any life. A person's fantasies of success are only the most recent versions of an elaborate personal history of such fantasies. If our earliest success is our own survival – our development into people who can have fantasies of success – we acquire, in the language of our mother tongue, the ideals of our culture. Fantasies of success are both given to us – our inheritance but not our invention – and, much like our gender identities, from which they are inextricable, constructed. And this leaves us, I think, with two questions pertinent to therapy. How do we make ideals for ourselves, those success stories that we try to live by? And secondly – and in some ways more problematic – how do we make them our own? How do we get to feel that to some extent we have chosen them – that they formulate what matters most to us – rather than had them imposed upon us? Ideals should feel like affinities, not impositions. It is striking how tyrannical – hypnotic and intransigent – people's ideals can be. And this is particularly vivid, I think, during adolescence and young adulthood.

Clearly, these issues reach a kind of crisis around the initiation rite of going to university, and leaving it. And what I am talking about, any adolescent – and any adult old enough to go on being an adolescent – will recognize. It is the difference between doing something that I believe is right and doing something because if I don't I will be punished. It is the difference between doing what I want – what makes me feel alive and can fill me with anticipation – and doing what other people want me to want. University, in other words, can be a crisis for the compliant self; and, of course, a crisis for the compliant self of the student counsellor or therapist who has to deal with such crises. Is the student counsellor to comply with the demands of the university institution and get the student back to productive work as soon as possible? Or comply with the student, understanding his or her symptom as an intelligent critique of the university? And what does the counsellor do when it feels like this kind of choice? The counsellor, like the student, has to answer a fundamental question: who am I working for? Success for the counselling treatment can mean failure for the university. The successful student counsellor may have to be a double agent, and is always a kind of spy.

III

For the moment I want merely to underline the words *the actual disorder of experience*.

William Arrowsmith, 'Turbulence in the Humanities'

It has become a conventional formulation, in the jargon of psychoanalytic theory, that people suffer when the disparity between their ego and their ego-ideal becomes excessive; that is to say, suffering turns up when there is too great a distance – too big a gap – between who a person feels himself to be and who he wants to be. When my ideal or preferred versions of myself begin to seem remote – or exclusively embodied by other people – so-called symptoms can be both a way of registering the distress and an attempt to mobilize resources. In fact, one could say that people come for any kind of psychotherapy or counselling because there is a problem in their relationship to success; because someone is letting someone else down, and that someone else can be a part of the self. Psychotherapy is about refinding the future.

Because we have come to think of ourselves as creatures who *aspire* – whether it be to survival or something grander – it is difficult to imagine (or describe) our lives without conscious and unconscious ideals. So I would like to try to work out why it is so difficult to imagine a (non-cynical) life without ideals, those objects we use to feel successful with (is a life without ambition a life without a future, or a life without a particular kind of future?). If, for example, my ambition in life is to see what happens to me, what kind of future am I imagining for myself? In this context we have to remember that the only contact we have with the future, so to speak, is in the form of wishes. But firstly, I want to look at the question of success – the conflict of ambition – from a developmental perspective.

Developmental theories offer us a repertoire of what can be called success stories – and success-anxieties. Developmental theories are the success stories against which we fail. Indeed, the idea of development itself – with its language of 'stages' and 'achievements' and 'fixation-points' – involves the idea of progress, of an ambition for something. And when we are faced with this barrage of theories of developmental competence, it can be easy to forget that the so-called patient or student might have quite different theories of his or her own of what a good life is; everyone has, and is, his or her own developmental theory. There is, of course, no rule that people have to grow up; there are just consequences to not doing so (and each person has a different sense of what this entails). It may, for example, be rather misleading to think that the child's *ambition* is to become an adult. Freud himself suggested that it was the child's ambition to become like the grown-ups; he didn't mention the fact that this also seems to be the grown-ups' wish.

Since every crisis about success, from a psychoanalytic point of view, has developmental antecedents, is full of reminders, it may be worth describing a repertoire of developmental puzzles. I want to suggest that these puzzles can be organized around a fundamental dilemma, that easily becomes (or perhaps is) a muddle; that after the earliest stages of infancy – the pre-linguistic stages – there is a fundamental ongoing internal relationship between desire and self-sufficiency. Development, one could say, is the continual process of working out what one cannot provide for oneself; and then one's relationship to such acknowledgements. There is a project of self-sufficiency and a project of wanting (these, of course, are conscious and unconscious fantasies); and in so far as these projects are felt to be incompatible, a person has an insoluble dilemma. If I am eager to learn something, but reading books about it exposes my lack of knowledge, the more I learn the less I seem to know. The books might seem like a mother who already seems to have everything I want. Since dependency, or the ways we have so far described it, seems such a pervasive conflict – no one ever says, for example, 'He's very good at being dependent on her' – at any transitional stage spurious alternatives are likely to turn up. Is success satisfying one's desire or escaping from it? Why, if I said I had an ambition to become more dependent, would I, at least in this culture, be politically and psychologically disparaged?

We can think of success, at any developmental stage, as being related to issues of self-sufficiency; and of wanting, of independence and dependence as the extremes on some imaginary spectrum. 'Success,' one of my adolescent patients said to me, 'is having everything you want.' I said, 'What will you want then?' and he said, 'Nothing.' Then there was a pause as he thought. After a few minutes he said, as though brightening up, 'After I've got everything I'll have to find someone else to give me some new ideas!' If we are living, at least in fantasy, between the extremes of having (or being) everything and the idea of there being something else, what are the available forms of success from a developmental point of view? Nearly all kinds of learning involve acknowledging what one does not yet know, and depending on a source outside oneself to acquire that knowledge. Successful learning is successful, or tolerable, dependence.

The psychoanalytic distinction between two-person and three-person relationships – between the pre-Oedipal and the Oedipal – can be useful here, because each brings with it different kinds of success and failure, different compromises and conflicts, different versions of dependence. Whether or not we believe in their chronology, they are ways of adding to our repertoire of kinds of relationship. From a psychoanalytic point of view these early relationships are the circumstances in which we begin to construct our ideals and depend on them, to formulate our wishes and watch them in action. So I want to build up a picture of what it would be, in psychodynamic terms, to be a pre-Oedipal and an Oedipal success, and consider how this can be linked to the conflicts and confusions of student life.

What are the ambitions of the infant and child, and what does it mean for them to fail? These pre-Oedipal and Oedipal issues can be usefully oversimplified by talking about envy and rivalry. We can say, for example, if we believe in these kinds of psychoanalytic story, that reading a book is a later version of feeding from a mother, a kind of visual eating. Or at least we can usefully describe the problems of reading in terms of this pre-Oedipal two-person mother–child relationship. A successful feed depends upon a number of factors: firstly, the coming together of the child's actual hunger with a mother ready and willing to feed. By the same token, perhaps, we can only really read – that is, take it all in and digest it – if we are really interested. Otherwise, we read with growing resentment; that is, with a compliant version of ourselves. The reading gets done, but not by us. So a student might come to a counsellor to recover, or rediscover, his appetite; to understand the obstacles to taking things in, and to work out what he or she is hungry for.

If there is real appetite, or curiosity, around, then quite quickly for the child there is the dawning awareness that these wants depend upon an external object for both recognition and satisfaction; and that this external object – the mother, father or a substitute parent – is both beyond the control of the child and seems, especially at times of acutest need, to have or be everything the child wants. So there is the shock of dependence and the disillusionment of not ruling the world. It is easy, in other words, for the child to envy the mother; and this envy – the spoiling of what is felt to belong to oneself – can get in the way. Indeed, the need for the mother might feel, or be made to feel, so unbearable that the need itself has to be destroyed. If somebody you are longing to see makes you wait too long for them, it is extremely difficult to appreciate them when they finally arrive; and to recuperate your desire for them.

All this infantile eating and envying might seem a long way from the student at university who finds himself or herself unable to study. And yet the one who knows, or seems to know – the teacher – might be experienced like a mother, or a father, as an object of envy. The frenzy of need – of felt inadequacy – baffles the learning experience. Or the student, aware somewhere in himself of his own envy, may, by the same token, be very fearful of becoming a successful student through fear of the envy of others. People can go to remarkable lengths to avert the catastrophe of their own success; or to ensure that they are not seen, even by themselves, to be, or to be trying to be, successful. It is certainly useful in the psychotherapy of adolescents to help them find ways of managing other people's envy of them as well as their own. If a book or a teacher can be experienced as being like a mother – and so has echoes of an earlier relationship – then in psychotherapy or counselling we are trying to understand the obstacles in the relationship. The exchange – the taking in and the being taken in by – is in some way being sabotaged.

A first-year undergraduate I saw for psychotherapy, who had developed an anxiety about remembering during her A levels, came to see me because she had become phobic about going into the university library. Going into the library, she said, was 'too much for her' and she felt faint. I said, 'Too much of what?' She said she 'couldn't take it all in'. I suggested that she had a belief that she had to take it *all* in. She then became huffy with me; it was a bit like a rather pious mother telling her delinquent child to be conscientious. I described what I thought was happening between us and asked her – she was a literature student – if she knew Oscar Wilde's remark, 'If a thing's worth doing, it's worth doing badly'? She was amused by this but then asked me, having recovered herself, what that had to do with anything. I suggested to her that going into the library felt like someone placing a huge meal in front of her and telling her that she had to finish her plateful; and that her faintness was a rage about this. And she replied, 'Perhaps I should blow up the library.' In this situation a person might feel that they have either to blow up the library, or blow up the need for the library. This student told me that when she found herself enjoying a book she would start on a fault-finding mission because 'the book was too good'. As with the library, it was as if her primary task was managing her greed. In a sense, she wanted it so much she couldn't take it in. She said to me at one point, as a joke: 'I really envy the library, it knows everything already.'

If there is envy *of* the desired object in the earliest relationship, there is rivalry *for* the desired object in the later three-person relationship. The child realizes, in other words, not only that the mother seems to have what he or she needs, but that there are rivals in competition for her – the father and perhaps siblings. From a psychodynamic point of view, acquiring, in whatever sense, the object of desire becomes the precursor for – the original picture of – success. Rivalry means competition, and competition brings with it winners and losers, and we have all had the experience of being both. Everybody knows what it feels like to be left out, and the first people who can leave us out – in fact, can't help but leave us out – are our parents. They do things together that exclude us and the ways we find of managing this formative experience have important repercussions. It may, for example, feel safer to be left out than to do the damage necessary to get in. And every student who gets to university has, somewhere, to cope with his or her triumph over all those who did not, or who never had the opportunity even to compete.

IV

Order at the centre is in this sense deceptive, being sustained by nonconforming and unacknowledged practices at the periphery.

James C. Scott, *Two Cheers for Anarchism*

If the successful pre-Oedipal infant can enjoy, or at least tolerate, the intensity of his appetite, the successful Oedipal child has to enjoy, or at least tolerate, his or her triumphs. To put it another way: he or she has to learn to share without sacrificing his or her passion. For the Oedipal child – or for that part of ourselves – success always means (unconsciously) someone else's failure; and this can feel intolerable, or worthy of punishment. Failure can sometimes feel like the only appropriate punishment for success.

A twenty-two-year-old patient – a graduate student – told me that she had bought a suit she really liked to go to the first seminar of the term. She felt very attractive in it and when she got there two of her female friends commented on how nice she looked. But instead of this confirming her sense of herself she suddenly became very 'jittery and self-conscious'. I suggested that she had heard this as though they had said to her, 'You look more attractive than us.' She replied that, unusually for her, she had made herself 'invisible' in the seminar. The conversation then rambled, as it does, until eventually, as part of an apparently inconsequential story, she described a memory of her mother and brother sitting on a sofa together at home and her feeling 'like a television set that no one wanted to turn on'. I wondered if it felt too dangerous to be turned on, to be so special that everyone would look at her? She said, 'If they all look at me, who'll look after me?' It was as though, for her, successful competition could feel like abandonment. Or that in order to be looked after she had to keep herself left out.

Envy and rivalry as essential ingredients of our failures and successes come from a picture of ourselves as acquisitive creatures driven by animal appetites and moral greeds. And this is a picture that psychoanalysis – and all the therapies derived from it – both endorses and partly created. Of any theory one can usefully ask, what is the drama that the theory is a caption for? Theories, that is to say, are interpretations of dreams. But I want to suggest, by way of conclusion, that it may be too limiting to think of ourselves and our clients with only this picture in mind. It is particularly difficult to entertain alternatives in a culture so bewitched both by the idea of success and by such a limited definition of what it entails. Because the idea of the enviable life has now replaced the idea of the good life, it may be difficult to hear, or to listen to, the parts of our patients or students that are not interested in success. There are, as we know, people around for whom being successful has not been a success. But there may also be people around – and I would guess there are a lot of them at universities – for whom success itself is a distraction, but for whom there is no language available to describe a good life free of success. We police ourselves with purposes. Our ambitions – our ideals and success stories that lure us into the future – can too easily become ways of not living in the present, or of not being present at the event, a blackmail of distraction; ways, that is, of disowning, or demeaning, the actual disorder of experience. Believing in the future can be a great deadener. Perhaps we have been too successful at success and failure, and should now start doing something else.

Contingency for Beginners

I

If one considers chance to be unworthy of determining our fate, it is simply a relapse into the pious view of the Universe which Leonardo himself was on the way to overcoming when he wrote that the sun does not move.

Freud, *Leonardo da Vinci and a Memory of His Childhood*

A fifty-five-year-old woman, whose coming to see me was prompted by the death of her mother, began, after about a year of treatment, to pick up a theme that she described as 'something she had never been able to unpuzzle'. I wasn't sure whether 'unpuzzle' meant talking the puzzle out of something – stopping it from being an enigma – or just taking the puzzle apart like a jigsaw so one could redo it. When I asked her about this we realized that there was an instructive uncertainty in her as to whether she was inviting me to help her keep the puzzle, albeit in different terms, or help her get rid of it. And this related to one of her dilemmas about mourning her mother; do you keep someone by getting rid of them, or do you get rid of them by keeping them?

The puzzle that she was constantly preoccupied by – and which was clearly linked to the death of her mother – was that whenever she had fallen in love with a man, or even made an enthusiastic friendship, she was haunted, indeed obsessed, by the other person, but he (and occasionally she), though usually keen on her, did not seem quite so distracted. She described herself as someone who 'always took her chances', and she was clearly someone people were much attracted to. But in these relationships it was as though the continuity of her life was ruptured, whereas the continuity of the other person's life was simply enriched. She described this predicament often as 'just her luck', and I was struck by the paradox of her having so often personalized her luck (one can often reconstruct very interesting bits of people's histories from their accounts of their luck); but of course her 'puzzle' seemed a dismayingly common, indeed banal, one. She had discussed this inequity in her relationships – which had begun, she knew, with her mother – with various friends and lovers over the years, and there had always seemed to be a kind of consensus that this was one of the differences between the sexes, and therefore one had to learn to manage this piece of alleged reality as a piece of biological bad luck. However, she had never been fully convinced by all this 'truth' and its relevance to her particular life, and so she had evolved a double-life attitude to it all: one part of her acknowledged the dispiriting sense of the conventional view, which at least simulated a solidarity with fellow-sufferers, but another part of her was keeping her ears open for a better story. The death of her mother had given renewed urgency to the question of her relationship to her own luck.

Since the asymmetry of the psychoanalytic situation – and of the mourning process – is one of its defining characteristics, we could obviously discuss her puzzle in terms of the transference, and this could be linked to the bewildering dissymmetries of the child's relationship with the parents, and the survivor's relations with the dead. But because this puzzle was such a crucial issue for her – it had become, as she put it, 'like a favourite walk' – she was very skilled at tolerating all the false leads and bits of folklore people could come up with when they talked about it with her. I suggested to her that she would recognize – register in some way through a stirring of curiosity – what was of interest to her, and she should let herself be ruthless with my contributions if they seemed irrelevant. Her evident relief at this showed me how much Wisdom she had had to endure in the past.

I should add by way of a parenthesis here that I think of these very idiosyncratic recurring personal preoccupations like this woman's puzzle – that often seem banal – as being (or being like) interpretations of a dream that a person has forgotten. So these insistent and consciously formulated issues put the patient and the analyst in the paradoxical position of having to reconstruct a dream from an interpretation. Or to put it another way, for people with these organized life-questions the aim of the analysis is not insight so much as reconstruction of the material out of which interpretation by the patient can be remade. It may be worth wondering why the idea of reconstructing dreams is so much more unthinkable than the idea of reconstructing personal histories. Even though we make our dreams, we think of them as beyond our own devices. We cannot – and this is integral to my subject – arrange to have dreams, or to have a dream again. (Nor, of course, can we arrange to have our histories again; we can only arrange to reconstruct them.) Analysis may be more of a search for dreams than of a search for insight. The fact that we may be able to interpret dreams does not make them any less contingent than the day-residues they use (dreams are accidents of desire).

As we worked on this puzzle over several months, my patient stopped remembering her dreams (previously it had been 'her luck' that she could always remember what she dreamed). Our conversations ranged from a version of common sense (people metabolize emotional experience in different ways) to the more distinctively psychoanalytic (that through projective identification there was a division of emotional labour in her relationships: she would be obsessed, they would be relatively uninterrupted). She was unable to hold inside her a more ruthless, taking-it-and-leaving-it relationship to a love-object, so she gave that bit to her partner; she was then swamped and sustained by the illusion of her partner's permanent presence within her. We talked of the pleasures of being swamped, and the terrors of not being dependent on someone one loves. Some of this fitted with and evoked some of her sense of her childhood, but none of it was enlivening enough to make her really thoughtful, or to make her fall back inside herself. Meanwhile I was aware of experiencing something in the counter-transference that began to be pertinent: a growing sense that I was always getting it a bit wrong, as though there was some rule I didn't know about. I was being left with a conversation in my mind between an abject person and a thoroughly and impatiently competent one. At one point I said to myself in one of these internal conversations, 'I can't keep my side of this bargain!'

The first thing that really redeemed her curiosity was something that gradually began to occur to me quite late in the treatment, although it seems in retrospect, as it always does, that she had repeatedly been giving us both clues, not the least of which was several sessions spent talking about marriage certificates and death certificates. I suggested to her that when she was interested in someone, or fell in love, she instantly drew up from the past a secret contract with the person about the nature of the emotional experience they were going to have. Although she herself was unaware of the contract, she was compelled to abide by it. So if she was not obsessed and haunted – which was her side of the furtive agreement, derived from earlier contracts in childhood – she would not only be letting herself down but letting her partner down as well. Thus she was, in a sense, tyrannized by her own integrity. The irony of the situation, if 'irony' is the right word, was that neither of them had ever consciously seen the contract. Immediately alive to the complications, the potential for farce in these kinds of pact, she said, 'It's like a peace treaty signed in secret by only one side.' We went on to discuss the kinds of war she was always unconsciously wanting her relationships to be.

Of course it is not news, from a psychoanalytic or a family-therapy point of view, that people engage in unconscious contracts with each other, though the extent of these contracts – the small print, as it were – should never cease to amaze us (not to mention those even more hidden and binding contracts we enter into with ourselves). Given the number of contracts we enter into without apprising ourselves or other people that we are doing so, it is not surprising that our more official social contracts – rule-bound games, legal arrangements, socially sanctioned rituals – as attempts to organize or put a frame around our luck, can be so reassuring. The psychoanalytic contract for treatment is unusual because at its most radical it disfigures (or even dismantles) the possibility of contract. It provides a transition between the world of contract and whatever it is that the world of contract tries to exclude. In fact, the psychoanalytic contract is kept in order to show, but not to enact, what it is that contracts, indeed all agreements and connections, are always vulnerable to – that is, the unconscious and the unknowable future. People can never know in any situation exactly what they are agreeing to because the agreement includes at the very least the unconscious history and desire of the participants and, in that bizarre phrase, whatever the future holds. So Don Juan is the anti-hero of my paper, for he is the parodist of contract who pretends to master contingency by identifying with it. It is surprisingly difficult, as the Jewish proverb suggests, to make time for time. No one can be exempted from chance. Even though our wishes try to convince us otherwise, the future is not available to be repressed. It is not only the home of wishes but also the resort of accidents. We can only think of our lives as a progress narrative through time – in terms of development – because we happen by accident to have heard of the idea of development.

The wars that my patient had unconsciously been wanting to turn her relationships into represented a wish for more abrasive forms of contact, more action. War was a way of getting uncertainty back into the picture. Indeed, what was especially striking about her particular kind of unconscious contract was not only her difficulty in acknowledging the separateness of her partner, and her pervasive assumption, derived from a grievance with her mother, that the partner's emotional experience should be symmetrical with hers; it was also the way in which the unconscious contract was used – as Claude Lévi-Strauss said of dreams – as a machine for the suppression of time. My patient's unconscious contract, much like a pornographic image, was an attempt to seclude herself and her partner from luck – the good and the bad luck, the accidents and chances we are negotiating and using all the time. The contract was like an emotional spell cast over the relationship at the beginning to exempt her from contingency, to pre-empt the inevitable uncertainties of evolving time. I began, in other words, to find it useful to listen for clues about her relationship to time. In fact, I began to think of the transference as a re-creation, or repetition, of three early relationships that were distinct and overlapping: the relationship to the mother, the relationship to the father, and the relationship to time. The unconscious contract was an attempt to encapsulate time, to seal it off and isolate it like a part-object.

It was by analysing her transference to time – which meant her finding out what kind of parent it was for her, and her allowing herself to experience it as no kind of parent, just the matrix of chance – that my patient began to find in herself more flexible forms of exchange with other people, a repertoire rather than a fate.

My conversations with this woman left me preoccupied with a range of rather obvious, and clinically pertinent, questions. What kind of love affair is a person having with time, and what kind of object is it for them? Is it, for example, something that needs filling or something that tends to get wasted? Is there never enough or does a lot of it have to be killed? What makes us feel there is plenty of it or that it is running out? If we spend so much time planning to use it, what is the risk of leaving things to chance? Entrusting oneself to a person is quite different from entrusting oneself to time.

In his novel *Foe*, the South African writer J. M. Coetzee describes it like this:

> In a world of chance is there a better and a worse? We yield to a stranger's embrace or give ourselves to the waves; for the blink of an eyelid our vigilance relaxes; we are asleep; and when we awake we have lost the direction of our lives. What are these blinks of an eyelid, against which the only defence is an eternal and inhuman wakefulness? Might they not be the cracks and chinks through which another voice, other voices, speak in our lives? By what right do we close our ears to them?

Perhaps it is not surprising that a novelist who grows up and writes under a totalitarian regime is alert to the voices of chance, the voices that cannot be coerced.

I want to suggest that in developmental terms the recognition of contingency, of what Coetzee calls 'other voices' – recognition of one's life turning on a series of accidents in time, of events beyond one's power – is every bit as problematic as and different from recognition of the object, and less amenable to psychoanalytic description. In fact, I want to offer here for consideration the hypothesis that the preoccupation in developmental theory with recognition of the object can be a defence against the full acknowledgement of contingency. It is one thing to recognize the object – another person – as separate and to make him or her available for use, and quite another to live in time and make accidents available for use. If it has been useful in psychoanalysis to think that there is an instinct-driven self, we may need to add to this a self immersed in its contingency. We talk, in the bizarre language of property relations, of owning our instincts as personal intentions, but we talk rarely, if at all, of the more paradoxical idea of owning the contingency of our lives. Another way of saying this is to wonder why it is so difficult for us to believe – to live confidently as if – our lives are subject to accident.

The *OED* defines the once philosophically fashionable word

'contingency' as, 'liable to happen or not . . . happening or coming by chance . . . subject to accidents'. Given the obvious contingency of much of our lives – we do not in any meaningful sense intend or choose our birth, our parents, our bodies, our language, our culture, our thoughts, our dreams, our desires, our death, and so on – it might be worth considering, from a psychoanalytic point of view, not only our relationships to ourselves and our relationships to objects, but (as the third of the pair, so to speak) our relationship to accidents.

Psychoanalysis began, after all, with links being made by Freud between instinctual life and the 'accident' of trauma, with remarkable descriptions of lives being lived with unchosen desires in unchosen families and unchosen wars. But in Freud's work a whole range of accidents began to be redescribed as unconscious intentions; in psychoanalytic theory bodies were bled of their contingency. Indeed one of Freud's most popular and immediately appealing ideas was the parapraxis: the accident that dared not speak its name until Freud authorized it. The Freudian slip – whose very name is a giveaway – is the accident that is meant to happen.

II

His basic question was: 'Can we ever find within determinism a way out of it?'

Jean-Paul Sartre, *Mallarmé, or The Poet of Nothingness*

The Psychopathology of Everyday Life, first published as a book in 1901, has always been one of Freud's most popular works – although it is perhaps more accurate to say that the ideas in the book are among Freud's most popular, because most people find the experience of reading the book through rather wearing. But

The Psychopathology of Everyday Life – the Mistake Book, as I will call it, to bring it in line with the Dream Book and the Joke Book – has been through more German editions and foreign translations than any of Freud's other books apart from the *Introductory Lectures on Psychoanalysis*. And as Freud's English editor and translator James Strachey tells us, it is like *The Interpretation of Dreams* and *Three Essays on the Theory of Sexuality* in that Freud added fresh material to virtually every new edition published during his lifetime. This seems particularly interesting given the fact that, as Strachey remarks in his Introduction to the *Standard Edition*, 'Almost the whole of the basic explanations and theories were already present in the earliest edition.' In fact, unusually for him, Strachey betrays some slightly bemused exasperation with Freud about this. 'No doubt he felt particular pleasure,' Strachey writes, 'both in the anecdotes themselves and in being presented with such widespread confirmation of his views. But the reader cannot help feeling sometimes that the wealth of new examples interrupts and even confuses the mainstream of the underlying argument.' Why then, in this book, subtitled *Forgetting, Slips of the Tongue, Bungled Actions, Superstitions and Errors*, are there so many examples? Why is so much evidence needed?

In a way it is not surprising, given Freud's professional allegiances and the uncertain status of his new and unusual science, that he should want to accumulate evidence as proof, even though in this case, as Strachey says, the quantity diminishes the quality. In so far as the Mistake Book is written in a specific genre – it was first published in a journal called the *Monograph for Psychiatry and Neurology* – it observes the conventions of a certain kind of scientific treatise. If one answer to the question of the book's excess has to do with genre, the equally obvious psychoanalytic answer would be that the insistence of the book betrays a doubt in Freud's mind; that the material evokes a resistance both in the writer and in the imagined audience that requires tenacious overcoming. It is as though Freud is saying, 'There really are lots of mistakes and accidents in life, and they really are meaningful, often in a sexual way.' Given Freud's interpretations of parapraxes, it is not surprising that he thinks we need persuading; but we all do, of course, know that life is full of errors and accidents. However, if the errors and accidents are meaningful in the way he proposes, they cease to be errors and accidents. With something akin to Freud's logic of dreams, the book describes a large number of accidents to prove that there is no such thing as an accident. By the end of the book, if we get through it, we have been absolved of error and introduced to the psychoanalytic world of multiple plots. We are not continually making mistakes, we are continually making alternative lives. But why can't we, as Freud suggested six years later in his book on Leonardo, consider chance to be 'worthy of determining our fate'? It may not be that all accidents are meaningful, but that meaning is made out of accidents. Freud uses psychoanalytic theory to turn accidents, apparently chance events, into significant intentions. But the excessive evidence of the Mistake Book may also be to counter the anxiety that chance is determining our fate and the potential loss of meaning this could entail. Freud, after all, has managed to make accidents entertaining.

The Mistake Book, a virtual encyclopaedia of errors and accidents, reveals with scientific sobriety the slapstick of everyday life; in which what Freud calls 'seemingly accidental clumsy movements', in all their minuscule violence and chaos, 'prove to be governed by an intention, and achieve their aim, with a certainty which cannot in general be credited to our conscious voluntary movements'. 'Falling, stumbling and slipping,' he writes, 'need not always be interpreted as purely accidental miscarriages of motor action.' He reveals that we are not making fools of ourselves, but that on the contrary we are as competent as we dream we are. We are suffering from an excess of meaningful intentions. Accidents become, in Freud's version, ways of securing unconscious gratifications, either self-punishment or other muffled fulfilment of forbidden wishes. And 'there is no sphere', he writes, 'in which the view that accidental actions are really intentional will command a more ready belief than that of sexuality'.

Accidents become disowned intentions; other voices speak through our mistakes. So the idea of accident – of the apparently unintended, the contingent – gives us access to otherwise unavailable desires or parts of the self, depending on one's language commitments. Accidents become the best way, indeed the only way, of doing some things. And conversely, without a notion of accident or contingency we would not be able sufficiently to disown them to make them known. Freud is showing us, in other words, not only that accidents are meaningful but how we use the idea of accident in the production of meanings that are most forbidden. Error is legitimate criminality. We are at our most transgressive when we fail. The Mistake Book contains, that is to say, both descriptions of what people use accidents to do, and what Freud can do by redescribing these accidents. And one of the many things he can then do by redescribing accidents in this particular way is to make them revelations of personal history. As psychoanalysis turns instinct into personal history, so there is no such thing as a mistake, only the continual disclosure of the past. If a parapraxis is a self-inflicted accident, why would one want to inflict such an accident on oneself? And Freud's remarkable answer is: to gratify, in compromised form, a forbidden desire, but also to recover the past, to link us to our history. There is a history that our competence conceals.

By way of concluding his book, Freud states:

> There is one thing which the severest and the mildest cases all have in common, and which is equally found in parapraxes and chance actions: the phenomena can be traced back to incompletely suppressed psychical material, which, although pushed away by consciousness, has nevertheless not been robbed of all capacity for expressing itself.

Suppressed desires are suppressed histories, or suppressed histories that were in the making. Through psychoanalytic interpretation Freud takes the luck out of accidents and makes them available as non-mystical sources of meaning. What looked like accident or chance was in fact voices from the past pressing for recognition; there are lives inside us competing to be lived. We must assume from what Freud says here that the 'suppressed psychical material' wants to express itself – that there are personal histories inside us, in conflict but clamouring for recognition. Accidents are reminders of unfinished business, that we are living too few of our lives.

III

I want to consider the idea that not only might we swallow an idea too quickly, but that we might accept an idea for the very purpose of not engaging with it.

Chris Higgins, 'Open-Mindedness in Three Dimensions'

Freud invented a method, a treatment, for the recovery of the past through reappropriation – to use the wrong word – of desire. Transformation, however circumscribed by the modesty of his therapeutic ambitions, involved the recovery through the transference of the possibilities of desire. But Freud also knew, because he was not an orthodox Freudian, that all sorts of experiences can remind us of who we are; that if chance is worthy of determining our fate anything might serve to transform one's life; that the past, as Proust devoted nearly twenty years of writing to show, can return by accident. But the Proustian accident, unlike the Freudian accident, does not appear to come from inside.

In the Overture to *Swann's Way* Proust writes:

One day in winter, on my return home, my mother, seeing that I was cold, offered me some tea, a thing I did not ordinarily take. I declined at first and then for no particular reason, changed my mind. She sent for one of those squat, plump little cakes called 'petits madeleines' . . . no sooner had the warm liquid mixed with the crumbs touched my palate than a shudder ran through me and I stopped, intent upon the extraordinary thing that was happening.

The extraordinary thing that was happening, brought on by the most famous cakes in literary history, was the memory of Combray, a crucial piece of his past. Proust conveys both the simplicity, the absolute ordinariness, of the event, and how it could easily have not happened. His mother needn't have offered him tea, she might not have had those cakes, he needn't have had any, and so on. Proust makes us feel that in that moment of hesitation – 'I declined at first and then for no particular reason, changed my mind' – his life and the writing of his extraordinary book were in the balance without, of course, his knowing it. It was, from his point of view, an entirely gratuitous event.

Secular epiphanies like this reveal the past, but one's personal history is an elusive god. In the world of Proust's novel there is always a tantalizing quality about people's lives, as though time were flirting with them. Our recovery of the protean past, and the selves we have buried there, cannot be arranged. 'There is a large element of chance in these matters,' Proust writes, 'and a second chance occurrence, that of our own death, often prevents us from awaiting for any length of time the favours of the first.' Proust's writing, as an essential parallel text to Freud's, provides an anti-psychoanalytic version of psychoanalysis. From a Proustian point of view the analyst is someone with whom one might, with a bit of luck, through the transference, stumble on a bit of the past. Proust writes:

It is a labour in vain to attempt to recapture it, all the efforts of our intellect must prove futile. The past is hidden somewhere outside the realm, beyond the reach of intellect, in some material object (in the sensation which that material object will give us) of which we have no inkling. And it depends on chance whether we come upon this object before we ourselves die.

'Depending on chance' is, of course, an interesting phrase. For Proust there is no organizing, no technique, for securing access to the past. The past is disclosed by coincidences that are in themselves meaningless: a smell, a tune, a taste. And there is no knowing beforehand which or when it might be. Both Proust and Freud, in quite different ways, make us think about contingency, as they elaborate their instructive accidents. Proust's accidental encounter with the madeleines — an encounter which in his view might never have happened — prompts an involuntary memory that transfigures his sense of himself and the shape of his life. It presents him with a new future. But the past that is inside us is not, for Proust, busily and furtively arranging for its own disclosure, is not seeking attention. It is not even, he implies, waiting to be found; though it is there, somewhere, in some 'material object', if we are lucky or unlucky enough to come across it. And we will probably only come across it when we are doing something else; we cannot organize a quest for the past, nor is the past pursuing us with its essential messages and unfinished projects.

For Freud the accident disclosed a counter-intention; and this counter-intention is an insufficiently repressed desire, a piece of urgent personal history wanting to be lived out, even in its compromised form. But the desire is not wanting, so to speak, to be decoded as history; it is wanting some version of gratification. The desire seeks satisfaction, but the psychoanalyst makes history. Freudian interpretation aims to extend the realm of intention, and diminish the empire of contingency.

Proust's secular epiphany becomes, in Freudian terms, another piece of unconscious calculation. Endorsing a paper by Otto Rank, Freud writes: 'Often not only losing objects but also finding them appears to be (psychologically) determined . . . It is obvious that in cases of losing, the object is already provided; in cases of finding it has first to be looked for.' All finding in Freud is a looking for, and an already having seen, a refinding. What is intimated in the Proustian scenario and is repressed – indeed is nonsensical, from a psychoanalytic point of view – is the idea that we are not looking but that we may find.

For the purposes of this paper I want to use Proust and Freud as figures for two possible versions of the self; so I don't mean Proust and Freud in their real complexity but rather those aspects of them represented by my two examples. Staged in this way the comparison reveals, I think, an important omission or disavowal in psychoanalytic theory (though I think psychoanalysis has repressed the Proustian in Freud). I want to say that there are two versions of the self that psychoanalysis, despite its dualism and commitment to conflict, always tries to resolve into one. One version of the self, the Freudian, knows, in the psychoanalytic sense, what it wants and is always wanting; we can call this 'unconscious desire'.

But there is another version of the self – not defensive, indeed radically undefended – that is not about knowing what it wants or is wanting (and that brings with it the question: why is it so difficult for us to really believe that we don't know what we want?). This version of the self – for which wanting is not the game – lives its contingency without contesting it. One could say it simply abides by its contingency. But in certain environments this version of the self can only be lived either as despair – my life is out of my control and that's what's wrong with it – or as scepticism – I don't know what I want and therefore doubt my capacity to know anything. Acknowledgement of the contingent self – that self which has no contracts to make and which is linked with one's own death in a way that the self of unconscious desire never can be – entails, I think, the belated recovery, or processing, of the earliest forms of experience.

Early emotional experience may be imagined as being like a

series of accidents – unarranged events like hunger or sleepiness – that are gradually redescribed as more than coincidence. A person's relationship to coincidence – or to the idea of coincidence, or chance or luck – is a complicated link to this earlier self. Development in its non-progressivist sense means taking one's chances. Coincidences belong to those who can use them.

IV

Something has to be done to get us free of our memories and choices.

John Cage (interview)

Coincidence simply means two things happening together, 'occurrence or existence at the same time'. But from a Freudian point of view, discussion of coincidence is inevitably tainted with notions of the paranormal, or the kind of mystical animism that psychoanalysts tend to pathologize. Freud clearly could not have written a book called *Synchronicity: An Acausal Connecting Principle*. The four pages on coincidence in the Mistake Book are a brief testament to Freud's new-found ability to 'resolve' coincidences, like most other apparent accidents. That our lives might be simply a series or collection of coincidences seems peculiarly unacceptable (though it could, of course, be comforting). Indeed, the word 'accident' usually signifies something going wrong. If we began to think of Oedipus, for example, as just extremely unlucky, psychoanalysis would be a very different thing. The play, after all, is full of extraordinary coincidences.

It is, I think, of interest that in Winnicott's description development begins with instincts experienced as contingent events, and their gratification as a coincidence (like the 'overlapping of two lines'). For the infant, he writes, 'the instincts are not yet clearly defined as internal to the infant, the instincts can be as much external as can a clap of thunder or a hit'. If the instincts feel to the infant like contingent events, then the mother's task, in the Winnicottian picture, is the personalizing or humanizing of an original and formative contingency. Instinctual experience, through the complementary relationship with the mother, becomes a discernible process, with something like a beginning, a middle and an end, or, at least, a pause. So the question of how one recognizes coincidences and comes to use them as such can be linked with Winnicott's description of the process of illusionment. In *Paediatrics and Psychiatry* (1948) he writes:

> Initially there is a condition which could be described at one and the same time as absolute independence and absolute dependence. There is no feeling of dependence, and therefore that dependence must be absolute. Let us say that out of this state the infant is disturbed by instinct tension which is called hunger. I would say that the infant is ready to believe in something that could exist, i.e. there has developed in the infant a readiness to hallucinate an object; but that is rather a direction of expectancy than an object in itself. At this moment the mother comes along with her breast (I say breast for simplification of description), and places it so that the infant finds it. Here is another direction, this time towards instead of away from the infant. It is a tricky matter whether or not the mother and infant 'click'. At the start the mother allows the infant to dominate, and if she fails to do this the infant's subjective object will fail to have superimposed on it the objectively perceived breast. Ought we not to say that fitting in with the infant's impulse the mother allows the baby the illusion that what is there is the thing created by the baby; as a result there is not only the physical experience of instinctual satisfaction, but also an emotional union, and the beginning of a belief in reality as something about which one can have illusions.

For the infant, desire is of a piece with satisfaction. For hunger to be virtually synonymous with being fed is, from the infant's point of view, no coincidence; from the observer's point of view it is as though one thing, the infant's scream of hunger, causes another, the mother's wish to feed. As waiting becomes a processible and therefore a tolerable experience for the child, the question arises: is being fed the consequence of being hungry, like cause and effect, or is it simply coincidental with being hungry? The answer is that both descriptions are available but one is much harder to take than the other.

At first, Winnicott writes, 'there is an overlap between what the mother supplies and what the child might conceive of'. But once the capacity for illusionment has been secured through sufficiently attentive care, the mother has the 'job' of disillusioning the child. It is what Winnicott calls 'the good-enough environmental provision' that enables the child to 'cope with the immense shock of loss of omnipotence'.

This immense shock occurs whenever the mother's presence is no longer coincident with the child's need (which in absolute terms, of course, it never can be). Given good-enough care the child accumulates a belief that he or she can create the coincidences he or she needs – what Winnicott calls 'a belief in reality as something about which one can have illusions'. From the infant's point of view, at the earliest stage, there is no coincidence because there are not yet two things to coincide; there is simply the infant's need. But once there is a glimpse that well-being or satisfaction is a cooperative venture, then it might seem as if – or be reconstructed as if – the infant or child causes his satisfaction through the clamour of demand. The child is no longer just the site of contingent instincts, but the agent of their actual appeasement. But it is integral to the process of disillusionment, the immense shock Winnicott writes about, that the child has to get beyond believing that the consequences of his actions are commensurate with his intentions. Desire is not an insurance policy for satisfaction. The mother is not his machine and neither is his body. Desires and needs – like thoughts and dreams – are as contingent as their gratification. The extent to which we socially regulate hunger suggests that appetite was once experienced as something of a surprise. (Though we, in that absurd phrase, eat between meals, we don't think between thoughts.)

For the sake of this essay I want to oversimplify and abstract the familiar process of illusion-and-disillusionment that in Winnicott's view organizes our lives. Infants, after all, have always been useful in psychoanalysis to attribute things to because they don't answer back. I want to impute states of mind to infants as a figurative way of asserting something that I think is of interest. So, from a psychoanalytic point of view, in the process of disillusionment it is as if the infant – and later the adult – has three choices. Either the infant is omnipotent, or the mother is omnipotent, or neither of them is; with this third option, which we can call the *Depressive Position*, there is, among other things, the acknowledgement that there is no such thing as omnipotence. People stop finding or being deities and have to do something else together. I want to suggest that there is a fourth choice – which looks as though it's somewhere between belief in omnipotence and the abrogation of that belief – though in actuality I think it is something quite different. It is called acknowledgement of contingency. It can be called luck, fortune, accident, coincidence, and is sometimes experienced and described as a kind of non-intentional or random agency. There is actually nothing behind it making it happen – though we can personalize it by projection – and its presence, in and of itself, says nothing about our power. It neither diminishes nor enlarges us, but we can use it to do both. Because it includes both the body and whatever is felt not to be the body, it is neither internal nor external; a bit like Winnicott's imagining of the infant's earliest experience of instinct. It would sound absurd to talk of a stage of contingency, or a Contingency Position, because what I am referring to is the enemy of fixity (of reification) but is always there. But as with the Depressive Position, or whatever one's preferred life-aim, psychoanalysis could be a process of understanding the obstacles to its full acknowledgement.

What are the preconditions, in terms of early experience, that allow the contingent self to emerge as such? What kinds of defence (defences are essentially contingency plans) blind one to coincidence? What prevents us from living, to repeat my earlier question, confidently as though our lives are a series of accidents? What is the cost of not considering chance to be worthy of determining our fate? And what happens when what I am calling the 'contingent self' is repressed or turned away from, since, from a psychoanalytic point of view, as Joseph Smith reminds us, 'Whatever is turned away from is marked as a danger to be faced or a loss to be mourned'?

Acknowledgement of the contingency of the self – and the contingent self that lives this acknowledgement – need not be exclusively a disillusioning or depressive experience, because somewhere one has never had illusions about it; in adult life it is contesting one's contingency that is productive of disabling illusion. (Classical tragedy could never be the preferred genre of the contingent self.) This contingent self, for example, is unable to engage in that bemusing activity that Leslie Farber once called 'willing what cannot be willed'. From the point of view of the contingent self, desiring – being drawn to someone or something – could only mean creating the conditions for a coincidence. (Or, to put it another way: we cannot make our relationships work; we can only make our compromises work.) And the idea of the contingent self has interesting consequences for our moral sense, because it is through our morality, as Bernard Williams has suggested, that we often try to make our lives 'immune from luck'. The contingent self enjoins us to imagine a life without blaming, a life exempt from the languages of effort and self-control.

The contingent self 'knows' nothing in the conventional sense; this is not a deficit, though, but a definition; because in the conventional sense there is nothing for it to know. Or perhaps I am closer to what I mean by saying that the contingent self is a weak epistemologist because it knows only one thing, and it is a paradoxical kind of knowledge. It knows that emotional experience is new at every moment; and since all our equipment to prepare ourselves for the future comes from the past, it is redundant and ironic. That is, we are all beginners at contingency because it is the only thing we can be.

The Uses of Forgetting

I

Remembering everything is a form of madness.

Brian Friel, *Translations*

People come for psychoanalytic treatment because they are remembering in a way that does not free them to forget. From a psychoanalytic point of view symptoms are reminders – 'indications', Freud writes in his essay 'Repression', 'of a return of the repressed'. A form of involuntary and disguised memory, symptoms are mnemonics of desire; and desire, for Freud – what he referred to as 'instinctual life' – is unforgettable. Repression, indeed all the mechanisms of defence that he described – the tropes of distribution and self-protection – are ways of retaining things by getting rid of them. The unconscious, that is to say, is what we know about when defences, like forgetting, break down (the phrase 'the unconscious' covers the whole spectrum from 'I'd rather not know' to 'I had no idea'). In symptoms, in dreams, in slips of the tongue, in free association and, of course, in memories themselves we are reminded of our disowned counterparts.

It is as though there are areas of our lives about which we can pretend to lose, or never evolve, our memory. And these areas can be called – depending on one's psychoanalytic language commitments – desires, thoughts, histories, trauma, parts of the self. This category of the unacceptable, or unbearable, is the target for psychoanalytic interpretation, which ideally frees the patient to resume contact with what he has never actually lost but merely hidden away, or been unable to process, or both.

He is encouraged to remember that he has forgotten these things, that he has actively mislaid them, for what might be called aesthetic reasons; that they were felt to be incompatible with whatever he had come to believe was good or desirable for or about himself.

Freud finds the analogy that he thinks of as the origin for this process in what he calls in his paper 'Negation' 'the language of the oldest – the oral instinctual impulses'. Judgement, or aesthetic valuation, is fundamentally a question of whether something is edible. But in talking about judgement in this way Freud is also giving us, by implication, one of his many pictures of memory and forgetting:

> [T]he judgement is, 'I should like to eat this', or 'I should like to spit it out'; and, put more generally: 'I should like to take this into myself and to keep that out.' That is to say, 'It shall be inside me' or 'it shall be outside me' . . . the original pleasure-ego wants to introject into itself everything that is good and to eject from itself everything that is bad. What is bad, what is alien to the ego and what is external are, to begin with, identical.

Everything bad is put outside by projection, or into the outside that is inside – the unconscious – by repression. You can, so to speak, forget outside or forget inside. But is forgetting – a later, more developmentally sophisticated, stage than the one described here – more like eating something or like spitting it out? Just as you can only repress something once you have acknowledged it, similarly you can only spit something out once you have tasted it. If Freud is describing here his paradigm for judgement he is also describing two forms of forgetting: if you spit something out you dispense with it once and for all; if you eat something you forget it through a process called digestion. Spat out it will be, as it were, metabolized by the world in a future you hope to have exempted yourself from; taken in, it will be metabolized by your body, and fuel your future. The question becomes not: what do I want to forget and what do I want to remember? but: which form of forgetting do I want to use? The picture of spitting something out, taken literally, adds to the repertoire a paradoxical notion, an absolute forgetting: that which can be put beyond the reach of memory, that which cannot be redeemed – in the language of the second-oldest instinctual impulses, an 'immaculate evacuation'.

There may be a cure for symptoms but there is, from a psychoanalytic point of view, no cure for memory, The past, ghost-written as desire, is driving us into the future; in fact symptoms, in this view, are a person's always unsuccessful attempts at self-cure for memory. And yet Freud intimates in his paper 'Negation' that there is a forgetting, which is a way of remembering, which becomes repression and that he encourages us to call 'eating'; and that there is a forgetting that is its own negation, that leaves nothing to remember. I want to suggest in this paper that Freud was in a continual dilemma as to which of these alternatives best represented the aims of psychoanalytic treatment. His disillusion with hypnosis as a cathartic treatment was an episode and not merely a watershed in his insistent preoccupation with the uses of forgetting. Was psychoanalysis exorcism or recycling? Can the past be forgotten, and then be turned into something that doesn't need forgetting?

One of what Richard Wollheim refers to as Freud's 'two momentous discoveries' – the other being his loss of faith in the seduction theory – directly raises the question of whether it is possible, in psychoanalytic terms, to spit out one's desire. 'Memories,' Wollheim writes, 'are found incompatible and repressed not because of the events that they are of but because of the impulses expressed in the events that they are of.' We use memories to forget with. Memory, in other words, was what Freud was to call 'screen-memory'; and these screen-memories were screens because memory, Freud had begun to believe, was *of* desire. Since desire was, by Oedipal definition, forbidden, 'the falsified memory,' Freud writes in his paper 'Screen-Memory', 'is the first that we become aware of'. Memories become forms of forgetting. 'It may indeed be questioned,' he continues, 'whether we have any memories at all from our childhood; memories relating to our childhood may be all that we possess.'

If memories are more like dreams than pieces of reliable documentary evidence, and are disguised representations of forbidden desire, it is as though desire can be remembered only by being successfully forgotten; which in this context means represented by a sufficiently censored dreamable dream, or an often banal replacement-memory. Forgetting, in its versions of disguise, makes desire accessible by making it tolerable. We can desire only because we can hide things from ourselves. The defences, as described by Freud, are a repertoire of forms of forgetting. But if desire, because of the threat of castration, can lead only to a furtive double-life of concealment, what, then, is the aim of psychoanalytic interpretation? The recycling of desire or the dispelling of it? If there was – as Ernest Jones suggested, with his powerful but now repressed concept of Aphinisis – a dread of the death of desire, perhaps also there was a wish to kill desire, to be able to forget instinctual life; a wish that psychoanalysis may (or can) be unwittingly complicit with? If, as Freud's description of the ego as a defensive structure suggests, we only pretend to forget, then what kind of remembering is psychoanalysis aiming to promote? And one answer would be: psychoanalysis is a cure by means of the kind of remembering that makes forgetting possible.

So in this picture of psychoanalysis Freud's later, and more obscure, notion of the death instinct is a way of describing a part of the self that wants to make memory impossible, that creates states of mind in which there is nothing left to remember; the death instinct was Freud's sublime of forgetting. If the body – that illimitable complexity of the self that the word signifies – is always in excess of the individual's capacity for representation, then the death instinct is that which shatters the possibility of representation.

In Freud's view man is the animal driven to forget, and driven by forgetting. If Freud's analysis of hysteria convinced him that we are never good enough at forgetting, it was his analysis of the Ratman that prompted him, perhaps unwittingly, to acknowledge the more paradoxical uses of forgetting; to give us his pictures of what forgetting might entail, for better or worse.

II

. . . the modern duplexity of reviving
the past as a search for the unknown

Robin Blaser, 'rose'

Once Freud had located the unconscious content of the Ratman's pervasive sense of guilt — that his 'criminal wishes' were actually directed against his father — the Ratman, in the following session, turned his doubts about himself against psychoanalysis and its father. When his now famous patient 'ventured', as Freud puts it delicately, 'to bring forward a few doubts' about the efficacy of psychoanalytic interpretation, of making the unconscious conscious, Freud gives him a curiously ambiguous account of the therapeutic value of remembering what one has tried to forget. It is as though the Ratman reminds Freud of his own uncertainty, of his own ambivalence about remembering, which his work with hysterics had obliged him to forget. Beginning his lecture to the Ratman, Freud writes:

I then made some short observations upon the psychological differences between the conscious and the unconscious, and upon the fact that everything conscious was subject to a process of wearing away, while what was unconscious was relatively unchangeable; and I illustrated my remarks by pointing to the antiques standing about in my room. They were, in fact, I said, only objects found in a tomb, and their burial had been their preservation; the destruction of Pompeii was only beginning now that it had been dug up. – Was there any guarantee, he next enquired, of what one's attitude would be towards what was discovered? One man, he thought, would no doubt behave in such a way as to get the better of his self-reproach, but another would not. – No, I said, it followed from the nature of the circumstances that in every case the affect would be overcome – for the most part during the progress of the work itself. Every effort was made to preserve Pompeii, whereas people were anxious to be rid of tormenting ideas like his.

If Freud had revealed to the Ratman his repressed, and so forgotten, murderous wishes towards his father, he suggests here that memory itself can be a form of murder, a way of disposing of things. '[T]he destruction of Pompeii was only beginning,' he reassures the Ratman, 'now that it had been dug up.' On the one hand, Freud says, forgetting, like burial, is a preservative; a kind of storage. And, of course, in his example of Pompeii, it is the storage of what has already been damaged. But on the other hand, remembering, like excavation, does something paradoxical: by linking the fragments – whether it be of the patient's story, or the shards of the city – it makes possible imaginative reconstruction; and yet this very reconstruction contributes, or even causes, the final destruction and disappearance of the material. What has made the reconstruction possible destroys the evidence (and from a psychoanalytic point of view this might make us wonder, for example, what happens to the dream once you have interpreted it, and what you want to happen to it).

The Ratman's question to Freud, after he has given him the example of Pompeii, obliquely registers the dilemma Freud has presented him with. He has compared his highly valued antiques, and the great city of Pompeii which he clearly considers worth preserving, with the Ratman's repressed death-wishes towards his father which he clearly considers worth, as Freud puts it, 'overcoming'. You render such wishes redundant, or at least relatively powerless, by making them conscious. But what if wishes, like antiques, should be preserved? How can Freud possibly forget his antiques once they are in his consulting room? His analogies produce an instructive muddle: is remembering a form of forgetting, or forgetting a form of remembering? If everything conscious, as Freud said, is 'subject to a process of wearing away', then isn't remembering a form of depletion, or even dissipation? And isn't Freud feeling guilty that his acquisition of the antiques contributes to their decay? It is as though one is evacuating the past, emptying oneself of it by remembering it. (It is perhaps worth noting here that it is a common clinical experience that bereaved people fear that talking about the person they have lost will dispel their contact with them; as though real remembering entails real loss.)

The alternatives that Freud offers the Ratman – remembering as a wearing away, or the repression of forgetting as 'relatively unchangeable' storage – are a vivid representation of Freud's perplexed preoccupation with the uses of forgetting. In fact, he presents the Ratman with what is at best a paradox and at its worst a double-bind: remembering is a way of killing off the past, and therefore so is psychoanalysis when it works. Either the most significant bits of one's past are unconscious, and available only in the compromised form of symptoms and dreams; or the past is released through interpretation, into oblivion (this is like a gloss on Rilke's famous remark that he would never have psychoanalysis because if he lost his devils he would lose his angels). Is the aim of psychoanalysis to make the past – the problematic past – available for disposal? If to remember is to relinquish, then memory may be a process akin to mourning; and forgetting may be either a refusal to mourn – a defence, as it were, against one's own entropy – or its completion. You can only forget when there is nothing to remember. Pompeii may have started to disintegrate only when it was dug up, but the antiques in Freud's consulting room, as I have said, were not apparently diminished by being taken from their tomb. By comparing the fate of

Pompeii with his own collection of antiquities, he makes a distinction that he fails to note: some things, like Pompeii, may be protected by being buried and forgotten, and some things may be destroyed by being dug up and remembered, like Pompeii and one's unacceptable wishes; but there are other things from the past that are, in fact, sustained by being recontextualized.

As a Jew in Vienna at the turn of the century, Freud may well have identified with the fate of his, by definition, non-Jewish antiquities that had changed places and come so far. His lecture to the Ratman, and to the reader of the case history, suggests that, despite his describing psychoanalysis as a cure by memory, there were things about the past that were, in a sense, nurtured by being forgotten. It has been the value of forgetting that psychoanalysis after Freud has most often repressed. Freud could describe a pathology of forgetting, but not an art. And yet his lecture to the Ratman represents, I think, his fundamental ambivalence about memory – his commitment to the uses of forgetting, and to the definition of its most benign and various forms. For Freud to have addressed more explicitly his ambivalence about remembering would have involved him in confronting his ambivalence about psychoanalysis itself – something every psychoanalyst has to work hard to disguise. For Freud, the aim of analysis was not to remember, but to establish sufficient states of forgetting.

III

Memories are killing.

Samuel Beckett, 'The Expelled'

If Freud described symptoms as forms of forgetting, and so a cure based on remembering, he produced – as a mirror-image, so to speak – a method of treatment, an explanation of artistic creation, and an account of sexual development based on the capacity to forget. Free-floating attention, the sublimation that is art, the fundamental configurations of the Oedipus complex, all depend upon the trope of forgetting. What Freud refers to as the 'defences' are all imaginative ways of losing one's memory, of pretending to oneself that the past has no future; that distinctively psychoanalytic forgetting (of concealment) that is the only way to remember. Psychoanalysis is, in fact, a phenomenology of processes – repression, repetition, transference, memory, dreams – that cannot begin without a forgetting. There are, in other words, two ghosts in this machine: the unconscious, and the capacity to forget. We are the creatures who refuse to remember who we are; and yet, from a psychoanalytic point of view, there can be nothing human without competent forgetting. If a life, in psychoanalytic terms, can be described as a relationship between the unconscious and a repertoire of forgettings, this relationship can only be understood, in psychoanalytic treatment, if the analyst has learned the art of free-floating attention.

Psychoanalysis, as a technique that aims to facilitate by interpretation the memory that is desire, depends, in Freud's view, on the analyst's ability to forget; to be able to tolerate not wilfully keeping things in his mind. And this, though Freud does not put it like this, is an act of faith. It implies a belief that there is a process inside the analyst that gets to work by not trying to remember; and for which conscious, as opposed to preconscious or unconscious, memory is a saboteur. 'It must not be forgotten,' he writes in 'Recommendations to Physicians Practising Psychoanalysis', using the pertinent word, 'that the things one hears are for the most part things whose meaning is only recognized later on'; the making of meaning, he suggests, depends upon deferral, on a certain kind of storage. 'The analyst,' he writes, 'should simply listen, and not bother about whether he is keeping anything in mind,' because 'a conscious determination to recollect the point would probably have resulted in failure.'

Listening, Freud says, is informed by forgetting; to try to

remember is not to hear in the sense that he is proposing. In his encyclopaedia article on psychoanalysis of 1923, he writes:

> Experience soon showed that the attitude which the analytic physician could most advantageously adopt was to surrender himself to his own unconscious mental activity, in a state of evenly suspended attention, to avoid as far as possible reflection and the construction of conscious expectations, not to try to fix anything that he heard particularly in his memory, and by these means to catch the drift of the patient's unconscious with his own unconscious.

In this picture, memory, as a function of the ego, is an obstacle: this 'surrendering' of the analyst to 'his own unconscious mental activity' so as to 'catch the drift of the patient's unconscious with his own' implies that conscious active remembering is a defence against contact; that memory obstructs communication. It is as though there is an unconscious analysing instrument that can function only when memory is abrogated (the Kleinian psychoanalyst Wilfred Bion advocated that the analyst should engage in the psychoanalytic session 'without memory or desire', but he had both to remember to do that, and want to). Understanding can happen – the analyst can 'catch the drift' of the patient's unconscious, a phrase which catches the drift of this kind of understanding – in the space cleared by relinquishing memory.

'Surrendering to one's unconscious' means temporarily forgetting who one is; Freud, that is to say, with the kind of instructive lucidity which can make it all sound like practical common sense, presents his listeners with something very paradoxical. The patient free-associates – every association being a memory, coming from the past – and the analyst does something complementary that Freud calls 'simply listening'. And yet he makes something quite clear that he cannot elaborate: that it is only when two people forget themselves, in each other's presence, that they can recognize each other. Because we can communicate only underground – only recognize each other in spite of ourselves, unconscious to unconscious – communication entails, indeed necessitates, a version of forgetting.

By explaining free-floating or evenly suspended attention, Freud is trying to describe a version of memory – or rather, a form of forgetting – that does not mystify contact between people. But there is, it should be noted, a curious conviction informing his method: that unconsciouses, so to speak, can catch the drift of each other; that there is recognition somewhere even if it does not lie in trying to remember what people say. So in this picture, once you have forgotten, once you've stopped trying particularly to 'fix' anything you hear in your memory, what have you got down to, or what do you start with? I assume it is not an accident that this is so difficult to imagine. One possible imagining, though it is bland in the range of analogy it suggests, is that when we can sufficiently forget – or forget, as Freud says, our 'reflection and the construction of conscious expectations' – we can process each other, meaning that we can make sense of each other, or at least the kinds of sense that psychoanalysis requires of us or that we may require of each other. Certainly, Freud intimates that particular kinds of sense-making are inextricable from, and impossible without, certain kinds of forgetting; it is as if people can meet only in anonymous encounters. And psychoanalytic theories are imaginative constructions of what happens in the gap between recognition and remembering – the gap we make by the act of forgetting.

Freud sometimes calls what happens in the gap we call forgetting 'dream-work'; and at other times, though he does not use this phrase, 'art-work'. The making of a dream, like the making of a work of art, in his account, is essentially a process of reworking, and you can't remember something, of course, until it has happened to you, or at least until something has happened to you. 'What memories, hysteria and works of art have in common,' Sarah Kofman writes in *The Childhood of Art*, 'is that they are phantasmal constructions from memory traces, and have a plastic or theatrical form.' And these reworkings, these phantasmal constructions, are akin to that protracted unconscious free-floating attention that Freud prescribed for the analyst. What the analyst does from outside, the dreamer and the artist do from inside: a sustained, forgetful self-listening. Each of them is finding ways of making the previously unacceptable accessible through redescription or redepiction. It is almost as though Freud is saying that the dreamer and the artist (and the ordinary rememberer) already have something like an analyst inside them, 'simply listening'; and that a person comes for analysis when this inner analyst can no longer sustain evenly suspended attention. That this internal figure has forgotten how to forget and needs to be reminded (not, it should be said, by a real analyst, which can only be internal, but by his external representative, a provisional impostor). In analysis it is as though everything has already happened, even the analyst.

For Freud, the psychoanalyst was, among other things, a way of describing a new figure with a particular way of forgetting called 'simply listening'; and in this kind of listening, meanings – or constructions – can be made only by way of deferral. A time lag is built into the system. You cannot remember something as it is happening; and you cannot know – or rather, predict – quite what it is you will remember. One cannot learn one's personal history off by heart.

IV

If all time is eternally present
All time is unredeemable.

T. S. Eliot, 'Burnt Norton'

It is perhaps unavoidable in this context to mention Freud's concept of deferred action; though it is significantly difficult, as it clearly was for Freud, to rework it. Deferred action seems to be something we can remember but not retranscribe. Freud himself could only repeat it – admittedly in different contexts: in a letter to Wilhelm Fliess, in the Dream Book, in the Wolfman case – he could not sufficiently elaborate on it. For such an illuminating idea, it is indeed surprising that he did not devote a paper to it. It is as if the idea itself were like a trauma for him, subject only to repetition, not to modification. 'Freud uses the term "nachtraglich" repeatedly and constantly,' Jean Laplanche and J.-B. Pontalis write in their dictionary of psychoanalysis, 'often underlining it. The substantival form "Nachtraglichkeit" also keeps cropping up, and from very early on. Thus although he never offered a definition, much less a general theory, of the notion of deferred action, it was indisputably looked on by Freud as part of his conceptual equipment.' After mentioning that it was Lacan who 'drew attention to the importance of this term' (they give no references), they introduce their own characteristically lucid account by saying, 'we do not propose to set forth any theory of deferred action here' (Charles Rycroft, incidentally, has no entry for 'deferred action' in his *Critical Dictionary of Psychoanalysis*). The question, intimated by Laplanche and Pontalis, is: did Freud set forth any theory of deferred action, and what might have been the problem of doing so?

In one sense Freud's theory of deferred action can be simply stated: memory is reprinted, so to speak, in accordance with later experience. As Laplanche and Pontalis put it, 'experiences, impressions and memory traces may be revised at a later date to fit in with fresh experiences or with the attainment of a new stage of development. They may, in that event, be endowed not only with a new meaning, but also with psychical effectiveness.' Freud, in a famous letter to Fliess (6 December 1896), writes of 'memory traces being subjected from time to time to a rearrangement in accordance with fresh circumstances – to a retranscription'. Memory is like a stock of material available for revision. And these ideas of rearrangement, retranscription, revision enable Freud to make sense of two central and related preoccupations: sexual development and trauma.

'Every adolescent,' he writes in his *Project for a Scientific Psychology*, Part 2, 'has memory traces which can only be understood with the emergence of sexual feelings of his own.' It is the forgetting of infantile sexuality that makes possible, and makes sense of, adolescent sexuality and therefore of the infantile sexuality that preceded it. Just as, sometimes, a memory can only become a trauma by being remembered; 'a memory,' Freud writes, 'is repressed which has only become a trauma by deferred action'. It is as though experiences are in search of a context to make them meaningful; in fact, to make them into experiences. Something happens that we can call a 'psychic event' which then, in some form or other, is repressed, only later to be called up into meaning. Something has to be forgotten which we then get access to by revision. Remembering, at any given moment, is a process of redescription; the echo can be different each time. The past is in the remaking. Remembering is a prospective project. But it is as though we are continually remaking something that to all intents and purposes never existed; or perhaps because we are making copies without an original – a representable original – all the copies are different?

Meaning is made, according to Freud, in the revision consequent upon deferral. The status, or the state, of what is forgotten is, in his account, indeterminate, so memory is a way of inventing the past. We are compulsive revisionists with an unknowable vision. Freud is very close here to making a nonsense point, though, of course, it is often at the nonsense points that psychoanalysis seems most interesting. He is almost saying here: there's no such thing as forgetting, there's only remembering; or rather, there's no such thing as the forgotten, there's only the remembered. I want to suggest here simply that Freud could not make much of his concept of deferred action because one cannot remember without having forgotten, just as one can only defer something that already exists.

Freud is close here to a picture of psychic life as something that lives in a continual present tense: nothing is forgotten, nothing is deferred, there is just intermittent redescription. In other words, he may have needed the idea of memory and forgetting to keep the past and the future apart. With the idea of deferred action it was as though he sensed the possibility of time collapsing. The concept of deferred action was like a conceptual fetish to protect him from the 'timelessness' he ascribed to the unconscious.

V

The mind is additionally burdened with a compulsion to repeat the past, and a compulsion to get away from the compulsion to repeat the past.

Leonard Shengold, 'The Boy Will Come to Nothing!'

In Freud's view the individual has to forget because the consequences of remembering are too painful, or too dangerous (or, in the analyst's case, sometimes too obstructive). But the forgetting that is in the service of self-protection can sometimes remake, as a way of refinding, what it has lost. In his essay on Leonardo, Freud writes:

> When in the prime of life Leonardo once more encountered the smile of bliss and rapture which had once played on his mother's lips as she fondled him, he had for long been under the dominance of an inhibition which forbade him ever again to desire such caresses from the lips of women. But he had become a painter and therefore he strove to reproduce the smile with his brush, giving it to all his pictures.

He had, Freud writes, 'remained true to the content of his earliest memory'. It is as though the past, a particular memory, was pushing Leonardo into the future to look for echoes. Replication is a self-cure for loss. 'Mona Lisa's smile,' Freud writes, 'awoke something in him which had for long lain dormant in his mind – probably an old memory. This memory was of sufficient importance for him never to get free of it when it had once been aroused; he was continually forced to give it new expression.' The very possibility of repetition signifies loss; one repeats only the unrepeatable.

But this initial forgetting under the aegis of the super-ego turns one kind of repetition – frequent caresses from the mother – into the other, displaced kind of repetition called art. Because Leonardo was coerced to forget – for fear of castration by the father – he had to find a substitute called remembering, reproducing the smile, as Freud, or rather his editor and translator James Strachey, put it, 'conjured up on the lips of his female subjects'. For Freud the logic of the Oedipus complex dictates that men must forget what they want (the mother) in order to remember something they can supposedly 'have' (other women). And according to the normative logic of this, women have to forget what they want (the mother) in order to find and be found by the father, whom they also have to forget in order to more successfully desire; they have to twice forget.

Leonardo, like everyone else – though, of course, Leonardo was also not like everyone else (psychoanalytic writing finds it difficult to show that everyone else is not like everyone else) – was in search of those substitutes that create the illusion of unique experience. But in order to find substitutes he had to forget what he had lost, make it absent. Forgetting is a way of describing the remaking involved in substitution (and, by the same token, the most dangerous insights, or revelations, are those one cannot forget: they become fetishes rather than objects for use, for forgetting). To make a substitute is to make a difference. Forgetting is the precondition for symbolization. It instigates the work – the dream-work – that goes on behind the scenes. The substitution we call symbolism is a reminder that what we call the past happened only once. And yet there is, of course, something that Freud refers to as repetition – indeed, a repetition compulsion that he increasingly regarded as a prime mover, or rather prime paralyser, of the psyche. But repetition for Freud is what happens when something cannot be remembered. 'Forgetting impressions, scenes or experiences,' he writes in 'Remembering, Repeating and Working Through', 'always reduces itself to shutting them off . . . The patient does not remember anything of what he has forgotten and repressed, but acts it out. He reproduces it not as a memory but as an action; he repeats it without, of course, knowing he is repeating it.' Freud discovered, in other words, that people were suffering not from their memories, but from their forgettings. They were forgetting in the wrong way, in ways that disabled them.

If a trauma is, by definition, that which you cannot experience until you remember, then repetition is evidence of an unwillingness – or, more disturbingly, an inability – to forget. The aim of psychoanalysis was to make emotional experience from the past available for transformation, subject to dreamwork; available, that is, for the kind of forgetting that would put it beyond the repetition compulsion. Freud realized, in other words, that there is always a risk – and psychoanalysis itself could be complicit with this – of foreclosing the future by making it merely another version of the past: the future being also, as it were, the wrong place for the past. 'In the end,' Freud writes, 'we understand' that the patient's repetition compulsion 'is his way of remembering . . . the patient yields to the compulsion to repeat, which now replaces the impulsion to remember.' This formulation brings with it the questions: what kind of actions would we be performing if we were not remembering; what would our lives look like without repetition? In our repetitions we have found a way of remembering something by never knowing what it is; and by not knowing we make it unforgettable. Those who can't, do; those who can, remember (or dream). And, as in the case of the Ratman, this leads Freud to formulate what might be called an exorcist aim for psychoanalysis: 'it is a triumph of the treatment', he writes with uncharacteristic triumphalism, 'if [the analyst] can bring it about that something that the patient wishes to discharge in action is *disposed of* through the work of remembering' (my italics).

Ideally, one rids oneself of the repetitive past through analysis, but does that make the analyst the accomplice of the death instinct, which ultimately disposes of everything and whose aim, Freud writes in *An Outline of Psychoanalysis*, 'is to undo connections and so to destroy things'? If repetition puts memory on hold, the death instinct kills it. If the aim of the organism, as Freud says, is to die in its own way, is this because it is remembering how to die – as though there were a 'death-memory', so to speak – or because it is forgetting how to live? The death instinct, as I suggested earlier, is Freud's figure for the most sophisticated forms of forgetting, perhaps the kind of forgetting that the analyst is in search of on behalf of the patient. The only way to truly forget the past is to dispose of it, to kill it, and the only way one can do that with any assurance is by dying.

Clutter

I think your analysis is right as far as it goes but if completed
leaves no word which is at all meaningless.

William Empson, note on a Commentary on
Hart Crane's 'Voyages III'

I

All psychoanalyses are about mess and meaning, and the links
between them; about the patient's and the analyst's relationship
to disorder, and their mostly unconscious fantasies of what disorder might entail, something orgiastic, something violent,
something inchoate, something longed for and feared. If our
lives have a tendency to get cluttered, apparently by themselves
but usually by ourselves, most accounts of psychoanalysis have
an inclination to sort things out. A kind of pragmatic clarity is
considered a virtue in psychoanalytic writing; it always has a
how-to ingredient as though its genre were the instruction man-
ual. The raw material of psychoanalysis – the unconscious desire
that is personal history – may be wildly unreasonable, but there
are eminently sensible vocabularies for summing it up.

Psychoanalysis, in the more empirical British tradition and the
more ego-psychological American tradition, aims to clarify
things; it is impressed by the lucidity it promotes without
acknowledging that this supposed lucidity is itself an effect of
language. Psychoanalytic theory – and indeed, its highly ritualized practice – has an aversion to clutter. Its categories of
pathology are always fantasies of disorder (there is, for example,
a well-known diagnostic category called a 'character disorder',

as though character could be anything else). Psychoanalysis, of course, wants us to be interested in – indeed, wants us to reappropriate, to redream – whatever we are keen to get rid of. And yet, in all its versions, it promotes the intelligibility of system; it repudiates chaos, even though the vagaries of our desires are often more revealing than their discernible forms.

So, in the inevitable to and fro we might prefer between idealizing order and idealizing disorder, clutter has rather an ambiguous status. It has the paradoxical implication of being something which may have no intrinsic or discernible order or pattern, and yet of being something that people make, wittingly or unwittingly, determinedly or helplessly. It invites us, in other words, to do something puzzling, or even uncanny; that is, to make meaning – as in, just say something about – the absence of pattern. Clutter, like all the orderly disorders we can describe in language, tantalizes us as readers of it. We can't be sure who the joke will be on if we say something intelligible or persuasive about it.

It is obviously unpromising to try to imagine representation without structure, or games without rules (if clutter was a game how would you learn to play it?). And yet our virtual passion for learning rules – if only by breaking them – lures us into situations where we can't apply them. All the now infamous psychoanalytic categories – hysteria, obsessionality, narcissism – are, among other things, parodies of rule-making. The obsessional neurotic, for example, in classical psychoanalytic theory, has an addiction to the clutter of order to conceal his instinctual life from himself. Winnicott's 'false-self personality', in his words, 'collects demands' to clutter up his life: to baffle and evade his desire, to protect but to starve his true self. If psychoanalysis is necessarily about the inevitable passions of losing and finding, about the terrors of the absence of meaning and desire, it is worth wondering how clutter is made, and what clutter can be used to do. It is, as everyone knows, a lot of work that makes a lot of work. Looking, say, at the clutter of one's desk it can sometimes seem the apotheosis of that wish that Freud saw as so insidious, the wish to frustrate oneself. But as the psychoanalyst Michael Balint once remarked, talking about defences, anyone who is running away from something is running towards something else. By the same token, when we are talking about clutter we should remember, anything that stops something happening is making something else possible. That if you lose something you might find something else in the process of looking for it. Indeed, this may be the only way you can find something else.

So in this case history of clutter, my first image, my emblem for the story, is the picture that mothers – not so often fathers – frequently conjure up for me of their adolescents' bedrooms. When they want to give a full account of how impossible their child is, the adolescent bedroom is *the* symptomatic scenario. This story is set in the crossfire between the parents' view of the adolescent's bedroom, and the adolescent's view of the adolescent bedroom. The adolescent, it should be noted, rarely complains about the parents' bedroom.

II

What, after all, could be more consoling than the knowledge that there can be no consolation?

Diane Fuss, *Dying Modern*

The person I want to write about, a painter in his early thirties, referred himself to me because he thought he was becoming 'mildly agoraphobic'. It was, he said, difficult to be sure because, obviously, he spent most of his time at home painting. He was not, he thought, a loner but had, ever since early adolescence, a passion for painting. He had a world of friends and a girlfriend; he knew something about psychoanalysis and it was clear to him, as far as he knew, that he did not especially have relationship problems. As he said, what 'people call relationship problems should just be called relationships'. I couldn't help agreeing, while also assuming that he was locating something about desire – about his link with other people – in his apparent symptom. His mild agitation about going out, and in particular the way he found himself steering clear of wider open spaces like parks and the countryside, had made him wonder, as he put it, 'what there was out there that he didn't want to see'.

Since, perhaps unsurprisingly, he thought of his fear in visual terms I asked him if he could see any links between this fear and his work. When I asked him this in our first meeting a curious thing happened. He said, 'When you asked me that, I suddenly had a very strong image of that famous photograph of Francis Bacon's studio. And I remembered thinking when I first saw the picture, "How could he find anything in all that mess?"' Then he paused and said, as an afterthought, 'And his pictures are so uncluttered.' I said, entering for some reason into a seminar on Francis Bacon, 'Yes, it's odd, isn't it? The paintings are uncluttered but rather claustrophobic.' And he replied, rather amazingly to me, 'You feel like the figures can't get out, but Bacon got them into it so presumably he could get them out.' There was a pause then, and I had so much to say that I couldn't think of anything to say. It was as though we had suddenly done a lot, and there was too much already. The word I want to use now is 'clutter'; but as it turned out, a sense of impossible excess was to be integral to this man's predicament, and hence the predicament he would put me in. What I did say was: 'Are you worried that I might get you out of painting?' And he replied, 'I will be in a mess if I come here with agoraphobia and you cure me of painting!' As is often the case, I think, when people fear that psychoanalysis will destroy their talent – and symptoms are a talent, if only for survival – they are often having to manage a very powerful wish to be cured of it.

One of the things this man had struggled with since adolescence was a great fear of – and intimidation by – other people's envy of his talent. One of the ingredients in what he began to call his 'space fear' was that when he went out people would know what he had just painted and would want to attack him or spoil it, or stop it being finished. He was, as it were, staying at home to protect his children. We established, in short, that he had only begun, or begun again, to feel hemmed in as he became successful. It was to be perhaps his only revelation in the treatment that it is possible to make envious attacks on oneself, that no one is more envious of one's gifts than oneself.

A lot of our conversation was about how space works, how one can make it work, how one finds the space one needs, and how often making the right space is the point, all else follows from there. The frame makes the picture; as he said, 'without it you wouldn't know where to stop, or start'. We could link this with the unframed quality of life outside his flat. And by the same token we talked a lot about the filling of space – indeed, that one can make space by filling it, as though space were simply an idea to house things in – and of the difference between filling space and filling time. He had never thought of himself as someone who filled time; but of course, being a painter, meant he was, in a sense, filling space all the time.

Psychoanalysis only begins, in any sense, to work when people begin to be impressed by their symptoms. It was the links between his present, apparently mild, symptoms and the initial dilemmas my patient found himself in when he began painting as a fourteen-year-old boy that brought the analysis to life. Faced with an empty canvas, in short, he would 'clutter it all up', and then he wouldn't be able to do anything with it. In his very eagerness, the way he painted stopped him painting. It was as though painting were too exciting, or too illicit, or too something, and he needed the clutter to stop what he thought of as the real painting happening. After all, what would he find himself painting if he didn't clutter up the canvas? The earliest sexual fear he could remember himself having – and it was painting that turned up for him when sexuality did – was of premature ejaculation. There was something he desperately wanted and something he had to get out of as soon as possible. And someone he must refuse to satisfy.

It is perhaps one of the most useful, indeed pleasurable, Freudian insights that the way we defend ourselves tells us, in disguised form, what it is we desire. If clutter was the obstacle to desire, it was also an object *of* desire. In clutter you may not be able to find what you are looking for, but you may find something else instead, while you are looking for it. Clutter may not be about the way we hide things from ourselves but the way we make ourselves look for things. It is, as it were, self-imposed hide and seek. I may clutter up my canvas, or my studio, to stop myself working – to sabotage the process – or I might do it to force myself to work in a different way. The problem with not being able to bear frustration is that you never notice the paradoxical nature of your acts: to frustrate one version of the self is always to gratify, to promote, to refind another version.

One of the reasons that Bacon had been so important to my patient – apart from the fact that he was powerfully affected by the paintings, even as a child – was because he had, in fact, shown him the way out of this problem of cluttering up his canvases. In an interview he had come across with Bacon, the artist had spoken about his now famous untechnique of, at a certain point, throwing paint at the canvas. When my patient had first read this, he said with his own almost unwitting irony, 'everything fell into place'. Not only did this idea fit with a whole nexus of then adolescent intellectual passions – Gide's gratuitous acts, Breton's random writing, the chance and indeterminacy of John Cage's compositions; in other words, a passion for loopholes, for ways of abrogating self-control in the service of contingencies – but it also fitted in with one of his own techniques for the uncalculated, which I imagine was an adolescent reworking of a childhood game. Little children often like dropping things behind them as a way of making them disappear. My patient, aged about fourteen, had invented a new way of dressing in the morning. For obvious and not insignificant reasons he could do this only during the holidays, when he wasn't going to school.

He invented this new method one morning when he couldn't decide what to wear. So he took a lot of clothes out of his cupboard, dropped them over his shoulder behind him, and took what came to hand, irrespective of whether it matched, or indeed, of whether he liked it. But as important was the fact that his method depended on accumulation, that is to say, in his view, it got better the longer he did it. The more clothes that piled up over time on the floor of his room the better it was. When he bought new clothes he would drop them on the floor, pick up the bundle of clothes, and drop it over his shoulder so they would be properly mixed in. To begin with, his, as he called them, 'bohemian parents' were amused by this – after all, the art of family life is to not take it personally – but eventually his mother cracked. 'But you can't find anything in this room,' she would say to him quite sensibly; to which he would reply, in one way or another, that that was the point. The clutter he created meant that things found him (he would say to his mother, 'our clothes should come and find us', which seemed rather profound to me). Sometimes, he acknowledged to himself, it was extremely frustrating not being able to find something that he was looking for, but this was more than compensated for both by the way he could discover things he didn't know he was looking for and, of course, that he would find himself wearing such apparently unusual combinations of clothes. Of course, as he now conceded, it wasn't all quite as random as he then liked to think – he was, after all, still selecting his clothes, but from a different way of organizing them.

Part of the freedom of being fourteen – or at least the freedom one has to fight for, is the freedom to sleepwalk; the freedom, that is to say, to do things in one's own way. This is why psychoanalysis can be so disruptive for adolescents – indeed, for anyone – because at its worst it forces a pattern. It can make the links that should be left to find their own way. It had never occurred to my patient, until we started talking, that there was a link between the problem he was having with his painting and what he called his 'mess-dress' method. By, as he put it, cluttering up his paintings it was as though he couldn't paint; by cluttering up his room he could dress in his own way. One was apparently a problem, one was a solution. Something that worked for him in one area of his life, was felt to be a kind of sabotage in another area. It is often true in psychoanalysis that solutions can be found by mapping one area of a person's life on to another, apparently disparate, one. When it came to dressing, clutter was useful to him; it was exactly what he needed, and so he deliberately made a mess. When it came to painting it seemed to take him over, he was making it but he couldn't get away from it. Ordinarily one might think one person's clutter is another person's . . . what? Pattern, beautiful object, whatever. For this man, from one psychoanalytic point of view, there was an unconscious project to keep these two selves separate. The self that dressed and the self that painted had to be kept apart. When he dressed he could make, at least from his point of view, a good mess. When he painted he made a bad one.

Clearly, a lot could be made of this, in psychoanalytic terms. The analyst doesn't merely tell the so-called patient what he thinks of him, he shows the patient what he thinks of himself. In this splitting of himself he managed to keep the destructive mess away from his parents; 'no one', as he once said to me, 'gets hurt if you fuck up a painting . . . except yourself'. Or you could think that his elaborate quasi-obsessional ritual of spontaneous dressing, exactly the same as cluttering up his canvases, was in fact an anxiety about allowing himself to fantasize, to really elaborate the thought of his desire. Faced with a wardrobe or a canvas he might start imagining – owning up to – dreams of what he wanted, who he wanted to be, what of himself he might want others to want. If paint, like clothes, was for him, at an unconscious level, a covering up, then what were the catastrophes associated with nakedness? What would he have been doing, what would he have been thinking about, if he had neither got dressed nor painted? If one was to be a crude old-style Freudian, in other words – not an uninteresting thing to be – one might think of clutter as a reaction formation against some simple crudities. Think how cluttered – how complicated and confusing – one's mind or indeed one's conversation can become faced with someone we desire.

All of this, to some extent, and at different times, seemed pertinent to my patient. But I want to consider here some more specific questions. First, what is a good mess? Which might mean from whose point of view is it good (or bad) and what are the unconscious criteria for deciding? In one mood I might think despairingly, 'This room is too cluttered'; in a different mood I might take it for granted, find it rather cosy, be impressed by being the kind of person who lives in creative chaos, and so on. In other words, what makes clutter work for us, and how does it work when it does? A good life, one might say, involves making the messes you need.

So, how does clutter work for us? After all, we may be able to tolerate, and even enjoy, our own mess, but nothing tests our feeling for other people more than our feelings about their mess. Indeed, our relationship to what we think of as the other person's disorder, or their disordering of us, is a picture, a synecdoche, of our relationship to them. Where we experience other people as disorder can be where we experience them as other. In this sense, clutter *is* other people, they get in our way. It's always worth wondering when we think someone is ruining our life what we imagine our life uncluttered by them would look like. I think all this is relevant because our relationship to clutter – what we identify as clutter, when we use the word – has a history. And personal history is always co-constructed, is always made in the context of relationship. So we may wonder, at the start, with whom did we first experience what we think of now, or even thought of then, as clutter? How did we learn it, and how were we taught it? Two different things.

My patient, growing up, as he said, with 'bohemian parents', had clearly spent some of his childhood longing for what he thought of as 'an ordinary home' like some of his friends had. Of course his friends found his home, crowded as it usually was, with things and people, incredibly exciting. 'We are ramshackle but we are comfortable,' his mother would apparently say, sounding like someone from an Edwardian or Bloomsbury novel. What my patient thought of as an ordinary home was one in which meals were regular and on time, and one in which the adults made more time for the children. It was only by going to other children's houses that he began to realize that there were other worlds. But as he remembered it, it was as though other people's 'more normal' homes crystallized something that he had always sensed but never quite realized, that he experienced his life as something of an obstacle course. A lot of things seemed to get in his way. The freedom of his parents' household could be sometimes just a mess for him.

At home there had been both too much space – the space created or imposed upon him by his parents' own absorbing preoccupations, which left him, he thought, too much to himself – and too little space; the house seemed cluttered with its unpredictable population of people and its various artefacts. And this was another ingredient of his present agoraphobia. Outside, with all that space, and no one keeping an eye on him, what might have happened to him? Which was the passive version of a more frightening question, what might he have done? The neglect he had felt at home had left him feeling uncontained; this was then, in adulthood, displaced on to the outside world, as a fear of freedom.

When he cluttered up his canvases as an adolescent he was inevitably doing several things at once. At a documentary level it was a representation of the clutter he experienced his home as – a clutter that could preclude his freer expression of himself. What he had, to some extent, suffered passively at home – his parents' chaos – he now actively inflicted on his canvas. There was a strong Oedipal current here – that is what the parents do, they prohibit, they baffle one's desire.

None of our parents gave us enough freedom; gave us the freedom we needed and deserved, the freedom to make them our partners. But also the clutter at home suited him – he could exploit it as part of his defence against his own desire. He could become addicted to the obstacles to his desire rather than to the objects of his desire. He could protect himself from his own delirium of wanting. The rage of frustration can be more comforting than the derangement of desire.

But, as is often the case, the solution is as interesting, as inventive, as the problem. When, following the lead of another father, Francis Bacon, my patient started throwing paint at his canvases, he was, as he put it, 'making a mess of the mess'. It wasn't, exactly, that he needed to unclutter his canvas, but rather that he needed to find a different way of cluttering it up. What mattered then was simply that it worked. His coming for psychoanalysis meant we could think about – in relation to his presenting symptom – what made this new kind of clutter work for him. 'While you're working in a certain way,' Bacon said in an interview, 'you try to go further in that direction, and that's when you destroy the image you had made; an image that you will never retrieve. That's also when something unexpected suddenly appears: it comes with no warning . . . What's most surprising is that this something which has appeared almost in spite of oneself, is sometimes better than what you were in the process of doing.' Bacon is saying, whatever destroys the image takes its place; that the act of ruining something produces something else. That the spoiled thing can not only – though not always – be better than the original thing, it can also be, indeed can't help but be, utterly unpredicted; in that sense, unique, unprecedented: that only by absolutely losing something – 'an image that you will never retrieve', as Bacon says – do you get the surprising thing.

Chambers Dictionary defines clutter as 'a clotted or confused mass: a disorderly accumulation: confusion . . . to clog with superfluous objects, material etc'. What Bacon suggests – without superstition – and, indeed my patient found, was that the disorderly accumulation of throwing paint, the act that could clog the picture with superfluous material, could also disclose something new; something that paradoxically was closer to one's heart by being beyond one's design. Clutter, as chaotic accumulation, could be both a thwarting and a source of revelation. One might think of the difference as being two different kinds of unconscious work, the good mess and the bad mess – the mess that can be used, and the mess that stultifies. It may be a more productive distinction than the one between clutter and pattern. Our vocabulary of disorder, by virtue of being a vocabulary and implying a grammar, is always glib.

In her wonderful book *On Not Being Able to Paint,* Marion Milner refers to a kind of personal aesthetic she discovered for herself through what she called 'free drawing', the visual equivalent of free association, the kind of doodling one might do in an idle moment:

> One thing I noticed about certain of my free drawings was that they were somehow bogus and demanded to be torn up as soon as made. They were the kind in which a scribble turned into a recognizable object too soon, as it were; the lines drawn would suggest some object and at once I would develop them to make it look like that object. It seemed almost as if, at these moments, one could not bear the chaos and uncertainty about what was emerging long enough, as if one had to turn the scribble into some recognizable whole when in fact the thought or mood seeking expression had not yet reached that stage. And the result was a sense of false certainty, a compulsive and deceptive sanity, a tyrannical victory of the common-sense view which always sees objects as objects, but at the cost of something else that was seeking recognition, something more to do with imaginative than common sense reality.

Milner counsels us to be wary of the pre-emptive imposition of pattern, of the compulsive sanity of reassuring recognitions. Of what we might be doing when we are too keen to clear up clutter. Clutter, that is to say, may be a way of describing either the deferral that is a form of waiting, or the waiting that is a form of deferral. Our eagerness for recognition can be a self-blinding.

Narcissism, For and Against

I

By decomposing groups of figures you compose
groups of movements.

May Sinclair, *The Tree of Heaven*

If much of the most interesting psychoanalytic theory today is sceptical of the whole notion of relationship (Freud, Lacan, Laplanche, Bersani), most of the best popular psychoanalytic theory takes relationship for granted (Klein, Winnicott, Bowlby). Either we are suffering from whatever it is that sabotages our intimacies, or we are suffering from the notions of intimacy that we have inherited. It is not clear whether better relationships are the solution to our suffering, or whether it is that very aspiration that we suffer from. Narcissism, unsurprisingly, has been a keyword in these debates, and what is loosely called morality is what has been at stake. What kind of regard we are able, and wanting, to have for other people, and how we might distinguish between the good and bad forms of so-called self-love have become abiding preoccupations.

It is not amazing that a Judaeo-Christian culture is unimpressed by, and suspicious of, states of self-absorption. Solitary contemplation of God (and His demands) and certain kinds of committed devotion to others (as one of His commands) have been for many people the prerequisites of a good life. Scrutiny of the self, but not celebration or adoration of the self and its less devout and considerate desires, has been integral to this project. What the secular narcissist – relatively untroubled by heresy – might be preoccupied by has become a contentious and disturbing issue. Whether narcissism gets a good press (in Freud and Kohut, say) or a bad press (in Klein and the post-Kleinians), it is always keenly moralized. Great claims, either positive or negative, are always made on narcissism's behalf; as though when people are talking about narcissism they are always talking about something else. Do 'creative artists' – the psychoanalyst's secular idols: all talk of creativity is quasi-religious in its allusion to a creator – need to be narcissistic, or is this what they suffer from, or both? Is masturbation bad for people because it doesn't involve other people? Are we primarily interested in other people, so that self-preoccupation is a symptom of thwarted involvements, or are we essentially self-involved creatures interrupted, every so often, by our unavoidable dependence on others? Or is it, as we are so keen to say, probably a bit of both? These are the old questions – with their oppressive historical baggage – that psychoanalysis has got bogged down in, and which are versions of a more interesting question: what should a good person – from a psychoanalytic point of view – be open to, and be closed to, apart, that is, from being open to this particular question? When people write about narcissism, in other words, they are persuading us about what we should value, what forms of exchange we should aspire to. They are writing about, in other words, what, ideally, we should be giving our attention to. It is worth, therefore, considering the narcissism of psychoanalysis. And, indeed, the fact that no one is more narcissistic than the enemies of narcissism. It is part of the function of narcissism – the aim of narcissism – to expose by provocation the narcissism of those with whom it comes into contact.

I want to start at one of the so-called beginnings – to which the more ambitious psychoanalytic theorists are always drawn – because it is one that I find particularly convincing; both evocative and instructive. It is Laplanche's notion of what he calls the 'enigmatic signifier'. Despite the extremely complex and sophisticated theory Laplanche has woven around it, it is a mercifully simple and compelling idea. That every infant – and so every person – begins life being given what he calls 'messages' by the parents (at first by the mother) that are beyond comprehension. These messages are not exclusively, or even predominantly, verbal; they may be gestural, olfactory, tonal, and so on. And they are enigmatic in a double sense. The parents themselves don't understand them – or even know about them – because they are unconscious. And the child cannot understand them because his powers of so-called understanding are so undeveloped, and because they are puzzling. What the child is able to 'translate', in Laplanche's keyword, he may be able to include, but the residue – which he intimates is always the larger share – constitutes an unconscious of 'foreign bodies'. 'The unconscious,' he writes (in *Essays on Otherness*, 1999), 'is thus in no sense an other "myself" in me, possibly more authentic than me, a Mr Hyde alternating with a Dr Jekyll, the one with his hatred, the other with his love . . . It is an other thing (*das Andere*) in me, the repressed residue of the other person (*der Andere*). It affects me as the other person affected me long ago.'

We are decentred in Laplanche's view because we have inside us the opaque messages transmitted by our parents, often in spite of themselves. 'To address someone with no shared interpretative system, in a mainly extra-verbal manner; such is the function of adult messages, of those signifiers which I claim,' he writes, 'are simultaneously and indissociably enigmatic and sexual, in so far as they are not transparent to themselves, but comprised by the adult's relation to their own unconscious, by unconscious sexual fantasies set in motion by his relation to the child.' And for Laplanche it is, as one might suspect, the child at the mother's breast that is the source, or exemplary scene, for this tragi-comedy of mutual confounding that makes us who we are. The other's desire – in this case, the mother's – is both primary and constitutive in its provocative enigma. As though the breast – as the precursor of all desirable cultural objects – is asking the infant a question. 'Can analytic theory afford to go on ignoring,' he writes in his *New Foundations for Psychoanalysis*,

> the extent to which women unconsciously and sexually cathect the breast, which appears to be a natural organ for lactation? It is inconceivable that the infant does not notice this sexual cathexis, which might be said to be perverse in the sense that the term is defined in the *Three Essays*. It is impossible to imagine that the infant does not suspect that this cathexis is the source of a nagging question: what does the breast want from me, apart from wanting to suckle me, why does it want to suckle me?

It is as though the mother's breast transmits an obscure sexual message that implants itself in the infant as a question he is ill-equipped to reply to. Whatever is being ascribed to the infant here in terms of proto-questioning, or a capacity for puzzlement, it does seem entirely plausible to imagine that parents convey far more than they intend, and that children take in, in whatever form, far more than the parents or the children suspect. In this view our lives become – and analysis becomes – the attempted translation and retranslation of these enigmatic messages our parents left us with; and our coming to terms with the limits of our capacity for retranslation. We can never pluck out the heart of the mystery. So what is inescapable in the genesis and development of every person is the presence inside them – the psychic force field, the aura, the atmosphere, the messages – of another person (at first the mother, Laplanche implies, then the father, and so on). There is no escape from the uncanny influence of those primary others, the parents (and their parents, and so on) but there is the possibility of some translation. So what kind of sense does it make to say that we were trapped by having the parents we happened to have? As though we could have had other parents. By definition the ineluctable isn't something we can think of as being available to escape from. We can wish that it was – we can wish that we and the people we love won't die, we can wish we didn't have to eat – but with these things we have to do something different.

It is noticeable in Laplanche's account that it is as if the child were captured by, in thrall to, these enigmatic signifiers, these radically perplexing decentring messages. Clearly there can be a way out of this (although there are no ways through), one of which, of course, is psychoanalysis itself. Indeed, it is the analyst's very attitude, how he positions himself in the project of analysis, that shows the patient that the only way out is through. Psychoanalysis, of whatever persuasion, always describes itself as anti-escapist; and it can only do this, in my view, by being unduly omniscient about what there is to escape from, and so about the nature of escapism. Narcissism, broadly speaking, becomes one of the keywords in psychoanalysis for those forms of life that, in various ways, have tried to escape from all those things that are assumed, by the different psychoanalytic theorists, to make a life worth living. A good life is one in which one has been able to escape from the right things. It is in their theories of narcissism – in their uses of the word, rather – that psychoanalysts can often tell us what they want from life, and so what they want from their patients' lives.

Laplanche conceptualizes what he refers to as a kind of oscillation of the human soul, and he describes it, rather wonderfully, as analogous to the Ptolemaic and Copernican cosmologies: the sun going around the earth as akin to the narcissistic relation. 'One is entitled to claim,' he writes, 'that the Ptolemaism of the human psyche, its narcissistic recentring, follows upon a Copernican stage as its presupposition, in which the nursling child is caught up in the orbit of the other and has a passive relation to its messages.' There is, he writes, an 'ineluctable narcissistic closure of the apparatus of the soul'. The infant, in narcissistic closure is, so to speak, in recovery from having been too open, too confoundingly receptive to the mother's messages. A familiar question returns: do we begin too open and need to find ways of closing, or are we born closed and need to be prised open? Laplanche's essence of the human soul is a traumatic but unavoidable – and therefore constitutive – receptivity to the other (the word 'relationship' here would not be quite right).

There is a systole and diastole of the soul; the picture is of an organ or an orifice that is too open and learns forms of closure (of course it isn't really *too* open because it couldn't be otherwise). It is as though the language is progressively or developmentally moralized; entrapment and escape get grafted on to open and closed.

But the correspondences are interestingly mobile. The infant is trapped by being open, but trapped in a different way by becoming closed. The way out, Laplanche intimates, is being able to bear reopenings. Indeed, his belief in psychoanalysis depends upon the possibility of reopening, and of what he calls 'a deconstruction of old constructions'. The aim of a psycho-analysis is to disturb the patient's inevitable narcissistic closure. And part of this closure has been effected by the patient con-structing coherent narratives about himself. Coherence, the self-story hanging together, is here a sign of closure. 'The aim here,' Laplanche writes, 'is not to restore a more intact past (whatever would one do with that?) but to allow in turn a deconstruction of the old, insufficient, partial and erroneous construction, and hence to open the way to the new translation which the patient, in his compulsion to synthesize (or, as the German Romantics might have put it, in his "drive to translate") will not fail to pro-duce.' The analyst and the patient collaborate to open the way for the patient's retranslation of those constitutive enigmatic messages he received unknowingly from the parents. 'The development of the human individual,' Laplanche writes, 'is to be understood as an attempt to master, to translate, these enigmatic traumatizing messages. Analysis is first and fore-most a method of deconstruction (ana-lysis) with the aim of clearing the way for a new construction, which is the task of the analysand.'

It is in a sense the virtue of the message that it is enigmatic because this makes it subject to, indeed irresistible to, retranslation. And this, in itself, breaks the rigid determinism that too easily stifles much psychoanalytic theory. It makes the child and his future collaborators necessarily inventive. It leaves them with something to work on if not work out. 'With the concept of enigma,' Laplanche writes, 'a break in determinism appears: to the extent that the originator of the enigmatic message is unaware of most of what he means, and to the extent that the child possesses only inadequate and imperfect ways to configure or theorize about what is communicated to him, there can be no linear causality between the parental unconscious and discourse on the one hand and what the child does with these on the other.' Meaning, fresh translation, is there to be constructed, and in Laplanche's view we are always translating a translation. Pathology is the conviction that there is a *Standard Edition*.

I have gone to such lengths here with Laplanche partly because, in my view, he offers us, in a psychoanalytic context, an exemplary myth of human origins; and for reasons I will explain. But also his myth is useful as a way into the broader question of the very real consequences of psychoanalytic myths of origin. What is inescapable for the infant and child in Laplanche's account is its proneness, its receptive openness to (in the first instance) the mother's messages; and it is unavoidable, beyond her conscious intent, that she should transmit such messages. And it is finally inevitable that the messages should be enigmatic, and so in need of translation (Laplanche simply reminds us that the parents have an unconscious, and the child has a relatively undeveloped comprehension). For Laplanche this is what might once have been called the given, the foundational experience, from which escape is not possible, of being the recipient of the mother's unconscious messages. Escape, one can say, is not an option here; it is not a question of how to get away, but of what can be done by way of continuing retranslation. So what distinguishes Laplanche's version of beginnings is the redundancy of escapism as a ploy. One can't escape from the opaque fact of one's parents' unconscious, any more than you can, in actuality, escape, in Freud's and later Klein's versions, from the imperious urgencies of one's instinctual life. And so the simple point of my essay is that in psychoanalytic theory – and not only there, of course, do such tautologies exist – *that which the subject wishes to escape from but cannot is considered to be his essence.*

It is in describing the individual in his self-deluded, self-misleading project of escape that the analytic theorist unavoidably describes his sense of what matters most to her. Every time we show the patient, in whatever way, that he is avoiding something we are impressing upon him, however obliquely, our sense of what is essential, of what matters most. We have always already posited a reality and then defined a good life as the talent, or the capacity, to abide by it. In other words, our accounts of the escapism of everyday life – our whole extensive vocabulary of defence and avoidance and flight – is the key to our most cherished essentialisms. If we want to find out what we take to be real – what we assume to be of the utmost value to acknowledge – then we must attend above all to what we think of ourselves as being on the run from. Our notions of escapism are entirely complicit with our fantasies of the real; and in this sense the real itself can be an escapist fantasy; in need of what Laplanche calls 'retranslation'. From a psychoanalytic point of view we are at our most absurd, at our most wishful – that is, at our most human – in our escapism; *because we try to escape only from that which is by definition inescapable.* We call this, of course, the now overly familiar 'divided subject'; in our flight from sexuality, aggression, dependence, gender conflict, grandiosity, even conflict itself, we make a mockery of ourselves. Man's preposterous project is to escape from himself. And in the full knowledge that one's nature by definition cannot be left. Or rather, that if one had the nature it is that which one cannot get round.

My hunch in this essay – which is a hint because I can't justify it – is that the kind of psychoanalysis I would prefer, if indeed it is conceivable, would be one in which the language of escapism had disappeared – no longer seemed useful, or relevant, or to the point of our new-found self-descriptions. I do realize, I hasten to add, just how silly this is. And I say this not by way of excuse, but by way of qualification. Psychoanalysts should not be earnestly breaking codes but revealing fabulous misunderstandings.

II

> Instead of asking, 'Are there truths out there we shall never discover?' we should ask, 'Are there ways of talking and acting that we have not yet explored?'
>
> Richard Rorty, 'Truth and Progress'

All escapist theories need a concept of the real; that is to say, they are all, somewhere, essentialist theories. Though this makes them no less valuable – as belief-systems, or heuristic devices, or possible facts or regulative fictions – it does make them morally and epistemologically suspect. These theories – of which psychoanalytic theories are a kind of quintessence – are themselves also enigmatic signifiers, puzzling messages that invite retranslation. Whereas Laplanche's essentialism of the message, of the enigmatic signifier, is by definition – almost by design – provocative of redescription, his myth of origins so open in its consequences for any given individual – there are consequences more pronounced, more delimited in the myths of origin of Freud and Klein, as taken up by some of their followers. It is indeed paradoxical that determinism and escapism so often seem to go hand in hand; escapism as the wishful burlesque of determinism. That which I cannot escape I must find ways of seeming to escape: this would be the comedy-as-farce approach. That which I cannot escape I must ultimately and impressively submit to, at exorbitant cost: this would be the tragic view.

For Shakespeare and Kafka, Lionel Trilling once remarked, the world was a prison; but in Shakespeare the company is better. For Freud and Klein the prison is our instinctual endowment in its fraught meeting with culture. But the essentials of their theories – the instincts, and so the unconscious and the Oedipus complex – are not themselves seen as contingent historical inventions. It is often intimated that they are virtually ahistorical, acultural universals. This is the prison – the war between the life instincts and the death instincts – and even though the company doesn't make the feast, it makes a difference. Both Freud and Klein, in theory, dramatize a flight from, or attack by, something deemed to be life-denying; and a flight towards something assumed to be life-enhancing. Narcissism – the keeping oneself company at the cost of other company – has come to be seen, in its various denominations, as a peculiarly undesirable prison; as an always tempting, some would say, unavoidable solution to the problem of bearing one's instinctual life. For Laplanche, we might remember, it was as though there was narcissistic closure as a temporary resort from the desire, the terror, the disarray prompted by the mother's enigmatic sexual messages; the ego's attempt to seclude itself, to hive itself off from the other outside and the other inside.

But the viability of psychoanalysis as a treatment was predicated on the individual's wish to reopen; to reopen the endless question of those messages. To offer up his associations for redescription, deconstruction, retranslation. If narcissism has been the traditional enemy of psychoanalysis – its collaborative antagonist, more agreeable than psychosis – then it must have some ideas about what the alternatives are to narcissism. If, as everyone more or less agrees, narcissism is a form of self-cure, then it might be better to describe the various narcissisms as the rivals of psychoanalysis. Its most difficult, recalcitrant siblings. If I can put this allegorically: the analyst and the narcissist – assuming that they are different – have alternative cures for a similar problem; but which is better and from what point of view are we going to arbitrate, or even discuss this? What does so-called narcissism offer the patient that the analyst wants to persuade the patient not to want? What are the good things worth seeking in life, and why would somebody want to devote their lives to more or less getting away from them? It is, for example, easy for us to forget that relationships are supposed to make us feel better; psychoanalysis can remind us of this. In the analytic descriptions of so-called narcissistic conditions, or narcissistic people, the patient and the analyst seem to be involved in some emotionally fraught debate about whether this is any kind of life for a person. Analysts who believe in something they call narcissism, I contend, have an especially strong sense of what a good life for a person is. If they did not have this largely unconscious sense they would have no way of recognizing what it was that the patient was supposedly in flight from. I don't mean by this that I think such analysts are more directive or even manipulative than others – though they may be – or indeed that their patients don't have comparably powerful beliefs about a better life for themselves. But rather that it is more interesting and useful analytic practice to have a glimmer of what it is one is promoting, and so be able to subject it to retranslation.

There can be nothing more narcissistic than believing in narcissism. So I want to take Narcissus – though there are, of course, other candidates, Oedipus, Jonah, etc. – as my exemplary escapist, for the sake of this essay, to suggest two things. First, that theories of narcissism are peculiarly complicit with ideas about escapism. And that the theorist of narcissism always runs the risk of getting himself into a cul-de-sac analogous to the one he describes his narcissistic patient as suffering from. Both the so-called narcissistic patient and his analyst get their entrances and their exits confused. I want to take examples from the British psychoanalytic tradition to show how John Steiner's notion of psychic retreats and Neville Symington's notion of the narcissistic refuge are logical conclusions of aspects of the Kleinian and Independent groups, respectively.

III

I do not like that presumptuous philosophy which in its
rage of explanation allows no XYZ, no symbol representative of the vast Terra Incognita of Knowledge, for the
Facts and Agencies of Mind and Matter reserved for
future explorers . . .

S. T. Coleridge, *Notebooks*

It is, above all, to psychoanalytic theories of narcissism that we
should go if we want to find out what the various psychoanalytic
visions of a good life are. We might go – and we would certainly
once have gone in the days of radical anti-psychiatry – to psychosis, to schizophrenia, for the apparently deeper meaning-of-life
stories, but that would be a different elaboration of my argument here. Theorists of narcissism always have a more drastic, a
more absolute, sense of what their nominated patient is escaping
from, or attacking, and so, by implication, what it would be better for him to prefer. I think it is good, not to mention inevitable,
that psychoanalytic theorists should each have their own good-
life stories, but not always good that we have to infer them from
their theories of pathology. If the so-called narcissist is the negative ideal of the psychoanalyst (in my allegory), then he is also
his double, his counterpart, his alter ego; and at worst his scapegoat. As we shall see, in some versions of Kleinian theory the
narcissistic parts of the personality are saboteurs, despoilers of
life, liars, cheats and tricksters.

And it is part of the covert link, the elective affinity between
the psychoanalyst and the narcissist, that her theories of narcissism,
like narcissism itself, tend towards closure, towards strict definition. But of a subtle kind because their whole drift – what they
explicitly proclaim and affirm – is in the direction of openness,

of acknowledgement of the otherness within and the otherness without. In other words, in my caricature of this, both the analyst and the narcissist might endlessly accuse each other of being too knowing, at the most interesting of cross-purposes. The analyst, of course, only gets to see the unhappy narcissist; the narcissist who, ironically, must be wanting something else, which is why he has come for analysis. But then, of course, this is the once philosophical question of what it is we should want in order to make our lives good; and what the relationship is, if any, between what we want and what we should want. My question is: can a psychoanalytic theory of narcissism avoid being what Coleridge called 'a presumptuous philosophy' with a 'rage for explanation'? Indeed, 'presumptuous' should perhaps be a keyword in any discussion of that great escapist, the narcissist. For 'presumption' the *OED* has: 'Seizure and occupation without right; usurpation; the taking upon oneself of more than is warranted; forward or over-confident opinion or conduct; arrogance, pride, effrontery, assurance . . . the taking of something for granted.' My discussion is about what the so-called narcissist and the so-called psychoanalyst take for granted.

IV

. . . We should remember that work may be unimaginative
not because it is badly argued but because it is
arguing with the wrong people.

Bernard Williams, 'What Might Philosophy Become?'

If Oedipus is the family researcher in psychoanalytic mythology, the explorer of origins, the man who was dying to get home, then Narcissus is the master of isolation and ignorance (Tiresias, we might remember, told Narcissus's mother Leiriope, 'Narcissus will live to a ripe old age, provided that he never knows himself' (Robert Graves, *Greek Myths*)). Oedipus, like the classic neurotic, keeps arriving at the place he is running away from. The ironic escapist, Oedipus is in flight from the family he keeps getting closer to. Narcissus, in love with his own beauty, his own image, is in flight from his desirous admirers; his path, Robert Graves writes in a sprightly retelling of the myth, 'was strewn with heartlessly rejected lovers of both sexes; for he had a stubborn pride in his own beauty'. After one such lover, Ameinius, killed himself, the gods agreed to take vengeance. Through the ministries of Artemis, Narcissus is inveigled to fall madly in love, unknowingly, with his own image in the water; and he kills himself because Artemis, as Graves plainly puts it, 'made Narcissus fall in love, though denying him love's consummation'. This is a story, to put it equally plainly, about someone who would rather die than have a relationship with anyone; and who, we are persuaded to believe, had a self-destructive, indeed, presumptuous relationship with himself. Narcissus's pleasure, we infer, was in refusing people, including, of course, himself. If Oedipus was escaping from his family – from their welter of desires for each other – what, comparably, is Narcissus deemed to be on the run from? We are told nothing by Graves about Narcissus's suffering (or its absence); we are told only that, beyond a certain point, there was something the gods wouldn't let him get away with. We might say, commonsensically, that you just can't go round treating people, including yourself, like this.

Oedipus is an epistemologist, a quester; there are things he wants to find out. He is characterized by his curiosity. Narcissus is the antithesis of these things; indeed, Tiresias told Narcissus' mother that his living to a ripe old age depended on his *not* knowing himself. That self-knowledge would not be good for him. This in itself makes Narcissus something of a problem for the psychoanalyst. And we could, of course, say that Narcissus was in flight from self-knowledge, and this makes Oedipus ultimately the success to Narcissus's failure. But there are, I suppose, two questions here: first, how do we think Narcissus's life would have been better if he had had – or been able to bear, against Tiresias's prophecy – self-knowledge? And was that, indeed, what he was trying to escape? Again commonsensically, we might imagine that he wanted to escape from the reproaches of his defeated lovers, and that he clearly couldn't escape from the wrath of the gods. These rather simple-minded suggestions are merely by way of pressing the question, what was Narcissus trying to escape from? Because this is the way the question has been posed by those psychoanalysts after Freud who have taken up the myth as a useful and provocative description of a contemporary predicament. In many ways I think the Oedipus myth has seemed less enigmatic than the story of Narcissus; it has sent us a more perplexing message, at the same time as it offers us a perfect amused emblem of the perils of interpretation. We gaze in fascination at something that is merely a reflection – a mirror not a window – and it does us no good at all.

I want to take as my psychoanalytic tag for this, Serge Viderman's formulation that the hell of the narcissist is the tyranny of his need for the other. All the quite various psychoanalytic theorists of narcissism agree, I think, that for the so-called narcissist, needing has become a specific kind of preoccupation; and that the narcissist, or the person in a narcissistic state of mind, is suffering from something to do with his apprehension of otherness, whether it is the other(s) within, designated as the unconscious, or the others outside. In ordinary language the narcissistic person is considered self-absorbed, and this self-absorption is experienced by the bystanders, onlookers and witnesses as both a shield and a weapon. Viderman's formulation interests me because it points us in several directions. On the one hand, it lets us wonder, what has to happen to needing, what has to be done to needing, to make it feel like a tyranny? What are the conditions in which needing is felt to be a tyranny? There are questions here about the nature of need, but also about the nature of tyranny. Need has become a tyranny, and tyranny, we would all agree, should be resisted.

What we tend to do with tyrannies is conform, resist, use secret ruses to evade and avoid them, overthrow them – but not, generally, negotiate with them. Because that is what makes something a tyranny, the impossibility of negotiation. And if there is also something intrinsically tyrannical about everyone's need for the other, is 'tyranny' the right word here? We don't after all talk about the tyranny of breathing or of sleeping; with these, as it were, solitary pleasures, there may be a kind of tyranny in being unable to sleep or suffocating. But the narcissist's predicament is both terrible and paradoxical in Viderman's version, because he is tyrannized by what he cannot do without. Hell, of course, is a place from which one is unlikely to escape.

In finding his need for other people a tyranny, this narcissist is immoral and apolitical. Or, to put it another way, the narcissist is at odds with democracy. The notion of collaboration is without meaning. For the narcissist in his unmisgiving project of self-sufficiency, there must be no outside. No others to ruffle his arrangements. He is not an object-relations theorist. And so he becomes, either as a diagnosed person, or as a figurative but prevalent part of everyone's self, the target, so to speak, of psychoanalysis. Addicted to his own propaganda, he is a fundamentalist of himself – or of one image or version of himself – and must be persuaded, convinced, seduced, encouraged, held, contained, loved, nurtured, 'appropriately hated', confronted, understood, not colluded with, reconstructed, analysed: I'm not sure what the word is – he must be shown the benefit of needing and being needed by others. I think the dialogue between the analyst and the narcissist – and calling it a dialogue already gives too many prisoners – is one of the emblematic double-acts of our time. It is one of our secular redemption myths; from insulated impoverished isolation to receptive, more generous free association. The conflict of need made more than bearable. In my story of this it might be as misleading to become card-carrying narcissists as to become qualification-carrying psychoanalysts. The miseries of so-called narcissism are often patent, and radically diminishing.

The narcissist, by trying to escape from the inescapable – his need for others, whether it is described as a need for gratification, for recognition, or for relationship – has found a dispiriting self-cure. But what does the analyst propose? Both agree, after all, that something called 'otherness' is both a problem, and the problem. There is, apparently, something else that has to be fully acknowledged – call it the unconscious, infantile sexuality, the life and death instincts, the object, people apart from oneself, the non-human environment – and a good life quite literally depends upon these things. The narcissist won't have any of it (other than the death instinct). The psychoanalyst can't imagine a morally and sensuously convincing world without virtually all of them.

I think it isn't merely facetious to say that from the psychoanalyst's point of view the narcissist, or the narcissistic parts of the personality, have got it wrong. But it is callous to put it quite like this because the analyst, ideally perhaps, is also mindful both of the suffering caused by narcissism, and the kind of suffering, of trauma, that it is an attempted solution to. At its most minimal and documentary, if external reality is unbearable, one needs at least the illusion of internal refuge. If thoughts and feelings and wishes and desires and affections feel persecutory one might need the asylum of psychic anaesthesia, a retreat or a seclusion where one is apparently exempt from such terrors and perplexities. These exits are entrances; these flights are a kind of release.

I said earlier that our descriptions of escapism were the key, by inference, to our notions of the real, the given, 'that which it is impossible not to know', in Henry James's words: it is our chosen, or unchosen, essentialisms that are our enigmatic signifiers par excellence; the culture's apparently untranslatable messages. And in this issue, which I am dramatizing, if not caricaturing, there is, in theory, a conflict of essences. For the psychoanalyst the essence can be called 'otherness'; for the narcissist the essence can be called 'the absence of otherness'. There is something else there other than me as I want to be, or there is nothing else there other than me as I want to be. I think it is worth wondering – if it is possible to do this without portentousness – what kind of essence otherness is? Which in the context of my essay means looking at the ways psychoanalysts write and talk in sympathetic antagonism with the narcissism they find so debilitating in themselves and their patients.

I think I should perhaps add here that I don't think sufficient consideration has been given to the eagerness with which analysts want to, in Neville Symington's zealous phrase, 'flush out' the putative narcissism in their patients; which is merely morally high-minded scapegoating. It is always people's narcissism, we should note, that calls up narcissistic rage in other people (the Socratic dialogues dramatized this fact). Any conversation, external or internal, without a strong narcissistic voice joining in, tends towards dreariness; it is only when the narcissistic voice tyrannizes – which is, of course, its forte – that the conversation dies into monologue and hush. Any good conversation about the unconscious usually needs someone who doesn't believe in it. This, of course, is always the most problematic voice to deal with in any analysis.

V

> . . . even if a non-human authority tells you something,
> the only way to figure out whether what you have been
> told is true is to see whether it gets you the sort of life
> you want.
>
> Richard Rorty, *Pragmatism as Romantic Polytheism*

Clearly the so-called narcissist has turned up for analysis only because what the analyst may call his 'narcissism' has not got him the sort of life he wanted. He may be, in my shorthand sense, wishfully committed to the absence of otherness, but he must want something else. Of course, in actuality there could be no such thing as pure narcissism; even Viderman's formulation requires of the narcissist that he experiences a tyranny. So the narcissist, we can more realistically say, wants to keep otherness down to a minimum. He goes about diminishing difference, stripping the world of its opposition, its separateness. A personal religion of closure is actively and passively practised. But forms of closure are perhaps more hospitable to description than forms of openness.

In his meticulous descriptions of what he calls 'pathological organizations' within the self, the British Kleinian John Steiner invokes, perhaps inevitably, Narcissus. These pathological 'structures' as he calls them (in *Psychic Retreats*, 1993), have a 'central function: to contain and neutralize . . . primitive destructive impulses'. Through projective identification – an active putting into another object the destructive impulses – states of mind are produced in the patient in which he feels 'stuck, cut off and out of reach'. 'A psychic retreat,' Steiner writes, 'provides the patient with an area of relative peace and protection from strain when meaningful contact with the analyst is experienced as threatening.' But the effect of this avoidance of contact with reality – through the ejection of so much of the patient's internal reality – is stultifying. 'The relief provided by the retreat,' Steiner writes, 'is achieved at the cost of isolation, stagnation and withdrawal . . . Typically an equilibrium is reached in which the patient uses the retreat to remain relatively free from anxiety but at the cost of an almost complete standstill in development.' The function of this retreat then becomes 'an area of the mind where reality does not have to be faced, where fantasy and omnipotence can exist unchecked and where anything is permitted'. Any 'aspect of reality which is difficult to accept' – and Steiner offers, as one might expect, death, ageing, difference between the sexes and the generations – is apparently abolished in the retreat. The analyst, Steiner writes quite sensibly, 'must try to understand what it is that the patient fears would result if he emerged from the retreat'.

It is a retreat because it is a psychic and/or environmental space fabricated by the patient to free himself of psychic pain. It is a pathological organization, a structure, because it starkly arranges, through the subtlest mechanism of projective identification, a certain relatively anxiety-free state of mind. And Steiner is characteristically lucid in his exposition of this, which leads him to Narcissus, and Freud's Leonardo. 'In the most straightforward type of projective identification,' he writes,

> a part of the self is split off and projected into an object, where it is attributed to the object and the fact that it belongs to the self is denied. The object relationship which results is then not with a person truly seen as separate, but with the self projected into another person and related to as if it were someone else. This is the position of the mythical Narcissus who fell in love with a strange youth he did not consciously connect with himself. It is also true of Leonardo, who projected his infantile self into his apprentices and looked after them in the way he wished his mother had looked after him.

Steiner does not describe his psychic retreats as specifically narcissistic; though narcissism and Narcissus himself are clearly implicated. It is perhaps worth mentioning that in Steiner's brief account of the myth, Narcissus must have projected something rather enticing into his reflection, in order to fall in love with it. Whereas Graves's description of Narcissus's path 'strewn with heartlessly rejected lovers of both sexes' would fit with Steiner's account of a projection of both destructiveness and guilt into the forsaken lovers.

But what I want to focus on here is what Steiner believes is being escaped *from* in these psychic retreats. There is reality, the strain of meaningful contact, 'any aspect of reality which is difficult to accept', particularly ageing, death and gender and generational differences, and primarily primitive destructive impulses. But at a more fundamental level, subsuming all these other things, as it were, is the sabotaging of, the attack on, the escape from, *development*. The Sadeian orgy in this retreat where 'reality does not have to be faced, where fantasy and omnipotence can exist unchecked and where anything is permitted' is an alternative to, a sanctuary from, emotional growth. Without this essential underlying principle of emotional development the whole project of psychic retreat, within this metapsychological system, loses its purpose, its telos (Narcissus as the great hater of time). What is to be escaped from – what is deemed to be too painful to bear – is development. And so all of Steiner's images of life within the retreat are an odd mixture of licence ('anything is permitted') and immobility, paralysis, isolation, stagnation, withdrawal, feeling stuck, cut off and out of reach. This escape – Steiner's bolt-hole – tells us that for Steiner time and emotional development are the reality. And the way in which his theory tends towards closure – itself a kind of retreat – is in its implicit claim to be able to recognize genuine emotional growth when it sees it. Is it not, after all, another kind of omniscience to consider oneself the arbiter of true development? Not to mention, of course, the assuredness of his conviction that there is such a thing as development. If, for example, we were to say that there is simply change, and thereby shrug off all the progressivist associations, we might say that different people prefer some kinds of change to others. Psychic retreats would then no longer look like retreats, but rather more like resorts and resources. By calling it a retreat one might have pre-emptively privileged the alternative. In other words, if we take up Rorty's quote, the point is not: certain ways of living sabotage something essential to your being called emotional growth, and that one must, if at all possible, be in contact with something called reality in order to foster this growth. The question would be rather: does doing this, living in this way, get you the sort of life you want? 'The way to solve the problem you see in life,' Wittgenstein wrote, 'is to live in a way that makes the problem disappear.' It would, I think, be inaccurate to say that one can make the problem one sees in life disappear by trying to escape from it. The reason psychoanalysis needs Rorty's pragmatism is because pragmatism encourages us to experiment with possible truths and their possible consequences; psychoanalysis, by contrast, assumes a knowingness about essences and origins. Psychoanalysis, at its worst, always already knows what a good life is, what it is for and what it consists of. Narcissism in psychoanalysis is always the enemy, the saboteur of that supposedly good life.

At their worst, both rhetorically and practically, the essences in psychoanalysis, like emotional development in Steiner's theory, function as a kind of implicit blackmail. If you don't do this – get in touch with what I call reality – then something terrible will happen to you. You will fail to do something I call 'develop'; you will stagnate. In other words, it's worth wondering how much otherness, or what kind of otherness, can be happily included in Steiner's system, before the patient or the patient and his analyst is assumed to be on the side of pathology. The analyst must be an expert at recognizing destructive, counter developmental behaviour. He cannot afford, say, to think of every act as morally equivocal, or paradoxical, or intrinsically unpredictable in its consequences.

As Steiner's interesting account makes clear we cannot promote otherness – that which is beyond fantasies of omnipotence, that which the narcissist struggles to disavow – without to some extent defining it; and by describing what otherness might include we must, to some extent, appropriate it, bring it within the range of our descriptions. In theory it tends to become either each theorist's open category, filled with what it is assumed the patient needs to acknowledge for a good life; but at its worst, of course, it becomes merely another tyrannical super-ego demand. Worse even than the command 'Be happy, enjoy yourself' is the command 'Allow something other than yourself as you would like to be.' The double-bind of this is self-evident. It might be, within its own terms, the apotheosis of narcissism to be as unnarcissistic as possible; to risk living outside the retreat. 'We wish to have,' Coleridge wrote in his lectures on Shakespeare, 'a sort of prophetic existence present to us, which tells us what we are not . . .' Only the omniscience of knowing what we are can produce the omniscience of knowing what we are not. The shock of the new, one might say, is the shock of just how knowing we have been about the apparently familiar.

VI

Only when you understand one another can you disagree.

Donald Davidson, *The American Philosopher*

So what is interesting about Neville Symington's *Narcissism: A New Theory* (1993) – which comes out of the British Independent or Middle Group tradition – is what Symington wants to add to the familiar theories of narcissism. Agreeing that narcissism is essentially destructive (of the individual and the group) and, as he puts it, 'deeply antagonistic to self-knowledge . . . projecting unwanted aspects of the self', he also believes it – against the grain of much psychoanalytic determinism – to be essentially 'chosen'. What he calls the 'narcissistic option' becomes the patient's decision in the face of trauma. He usefully divides up previous theories of narcissism as trauma theories or phobia theories. Steiner's more Kleinian theory would be phobic in that the narcissist is deemed to be in flight from innate destructiveness that has been projected in and out. Fairbairn and Kohut would be trauma theorists because for them the narcissist is managing an environmental deprivation, or impingement or insult. Both kinds of theory are a kind of pernicious bad faith for Symington – though that is not a phrase he uses – because they both covertly shift responsibility from the patient. The phobia theory implicitly blames some putative death instinct (or innate aggression), the trauma theory blames parents (and this means usually mothers). For Symington, in his unembarrassedly essential language, 'the *core* of narcissism is hatred of the relational – a hatred of something that is *inherent* in our being'. In what he calls, advertently, 'the narcissistic disposition, it goes profoundly against the grain to have to acknowledge that one is affected by another'. The narcissist is a kind of Satan, an anti-life figure attacking the putative *core* of our being, our relation with others. So the narcissist, or the person of a narcissistic disposition, is both deemed to know what is the core of our being, that is, he is himself a committed essentialist, and because he knows so exactly what nurtures the relational he can so accurately spoil it. The narcissist and his theorist (or therapist) have a kind of symmetrical or complementary knowledge. Both of them know – though quite how we are not told – what is life-enhancing. 'The therapist's task,' Symington writes with a degree of assurance provided by his theory, 'is to protect the struggling life-enhancing side against the side that desperately wants to keep within that narcissistic refuge and remain anaesthetised.'

I am myself now taking up a knowing position in relation to Symington's theory; but this fact, I think, is illustrative of the predicament I want to illustrate. Just as Symington believes 'Narcissism always has to be flushed out,' presumably in both senses of the word – something all theorists of narcissism must be committed to a version of – so I want to flush out the omniscience in myself and others that makes such theories plausible. Everyone in psychoanalysis is against omniscience, this is not news; it should be more interesting news that so-called otherness is so difficult to really write and talk about without fetishizing it as a concept. And obviously this has implications beyond the psychoanalytic consulting room. If it might be better to talk about preferred worlds rather than narcissism and its alternatives – different worlds inducing different kinds of pleasure and suffering – it is not clear whether psychoanalytic theory can accommodate such frank pluralism, or would even want to.

I, too, want to escape from the dangerous escapism that is

omniscience, and that gets to be called in psychoanalytic theory 'narcissism'. Indeed, the ordinary image of the narcissist – in Symington's words, 'enclosed, shut off from the other . . . not interested in communicating' – is, by seeming definition, a negative ideal. And yet, as I have suggested, there is a dispiriting tautology or double-bind. What could be more omniscient than knowing that I do not know myself? But I don't think we should get out of this dilemma, or find ways around it, so much as be in it in better ways. Perhaps, like many other people, I find Steiner and Symington's accounts both meaningful and clinically useful, and doing in their theory-making what theorists of otherness cannot help but do; but that is partly, I think, because they appear to solve a problem, when the problem itself might be more interesting than the solution. The question becomes obscured by its answers. How *do* we know what is good for ourselves and someone else? Or indeed, how do we know – by what criteria, as it were – what is good about ourselves and others? Clearly they are not always the same. Psychoanalysis does not get around these moral questions with the language of pathology. If what we think we want to escape from is a key to what we think of as real – and the real in psychoanalytic theory is deemed to be of essential value to a person – then perhaps we should always treat our notions of the real as what Laplanche calls 'enigmatic signifiers', confounding messages that we inherit and need to retranslate. Anything, after all, can be used as a refuge; so we should ask of each psychoanalytic theory what it might be a refuge from. Not as a way of invalidating it, but as a way of elaborating it, of retranslating it.

When Freud wrote in 'Group Psychology and the Analysis of the Ego', 'Love for oneself knows only one barrier – love for others, love for objects,' he was retranslating, among other things, the enigmatic signifier of a supposedly altruistic Christianity. But he was also leaving a kind of riddle for the profession he had invented. After all, what happens when the patient becomes a barrier to the analyst's self-love?

Bombs Away

I

It took bombs to deliver us.

J. B. Priestley, *Margin Released*

The year before war was actually declared – the possibility of war having been in the air, so to speak, for some time – T. S. Eliot had spoken of wanting to participate in some way in the war effort. He had hoped, in Peter Ackroyd's words in his biography of Eliot, 'for occupation in some form of National Service without that official status which might shut his mouth, and that he would be free to take part in any work for the future that was possible'. He ended up becoming an air-raid warden for the area of Kensington in which he lived, which involved watching for air raids and 'rehearsing the procedure for marshalling people in the event of an air raid, and practising his fire-drill by putting out bonfires'. This work, which seems so incongruous with our image of Eliot, did not shut his mouth. Despite being uncertain in September 1939 about whether he would write poetry again, within three or four months of war being declared Eliot started work on 'East Coker', the second of his *Four Quartets*, which would eventually be published together in 1944. It is not always easy to remember – given the lack of explicit reference – that the *Four Quartets* are war poetry, partly written in London during the Blitz. Although the poems are very much preoccupied with continuity and rupture – and indeed with the idea of England and its Christian heritage – the landscape of the poems, though sometimes eerie and desolate, is not, as it were, bombed. The opening of the second section of 'Little Gidding' makes perhaps most obvious reference to the landscape from which the poems came:

> Ash on an old man's sleeve
> Is all the ash the burnt roses leave.
> Dust in the air suspended
> Marks the place where a story ended.
> Dust inbreathed was a house –
> The wall, the wainscot and the mouse.
> The death of hope and despair,
>   This is the death of air.

Apart from its apocalyptic associations, 'This is the death of air' means also this is the death that comes from the air, the bombs that turn houses and lives to dust.

There is, of course, no reason why this or any other poem should be a documentary reflection of the world in which it came about. But what I want to look at briefly – by way of an implied comparison with the psychoanalysts – is one localized example of what Eliot, consciously or unconsciously, uses the war to do, and especially the air raids with which he and indeed all Londoners were much preoccupied during several of the war years. The word 'raid' is used only once in the *Four Quartets*, and it is in the passage in 'East Coker' in which Eliot is writing about writing poetry. The language of war is recruited to articulate something about articulation, but with the strangest implications: 'And so each venture,' Eliot writes about himself writing poetry:

> Is a new beginning, a raid on the inarticulate
> With shabby equipment always deteriorating
> In the general mess of imprecision of feeling,
> Undisciplined squads of emotion.

In what in psychoanalytic language might be called the dream-work of the poem, Eliot has turned the air raid into one of his pictures for the struggle to write poetry (air raids were effectively 'a raid on the inarticulate' in that the victims couldn't speak nor be understood by the German bombers). In what sense is each new venture of writing like a raid on the inarticulate? Does a raid, as in a robbery, steal something back? To use the word 'raid' in this context could not help but bring with it the immediate history, the association of air raids, and by doing so, suggest something of the poetry of war. A poem is an air raid, a surprise attack, it conquers internal countries of inarticulacy. And this is not worlds apart from Freud's now famous slogan of usurpation, where id was there ego shall be.

This essay is about what British psychoanalysts – especially the increasingly important child analysts – used the war, wittingly and unwittingly, to articulate about the child's putative nature. And so it is about the conflict – not always articulated as such – between those who worked as if the unconscious, and therefore most starkly the child, were outside history, 'timeless', exempt from contingency; and about those for whom whatever was being described by the notion of the unconscious was utterly contingent, entirely a period piece; those for whom the war would confirm psychoanalytical theory, and those for whom it could not help but put it into question.

This essay is about, then, how the Blitz got into the poem that is psychoanalysis; and how the child in the Blitz is perhaps the dream-image – the emblem – of which most psychoanalysis after the war is the interpretation.* The child, from a psychoanalytic

---

*I think it is more illuminating to read psychoanalysts as poets – mostly, of course, poor ones – rather than failed or aspiring scientists; if we do this we need not worry about whether they are right or wrong, or whether they are making progress, we can just argue instead about whether their words are persuasive, eloquent, evocative or beautiful. Whether they have made something haunting rather than true.

point of view, was living in a Blitz. In what was beginning to be called the child's 'internal world' there was always a war going on. But I want to begin with a clinical vignette.

A sixteen-year-old boy came to see me after the sudden death of his father because he found himself, as he put it, 'absolutely obsessed' by his father; for the first time in his life feeling really close to him, feeling the affinities between them. His presiding grievance with his father had always been that his father refused to really fight with him, to take him on. And this had been particularly strange to my patient, when he was a young boy, because his father was a war hero, with medals that he refused to show anyone, for bravery. How could he find out about his father's war if he literally refused to fight with him, when he quite explicitly, though gently, discouraged the boy from being rough. When it came to Oedipal conflict his father had been, as it were, a conscientious objector. My patient told me:

After the war, my father became obsessed by books about Germany: social histories, biographies of Nazis and German statesmen, memoirs of the period, all that stuff . . . he believed – and he would often say this to my mother and I – that you had to find out what the enemy were really like so you could make yourself absolutely different . . . my father developed a kind of private cult of inefficiency and gentleness . . . he was a sort of hippy . . . I was always trying to find the hard man in him. I did everything I could to make him an enemy.

I said: 'I am trying to imagine a life – or a war maybe – in which you never know who the enemy is, never know how to find him.' And he said, 'If you never knew who the enemy was you wouldn't know how to be good, that's what my father believed.' I said, 'So the enemy makes you good, makes it possible for you to be good'; and he said, 'Yes, gives you a picture of goodness.'

The complications of this attempt at generational unhaunting were obviously bemusing. From his experiences in the war – whatever kind of trauma they had been – the father was left still looking for the enemy. His obsession had been to understand and define the enemy as a negative ideal; he would never be like them: it would never happen again. His son also needs an enemy but comes up against something bewildering; the father who is an enemy by refusing to be one. For the father to refuse – or rather to try to refuse – to be the son's enemy could be a consummate act of unconscious Oedipal aggression. The son says to the father: I want/need to fight with you. The father says to the son: You need enemies in order to be good, but I won't be your enemy.

For the sake of this essay there are two emblematic things here. First, the need to locate, describe, understand the enemy. And second, as an inevitable corollary of this, the need for intimacy with the enemy (if you don't know who and where the enemy are they may be having a relationship with you without your knowing). For this man's father after the war, it seemed that, at least to his son, the most passionate relationship of his life was with the Germans; his wife and his son could rarely impinge upon this. For my patient his father reading books about Germany was a primal scene. (Indeed, one could think that the first couple that the child experiences – the child's first primal scene – is the mother's internal relationship to the enemy, the unacceptable within herself.) For my patient, after his father's death, found himself obsessed, once again, by his father's obsession: by the kaleidoscopic shifts between triangles: father, mother and son; father, mother and Germany; father, son and Germany, and so on. In identification with his father he lived as if his partners and friends – the people about whom he was passionate, whose company he craved – were enemies. He lived, that is to say, as if knowing people was, unconsciously, a project of disidentification. He knew people in order to be unlike them.

In Franco Fornari's book *The Psychoanalysis of War* (1975), the critic writes that, 'war serves to defend ourselves against the "Terrifier" as an internal, absolute enemy . . . in this manner we arrive at the incredible paradox that the most important security function is not to defend ourselves against an internal enemy but to find one.' As armchair psychoanalysts it is obvious to us that this solution – this security function – is a problem. But you can't fight a war, of course, as though it were the internal problem of the combatants. What do we imagine it would be like if, by magic, all the people in a war – in the middle of a battle – suddenly withdrew their projections, owned and acknowledged their personal terrifiers? Would they start attacking themselves?

In this cartoon there would be a stunned silence and then some people would go mad, some people would become sad or depressed and some people would feel a lot better; but how would they then see each other? What kind of relationship would they have next? What would they use each other to do?

In order to understand a lot of psychoanalytic theory we have to fast-forward it to the moment after the cure: the aftermath or the fallout after the successful treatment. After my psychoanalytically cured war there would be more internal conflict – people would be really and most immediately up against themselves – but apparently less, or certainly different, external conflict. Because we cannot bear the battle within, psychoanalysis tells us, we have our battles, whenever possible, outside.

I want to suggest in this essay that, in the first instance, the experience of the Second World War, in London, consolidated the psychoanalytic picture of the child that Melanie Klein had been developing since the twenties; because the child, the Kleinian child, was assumed to be already at war, though essentially with himself. But it was the unconscious dream-work done on the war, the deferred action of that trauma – and of the Blitz in particular – that made of the child a site for contested accounts of both the nature of the child herself, and the child in the adult on which much of psychoanalysis depended. There was a war being fought, during and after the war, and not only between Klein and Anna Freud, to produce a privileged description of the child. As we shall see, the immediate experience of the Blitz confirmed much of Kleinian theory; the more gradual psychic processing of the experience – of both its practical consequences (the pragmatics of evacuation), and its emotional cost – produced a proliferation of competing descriptions, most notably in Britain from D. W. Winnicott, John Bowlby and W. R. D. Fairbairn.

If we cannot imagine psychoanalysis without the notion of war – psychoanalysis was partly made out of the materials of war, its casualties and its language – then the immediate experience of the Second World War seemed to put the finishing touches to a new description of the child that analysts had been struggling to articulate since before the First World War. If it was the workings and the provenance of the unconscious that Freud began with in *The Studies in Hysteria* (1895), in the Joke Book (1905) and the Dream Book (1900) and the *Three Essays on Sexuality* (1905) before the First World War – then we cannot help but notice that between the wars psychoanalysis changes. On the one hand it simply proliferates; there are more practitioners and theorists and psychoanalytic societies. Freud's work is translated and reprinted; psychoanalysis finds an obvious use for itself in understanding and treating the psychic consequences of war. But with the concepts of the repetition compulsion and the death instinct (in *Beyond the Pleasure Principle*, 1920) Freud produces a kind of psychic essentialism that, if we believe in these concepts, seems to have immense explanatory force. What now can't be explained by the war between Eros and Thanatos, and the drive to repeat? If the unconscious becomes more intelligible – a source of coherent narratives – it also begins to be usurped by a new figure called the child. For some psychoanalysts – most notably Sándor Ferenczi, Melanie Klein and Anna Freud – describing the child replaced describing the unconscious, or the dream-work. Or rather, in their view, describing the child *was* to describe the unconscious. The child was, as it were, the unconscious *live*: you could see it in action. It had been found; in fact, you could virtually talk to it. With the advent of child analysis there was a growing sense that we could get closer to the source.

But in these new descriptions of the child – despite the great differences between Klein and Anna Freud with the ferocious controversies they inspired (see Pearl King and Riccardo Steiner's book, *The Freud–Klein Controversies 1941–45*, 1991) – the child had intelligible projects, the child had needs. It is infinitely more reassuring to have needs than to have an unconscious. (Need, one might say, could be defined: unconscious desire could only be tracked.) The war, *The Times* said, makes us 'think about essentials'; in other words, makes description of need urgent. The psychoanalytic child that emerged from the Second World War in her various guises – Kleinian, Anna Freudian, Bowlbyan, Winnicottian – was equipped with, indeed constituted by, a discernible set of needs and was, in fact, equipped for a war of need. The child who came out of the Second World War had a variety of different wars inside her, depending on which psychoanalytic theorist you read.

'In the popular sociologies of the 1950s,' Denise Riley writes in *War in the Nursery*, '"we all know" that children need their mothers at all moments; and child psychology, ostensibly drawing on the "experiences of war" was scientifically reiterating "what everyone already knows".' The internal war that psychoanalysts had been refining in theory and practice between the wars came true, as it were, with the experience of the Second World War. What 'we all knew' about children after the war came, in part, from the complex relationship, the enmeshing, of war experience in Britain, and in London in particular, with the war which psychoanalysts increasingly believed constituted our being. For the psychoanalysts – and particularly the Kleinians – a war was another word for a person. So, what was the difference, if any, between the war outside and the war inside? And what were wars about, and so what did we need to cope with them? If the war with its bombings and evacuations, and mothers working, and fathers away indefinitely, showed people starkly what deprivation was for a child and so, by inference, what a child needed, then the child could tell us what a war was.

'If we accept the notion,' Winnicott writes in his 1940 paper 'Discussion of War Aims', 'that basically in our natures we are like our enemies; our task is immensely simplified.' This, of course, is far from being a simple statement. The task he refers to is at once psychoanalysis, and the understanding of the war. This, one could say, is a virtual summation of psychoanalytic theory; basically in our natures we are like our enemies. Real wars, of course, make us believe we know what an enemy is: someone essentially different from us. If there is so little difference between ourselves and our enemies we are clearly, as Freud suggested, a danger to ourselves.

I want to suggest that the Second World War was, so to speak, an ideal setting – and psychoanalysis was a more than suitable discipline – to ask, what is an enemy? And in child analysis it was as though one could be in on the beginning of the answer. Was what was increasingly being called development – or, in the Kleinian schema, more or less primitive positions – merely a process of locating the enemy and then of having a good-enough relationship with it? Was child analysis – or indeed living a life – about winning wars, or finding suitable truces? In short, was a child someone in the process of locating the enemy; and where, if not from the adults, was the child going to acquire her sense of what she was up against? Acculturation, as the child analysts would formulate it after the war – and practise it in the consulting room – was teaching the child, and re-educating the child's mother, to recognize the enemy.

In 1944, Ernest Jones, the founder of the British Psychoanalytic Society in London, who had been instrumental in the promotion of Melanie Klein's work in Britain, gave a lecture in America entitled 'Psychology and War Conditions'. Fresh, so to speak, from the Controversial Discussions in the British Society – the discussions themselves something of a war within a war – Jones used the opportunity of his lecture to explicitly reflect on the effect of war conditions in Britain, and, more obliquely, on the war conditions in the British Society. Indeed, his title, which could have been 'Psychology *of* War Conditions', is itself suggestive of a necessary or even enabling link. Psychology, at least the psychology that is psychoanalysis, and war conditions go together.

In this paper Jones makes two related points. First, that it was only when we, the British, realized how evil the Germans were, that we began to feel better. It was, he says, with 'the apparently irresistible form of the Blitz-krieg', 'when we saw the Germans marching at will' into France, when we realized their 'invincibility', that they were so much more 'implacable' than in the last war, that we could then locate our resources, the good things that would protect us. 'At such a moment of mortal peril,' he writes,

> the country was seized with a united determination so admirably voiced by the genius of our prime minister, and it was this sense of unity that gave us the conviction that there was something we could believe in and trust, namely each other. This conviction was so strong as to be quite impervious to the pessimistic anxieties in the rest of the world concerning our fate.

It is the mortal peril – a clear sense, a vivid definition of the enemy – that turns the country into a strong positive group, providing what Jones refers to as the 'sense of unity'. The enemy, Jones implies, by the sheer force of the terror it inspired, made us a strong positive country, with a genius as a prime minister. In fact, Jones intimates, sheer horror of the Germans made us practically invulnerable, 'quite impervious to the pessimistic anxieties in the rest of the world'. What could be more inspiring than an enemy? How else, we might wonder in the light of Jones's fervent account, might we acquire such virtues and strengths? Without this much evil would there be this much good; would there be something that had the kind of unity that allowed us to call Britain a nation? Satan's dare in *Paradise Lost* (written after another war) – 'Evil be thou my good' – comes ironically true. Or to use Jones's preferred Kleinian language, though not in quite the way Klein intended, the Bad Object inspires the Good Object. We become good reactive to the defined presence of the bad. The moral question here – redescribed in the new language of psychoanalysis rather than the old language of theology – is: what would we be without the Bad Object? The second and related point that Jones makes is that in his view – and this of course would fit with some of his psychoanalytic assumptions – the war made people feel better. 'There is no evidence I know of,' he writes,

> to indicate any increase in psychoneuroses in these five years (of the war), and there was a very general impression during the most dangerous period of the war that would explain this by the reciprocal relationship that exists between so-called 'real' suffering or danger coming from without and neurotic suffering; when fate inflicts suffering there is less need for the self-punishing functions of the neurosis.

What the war confirmed, and air raids in particular, was '. . . how very much easier it is for the human mind to tolerate external danger than internal dangers'. The war, Jones intimates, is just what a lot of people needed: 'the higher degree of single-heartedness in this war', he writes like a man with a proof in his hands, 'results in a mental harmony that fortifies endurance against discomfort and distress'. Does Jones – and, by implication, do psychoanalysts of his own persuasion – think that war is a good, indeed necessary, thing? Or rather, does war between nations, or between opposing factions in psychoanalytic societies, function as a cure for the intolerable war going on all the time inside the individual? Being a person is virtually or potentially intolerable unless you are lucky enough to live in a time of war. Or putting it the other way round, what, from a psychoanalytic point of view, is peace?

In Jones's view here – echoing Freud but not exactly echoing Klein – external danger makes us feel better (Klein's implicit point is that it doesn't really make us feel better, it is a delusionary imitation of the problem). The defence of projection, coupled with either or both the neurotic need for self-punishment and the implacable danger of the death instinct, make up a virtual instinct or need for war; which, paradoxically, is in the service of the individual's self-protection, and moral well-being.

This discussion about war reveals a battle of theoretical allegiance in Ernest Jones himself. In at least one reading of Freud, war – or at least the evacuation of the bad or destructive – is a necessity for psychic survival. This, in a sense, is Freud as tragic realist. We are at war with ourselves and with culture. Real wars enliven us because they give us something to do – they give us both a target, and a performable project, a theatre – for our inner divisions; and they provide sufficient punishment, in terms of suffering, to make us more light-hearted. And yet, as Jones almost won't let himself notice in his lecture, this rather complicates the practice of psychoanalysis, especially Kleinian analysis with its essential project of enabling the patient to restore his destructiveness, to return the projections to their source, to facilitate the acknowledgement of a severe ambivalence in the service of entry into the depressive position. Or, to put it slightly more straightforwardly, if we are mad and bad, is psychoanalysis driving people mad by encouraging them to take their mad badness back inside themselves? Better out than in, or better in than out? Is psychoanalysis the alternative to war, or an art of war? If there is such a thing as mania – at least in Klein's description of it – then war is only ever going to be a temporary or provisional solution to inner depression and the madness that is an attempted self-cure for depression. And yet, as Jones is eager to assert – partly it confirms certain central psychoanalytic descriptions – the real war seemed to be every bit as curative for many people as he might have hoped psychoanalysis would be. War might be psychoanalysis's great rival. In fact, ironically, the real war, by validating some of Freud's still embattled ideas, could make psychoanalytic treatment itself a poor substitute for war. If war can do us good, and psychoanalysis can do us good, how should we choose between them? War and psychoanalysis might seem mutually complementary, each a proof, a validation of the other.

In child analysis it seemed as though we could find out, as it were, how wars started. Child analysts, in the unique setting of the war, were trying to find out what a good war was. 'Very notable,' Jones wrote ominously in his lecture, 'was the adaptation displayed by children provided their parents showed no neurotic terror.' Here we have, in miniature, the child analyst's question: what does the child depend upon to sustain his or her emotional well-being? And who is in a position to decide – to provide the privileged descriptions of – emotional well-being or health?

The child analysts had a good war. But Jones, as a virtual but still ambivalent Kleinian, was, at least in this sentence, putting a great onus on the parents, as Winnicott and Bowlby were to do after the war. '[P]rovided the parents showed no neurotic terror,' Jones observed, the children adapted well during wartime. But what kind of adult would it be who showed no neurotic terror during a war? Or, as it would soon turn into in theoretical discussions after the war, what kind of mother would it be who showed no neurotic terror in the war of child-rearing, the war in the nursery? No neurotic terror can only mean: bringing no personal history to the experience.

Psychoanalytic theory always runs the risk of dehistoricizing wars; as though there is something more or less universal called war that has certain more or less generalizable psychic effects. As though, say, technological developments would make no material difference to the psychic experience of war. War, from the psychoanalytic perspective endorsed by Jones, is a great relief for two reasons; it places the enemy fairly and squarely outside. And it defines the enemy, gives it definition, tells us who they are, what they are like, how they work. 'It might be said,' Freud wrote in 1915 in 'Thoughts on War and Death', 'that we owe the fairest flowerings of our love to the reaction against the hostile impulse which we sense within us.' We are, in this sense, dependent on the enemy, either within or without, to react against; to free us to construct our goodness, our virtues.

The experiences of the war in London – both the immediate experience of air raids, rationing, etc. – and the second-hand experience of media reports and rumour – were the raw material, the day-residues, out of which child analysts in London elaborated psychoanalytic theory to redescribe the enemy within. The war provided a ready-made set of representations out of which the Bad Object could be constructed – and reactively the Good Object. The good mother would be one who could absorb and process the infant's air raids – who would be undestroyed by his bombs; she would never mastermind an implacable invasion. In other words, by looking at one of the many experiences of the war that dominated people's lives – the air raids on London – we can glimpse something of the inevitable contingency – and historical occasioning – of the theorizing of unconscious fantasy, the sense in which psychoanalytic theory is always local history, and the way it attempted to privilege its descriptions by apparently exempting them from the specificities of history. We can see something of what happens when Freud's privileged description of the instinctual war that constituted the individual met the experience of a real war. Bombs, and the real possibility of invasion, seem, in retrospect, to have been just what child analysts needed to extend their account: the invasion by mothers, by their separateness or their intrusiveness; the invasion of the mother by the child; the child invaded by his instinctual life and needing maternal protection. These were the images that would organize psychoanalysis after the war; and the fathers who were mostly absent during the war would be mostly absent from the theory.

So, what did child analysts use the experience of war to do, what was the work of inner transformation, the dream-work, coming up with in terms of theory and practice? What was it like doing child analysis under the threat of invasion, in the expectation of air raids?

In 'On The Theory of Anxiety and Guilt', written in 1948 – a summation of her then present position – Melanie Klein explains how the war had vindicated, indeed proved, the validity of her most cherished theoretical conviction. 'If external danger is from the beginning linked with internal danger from the death instinct,' she writes,

> no danger situation arising from external sources could ever be experienced by the young child as a purely external and known danger . . . This was clearly shown in the analysis carried out in wartime. It appeared that even with normal adults anxiety stirred up by air raids, bombs, fire, etc. – i.e. by an 'objective' danger situation – could only be reduced by analysing, over and above the impact of the actual situation, the various early anxieties that were aroused by it.

War, she is quite clear, is fundamentally an internal problem; 'over and above the impact of the actual situation' – over and above being where the air raids came from – there are what she calls the 'various early anxieties' that are aroused. War reminds us, like a prompt, of our early selves; and our early selves are terrorized by the mysterious workings – the 'silence' Freud called it; and a silent war is indeed a terrifying notion – of the death instinct inside us. And because Klein takes the insidious, ineluctable death instinct so seriously, war cannot, in fact, provide sufficient relief. No danger for the child, or for the adult, can be 'purely external and known' because of its link with the death instinct. The Germans, with the air raids and their bombs and their threats of invasion, were merely reminders of a far greater danger within; a surplus or excess of inner danger that the enemy simply hinted at. Our fear, one might say, echoing Freud, is always in excess of the object's capacity to satisfy it.

This, for Klein, was what analysis during the war had 'clearly shown'. It had clearly shown something that was terrifying partly because it could never be clearly shown, was already beyond representation.

From Klein's point of view, paradoxically, the war worked for people – made them feel better – for two reasons, which needed to be carefully distinguished: one, as it were, genuine, and one spurious. For 'many people', she writes, the excessive anxiety produced by the war, 'led to a powerful denial (manic defence) of the objective danger situation, which showed itself in an apparent lack of fear'. War, that is to say, inspired in people the attempted self-cure of mania, the flight into invulnerability that itself spells our horrifying vulnerability to the death instinct. This, for Klein, is, as it were, the bad gain of the war; that as it mobilizes primitive terrors, it mobilizes primitive defences. But the good gain of the war, she writes, was that there were other cases in which,

> the relative stability of children in spite of war-time dangers was not determined so much by manic defence as by a more successful modification of early depressive and persecutory anxieties, resulting in a greater feeling of security regarding both the inner and external worlds, and in a good relationship with their parents. With such children, even when the father was absent, the reassurance gained from the presence of the mother, and from home life, counteracted the fears stirred up by objective dangers.

Instead of the internal, false solution of mania, these children, in Klein's view, could allow themselves to depend on, to gain reassurance from, their family. What Klein calls, rather vaguely, 'the good relationship with the parents', 'the reassurance gained from the presence of the mother, and from home life', counteracts and modifies the death instinct by showing comfort and reliability in action. The child sees that destructiveness can't destroy everything, that there are goodnesses sufficiently resilient to withstand the bad. That, in moral terms, virtue has a place because it works. The outside world is our only consolation for – our best refuge from – the internal world.

So, for Klein, the Second World War had been such a problem for people because it linked them with their earliest anxieties. It jogged their memories of their primitive selves. And it had made people feel better either spuriously, by restoring their primitive defence of mania; or more realistically, in her view, by making possible good external reassurance. Group spirit, the pooling of human resources, courage and resilience in action, all showed the children – and the adults – that they could be successfully protected, if not secured, from the death drive within. And at a different level, the war provided a reassurance for Klein herself by apparently validating her controversial theoretical convictions. The war inside is always worse than the war outside. The war inside is ahistorical and beyond contingency; the war inside is the truth of our being; the war outside is merely history. The enemy outside is a weak impersonation – an accident of history – compared with the enemy within. The war outside ghost-writes the internal drama. The historical reality of the war, confirmed for Klein and her followers, the fundamentally ahistorical nature of the internal world. Wars were contingent: Eros and Thanatos, and the theories that promoted them, were not. Because the real psychic war was always already going on – the war before the war was already happening – there is a sense in which the war did not impinge on Klein; it was not a difference that made a difference. It was, as it were, a confirmation, not a new experience. The extraordinary and virtually unprecedented threats of air raids, of bombings, were easily assimilated into the theoretical apparatus; but they were often assimilated rather than transformed. The dream-work of theory did not make them strange (or disclose their actual strangeness). In the conventional symbolic they were merely the most recent – the most up-to-date, contemporary, representation of the death instinct (or of related primal-scene material).

When Richard, for example, the ten-year-old hero of Klein's *Narrative of a Child Analysis* (1961), conducted during the war, drew pictures of bombers in his sixteenth session and told Klein the shameful secret that he had dirtied his pants the previous night, she had no problem interpreting that 'the thought about the secret had occurred at the moment when he had recognized that in the drawing he was the bad German bomber', and she added that his big job was felt to be the bombs. 'His fear lest he might bomb his family with his faeces might have been the cause of his dirtying his trousers last night . . .' and so on. Klein, in a sense, doesn't need Richard's personal associations to bombs, because she already knows what they are. They are exempt from dream-work. Dream-work – the process of inner transformation – is the making of history. Richard, one might say, in the context of Klein's treatment, can't make enough history out of his bombs. 'The outbreak of war,' Klein writes in the Introduction to the case history,

> had greatly increased Richard's difficulties . . . the war stirred up all his anxieties, and he was particularly frightened of air raids and bombs. He followed the news closely and took a great interest in the changes in the war situation, and this preoccupation came up again and again during the course of his analysis.

A trauma is that which is beyond, or resistant to, psychic transformation. The preoccupation that comes up again and again. When Richard's personal and contingent bombs meet Klein's ahistorical death-instinct theory; when, that is to say, Richard's material is met by Klein's theoretical preoccupation that comes up again and again in the treatment, it is as though both Klein's and Richard's personal history become secluded, set aside (they were in actuality safely away from the war, in a village). The meaning of bombs and air raids is self-evident – or rather the penumbra of possible, evolving personal meanings is foreclosed. Bombs, like the death instinct itself, are outside history.

The theory of the death instinct – that for Klein found its ultimate confirmation in the war – was itself like a trauma. And like all trauma, it appears to stop time. In so far as a trauma is not subject to inner transformation, it insulates one from history; it makes history impossible. Or to put it more straightforwardly, for those psychoanalysts who believed in the death instinct – and it was, and still is, one way of telling analysts apart – the war could seem, in one sense, rather unreal. Margaret Little, one of Winnicott's analysands, reported that at the first scientific meeting of the British Society she attended during the war, there were:

> bombs dropping every few minutes and people ducking as each crash came. In the middle of the discussion someone I later came to know as D. W. stood up and said, 'I should like to point out there is an air-raid going on,' and sat down. No notice was taken and the meeting went on as before.

'No notice was taken and the meeting went on as before.' This, one might say, is a formulation of the problem; how could you make the war real for the psychoanalysts of the British Society, get them to notice it, or pay attention to it, so that the meeting is interrupted? What kind of conversation would it be that could prevent the contingent historical situation – an air raid during the war – from stopping the meeting? In this emblematic moment – farce that presumably could have ended in tragedy – Winnicott, in his polite English way, points out that there is a war going on; nobody takes any notice and 'the meeting went on as before'. Winnicott, of course, would go on reminding the Klein group that there was a real war outside – that the real world had its real dangers – but the air raids did not impinge upon the meeting. So my question is, what is it about psychoanalysis – its theory and its practice – that meant, despite the air raids, despite the bombs, that the meeting went on as before? Another way of saying this might be to ask why, in the reported analyses of children during and immediately after the war – the accounts, say, of Klein, Winnicott and Milner – the analysts always know what bombs stand for? From a psychoanalytic point of view there was nothing enigmatic – nothing requiring associations – about this historically unprecedented experience when it turned up, as it inevitably would, in children's play material.

II

. . . one of the central puzzles of English history: how England came to represent reason, civility and moderation to a world it slowly conquered.

Ethan H. Shagan, *The Rule of Moderation*

In his *London at War: 1939–1945* (1995) Philip Ziegler makes it clear in some detail that, as he puts it, 'the population of London as a whole endured the Blitz with dignity, courage, resolution and astonishing good humour'; that Londoners effectively manufactured and lived out their own myth of themselves during the war, which made possible what seems, at least in retrospect, a spectacular accommodation to a terrifying predicament. Though in part clearly government propaganda, there were, in Ziegler's view, two main elements in the myth of the Blitz: 'the comradeship and sense of unity which it inspired among Londoners and the cheerful good humour with which it was endured'. The war in London, as many people acknowledged, brought out the best in people. Indeed, what was so remarkable about the Blitz was how surprisingly, or apparently, untraumatized most people were by it: the myth of the Blitz was the truth about the Blitz. Melanie Klein's daughter, Melitta Schmideberg, published a long paper with lots of clinical examples in the *International Journal of Psychoanalysis* in 1942 entitled 'Individual Reactions to Air-Raids'. What she demonstrated at great and tedious length was that reactions to the air raids weren't that individual. 'There were far fewer dramatic reactions to the raids than had been expected,' she writes in the summary of her paper:

> It is true that a number of cases of raid shock have probably escaped observation and that many of those who could not stand the raids left for the country. But the majority of the population adapted itself to the new Blitz reality. It did so by acquiring new standards of safety and danger and by gradually learning to take the bombing as an unpleasant but unavoidable part of life. Fearlessness was usually based on the secret conviction 'I cannot be hurt' – an emotional denial of the possibility of being hurt and regression to the narcissism of the baby. Adaptation was helped by identification with those less frightened than oneself and 'projection' of the frightened part of oneself on to more timid people. Activity, providing a sublimated outlet for aggressiveness and countering the feeling of helplessness, was a help. Rational fears were increased by irrational ones. Yet the Blitz situation also provided ample libidinal, sadistic and masochistic satisfaction. The condition of certain neurotics improved.

In this psychoanalytic account – not dissimilar from many others – it is as though war brings out the best in people's defences. Denial, regression to narcissism, identification, sublimation: people reaped the full benefit of their psychic repertoires. The Blitz provided unique opportunities for the satisfaction of perverse or component instincts of masochism and sadism ('The condition of certain neurotics improved'). The Blitz enlivened people because it freed them to perform gratifying defences and forbidden instincts.

Air raids, as a specific version of the war, were successfully, indeed triumphantly, adapted to by the people of London.

'In 1940–1941,' J. B. Priestley wrote, 'for once we felt free, companionable, even – except while waiting for the explosions – light-hearted. It took bombs to deliver us.' Air raids, in a quite different sense, were easily assimilated into psychoanalytic theory and practice. The Blitz appeared to in no way modify or indeed falsify psychoanalytic theory ('the meeting went on as before'). In fact, it confirmed it in most of its particulars. For the people of London the war disclosed unprecedented resources of communal feeling and personal resilience. For the psychoanalysts – especially for the Klein group – the war was reassuring proof. War was no surprise. War becomes, with the experience of the Blitz, that most paradoxical thing: the trauma that is apparently easy to incorporate. 'The majority of the population,' Schmideberg writes, 'adapted itself to the new Blitz reality.' The new Blitz reality is an unintendedly interesting phrase in this context (inviting us to construct a new Blitz reality principle). For some psychoanalysts the new Blitz reality was apparently not that new.

And yet, of course, the trauma of the Blitz, the new Blitz reality, was inevitably subject to those personal processes of history-making that psychoanalysis calls dream-work and deferred action, and that were to issue in disguised form after the war as theories of the mother–child relationship. And I think it is in psychoanalytic descriptions of the child after the war, and indeed prompted by the war, that the psychic transformation of war experience is most vivid. The child is, and comes to represent, the person most vulnerable to devastating interruption: from inside by the instincts, from outside by the nurturing environment; the mother who is, herself, an independent subject. The child is addicted to routine, to reassurance, to attachment, to going on being, to continuity of care: in this post-war story the radical antitheses of the new Blitz reality. When the new Blitz reality is not the child's death instinct in action – the bombed familiar cityscape an image of the child's depredations in and on the mother's body – it becomes the traumatic mother: tantalizing, invading, unpredictable, implacable, retaliating, impinging; unable to metabolize the infant's bombs, which are called projections. Air raids destroy the familiar landscape, rupture attachments, create the need for evacuation. For Winnicott, being dropped, in the psychic sense, is the primal catastrophe. A dropped baby is a bomb. For Bowlby the new Blitz reality and its consequences proved how much children needed their mothers. When the new Blitz reality was not being used as a picture of the child's internal world, it was being used (and exploited) as a kind of negative ideal of mothering. Mothers mustn't Blitz their children; mothers must be like Londoners during the war – flexible, good-humoured, resilient, generous. The child's invasion bringing out the best in them.

In the attempt to legitimate itself, some psychoanalytic theory has attempted – wittingly or unwittingly – to dehistoricize the child, to assume that the child's material in the clinical session is merely a local example of a universal and trans-historical predicament; that, in the terms of this essay, bombs and air raids are nothing special, are not being used to articulate some recalcitrant piece of secret personal history. But whether we like it or not, it is always the dream-work that is putting history back in the picture. It is always free association that is linking us to our unprecedented specific pasts. In psychoanalytic theory and practice after the war there are bombs everywhere. What some of the analysts forgot was that children take history personally.

Against Inhibition

for Joyce Lindenbaum

I

What begins in recognition, –
. . . ends in obedience.

Frank Bidart, 'By These Waters'

In his book *The Last Avant-Garde*, David Lehman tells an instructive story about Kenneth Koch's becoming a poet – acquiring the sense that it was poetry he was writing and wanted to write – in Ohio in the 1940s. It depended a great deal, according to Koch, on a teacher he was fortunate enough to have had in high school called Katherine Lappa. 'Lappa inspired him to a lifelong love of poetry,' Lehman writes,

> when she told him it was OK to allow his anti-social impulses into his poetry . . . The sensuality and violence that the boy felt he had to repress in his daily life found their way into the stream of consciousness writing he set himself to do. In one piece he wrote of the urge to 'step on a baby's head because it is so big and round and soft like a balloon, and would go squash under my feet'. Katherine Lappa remained unflappable. 'That's very good,' she said, 'that's just what you should be feeling – part of what you're feeling. Keep doing it.' Koch would come to regard this as an 'instance of the benevolent influence that Freud has had on my life. I was able to enjoy the benefit of a teacher who in Cincinnati in 1942 had undergone psychoanalysis.'

The benevolent influence of Freud is not much publicized these days; and yet there must have been many Americans of Koch's generation – he was born in 1925 – and many people subsequently who have experienced something akin to the thing Koch describes. It was part of the initial exhilaration of psychoanalysis – the thing that made it seem to some people both a liberation and an inspiration – that it seemed to extend the range of the permissible in thought and feeling. That by acknowledging the sheer morally ambiguous complexity of what people might have to say – and acknowledging the very real difficulties involved in saying it – new kinds of life seemed at once possible and plausible. If what we regard as the anti-social inside us is more social – more useful and interesting – than we thought; if it is the unacceptable, paradoxically, that might make us more acceptable to ourselves and others, then a remarkable piece of magic, indeed secular alchemy, has been performed. What the culture discourages, the culture, unbeknownst to itself, needs. Without the sensuality and violence repressed in daily life, Koch's poetry, and therefore his daily life, would have been enervated. His teacher disinhibited him through her affirmation; it is worth wondering whether an analyst would have freed him in this way.

I think it's possible that the more important truth in this story is that Koch's teacher was psychoanalytically informed. She perhaps could see the potential poetry in his words whereas an analyst might have seen, say, sibling rivalry. Who doesn't want to stamp on babies' heads would be the more or less glib assumption of most analysts. Obviously we can't really assess the pros and cons here; but in Koch's account – the only one worth having – he was the beneficiary of something that helped him become the remarkable poet that he is. Of whom, as he himself wrote in his poem 'To Frank Kermode', we might say, 'To know that such a person is there! It makes our years.'

Psychoanalysis is about inhibition, one might say, though it is not necessarily against it. And Koch's story is useful – and, I imagine, not that unusual – because it raises questions about whether what we are feeling is what we should be feeling; and why we call certain experiences inhibitions, and not others. Indeed some of the inhibitions that we don't tend to call inhibitions are among our most valued achievements: respect and consideration for others, sexual etiquette, continence, and so on. Why then, to keep close to our example, is it better to be able to write such things as Koch found himself wanting to write, about stepping on babies' heads and so on? How has it come about that the transgressive, in thought and feeling and expression (if not in the other kinds of action we call action), has come to seem to be good for us? After all, we can imagine a world – and a lot of people have lived in one – in which, faced with Koch's writing, Katherine Lappa might have been appalled and either punished or reported Koch, or referred him to a psychiatrist. For those of us who are fans of Lappa's approach – 'That's very good . . . that's just what you should be feeling – part of what you're feeling. Keep doing it' – the answers to these questions would be something like: first of all, writing about crushing babies' heads is different from, if not actually a virtual surety against, doing it (in other words, such freedom of self-representation is better than its alternative); secondly, such unexpressed things, whatever they are (or are like), may turn up somewhere else if they are disavowed, and far worse consequences will ensue. The image, as in Freud's famous paper of 1915, 'Repression', is that what is repressed

> proliferates in the dark, as it were, and takes on extreme forms of expression, which when they are translated and presented to the neurotic are not only bound to seem alien to him, but to frighten him by giving him the picture of an extraordinary and dangerous strength of instinct.

The repressed – Koch's 'sensuality and violence' – will return as terror and/or symptom. Freud and Lappa believe that the work of repression and suppression can denature us (in both senses).

By celebrating what Koch is tempted to suppress in his writing she opens up in front of him a vista of possible future phrases; there is, and in fact was, a new world of poetry to be written if certain inhibitions, certain apparently natural aversions, were deemed unintimidating. At least when it comes to writing, Lappa and Koch assert, the pleasures of repression are inferior to the pleasures of gratifying that repressed impulse in and of the poetry.

And yet the way Freud describes the working of repression in this particular image – and of course there are others, with quite different kinds of emphasis – seems to present a kind of unspoken dilemma. In one straightforward sense Freud is saying that the 'neurotic' terrorizes himself by repression. But also, it is intimated by Freud, this neurotic figure excites himself as well. The picture is of quotidian reality turned to grand opera, the ordinary made hyperreal, if not surreal. If we didn't repress our instinctual life – which for Freud is not an option – the implication is that we would be less daunted by it, that repression is a way we sustain the intensity, the gothic glamour, of our passions. The banal becomes the demonic through repression; our desires proliferate in the dark, take on extreme forms of expression, seem at once alien and of an extraordinary and dangerous strength.

In terms of the familiar distinction between freedom for and freedom from, these two descriptions lead us in different directions. What Koch's teacher did for him, as an aspiring adolescent writer, was to free him to follow his words wherever they might take him ('what is most serious for art to get to', Koch once said, '[is] ecstasy, unity, freedom, completeness, dionysiac things'). Freedom for writing was freedom from the inhibitions of social and personal niceties. His poetry, Fairfield Porter wrote, has an unusual kind of innocence. Koch's 'irony', he writes, 'recognises the childishness of ordinary feelings which he shares with the reader, and this irony washes away conventional sentimentality, until you are left with the emotions of childhood again, seen now with an innocence of maturity'.

Freedom from inhibition, acquired at least partly from his teacher, leading to freedom for the childishness of ordinary feelings. And Koch's freewheeling, canny whimsicality – the extraordinary shrewd ingenuousness of his poetry – so unlike anything obviously sponsored by psychoanalysis, may be one of the more obvious benefits, however indirectly entailed, that we will get from American psychoanalysis of the 1940s. This, one could say, is one of the great boons of psychoanalysis at its best; that it can inspire things so at odds with itself.

For Freud's 'neurotic', however, it is a different story. The quotation from 'Repression' itself assumes Freud's elaborate and often convincing account of the rationale, indeed the necessity, of repression. And even though the ingredients – the instinctual drives and the nature of trauma; the Oedipus complex and the nature of infantile sexuality; the discrepant logic of primary-process thinking – are complex, the project of repression is simple. We repress things because we believe that we will suffer more if we don't. But freedom from a certain kind of suffering, Freud suggests, frees us for a different kind of fear. The repressed instincts now become like foreign bodies – 'alien' is Freud's word – and there seems to be, once the analyst re-presents the patient's disowned instinctual life to him in the form of interpretation, 'an extraordinary and dangerous strength of instinct' where once, we must assume, there was not. Ideally, when the analyst translates (as Freud puts it) and presents the repressed back to the patient, he will be freer to love and work. The great work, the Sisyphean task of repression – so energy- and time-consuming – will be diminished. The so-called neurotic, like the poet Koch, will be released into more satisfying forms of expression.

And yet there is an implication in what Freud writes that may not have been sufficiently acknowledged. If it is possible at all to undo repression then the repressed is not absolutely, not terminally, unacceptable. Indeed, one could say – and here Koch's new-found freedom to write is pertinent – *it isn't that what had to be repressed — unacceptable or forbidden desire, overwhelming trauma — was intrinsically unacceptable, but that it was presented, that it presented itself, in unacceptable form.* This has two implications for psychoanalysis; one is, that the unacceptable is unacceptable only until it has found a description that makes it acceptable (writing about stepping on babies is fine because it's part of what you're feeling). So there is nothing innate in human nature that is, to use the old-fashioned word, evil; there are just parts of ourselves, or rather things that we can do, that we will go on deeming to be evil until someone describes them differently. So we may have thought it was evil to kill Jews until people came along who made it sound more viable. The repressed, that is to say — and psychoanalysis as a therapy, among other things, depends upon this being true — can be made acceptable, and the only way to do this is in language; to sufficiently redescribe the unacceptable so it can be more knowingly included (the acknowledgement of this — of the power of redescription — is the shared scandal of pragmatism and psychoanalysis). The second implication of this — which I will come back to — is that it is conceivable that it would be possible to do psychoanalysis with their being no resistance involved. Or rather, there would be resistance by the patient for only two reasons: either the analyst has got it wrong, or the analyst isn't doing the analysis properly. And that means the analyst hasn't (yet) managed to find the words that will render what is intolerable to the patient easy to take. The food is not yet ready to eat; but the good analyst makes it appetizing, if not delicious. You experienced this as terrible, the analyst will seem to be saying, but actually it was, say, fascinating. The patient wants to repudiate it, the analyst has to make it interesting; or at least hearable.

In this sense the inhibition is as much in the analyst as in the patient. Something is stopping the words doing the work they at least sometimes can do. Good writing, like good conversation or interpretation in analysis, seems to free something in us. It is as though mobility has sprung from paralysis; but only once we start moving do we realize quite how stuck in we had been. The picture in our minds, in our language, is usually of blockage and release. We, or something in us, is felt to be trapped or constrained. Whether it is the repressed instincts proliferating in the dark, buried alive, or the poetry flowing through descriptions of squashing babies' heads, the aim is to re-create fluency.

II

Up to a certain point every man is what he thinks he is.

F. H. Bradley, *Aphorisms*

Sándor Radó, reminiscing about Karl Abraham and the Berlin Psychoanalytic Society in the 1920s, was insistent that inhibition is a keyword. 'It might be thought that the libido theory gave a framework,' he says in a book of interviews called *Heresy*,

> but it could never tell you how it happened that a person suddenly at this point did such and such. The actual development of symptoms was a mystery. The libido theory underplayed the whole idea of pathological inhibition. The first understanding came when Freud began to emphasise inhibitions, symptoms and anxiety; but that was in 1926. The first real insight came when we grasped that pathology starts when useful healthy activities which are being carried out by all normal people suddenly become impossible because the person is inhibited.
>
> The compensatory miscarried repair work, the symptoms and fantasies of the patient, completely diverted attention from the fact that without inhibition there would be no need for symptomatology.

It is still an interesting idea that fantasies and symptoms may themselves be 'miscarried repair work' – unsatisfactory attempts at self-cure – and that the fundamental thing is inhibition. Certain activities, 'useful healthy activities' that all 'normal people' can do, as Radó puts it rather quaintly, can become impossible. And it is where a sense of impossibility turns up in a person's life that we should be looking. And of course the implications of this extend far beyond the boundaries of clinical psychoanalysis because freedom – a sense of what is possible for ourselves – is integral to our more modern descriptions of ourselves as subjects and citizens. 'Arguably the chief conviction of modern Western societies,' Larry Siedentop argues in *Democracy in Europe*, '[is] the belief that freedom is a prerequisite of moral conduct. That, it can be argued, *is* the important consensus achieved by the liberal West . . . These assumptions about man and society have underpinned the long-standing liberal attempt to found social arrangements on consent.' It is as though we assert that freedom is the precondition for most things we value, and yet we tend to produce theories – of which psychoanalysis is one – that at best ironize the idea of freedom and at worst show it to be impossible; indeed, to be the constitutive human delusion. If, like Radó, we make inhibition the heart of the matter, we can't help but put some ideas about freedom back in circulation – and in the full knowledge, odd though it is, that freedom is not, as it were, a psychoanalytic term. Or, to put it another way, those of us who are impressed enough by psychoanalysis to want to practise it have consented to a theory of, in the words of Freud's title, inhibitions, symptoms and anxiety which has remarkably little to say about the alternatives to inhibition.

So I want to ask, what is it that stands against inhibition, what is its opposite? And what would it be to be against it; what would one be free of, what would one be proposing? In the Index of the *Standard Edition*, after many entries under 'free association', there are two references for free will and determinism, one under 'free will, the illusion of', and two under 'freedom, desire for'. (The entries for 'freedom, desire for', perhaps needless to say, come from *Civilisation and Its Discontents*).

What, from a psychoanalytic point of view, is there freedom for, when it is quite clear that there can be no freedom from? If, from a psychoanalytic point of view, it is literally a contradiction in terms to talk of freedom from instinctual life or from death, and yet we experience ourselves at any given moment as more or less free, it would indeed be worth figuring out something apparently so common or garden, something so familiar, as inhibition.

It is, I think, impossible to imagine a person without inhibition, or a person who is not somewhere curious about what it might be like to be disinhibited in just those areas of one's life where one feels most plagued by hesitation. So this paper is not exactly or wholeheartedly against inhibition, so much as wondering what thinking about inhibition brings us up against. It would make sense that we would be at our most inhibited in thinking about inhibition. And yet, of course, questions of free will and determinism have been the staple subjects of theology and academic philosophy. The issues are not new; but freedom, one could legitimately say, is a new idea for psychoanalysis.

III

Acknowledgement of the infiniteness of need and, more generally, of emotion . . . is an important aspect of the sparing of the object.

Jorge L. Ahumada, *The Logics of the Mind*

In one of the philosopher G. E. Moore's notebooks – written between 1948 and 1953 for his own private use – there is a section on free will in which, like many philosophers before him, he experiments with descriptions of free will; tries to find what, if anything, the phrase refers to, or what other words follow on from it. 'My will is free,' he writes, 'if & only if both (1) IF I had CHOSEN (or DECIDED) to make a "voluntary movement" which I did not make, I should have made it; and (2) I COULD have CHOSEN (or DECIDED) to make it.' In other words it must be within my power to have done something other than what I actually did. If it wasn't within my power to do otherwise, 'decision' is the wrong word to describe my action. The idea of free will depends upon there being genuine, practicable alternatives for me to do. So as an initial working definition we could say that it is interesting to talk about inhibition only where it is to all intents and purposes true that we could actually do the thing we feel ourselves to be inhibited from doing. I am not inhibited from flying through the air now, but I may be inhibited about doing a head-stand (I could, perhaps, learn to do one). To choose or to decide, we must, Moore reflects, have viable alternatives in mind. 'I think that in general we only talk of "choosing" or "deciding", when we have the idea of NOT making the movement, & PREFER making it to not making it.' For the idea of choosing to make sense we have to be able to imagine and enact not doing the chosen thing, and be alive to a sense of preference in ourselves. That we have the capacity to prefer – that we can perceive difference – and that we can act according to preference is what matters.

Radó, we may remember, said that 'pathology starts when useful healthy activities which are being carried out by all normal people suddenly become impossible'. The inhibited person, that is to say, definitely prefers something, but it is no longer felt to be within their power. They are suffering from a curious compromise in terms of Moore's description. They believe that they could do otherwise – or rather, it is at least possible to do otherwise; other so-called normal people are doing these things after all – and yet the idea of not, in Moore's words, 'making the movement', holds them in thrall. They really know something else could be done, but not by them. But, of course, they can think of themselves as inhibited only if somewhere they have a strong belief in free will. The inhibited person – and/or his analyst – believes that his free will has been constrained by something; as though something in him taunts him with a free will he has but is not permitted to exercise. He has inside him a free will, but it is not for him. It seems like a kind of nonsense to say that somebody has found a way of inhibiting their free will.

It is obvious that we need some notion of freedom as a precondition for believing that there is something we can usefully call inhibition. And when someone describes themselves as inhibited – as finding certain areas of their lives, certain actions impossible – we might be wondering what makes them think that it is nevertheless possible for them to do this thing. Would it make sense to think of someone as inhibited in their mourning, in the same sense as we might think of them being inhibited in their sexuality? Inhibition, in other words, is always a form of omniscience, an all too knowing prediction. We always need a picture, a description of the thing they believe they could be doing but can't because they find it impossible.

Radó's reference to 'useful healthy activities which are being carried out by all normal people' raises the question of whether, if some or even most people can do something, therefore everyone can; because we can get our picture of what is possible for us only from what other people have done. Radó's constituency of normal people and their useful healthy activities become our picture of what we are choosing between. In anyone's sense of their own inhibition they are always measuring themselves up against real and imaginary others, who are more or less capable of the things the inhibited want to do but find impossible. If I find it impossible to be rich or to get a job – to take two topical examples – to talk about this in terms of free will and inhibition could feel like an imposition. Whereas if I find it impossible to get to sleep, or to masturbate, or to get on with other people, it would be realistic, we might assume, that these things could be within my range. But it is clear that the impossible quickly becomes a difficult category, because it involves our wondering about where (or from whom) we have acquired our sense of the possible. If freedom is about anything it is about – it is a way of talking about – possibility. And this, of course, is where we come up against the Scylla and Charybdis of the law and of biological constraint, and the attempt to make them seem compatible, the making of taboos. Incest is illegal because it leads to biological degeneration; incest is biologically degenerate because it is illegal. No one is quite sure what's wrong with incest, but virtually everyone – certainly all normal people – are horrified by the idea of it. All these statements are both thinkable and contentious.

IV

Before nourishment there must be obedience.

Eduardo C. Corral, 'Slow Lightning'

When psychoanalysts, at least, talk about inhibition, their thinking is magnetized by what they consider to be the two constitutive human experiences: the dependence into which we are born and that continues throughout life; and the Oedipus complex, everybody's lifelong negotiation of three- (and more) person relationships and of the strange fact of there being two sexes. The fear of damaging (and losing) the people one loves and needs, and the taboo against sexual intimacy with the parents, are deemed to be the breeding ground of inhibition. But what is so striking about the notion of the forbidden – about the idea of transgression – is that it always invites us to imagine the thing we must not do. Indeed, if we can't to some extent imagine it – whether consciously or unconsciously – we wouldn't know not to do it, or how to go about avoiding doing it. The forbidden is the impossible with a capital I. But the forbidden must be possible – for someone – otherwise there wouldn't need to be a rule against it. It's not forbidden to have three arms. So in actuality the forbidden is the possible that has to be described as beyond possibility; either biologically unviable, or entailing unbearable punishment. When it comes to the forbidden we have, in Moore's terms, free will; I believe I could, in some way, do the forbidden thing, but I believe I would prefer not to, and that I can act according to my preference. Forbidden experiences are the ones we are supposed to be inhibited about. There is no sexuality without inhibition because all sexuality has echoes of the forbidden; and the forbidden is the place we are obliged to hesitate. The taboo gives us pause. There is no such thing as a free transgression.

But transgression describes something that some people actually do, and that many people fantasize about doing. Faced with at least two options that are entirely possible for them, they choose the forbidden thing, and therefore implicitly the consequences that come with their decision. But just as the idea of inhibition requires some notion of freedom to back it up, the idea of transgression doesn't make sense without the possibility of choice; without Moore's sense of the pragmatics of preference. In a world of absolute determinism – in a world without free will – transgression, in this sense, would not be possible. There are only so-called forbidden things because there are things we can decide not to do. It is part of the cruelty of the super-ego that it says, in effect, you must not do this thing that you could do and that certain other people are doing (the father says to the son, do as I say, not as I do). To be judged if we are not actually able to make choices is an unspeakable cruelty. The existence of laws – secular laws that are known to have been made by people – tells us that we have the capacity to make choices. Determinism tells us that we are punished for things we are unable to choose not to do.

To describe someone as inhibited is to assume – at least in this particular area of their lives – that they are not the victims (or the beneficiaries) of an absolute determinism. That for reasons of which they may be largely unconscious they have chosen to do one thing rather than another; to go to bed with someone, say, but not to have sex with them, to go to a party, but not to mix in. They are, in Moore's terms, acting according to preference. So to understand something about inhibition, we need to say something about the nature of preference. Because at its most minimal, preference implies a sense of purpose, a project (however unconsciously conceived); and a sense of satisfaction in the offing, of moving towards our pleasure, even if one of our pleasures is safety, or frustration, or uncertainty. To fail at one thing is to succeed at another, and vice versa.

But in an essentialist theory like psychoanalysis – a theory which already knows what we are most likely to be inhibited about or around – what we have failed to do tends to be privileged over what we have succeeded in doing. Is the impotent man, for example, more failing to be fully sexually alive than, say, succeeding at eliciting sympathy or dismay from his partner? In other words, if we are to describe inhibition in terms of preference – as I think we must – we are likely to get bogged down in preferring some preferences to others. To tell a persuasive story about inhibition we need to be as imaginative about its hidden successes as we are about its more vivid failures. And if we do this, what is more often than not disclosed is a complex array (or disarray) of projects afoot. There is something strangely reassuring about witnessing the familiar parade of one's putative failings. The free will that inhibition entails is a complicating factor. Not only are there two things we might have done, one of which we have chosen; there is also the many things we are doing or intending to do in doing one and not the other. Inhibition turns out to be an exhibition of more than we realized. In our inhibitions – in the areas of our lives where certain things seem impossible – we are over-achievers. We are doing too much where we seem to be doing so little.

V

To taste the pleasure one is giving would be to violate
as grave a taboo as that of incest.

Denis Hollier, *Absent without Leave*

Freud's title *Inhibitions, Symptoms and Anxiety* (1926) seems to propose a kind of causal chain: we suffer from an inhibition of a vital practice (something supposedly normal becomes impossible), we develop symptoms, and we suffer from anxiety. Freud defines an inhibition here as 'the expression of a restriction of an ego-function'. And what he means by an ego-function, broadly speaking, is what Radó meant by useful healthy activities carried out by normal people, which Freud lists as 'the sexual function', 'the function of nutrition', 'locomotion' ('a disinclination to walk or a weakness in walking') and work. And these restrictions, he suggests, are the consequences of a person's attempt to avoid conflict.

Inhibition is a person's cure for conflict (it is worth remembering Money-Kyrle's remark, that the aim of psychoanalysis is to render the inhibition irrelevant). If this particular activity became a possibility an unbearable conflict would ensue. Whether, in Freud's language, the ego represses sexual desire to avoid punishment from the super-ego or further assault from the id; or whether, in what he refers to as 'more generalised inhibitions' – as happens in mourning, or the management of excessive feeling or overpowering sexual fantasy – in which the 'psychical task' involves so much energy that a person is inhibited through sheer depletion of energy, either way a particular course of action is prevented. 'As regards inhibitions,' he writes, 'we may say in conclusion that they are restrictions of the functions of the ego which have either been imposed as a measure of precaution, or brought about as a result of an impoverishment of energy.' Inhibitions protect one from danger and exhaustion. They are self-preservative: conservative not innovative.

As so often with Freud's writing, this account of inhibition sounds like a version of common sense. To be uninhibited, in certain areas of one's life, would feel like being unprotected. It would be like making oneself available to danger. It would be like being too freely associated with one's instinctual life – and therefore too involved with others – and it might, as overexertion, literally extinguish one's energy. And yet the question in the background – the consideration that makes this kind of language intelligible – is, what would it be like to be disinhibited? What might actually happen, what would one find oneself feeling? At its most minimal, Freud intimates, one precondition for being uninhibited is being able, being, as it were, more than willing, to bear conflict. As though one might come to see that the value, the point of being able to bear conflict, is that one can be less (and not more) inhibited. And it is not only, or just, conflict the uninhibited have to bear; it is also the possibility of being suffused with feeling, or what Freud calls 'a continual flood of sexual fantasies'. This is an interesting phrase in that presumably a *continual* flood ceases, eventually, to be called a flood, and becomes, say, a lake, or a river. In other words, following the image, sexual fantasy would become in time no longer invasive or overwhelming; it would be just what we were, what was in our minds, or just what our minds were. It would not be alien, but integral. The imagined uninhibited life would be a radical metamorphosis. We would no longer feel flooded, we would be a flood.

Indeed, it is sexuality, as usual, that provides Freud, in *Inhibitions, Symptoms and Anxiety*, with his most vivid examples of neurotic inhibition. And strangely, they echo the juxtaposition in the poet Kenneth Koch's life of writing and treading on people: though in Freud's example, it is a mother, not a baby, that is stepped on:

As soon as writing, which entails making a liquid flow out of a tube on to a piece of white paper, assumes the significance of copulation, or as soon as walking becomes a symbolic substitute for treading upon the body of mother earth, both writing and walking are stopped because they represent the performance of a forbidden sexual act. The ego renounces these functions, which are within its sphere, in order not to have to undertake fresh measures of repression – in order to avoid a conflict with the id.

One version of common sense might say: writing and walking could become even more enticing, even more irresistible, having been sexualized. But of course, if the sexual is the forbidden – or always has an insistent echo of the forbidden – then that is exactly where we are likely to hesitate. So inhibition occurs, for Freud, when any action is contaminated by, or unconsciously likened to, forbidden sexuality. In this view we are never out of control, or indeed losing control, we are more or less doing forbidden things. And when we inhibit ourselves – which we often refer to as controlling (or overcontrolling) ourselves – we are in fact choosing safety in preference to transgressive excitement. But there is a bind here which could be crudely stated as: why bother to write if it doesn't in some way feel sexual, if it doesn't smack of risk-taking? If we take the forbidden out of the picture there's no keen edge, no passionate necessity to our excitement; but if we put too much forbidden in – if writing becomes incest in our minds – we are stopped in our tracks. The inhibited person, we might say, can't take on the forbidden, can't face it; so at its most extreme everything is safe, but there is no anticipation; there is certainty, but there is little suspense. Inhibition, once again, as a form of omniscience.

Put like this, what I am saying begins to sound like a rallying cry, as if we should just all be a bit braver. And yet one of the many merciful things about psychoanalysis as a therapy is that it doesn't tend to make appeals to what used to be called the will. Indeed, to think of willpower as the cure for inhibition would be a perfect example of what Leslie Farber called, in a memorable phrase, 'willing what can't be willed'. So if inhibition is all to do with the forbidden, and we can't have a wilfull relationship to either inhibition or the forbidden, what can we do if a greater degree of freedom is one of our aims? Clearly, how we describe the forbidden will dictate what kind of relationship (if that's the right word) we can have with it. And Freud tells us that any activity – or 'function', to use his scientific term – has to feel sufficiently forbidden to be of genuine appeal to us; but it must not seem too forbidden or we shall be paralysed. If we were to speak in the absurd language of quantity we would say, when it comes to the forbidden we have to have just the right amount.

To think about the forbidden is to wonder, or perhaps remember, what parents seem like to children. And to wonder about the limits of redescription. From a brashly pragmatic point of view we could, for example, simply say that the forbidden is just something we haven't yet been able to describe in a way that makes it accessible. Along the lines of my earlier discussion, it would be that the inhibited person keeps describing certain of his activities in ways that make them too terrifying to enter into. Freud's writer insists – consciously or unconsciously – on describing writing to herself as copulation, so of course she mustn't do it. So as happy pragmatists we can say: she needs both a new description of copulation and then, maybe or maybe not, a new account of writing. In other words, it isn't the writing that's the problem, it's whatever she – in unconscious fantasy – thinks is going on in intercourse that's inhibiting her. For the happy pragmatist – about whom I do not feel facetious – the only problem about sex is the way we describe it. In childhood – for all sorts of reasons that psychoanalysis can help us with – we come up with the wrong stories about sex. We really begin to live as if sexuality is, say, a torture chamber, a devour-and/or-be-devoured orgy, a mutilation, an endless game of hide and seek, and so on. We are inhibited; we cannot possibly prefer the frightening representations we have found whatever it is that goes on between people when they are intensely (and intently) drawn to each other. Or we are so excited, or so shamefully excited, by these lurid options, that we have to refuse them in order to sustain a preferred image of ourselves that seems essential to our very being. Because when we are talking about inhibition we are also talking about the kinds of people we want to be and fear turning into. As Alex Coren has said, can we imagine being the kind of person who could be anything? To think about inhibition is to think about the constraints on self-fashioning, on self-invention.

And yet most of us will have a strong sense that it just isn't as simple as this, and I think we should be more curious, more genuinely perplexed, about why it isn't this simple. Or what we might need to add to the pragmatist's account to make it sound more convincing. Anyone who has experience of psychoanalysis – and perhaps of other forms of therapy – knows that both the analyst and the patient can come up with a very good, facilitative redescription of an inhibition and that it can be either resisted by the patient or, more interestingly, accepted by the patient (if not actually considered to be something of a revelation) and still not make a blind bit of difference. An inhibition is always an inhibition until it isn't one. We are talking about the feeling of not being able to do something; of the act of preferring, and the sense of impossibility.

When there is something we can't consent to ourselves doing, we must have a belief that we could do it if certain conditions prevailed, if there could be guarantees, as it were, that in the doing of it, certain feelings would not be felt. Radó's 'impossible' refers, I think, to whatever must not be felt. If I do the thing I can't do, certain feelings will be repeated, or at least disclosed, that I assume (perhaps rightly) that I cannot or must not be able to bear. Whether it is about incapacity – I actually don't have the equipment, the wherewithal to feel these feelings – or whether it is about permission – I can't allow myself to be the

who feels such things – is not always clear. To
[ ] ge of one's preferences is to have the courage of
[ ] Every wish is an experiment in consequences.

VI

The real is the only thing in the world we can never get used to.

Clement Rosset, 'Reality and the Untheorisable'

In cognitive terms one could describe inhibition as the inability to believe something about oneself; to believe, say, that one could be the kind of person who could feel such feelings, or carry out such acts. And this links the experience of inhibition with the more pervasive experience of not being able to believe in something; and especially not being able to believe in something that one should be able to believe in. I am thinking, for example, of the many powerful nineteenth-century narratives of people unable to believe in God any more, or unable to accept the religious observances of their families. And there is a difference, of course, between losing a faith one has acquired and being unable to acquire this faith in the first place (in psychoanalytic language it is the difference between illusionment and bearing disillusionment). What was then called the spiritual struggle of the protagonists of these dramas – as in Froude's *Nemesis of Faith*, say – is usually posed as a question: is it an incapacity, or is it a refusal in the hero that he is unable to believe? And if it is not, then, what we might call an inhibition, what else could it be? Is impotence – to take a secular, more carnal, analogy – a new version of the self, or merely a fear? Is it a resistance, or a revision of the self, and how are these two things different? I am putting it in this more cognitive, more sensibly intelligible, way to draw attention to the difficulties of putting it more psychoanalytically. And by psychoanalytically I mean closer to the confounding irrationality of feeling inhibited, of being patently and unavoidably divided against oneself. Unable, that is, to will oneself out; knowing what the wished-for good is and unknowingly (or, unconsciously, *too* knowingly) preventing oneself from attaining it. What, in other words, would be a good psychoanalytic description of what, in more traditional language, would be called a crisis of belief? A situation in which it is not just that someone cannot, or can no longer, believe in God, but that he can no longer believe in himself as a believer? If I am unable to believe in something – unable to perform something like a belief or a sexual act, unable to believe in or imagine myself doing such things – I might ask myself, in a psychoanalytic way, what pleasures are being courted or compromised, what punishments are being sought and averted in my being like this. And yet, even put like this, it sounds very close to a certain version of behaviourism. To find what I would think of as the psychoanalytic thing – the object, for want of a better word, of specifically psychoanalytic acknowledgement – we have to find what is, as it were, insolubly irrational about inhibition. We have to be able to render something intelligible – find a useful and interesting redescription of it – without rendering it only intelligible. Or, to put it another way, we have to redescribe it in a way that shows it to be subject to further – unknowably further – redescription.

What I make of my inhibition will be different at different times; that is, I will be using it to make different kinds of futures possible at any given moment. I am saying this at such tedious length because I think inhibitions are spectacular – are central to psychoanalysis in the way Radó emphasized – because on the one hand they seem only to be intelligible by presupposing an unconscious; and yet the unconscious disclosed by psychoanalytic accounts of inhibition too often seems just like another consciousness, a hidden one. As though we have two minds for the price of one. We want one thing, but unconsciously we want something else, and we want it more; and what we actually do reveals what we actually want. As though our wants are not so much irrational as unacceptable. All the analyst has to do is show the patient the multiplicity of his competing, and mostly hidden, wants. And perhaps also, ideally, to show the patient how such wants have come to seem, or indeed to be, unacceptable. Then the patient can evaluate his wants; the lights go up in the supermarket and he can choose. Where once he hesitated, now he can consume. Inhibition as a complaint – my sense of my own unfreedom, my sense of self-imposed restriction – could, in other words, make us too pragmatic in our apprehension of ourselves; too knowing of what we want; too incorrigibly rational in the way we figure the future.

VII

Cruising, like sociability, can be a training in
impersonal intimacy.

Leo Bersani, 'Sociability and Cruising'

Psychoanalytic theory always deduces a rationality from irrationality; what looked as though it was excessive, obscured or unintelligible turns out to be, becomes, explicit, if not entirely explicable. And this, of course, should give us pause. All versions of psychoanalysis tell us that we are not as opaque as we thought we were, or that we are not opaque in the ways we thought we were. Descriptions are available to us that can leave us less puzzled. The drift towards clarification – however sophisticated in its theorizing or glib in its acknowledgement of mystery – might make us wonder what a psychoanalysis would be like that sponsored neither the good sense of the ego nor the brash moralism of the super-ego; nor took flight into an idealization of the id. Surrealism is so easily tedious because it so quickly seems like more of the same. And being rude and cruel are not, broadly speaking, impressive ideals. In the different immersion experiences provided by the different schools of psychoanalysis – with their different stories about the past, childhood, sexuality, development, not to mention the unconscious – an interesting dilemma keeps resurfacing when people start discussing the so-called aims of analysis. And it can be simply stated as a question: is the aim of psychoanalysis to make people kinder, or to make them more unpredictable?

Some people – many people – would say that the aim of analysis is not to *make* people anything but, one way or another, to let people be who they are; to find out the more about themselves that they have needed to not notice. I think people are always making themselves and other people into something; that psychoanalysis itself is a story about how we are made up, and how we are – albeit unconsciously – making up our lives. And that psychoanalysis, by its own definition, could not be the place where this stops. The analyst and the so-called patient are, among other things, wanting to persuade, and, more indeterminedly, influence, each other (as do parents and children). And as the aims of psychoanalysis are always a reworking of – and so a reflection on – the aims of child-rearing we return to the original question. A question, as I say, that a parent as well as an analyst might ask: is the aim of psychoanalysis to make people kinder, or to make them more unpredictable? And just before we sensibly say both, it's worth noticing that unpredictability and kindness have, as philosophers say, quite different entailments. Or, as *we* might say, this is rather more complicated than it looks. We might, for example, think that we know what being kind involves; but we know what unpredictability involves in a quite different sense. Our own and other people's unpredictability does something to us that our own and other people's kindness doesn't. Perhaps we can get the gist of this if we imagine what our lives would be like if we preferred unpredictability to kindness; or if, in any given situation, we intended to do the kind thing rather than the unpredictable one. Inhibition, I want to suggest, is a crisis of unpredictability, in which questions of kindness are never far away.

Clearly, what it is to be kind is every bit as contentious as what it is to be unpredictable (as the idealization and the use of the word 'spontaneity' always reveals). And yet, 'be kind' is not so much of a double-bind, so to speak, as 'be unpredictable'. And 'be unpredictable' is often the frightening injunction the inhibited person is giving himself (or giving other people in the hope that they might free him). Indeed all the psychoanalytic diagnostic categories describe ways which people have found of being predictable to themselves, despite themselves. That's what a symptom is; it's a repetition, an unconsciously motivated self-prediction (and, by the same token, the 'patient' in psychoanalysis is cured when his past is no longer of particular interest to him). At best we flirt with our own unpredictability through our symptoms; at worst we are overcontained by them. Inhibition stages this as a drama. It is not always, or only, the inability to do something; it is also a cover story, a protection against not quite knowing what it is one wants to do. And what one might turn into, what one might feel, in the doing. The inhibited person, that is to say, has the most acute sense of the experimental nature of our acts. Of how doing something, doing anything, consigns one to the future, to the irreversible. To a future of unknown feeling; to the shock of the unprecedented.

Inhibition at its most minimal, one could say, is a kind of doubleness; and from a psychoanalytic point of view its ultimate referent, its centre of gravity, is the forbidden. What I want to do that I cannot do – what my preferred self would be capable of – either I must not do (because it is forbidden), or I am quite literally unable to do (I don't have the capacity for). I may be inhibited about public speaking, but I cannot honestly say that I am inhibited about choreography. What we tend to call inhibition has something to do with realistic possibility; but in a way that what we call unconscious fantasy does not. Indeed the irony of it is that the inhibited person has managed to transform the possible into the impossible, the realistic into the utterly implausible. In its most benign yet tantalizing form, the difficult act is imaginable; at its most extreme, it may be literally unthinkable. That, the inhibited person says to himself, is a pleasure only for others: they will have to do it for me. But what is most striking is the tyranny of the relationship with the other who can perform the forbidden act. The doubleness of inhibition, in other words, could be described as a sado-masochistic relationship with the self; an internal problem that is unusually suited to, and suitable for, public performance. Indeed, at its most extreme, the inhibited person begins to have his primary relationship with his imaginary uninhibited other. A game for two that only one can play.

From this point of view the uninhibited one is a gleeful, sadistic triumphalist. He is uninhibited only as part of a more pressing project, which is to make the other masochistic one feel abject and inhibited. And by the same token, as it were, the inhibited masochist goes on failing to perform, to make the relishing sadist feel potent and pleasured. Because of the collusive mutuality of this deadly *pas de deux* neither must be seen to be ultimately succeeding (the sadist never kills the masochist, if he can avoid it, because then he will lose the game that sustains his identity). It must always seem slightly possible and virtually impossible that the feared act could be performed (sado-masochism, that is to say, is a perversion of hope). The sadist tempts and mocks the masochist with the forbidden act, and the masochist consents to his oppression and absurdity. What is sustained is the paradoxical sense that a choice is being made in a situation in which there is really no choice. In fact the whole notion of choice seems like a spurious fiction, a lure invented by a sadist; the sadist says, you can choose to do what you want to do, and the masochist finds that he can only choose what he doesn't seem to want to do. The sadist says, of course you can make choices, but you are only able to choose what you least want; the sadist says, of course people choose what they want, but they don't really know what they want. And the masochist says, glumly, or ironically, or bitterly, what I seem to really love is my own frustration; the self I like to keep fashioning is an abject, self-depriving one.

In this variation of the Faustian pact – in this sado-masochistic loop, this closed system – it is often the sadist that chooses the objects of desire so as to better stage the humiliation. What is being so well arranged is a familiar kind of frustration. And I think it is worth stressing just how well managed these scenarios usually are, however unconscious a person is of what they are doing. Indeed one of the things one might be doing in analysis is showing the so-called patient just how he goes about choreographing his favourite dispiriting drama.

But, of course, the crucial 'how' question is usefully shadowed by the 'why' question. Why would someone go on doing such things? The answer will be different for each person, integral to each person's different and always differing history. And yet it may be possible to say something more general in scope, that can be useful when it is made particular. This great unkindness, this inventive cruelty to oneself, always has one overriding consequence; it renders a person apparently predictable to themselves. The shy person will always either not go to the party, or go to the party and suffer. What is then occluded, what is concealed or even supposedly abolished, is the unpredictability of the self. Where unconscious desire was – the person risking themselves in the search for pleasure – there a (albeit abject) surety will be. Where there was contingency, there will be repetition. Where there was a text, there will be a set text. Inhibition – the whole sado-masochistically staged drama of it – is like a ruse of the ego in its relentless project of negating the unconscious. Like a charm or a spell, the endlessly compelling sado-masochistic project – with its virtually mechanical forms of reproduction – distracts a person from the only freedom they have, the freedom to choose an unpredictable future for themselves.

Superiorities

I

. . . stability does not depend on the immutability of individual particles but solely on the dynamics of their interaction.

Evelyn Fox Keller, *The Century of the Gene*

In 1945, just after the end of the war, Lacan came to London as a French psychiatrist to find out about the effect of the war on British psychiatry. His report on his visit, *British Psychiatry and the War*, was published early in 1947. What Lacan is evidently most impressed by is his meeting with Bion and Rickman, and their accounts of their work in small groups with soldiers who, for various reasons, were debilitated and needed some kind of help. There are, as one might expect given the historical moment and the personalities involved, many fascinating things in Lacan's impressions and celebrations of this early psychoanalytic work with groups that has turned out to be so influential. But there is a thread running through Lacan's paper, a preoccupation that punctuates whatever else he is saying, that is clearly linked with his first official contribution to the psychoanalytic group on the mirror stage. What Lacan keeps returning to – perhaps unsurprisingly after the devastations of the war against fascism – is the idea, the modern political ideal, of equality. In the mirror-stage paper Lacan shows how we are never equal to our (unified) image of ourselves; that what the child sees in the mirror is, as it were, his complementary rival. If Freud had proposed in his structural theory of the mind that there was not, and could never be, internal equality between his various 'agencies', Lacan had added to this unending uncivil war an image of the child diminished, tyrannized and enraged by his wished-for self-representation. We are tyrannized by our picture of ourselves as we would prefer to be; we organize our lives around it. Whether or not Freud or Lacan (at this time) thought of themselves as democrats, or believed in equality as one of the rights of man, there is nothing in their psychoanalytic accounts of what people are really like that is conducive to the kind of social hope invested in ideas of equality. Indeed one might think, from a psychoanalytic point of view, that equality – like many of the other so-called rights of man – was ripe for ironization. Something, perhaps, along the lines of Joan Riviere's infamous, and possibly apocryphal, remark that socialism was the religion of younger siblings.

And yet in Lacan's paper – even in its tone of idealistic pessimism generated by the experience of the war – it is as though he cannot give up on something about the notion of equality. Despite Freud's work on group psychology, despite the daunting, invasive subtleties of forms of identification; despite the fact that, as he puts it, 'the dark powers of the super-ego make alliances with the most cowardly abandonments of conscience', he is interested in this paper in what might be called alternatives to leadership. If his early work on the family was about the consequences of the modern destitution of what he called the 'paternal imago', it is to redescriptions of the notion of leadership – of what we might call, sociologically, the problem not only of authority but of the fantasy of the authoritative – that he is drawn through his encounter with the British. In Bion's work, Lacan writes, the analyst, as group leader, 'will undertake to organize the situation so as to force the group to become aware of the difficulties of its existence as a group, and then render it more and more transparent to itself, to the point where each of its members may be able to judge adequately the progress of the whole'. As Lacan puts it, this is a version, to use his word, of forcing people to become equals. Clearly the aim of arriving at a point 'where each of its members may be able to judge adequately the progress of the whole', is to arrive at the point at which the position of leader disappears. It is a description of what one might want to be going on, ideally, in a certain kind of democracy. But of course it has to be noted, firstly, that it requires a group leader to get the members of the group to this point, through his psychoanalytic method. And secondly there is, and will always be, the question of who decides what it is to 'judge adequately the progress of the group'. Where, one can ask, do the criteria for adequate judgement come from? What has the group consented to when it acknowledges any judgement as adequate, or even unusually valuable? When what Lacan refers to as 'the crystallization of an autocritique materializing in the group' occurs, it is as though the psychoanalytic method of inquiry has given each and all the members of the group a shared, and therefore consented to, genre of useful judgement. They enjoy a new sense of know-how in common. But what is this autocritique like? It could, for example, be like the group having agreed to the rules of a game; but agreeing to the rules of a game doesn't stop some people being better at it than others. Indeed, one could say it creates the conditions under which people can distinguish themselves. It is only because there are rules that have been consented to, that prestige, that inequalities, begin to emerge. To consent to a set of rules is to set up a potential hierarchy. By putting a basic structure of equality in place, by providing a baseline of sameness, differences can come through. The question lurking here – which seems like a question tailor-made for psychoanalysis – is: why is hierarchy the reflex response to difference? But Lacan intimates here that, at least in his description of the Bion group, the psychoanalytic method can make possible the enjoyment, the productive use, of difference. If everyone gets to the point of being able to 'judge adequately the progress of the group' they must have some shared sense, however tacit, of what constitutes progress; of what it is better for the group to be doing. And yet, of course, we know that too much consensus, just like too little, is the enemy of democracy.

It is when Lacan refers in his paper to a comment made by Rickman that he begins to form, if not quite to formulate, his question. Rickman, he says, 'makes the following remark, which to some will seem striking, that if one can say that the neurotic is ego-centric and loathes any effort of cooperation, it is perhaps because he is rarely placed in an environment where every member would be on the same footing as himself when it comes to relating to one's counterpart'. One's immediate response to this striking remark is, where could there be such an environment? Because this, surely, is an environment of absolute equality. And yet to behave as if one is on the same footing with others – or on the same footing with regard to certain conditions – is a virtual definition of equality, if not of democracy. What would it be, for example, what would psychoanalytic treatment, which Lacan preferred to call 'psychoanalytic experience', be like, if the analyst considered himself to be on the same footing as the so-called patient? It is the need for superiority, the need to be the exception, the need to exempt oneself from something, that Rickman is using the word 'neurotic' to describe. As though a neurotic were someone who needed to believe that he had a distinguishing feature, that there was something special about him (and this might lead us to wonder how free we might feel if we were nothing special). Lacan refers later in his paper to what he calls, with a certain necessary archness, the '*noli me tangere* that one finds more than frequently at the root of the medical vocation no less than that in the man of Law and the man of God. Indeed these are the three professions which assure a man that he will find himself in a position in which superiority over his interlocutor is guaranteed in advance.' Of course Lacan's omission of the analyst – of psychoanalysis as the fourth profession that is a bit like each of the three he mentions – is essential here. In psychoanalysis there is no touching and it is, as it were, the redemptive wishes that are to be analysed.

And yet here we have, in a paper that is nothing if not celebratory of what Lacan calls the 'revolution' created by psychoanalysis, the juxtaposition of two images, of two insinuating descriptions. We have Rickman's neurotic, ego-centric and loathing of cooperation, because he is rarely placed or indeed places himself 'in an environment where every member would be on the same footing as himself when it comes to relating to one's counterpart'; and we have the doctors, the lawyers and the men of God, 'professions which assure a man that he will find himself in a position in which superiority over his interlocutor is guaranteed in advance'. The neurotics, like these great and legitimate professionals, need to exclude themselves from something, need to reject something in advance. They must, in one way or another, be untouchable. It is, to exaggerate, as if their lives depended upon their not having equals. It is some notion of equality that they are phobic of. So what could it be about equality – what does equality entail, or involve us in – that could make it so aversive? To be treated by one's interlocutor as superior or different in advance places one's interlocutor in a threatening position; as though what could be lost in losing one's superiority, one's prestige, however variously defined, is deemed to be catastrophic. The analyst, Lacan will later famously say, is the 'one who is supposed to know'; the person, perhaps, in whom the patient delegates his superiority. And among the targets of Lacan's later critique of the psychoanalytic establishment will be those psychoanalytic institutions and theorists who put themselves in a position in which their superiority over their interlocutors is guaranteed in advance. In other words, for Lacan psychoanalysis is about the way the individual suffers – and loves to suffer – his terror of equality. Psychoanalysis addresses how an individual excludes himself, exempts himself, distances himself from certain kinds of association. As though the modern, the 'civilized', form of what anthropologists called participation mystique is a horror of participation mystique.

There is something about equality, something about the

absence of superiority guaranteed in advance, that psychoanalysis has something to say about. And it is not merely one's own superiority; it may simply be the need to believe that there are some people – and that we can have some kind of connection with them – whose superiority is guaranteed in advance. It could be a deity or a celebrity, it could be a race or a nation-state; it could even be a psychoanalytic training institute. But without this superiority existing somewhere in a person's orbit, they – we – are destitute. Clearly, it is not incompatible to be committed to democracy and to dread equality – and so, in the name of democracy, to foster forms of prestige. The forbidden thought may be that there is more pleasure in being less special; that self-importance is the enemy of self-satisfaction.

There are two questions here: what would equality feel like such that people might organize their lives to avoid it? And does psychoanalysis, as Lacan intimates in this early paper – and the trials and tribulations of his life's work bear witness to the demanding perplexities of this – have anything akin to a cure for the wish for a superiority guaranteed in advance? Or, to put it rather differently, has psychoanalysis got anything to do with democracy?

II

The fact that the presence of deliberately introduced extraneous stimuli frequently improves performance has been regarded as a curious paradox . . .

Harry Scott, quoted in *Harry's Absence* by Jonathan Scott

'When we envisage democratic politics from . . . an anti-essentialist perspective,' Chantal Mouffe writes in *The Democratic Paradox*, 'we can begin to understand that for democracy to exist, no social agent should be able to claim any mastery of the foundation of society.' They would be unable to claim it because from this point of view there is no foundation of society available to be mastered. Indeed, one could say that it is the existence of foundations – or rather, the fantasy of their existence – that itself makes mastery possible. No one in a democracy, in Mouffe's account, has a superiority guaranteed in advance, at least when they are acting democratically. Would it not, after all, be constitutive – would it not be a virtual definition – of Lacan's notion of the superiority of the medical profession, the judiciary and the Church that each of these professions claim some kind of mastery of the foundations of their own society, if not of every society? The kind of equalities implied by democracy – what each person in a democracy relatively freely consents to – has to set new kinds of limits to mastery. Democracy, as Mouffe describes it, involves redescribing the whole notion of leadership, and the value of conflict.

Defining antagonism as the struggle between enemies, and agonism as the struggle between adversaries, Mouffe proposes what she calls 'agonistic pluralism'. 'The aim of democratic politics,' she writes,

> is to transform antagonism into agonism . . . One of the keys to the thesis of agonistic pluralism is that, far from jeopardizing democracy, agonistic confrontation is in fact its very condition of existence. Modern democracy's specificity lies in the recognition and legitimation of conflict and the refusal to suppress it by imposing an authoritarian order . . . a democratic society acknowledges the pluralism of values.

From a psychoanalytic point of view, Mouffe's version of democratic politics is an interesting provocation. We are more likely, for example, to feel superior to our enemies than to our adversaries. Indeed the whole idea of an enemy makes the idea of superiority possible, if not plausible (it may not be enemies we are in pursuit of, but states of inner superiority). If we use

Mouffe's picture as what used to be called a model of the mind – and what I would prefer to call a conjecture about what people are really like – and if we map her model of democracy back on to what some psychoanalysts call the internal world, we will at first find a great deal of reassurance. Isn't it, after all, one of the aims of at least some versions of psychoanalysis to transform enemies into adversaries; to free a person to be at odds with himself (and others) rather than in lethal combat. If agonistic confrontation is the very condition of democracy's existence, can we not say that, by the same token, conflict is the individual's life-support system? And yet, of course, psychoanalytic schools can be defined by the internal and external points of view they are prepared to credit. What, for example, would be an internal pluralism of values? Could the racism of the self find a voice here, and what kind of voice would that be? What is perhaps most interesting in Mouffe's formulation is the definition of the authoritarian as that which suppresses conflict. As though it is the very existence of conflict itself that certain versions of authority cannot bear. And this might be a clue to what is intolerable about equality. What the person whose superiority is guaranteed in advance cannot bear is the protracted sustaining, indeed existence, of conflict. Equality then is the legitimation, if not the celebration, of conflict. Is it then possible, from a psychoanalytic point of view, to think of a person as – or to free a person to be – internally adversarial? That is, more of a democrat through and through? It could legitimately be said that people come for psychoanalysis, people suffer, because they have suppressed a conflict by imposing an authoritarian order. They feel coerced, and they are coercive (the coerciveness is called symptoms by the so-called patient and transference by the so-called analyst). People experience and describe themselves as living under various forms of domination and oppression. The analysis discloses an unconscious authoritarian order called the super-ego. And it is indeed illuminating to think of the super-ego not as the cause of conflict but as the saboteur of conflict.

And yet, if we take up Lacan's evident privileging of psychoanalysis as being somehow part of a project to free the individual – without exaggerating or idealizing the kinds of freedom that may be on offer – as having found, through the experience of war, defining opportunities and occasions to think about the direction, the project, of psychoanalysis; both what it might have to offer and what it might want to offer; that is, to consider the values it promoted; then we have to think carefully about psychoanalysis in the light of Chantal Mouffe's sentence. 'Modern democracy's specificity lies in the recognition and legitimation of conflict and the refusal to suppress it by imposing an authoritarian order.' The authoritarian order pre-empts conflict, which is in and of itself a primary value. And to value conflict – to prefer the openness of conflict to the closure of intimidation – necessitates some notion of equality. Conflict that is not between equals ceases to be conflict very quickly. It becomes the simulacrum of conflict called sadomasochism. We may wonder what the preconditions are, both psychically and politically, for keeping conflict alive and viable. And in wondering that we might wonder both what a democratic psychoanalysis would be like; and what, to put it as modestly as possible, psychoanalysis may have to offer, if anything, to the making of democrats (better and better descriptions of the nature and value of conflict could be one candidate). Whether its practice – its writings, its trainings, the set-up of its clinical work – persuades people to identify with democratic values. It would be good, for example, if as Laplanche says a transference is never resolved, only displaced; that the outcome of a successful analysis would be that a person would be able to bear to listen to what other people have to say. That through the experience of analysis a person might rediscover an appetite for talking and for listening and for disagreement. Which is an appetite for democracy.

The subject who is supposed to know turns into the person with a passion for listening; for the after-effects of listening.

Speaking becomes worth doing because it is conducive of conflict. But conflict is not a version of pastoral. The equality in Mouffe's version of democracy, such as it is, could never be an equality of wealth, or talent, or beauty. The only equality that exists in it is in each person an equality of rivenness, an equality of unknowingness, the equality born of there being no foundations to master. In a mix of languages we might say that the will is displaced by the idea of the unconscious: and mastery is displaced by temporary forms of consensus. We do not know what we are doing but we have things that we must do. We are, like all creatures, creatures who want; and yet, for some reason we are unable to dispense with the idea of justice (even the immoral seem obliged to give moral justifications for their actions). So what then would a psychoanalysis be like, in practice, that recognized and legitimated conflict, and refused to suppress it by imposing an authoritarian order?

For most people, of course, this is merely a description of what, as analysts, they are already doing. After all, no one likes to think of themselves as imposing an authoritarian order; and no psychotherapist would want to see themselves as suppressing conflict. And there are also further puzzles in all this. Because the implication – which is so vivid in a political context – is that the more authoritarian the regime, the less conflict is permitted, but the more it is cultivated. The conflict is with the authorities, with the ones who are supposed to know. In other words, would a democratic psychoanalysis end up as, or begin as, a conversation between equals? Because the advantage, the beauty, so to speak, of the one who is supposed to know, is that what he knows suppresses conflict. He can tell us the truth about ourselves which will apparently dispel the rival truths. Instead of having to conciliate rival claims on ourselves – by ourselves and others – we can attain a superiority of knowledge.

From Bion's small, potentially leaderless groups, to Lacan's professionals whose superiority to their interlocutors is guaranteed in advance, to Chantal Mouffe's democracy that depends on conflict, on agonistic pluralism; in each case something about equality is being contested, something about its provenance and its value. As though a great deal might depend upon finding a good description of it. As though we are not sure whether equality as an ideal is our most pernicious mystification, or one of our best inventions. And perhaps one useful – usefully circumscribed – way of looking at it is through the issue that has haunted and informed the history of psychoanalysis: the equality, or otherwise, of the analyst and the unfortunately named patient. If he is a patient, the analyst is a doctor; if he is a client the analyst could be a solicitor; and if he is a lost soul the analyst is a member of the third of Lacan's professions based on superiority. So what, in the abstract, could be described as being equal about the analyst and the person with whom he will have what Lacan calls a psychoanalytic experience, a psychoanalytic opportunity? And why, if at all, would it be better to think of them, in any senses, as equals? What are they equal to, and what might they be equal for?

III

. . . a common ear for our deep gossip

Alan Ginsberg, 'City Midnight Junk Strains'

Psychoanalysis as a treatment and an experience, like democracy as a political process, allows people to speak and to be heard. Indeed it encourages people to give voice to their concerns, to be as difficult as they can be, because it depends upon their so doing. Of course lawyers and priests and doctors also require that people speak of their discontents. But they expect people to speak, or listen to them, as though they are speaking with deliberate intent and with a view to decision. After such conversations, ideally something specific will be done. And even if the kind of democratic forums we are familiar with are less overtly specialized – and even if they encourage dissent and debate and competing accounts – they press for some kind of consensus with a view to significant action. A democracy may consist of doctors and lawyers and priests, among others, but each of these individuals may be more or less democratic, more or less free to be democratic, in their practice. Expediency doesn't allow for endless debate. The idea is not to sit around all day having interesting conversations, and entertaining points of view. It is with a sense of some kind of urgency – with a sense of something being at stake, of something that can't be set aside or ignored – that people enter the political arenas, and consult their respected professions. Similarly, people don't seek out psychoanalysis, even if they think they do, or would like to, for a bit of armchair philosophy (indeed, from a psychoanalytic point of view there is no such thing as an armchair philosopher, there is only the negotiation of distances). Presumably all cultures provide settings or forums, places people can go to, and people they can go to with their most intense feelings, their most urgent dissatisfactions. Whatever troubles people, and they can't talk themselves out of, seeks expression.

One way of talking about this is in terms of what people recognize as a solution. And to talk about solutions – and whether 'solution' is the word at all – is to talk about forms of satisfaction. Democratic process, for example, may not be simply the best way of making decisions, or of conciliating rival claims; but the being in a democratic forum – hearing all those voices, in oneself and others, being drawn out by contact with all those speaking bodies – may itself be a kind of happiness. Or not, as the case may be. If, as Stuart Hampshire says in *Justice in Conflict*, 'The value of a democratic constitution lies in the defence of minorities, not of majorities,' and that 'Even the fanatic who is sure that he knows best in discriminating justice from injustice also knows that he must prepare himself with arguments to meet disagreement,' then disagreement is taken for granted. Or, to put it differently, disagreement – with oneself and others – never comes to an end; but an end, more or less provisionally, can be put to it. What is difficult about some versions of psychoanalysis and some versions of democracy is that they value disagreement as much as, if not more than, the solutions it occasions. Indeed, from a psychoanalytic point of view, disagreement is itself a solution. Violence can be the attempt to make disagreement disappear. And it is, of course, the violence people do to themselves and others that the psychoanalyst hears so much about. Psychoanalysis investigates what people can say without the relief of violence.

There is on the one hand the need to make decisions, to have a capacity for choice; and on the other hand there is the willingness to sustain disagreement. And choice, of course, without conflict, without competing alternatives, is nugatory. There is only choice when there are things to choose from. And this, again, I think, is where equality comes in. If choice and conflict are inextricable, the conflict only exists as such because the conflict is in some sense between equals. And equality here doesn't mean sameness; it means differently appealing but equally compelling good things. Desiring one's mother and desiring one's father; wanting to be independent but needing to be attached; wanting to be excited and wanting to be kind; both have much to be said for them. They can either be usefully sustained as conflicts, or the conflict can be suppressed by authoritative imposition. I can become unassailably either heterosexual or homosexual; I can be invulnerably arrogant or abjectly needy; I can become more or less sado-masochistic; I can become altruistically ascetic or brutally promiscuous. I am not suggesting, of course, that these are ever, or ever could be merely (voluntaristic), conscious decisions; but they are, in overly schematic form, the conscious and unconscious self-fashionings that we come across in this culture, in ourselves and others. The aim of psychoanalysis, one could say, might be the precondition for democracy; that a person be able to more than bear conflict, and be able to see and enjoy the value of differing voices and alternative positions. That a person might want to confer some version of equal status on the conflictual voices that compose and discompose him. We could then say, for example, that most people are homosexual and/or heterosexual until or unless they meet someone who makes them feel otherwise; that our bisexuality is waiting to happen, so the most interesting thing about one's so-called sexual identity would be the surprises it springs rather than the programmes it entails.

And from this point of view aggression would not be seen simply, or merely, or solely, as some kind of innate, quasi-biological essence. It would be seen as, or also seen as, the voice called up in the self to put a stop to conflict. Aggression would be seen to be creating a certain kind of conflict as a way of suppressing vital conflict. The analyst, like the democrat, would be attentive to – would be vigilant about – attempts to suppress both the possibility and the sustaining of conflict within the individual and the culture. The analyst would position herself as a democrat, wherever the so-called patient placed her through the transference. So in my version of analytic neutrality, 'neutrality' would never be the right word; because to think of oneself as neutral in a democracy doesn't make sense. It would only make sense that the analyst would be finding ways of sustaining the conflict that is a form of collaboration, that democracy speaks up for. The analyst, or the whole analytic setting, would be like a rendezvous for the conflicts entailed by the refusal, the suppression, of conflict.

The analyst would be wanting to be, in other words, the opposite of Winnicott's definition of a dictator in his 'Some Thoughts on the Meaning of the Word Democracy'. 'One of the roots of the need to be a dictator,' he writes, 'can be a compulsion to deal with this fear of woman by encompassing her and acting for her. The dictator's curious habit of demanding not only absolute obedience and absolute dependence but also "love" can be derived from this source.' The dictator is, as it were, the ultimate version of the figure Lacan refers to, whose superiority to his interlocutors is guaranteed in advance; and in this sense democracy is the heir of the Oedipus complex because the couple are exchanged for, are replaced by, the group; fascism is the triumph of the couple, of the dictator and his people.

Psychoanalysis has always been involved, one way or another, in the war against dictatorship; in the difficulty, if not the impossibility, of equality between people (and within people). If for Winnicott the meaning of the word 'democracy' takes him straight back to the meaning of the word 'motherinfant', it should also take us back to the meaning of the word 'psychoanalysis'. After all, from a psychoanalytic point of view it would not be surprising to find – whether or not individual psychoanalysts think of themselves as democrats – that the battle between dictators and equals has always been fought out in every area of psychoanalysis; from the teaching of it to the practice of it. And it has, perhaps, been exemplary as a profession in the way that it has kept the whole question of superiority – of the nature of prestige and dictatorship – on the agenda. Issues to do with equality are never far away when psychoanalysis is discussed, celebrated or disparaged.

IV

Efficient practice precedes the theory of it.

Gilbert Ryle, *The Concept of Mind*

If one wanted to reflect on psychoanalysis and democracy – on psychoanalysis and the meaning of equality – it might seem sensible at first to give some definition of democracy, but the difficulties of doing this are instructive in themselves. And it is worth remembering that democracy, like psychoanalysis, is a quite recent phenomenon. 'Until half a century ago,' the political theorist Larry Siedentop writes in *Democracy in Europe*,

> democracy was a word unknown to most of the non-Western world. Even in the West, until two centuries ago, the word carried decidedly unfavourable connotations. Until then the role of the idea of democracy was not unlike the role of the id in Freud's theory of the psyche – both suggested a dark, inscrutable and fathomless threat from below. The upper classes of European society and the established churches looked upon democracy as something almost demonic.

It is, of course, interesting that he should have recourse here to Freud's id by way of analogy and comparison. The threat posed by democracy was to assert that certain kinds of liberty, and certain kinds of satisfaction, were not reserved for the privileged. It is curious, if we read the analogy both ways, to think of the ego and the super-ego being somehow akin to the aristocracy and the Church. And yet when Freud showed us how what he called the ego was no longer master in its own house, or that the ego drove the horse in the direction the horse wanted to go in, he was intimating something similar. As though the id was the new, alternative, previously repressed voices which either are sexual and aggressive, or are described as sexual and aggressive to represent their primary quality, which is to be disruptive of the previously established order. Something else was demanding its right to be represented and heard. And put like this, the psychoanalyst is both herald and sponsor of the new democratic world.

It is very clear and entirely appropriate that the nature of democracy has been greatly contested. In Siedentop's view, democracy evolved from Christianity with

> the assumption that we have access to the nature of things as individuals. That assumption is, in turn, the final justification for a democratic society, for a society organised to respect the equal underlying moral status of all its members, by guaranteeing

each 'equal liberty'. That assumption reveals how the notion of 'Christian liberty' came to underpin a radically new 'democratic' model of human association.

It is the valuing of the individual despite his social status, and not because of it, that both Christianity and democracy promote. It is as though people are deemed to be something – to have something inside them – that is of equal value; and of a value greater than any worldly assessment can encompass. It is paradoxical that what exempts people is the ground for their inclusion. And it is, inevitably, the forms of equal liberty and the nature of this supposed 'underlying moral status' that have been, and are, ultimately contentious. What, I think, is less debatable is that there has been 'a radically new "democratic" model of human association'. More people associate with, have access to, more kinds of people from different classes and countries and histories now; and they associate with these previously isolated others from a quite different position. Some of them, for example, may assume that despite their manifest differences from these other people they have some other things – perhaps more important or 'deeper' things – in common. And the keyword, as it is for psychoanalysis, is 'association', as the way into something new. Indeed the only time the word 'free' ever gets used with any kind of regularity in psychoanalysis is with reference to free association, in which words are encouraged to consort with each other to unpredictable effect. Psychoanalysis, like democracy, works through the encouragement and validation of new forms of association and the conflicts they inevitably reveal. To have an appetite for association – of a political or psychic kind – is to have an appetite for, if not to actually seek out, fresh forms of conflict; and to see conflict as the way we renew and revise our pleasures. Democracy, one could say, extends the repertoire of possible conflict. It fosters an unpredictability of feeling and desire. It makes people say, or people find themselves saying, all sorts of things to each other.

When Chantal Mouffe says that 'for democracy to exist, no social agent should be able to claim any mastery of the foundation of society', I take her to mean that there can be no superordinate expert, nobody tuned in to the real or true nature of things (as a dictator would claim to be), because there is deemed to be no real, or true, or absolute foundation of society. Indeed it would be a monarch, or a dictator, or an aristocracy, or a Church who would represent themselves as essentially the representatives and the masters of the foundations of a society. And the notion of a social agent mastering the foundations of society is not worlds apart from Lacan's account of those whose superiority to their interlocutors is guaranteed in advance. Because democracy, in Mouffe's version, doesn't provide foundations in that sense – ones that can be mastered – it is again similar to psychoanalysis; whose paradoxical foundation is the unconscious, which by definition is not subject to mastery, even if what it is subject to is always in question. The new, both similar and different, kinds of association promoted by psychoanalysis and democracy are not, though – or not only – ends in themselves. What, after all, is all this new association in the service of? Is it merely a way of enlarging the market? How does it bring us the lives we want, and what is it about these particular lives that we do seem to prefer? We may not want to be so overtly dominated by absolutist tyranny, or corporate enterprise, but what do we want these new kinds of conflicts to do for us?

If it is perhaps more obvious what these forms of free association are freedom from, it is less clear what they are freedom for. Free association, in a psychoanalytic context, is designed to reveal the strange orderings of unconscious desire. 'When conscious, purposive ideas are abandoned,' Freud writes, 'concealed purposive ideas assume control of the current of ideas.' Freedom from censorship is freedom for the disclosure of unconscious desire. And desire, one could say, is always desire for exchange. Or, if one wanted to put it a little more circumspectly, one could say desire is always a person's question about exchange. Freud's 'conscious, purposive ideas' could be translated as the accepted entitlements of those with status, and 'concealed purposive ideas' could be read as the voices of the subordinated. Freedom from acknowledged forms of regulation is freedom for economic and erotic exchange. What proliferates is proliferation itself. The reaches of appetite can be explored. And in providing a setting for such freedom – and in defining a space as being for this and nothing else – what is so quickly revealed are the obstacles to free association, the difficulties, the hesitations, the pauses, the knots and shames and ruses that occur, and occur to someone when they are encouraged to speak.

When Ferenczi said the patient is not cured by free association, he is cured when he can free-associate, he was acknowledging the very real difficulty everyone finds in sustaining and making known an internal democracy. People literally shut themselves up in their speaking out; speech is riddled with no-go areas; internal and external exchange, as fantasy and as practicality, is fraught with resistance. Psychoanalysis reveals just how ambivalent we are, to put it mildly, about freer forms of association (from a psychoanalytic point of view there is no such thing as a free enterprise). And this must surely be where the analyst comes in. If the so-called patient is deemed to be suffering from one form or another of association-anxiety, presumably the analyst has something up his sleeve, so to speak, for precisely this predicament.

Encourage the patient to free-associate, Freud says; call this the 'fundamental-rule' of analysis and what will come to light, in detail, are the patient's misgivings about doing this. Let someone talk and they will start showing you that they can't and how they can't. They are always, in Chantal Mouffe's words, from a quite different context, 'suppressing [conflict] by imposing an authoritarian order'. And, in all probability, delegating to the analyst this thankless task of ordering them about. In this sense psychoanalysis reveals – whether or not the analysand recognizes himself as a democrat, as someone who professes democratic rights and obligations – the anti-democratic voices and urgings, and their complex history. And as anyone knows who has had a psychoanalytic experience there is often a great and shocking immediacy to these unconscious authoritarian impositions of order. One can't help wondering just what conflict is experienced as such that it calls up such violent hatred. The protest against, the hatred for – not to mention the desire and longing for – the figure whose superiority to his interlocutors is guaranteed in advance must be as nothing to the agonies and terrors of conflict. As though the alternative to there being a subject supposed to know, rather than a subject who can only live his dividedness by not trying to abolish it, is felt to be catastrophic. So what can the analyst do, where can she put herself, so to speak, to make conflict – and the pleasure conflict involves – the desirable and desired state of being? How does one acquire a taste for democracy, a desire for democratic values?

John Dunn begins the Preface to his book of essays, *Democracy, The Unfinished Journey: 508 BC to AD 1993*, with the words:

> This is a book about the history and significance of an old but vigorous idea; that in human political communities it ought to be ordinary people (the adult citizens) and not extra-ordinary people who rule. This is not a very plausible description of how things are in the world in which we live. But it has become the reigning conception today across that world of how they ought to be. The idea itself is devastatingly obvious, but also tantalizingly strange and implausible.

The idea of something at once 'devastatingly obvious' and also 'tantalizingly strange and implausible' is as good a definition as any of what used to be called making the unconscious conscious. That which has been rendered unconscious tends to have an elusive strangeness, even uncanniness about it; and is both hard to believe and hard not to. And yet here, of course, John Dunn is talking about an idea of political community and organization called democracy, which Dunn's faintly amusing subtitle points to as having been something of a long-term struggle; that is to say, as something with potent adversaries and enemies.

The whole notion of extending effective political power to more and more people; the idea of people having a right to choose their own government and, in some sense, rule themselves by themselves – by their own consent – without the need for people (or deities) of extraordinary and superior status; this, as an ideal and a political struggle, turns the world upside down. And it does this in part by making new kinds of association between people both possible and necessary. The whole idea of an extraordinary or superior person, or group of people, has to be redescribed. The old tautologies – the King is superior because he is the King – no longer hold. Hierarchy becomes a matter of consensus rather than divine or any other kind of right. Agreement and disagreement have a whole new status; they become the new effective currency of political life (democrats are not magicians). And psychoanalysis, of course, has something to say, or something to add, about the causes and reasons of agreement and disagreement; about the function of the agreeable and the disagreeable in people's lives.

From a psychoanalytic point of view this has to do with the inequalities – for want of a better word – that human development involves and entails. The gist of this might perhaps be captured in the absurd question: what would it be for a child to be the equal of its parents? What might there be in this obvious but also tantalizingly strange and implausible question that might be cause for resistance? To identify with democratic values and institutions requires, among many other things, that children no longer need, for their psychic survival, to think of their parents (and so of anyone else, including, particularly, themselves) as extraordinary or superior creatures. In psychoanalytic language, the enemy of democracy is not so much admiration as idealization. And this means, in Chantal Mouffe's terms, that it is essential to the viability of democratic values that they are not themselves idealized. Stories about equality, stories about self-government, stories about consent are there to be continuously reconsidered, not fixed (or reified) by idealizing them (the whole notion of mastery being both the cause and the consequence of idealization). If we speak in the psychoanalytic way of mothers and fathers and children, the democratic idea and ideal of people's right to choose and participate in their own government comes out as, however consciously or unconsciously conceived, people's right to choose their own parents and siblings. I cannot choose my parents – my family and its histories – but I may be able to choose the form of government I live by. It is obvious why for some people – and perhaps for most people some of the time – democracy can seem unnatural and transgressive. We don't speak enough, in other words, of democracy as a forbidden pleasure. And if we were to do this, we would get a clearer sense of the profound ambivalence in psychoanalysis about democratic values; an ambivalence reflective of, or simply of a piece with, this same ambivalence in the wider culture, of which psychoanalysis is always a part.

When I was training to be a child psychotherapist about twenty years ago we were asked by the committee running our course for suggestions about what we would like to be taught. When some of these suggestions were turned down, and some of us got rather cross, we were told by a member of the training committee that 'children can't bring themselves up'. As it happens I was a child then, but some of my contemporaries were in their thirties and forties, and had children themselves. So unsurprisingly, perhaps, they were rather affronted and bemused by this. It is integral to the point I want to make that, in retrospect, I think of this as an emblematic story about ambivalence, in both parties, about democracy; about the anxieties of equality. To be told either rather abstractly or rather dogmatically that sanity depends upon acknowledging and respecting the difference between the sexes and the difference between the generations doesn't always clarify this issue. Because the issue is: what kind of equality is viable in the light of difference?

It is peculiarly difficult to produce descriptions in psychoanalytic language – from a psychoanalytic point of view – of equality. Or, rather, of what kinds of equality might be emotionally viable for people rather than just more spurious ideals, or too-wishful propaganda. All versions of psychoanalysis are informed by the relative helplessness and dependence of the human infant, the centrality of the Oedipus complex, and the excessive power and logic of unconscious thought and desire. All this provides at best a sense, to use Dunn's phrase, of an unfinished journey in psychoanalytic theory and practice towards any feasible ideas of equality, or indeed of freedom.

It would be extravagant to say that psychoanalysis is essentially a story about why equality is impossible for human beings. But in the most cursory reading of Freud, Klein or Lacan, equality, in any form, doesn't spring to mind as a keyword. If psychoanalysts are mindful of the ways in which people are not equal to being themselves, not equal to the task of living; are unable, or unwilling, or overly enthusiastic about treating others as equals; if psychoanalysts tend to produce accounts of what people are really like that stress desire, dependence, greed, rivalry and abjection, the question of equality, in one way or another, has arisen around issues of treatment and training. All analysts agree, though they have different ways of saying this, that people are split subjects; but people are not assumed to be, as it were, equally split. All analysts agree that everyone has or is an unconscious; though people are not assumed to be, as it were, equally unconscious. But when it comes to training and treatment these issues become particularly pertinent.

Though training and treatment, as in all professions, are inextricable, I want to concentrate by way of conclusion on the question of the connection, if any, between equality and psychoanalytic treatment – a connection that would have to be privileged if there could ever be a democratic psychoanalysis.

Or rather a psychoanalysis that declared itself as democratic in intent. And by that I mean a treatment that saw itself as being about, whatever else it was about, the difficulties every person has in identifying with democratic values. Psychoanalysis of course was not conceived as, is not supposed to be, a political training camp; but that it has pretended not to be one, that it has at its worst created the illusion that it is possible to exempt oneself from group life, from politics, has, I think, been more damaging and misleading than need be. All social practices transmit preferred values. So just to localize the larger question, I want to ask in what sense it may be useful or true, or useful and true, that there is any equality between analyst and patient. And I don't mean by this that some kind of equality is the aim or the consequence of a good psychoanalytic experience; I mean, what kind of equality could be considered as a precondition for a democratic psychoanalysis? What would it mean – both for psychoanalysis and for the so-called treatment – for the analyst to assume, at the outset, any kind of equality between herself and the patient? Treating someone as an equal, as psychoanalysis shows so well, is not as simple or easy or uncostly as it might seem. But then, not treating people as equals is also its own kind of prophecy, its own kind of project.

There have, of course, throughout the history of psychoanalysis been various statements by psychoanalysts – Ferenczi, Winnicott and Laing among others – to the effect that the analyst and the patient are above all two human beings. Though sometimes saying this doesn't quite say enough; or rather it begs the question that needs to stop begging and being begged. 'A sign of health in the mind,' Winnicott writes in a paper called 'Cure',

> is the ability of one individual to enter imaginatively and accurately into the thoughts and feelings and hopes and fears of another person; also to allow the other person to do the same to us . . . When we are face to face with a man, woman or child in our speciality, we are reduced to two human beings of equal status.

The idea that when we are face to face we are two human beings of equal status leaves open the question of when we are not face to face, when one person is on the couch, facing away. The phrase 'two human beings of equal status' requires us to describe what this equality could consist of, just where it might be located. It is interesting that Winnicott's sense of equal status overrides here the differences between the generations and the sexes: 'When we are face to face with a man, woman or child . . . we are reduced to two human beings of equal status.' But why is 'reduced' the word here? Because it is akin to one of Freud's antithetical words meaning at once diminished and restored? Winnicott implies that the equality resides in each person's ability – though 'freedom' would be a better word – to 'enter imaginatively and accurately into the thoughts and feelings and hopes and fears' of another person; and, as integral to this, to have the freedom to 'allow' the other person to do this to oneself. This reciprocal entering into, this mutual intercourse between people that he sponsors here is, at least in a psychoanalytic context, a radical new form of association. It implies that the analyst allows himself to be, for want of a better word, known by the so-called patient. It would be the mark of Lacan's professional whose superiority to his interlocutors is guaranteed in advance, that he would have to set certain kinds of limits to intimacy. Like Rickman's definition of the neurotic who is ego-centric and loathes collaboration, this person has always decided beforehand, however unconsciously, on the nature of the exchange that will take place. The entering into of each other will be severely regulated. What Winnicott doesn't tell us – and it seems rather important in the context, though also perhaps forbidden to broach – is how this mutual imaginative intercourse is compatible with psychoanalytic practice, with the gathering of the transference.

In the more democratic forms of analysis it would be assumed that the analyst and the analysand need to find ways of knowing each other – or experiencing each other – such that the idea of the superiority of either of them disappears. It ceases to be relevant to the matters at hand. Because superiority – as Lacan's respectable professional and Rickman's neurotic make clear – is a function of distance. In a more democratic psychoanalysis the aim is to transform superiority into useful, or bearable, or even pleasurable difference. But perhaps this need not be merely the aim of psychoanalysis, so much as the precondition of its possibility. The analyst, that is to say, starts from a position – a listening position – in which there is no such thing as superiority because there is nothing to be superior about. And that, of course, is as much to do with his manner – who he happens to be and happens to want to be – as to do with his so-called technique. Indeed the whole notion of technique, at its most extreme, is complicit with fantasies of superiority.

If we think of psychoanalysis as a listening cure, as an agreement that two people will bear together the consequences of their listening (to themselves and each other), we could then start wondering about something I want to call 'free listening', in counterpoint to the notion of free speech. We could think of psychoanalysis as an inquiry into the equality of listening; into the senses in which we can be equal to what we hear. And into what we might do when we are not.

Making It Old

Living in history but not living in the past.

Charles Wright, 'Chickamauga'

In E. M. Forster's novel *Howard's End* there is a scene in which, to initiate their courtship, the businessman Mr Wilcox takes Margaret Schlegel to Simpson's in the Strand for lunch. Margaret is not used to restaurants like this but she is involved in a kind of conversion experience to Mr Wilcox's belief in business, and so with the versions of the past that this belief in business recruits to sustain itself. '. . . while Mr Wilcox made some preliminary enquiries about cheese her eyes surveyed the restaurant', Forster writes, 'and admired its well-calculated tributes to the solidity of our past. Though no more Old English than the works of Kipling it had selected its reminiscences so adroitly that her criticism was lulled, and the guests whom it was nourishing for imperial purposes bore the outer semblance of Parson Adams or Tom Jones.' There is, as Forster makes clear, the past that people have arranged for us, and with purposes in mind, more or less imperial. It is, if it is done persuasively and well, a well-calculated tribute to the past, if not to the past's solidity. Indeed these days it is more likely to be a well-calculated tribute to the ways in which what we call the past has nothing that we can call solidity.

Whether it is in restaurants or galleries, or reading lists or history books, or television costume dramas, a past has been arranged for us — reminiscences adroitly selected — in which an individual or a group or an institution agree to persuade us that this particular version and bit of the past should matter to us now. This provisionally consensual past will carry a range of conscious and unconscious projects with it. It may be literally trying to sell us something, but it will be trying to convince us of the value of something. It will have what Keats calls a 'palpable design' on us: it directs our attention and tries to fashion our sense of ourselves, and what these selves are supposed to want. But however seductive or persuasive or convincing this exhibition, this narrative, this costume drama is, its coercions are tempered by whatever else is going on inside ourselves at the time.

Keats went to medical lectures and found himself daydreaming about poetry; Freud went to the opera to think about psychoanalysis. And yet something else, lots of various other things, were going on in their minds. The question is, what are these other things, which are also coming from the past because there is nowhere else that they could come from? Psychoanalysis would call all these thoughts and feelings and apparent distractions and attractions, unconscious desire. And psychoanalysis would call unconscious desire itself a form of memory. Our preoccupations are the way our pasts go in search of a future. From a psychoanalytic point of view memory is of desire; we are formulating, we are picturing, in what we call our memories disguised descriptions of previous and longed-for satisfactions and terrors. In other words, when a person enters a gallery their own unofficial, largely unconscious, past meets, meets up with, representations of a past that has been arranged for them. One is always bringing one's own past to the past.

Indeed there is, Freud seems to suggest, a desire for memory. We seem to want to, as it were, get bits of our past back, but in a very unscholarly way. There is the past we decide, more or less methodically, to find out about; we may research it, we may go to a gallery, we can read books. And this feels more like a choice. I may not know why I am interested in the French Revolution, and I may not need to know why, but I know how to go about finding out about it. We have some idea of what constitutes evidence of this more official, legitimate past that is a subject called history. But the unofficial past usually takes us by surprise; a song, a smell, a dream, a colour, a shape can take us back, unsuspecting. There is, in other words, the past we can research and pursue, and the past that springs on us. There is the past that can seem to be searching us out, while we go in search of other pasts. There is the idiosyncratic past and the more consensual past. So when we talk about the presence of the past we may need to remember – to include in our calculations – the unpredictable personal past that lurks in the pasts that are prepared for us by our curators and teachers and writers. An informative object is not necessarily an evocative object. When, in Forster's words, reminiscences are so adroitly selected that criticism is dulled, it is the past as propaganda that is being described. What Forster calls criticism here we could just call our relative freedom to have our own thoughts and feelings about what is on offer. The freedom to dream rather than merely imitate or repeat. From a psychoanalytic point of view the challenge for the curator or the historian is how to adroitly select reminiscences so that reminiscence is not dulled.

Trauma is when the past is too present; when, unbeknownst to oneself, the past obliterates the present. It is the traumatized person – all of us, to some extent – who says that there is nothing new under the sun; that nothing ever changes. It is the art of art to make the past bearably present so that we can see the future through it. The problem, in other words, is not in making the past present, but in making the past into history.

The Master-Mind Lectures*

There are many things the good life is not. But no one thing
it is bound to be.

John Gray, *Two Faces of Liberalism*

There is a nasty, perhaps Freudian, moment in Ford Madox
Ford's novel of 1924, *Some Do Not*, in which something suddenly occurs to the hero, Tietjens, in the middle of a conversation:
'Suddenly he thought that he didn't know for certain that he
was the father of his child, and he groaned . . .' Tietjens, Ford
continues, 'proved his reputation for sanity' by carrying on the
conversation he is ostensibly having, but without reference to
his daunting thought. As though sanity for this Englishman is
about being apparently undisturbed by one's most disturbing
thoughts. It is exactly and exactingly about what one is able not
to say. Keeping to the topic, keeping the conversation going, is
the kind of sanity for which one could have a reputation. 'But it
gave him a nasty turn,' Ford writes: 'He hadn't been able to
pigeon-hole and padlock his disagreeable reflections. He had
been as good as talking to himself.'

This is perhaps a Freudian moment not because Ford was in
any sense a Freudian – whatever that is; and, as we shall see, that
is something that Freud himself made it impossible for anyone
to be. But rather because Freud gave us a language to redescribe
these moments of stray thought, these spots of distraught
time, in which we are unable to 'pigeon-hole and padlock' our
more disagreeable reflections; in which, in Ford's extraordinary

* This was originally a lecture on Freud given in the Master-Mind series at
the British Academy.

phrase, we are as good as talking to ourselves because, for some reason, we can't speak these thoughts to others. And also because, as Ford intimates, the 'we' is ambiguous; at such moments I am being addressed, but who is addressing me? I am talking to myself, but who exactly is doing the talking, the strangely silent talking we call thinking; and who, perhaps more per-plexingly, is the listener when we are talking to ourselves? And it is paternity, as it happens, that is at issue. Tietjens may not be the father of his son, but is he the father of his own thoughts? Something that belongs to you, something as intimate as one's own thoughts, could be illegitimate; could come from someone or somewhere else. A lot turns on these nasty turns we have.

But Freud didn't merely draw our attention to such nasty moments, or redescribe the provenance of our more nomadic thoughts. He invented a therapeutic method that encouraged, that traded in, such nasty turns. And the aim of this method – called, as everyone now knows, free association – is that people should be able to have their disagreeable reflections without feeling the need to pigeon-hole or padlock them. The people Freud saw were suffering, in his view, not only from the insist-ent, inherited forms of anguish that everyone is prone to, but also from their forms of classification, and the confinement of their narrow-mindedness. What do we imagine these disagree-able reflections – these unflattering mirrors that our thoughts can provide – are like? What is it that is being clichéd and crim-inalized (pigeon-holed and padlocked), and why is this what we are inclined to do with the thoughts we have but can't agree with? Tietjens didn't know for certain that he was the father of his child, and he didn't know for certain what to do about this horrible thought. So he carried on talking about the thing he was supposed to be talking about, but 'he had been as good as talking to himself'. Freud says that these moments of not know-ing for certain – these nasty turns that we are prone to – are akin to secular epiphanies. It is when our thoughts throw us, when, however fleetingly, we have lost the plot – when, in short, we can bear to lose our reputations for sanity – that we begin to get some news. But to hear the news we need to do what Tietjens would never do: we have to tell our nasty turns to another person; we have to fall through the holes in the conversation when and if they occur. In the therapeutic conversation that Freud invented, and called psychoanalysis, the so-called patient has to be as good as talking to himself, but aloud, in the presence of another person. He is persuaded to make known the interruptions and disruptions he is heir to. What used to be called, in the secular and sacred traditions that Freud was heir to, self-examination, self-questioning, self-doubt, could now be called making a Freudian slip. And being able to make something of that particular making that happens in spite of ourselves, inadvertently. That we think of ourselves as making rather than having Freudian slips is something I shall come back to. Where once, in the service of self-knowledge or religious instruction or medical examination, questions were asked of the self, now, in psychoanalysis, all that was asked of the patient was that he should, in so far as he was able, say whatever came into his head. He is invited to speak as freely as possible; as though reporting back from somewhere that he usually calls himself. 'The treatment is begun,' Freud writes in his 'Two Encyclopaedia Articles',

> by the patient being required to put himself in the position of an attentive and dispassionate self-observer, merely to read off all the time the surface of his consciousness, and on the one hand to make a duty of the most complete honesty while on the other hand not to hold back any idea from communication, even if (1) he feels that it is too disagreeable or if (2) he judges that it is nonsensical or (3) too unimportant or (4) irrelevant to what is being looked for. It is uniformly found that precisely those ideas which provoke these last-mentioned reactions are of particular value in discovering the forgotten material.

Questions are always a queer species of prediction. And it is noticeable in what Freud refers to in this article as 'Psychoanalysis as an Interpretative Art' that questions are not being asked. It is a matter, as Freud says, of reading off the surfaces; of abrogating our conventional criteria. The disagreeable (also Ford's word), the nonsensical, the trivial and the irrelevant are all to be included. Indeed, the thoughts that provoke precisely these reactions are, Freud insists, 'of particular value in discovering the forgotten material'. All the moral and aesthetic criteria we use have to be set aside in order to recover what Freud calls 'the forgotten material', as though these criteria were themselves forms of forgetting; that what we pride ourselves on – our judgements of the appropriate and the pertinent, our aesthetic standards, our selection of the good – are cover stories, disappearing acts. Freud is interested in what we exclude by our inclusions. He and his patients are fascinated by the aesthetics of memory; and so by the choices made in every moment of speech.

All the psychoanalyst has to do, Freud proposes, is suggest to the patient that he speaks as freely as possible – as though, attentively and dispassionately, like a scrupulous empirical scientist, reading off the surface of his consciousness – and then attend to the difficulties people always get into in the telling of themselves. We don't need questions (or authoritative information) to interrupt us, Freud says, because we will interrupt ourselves given half a chance; because there's something about what we have to say that we can't bear. And this is called, as everyone now knows – or as everyone now knows that Freud knows – sexuality. Sexuality, or what Freud more interestingly refers to as 'the forgotten material'. Memory, Freud asserts, is of desire; the thing we keep needing to forget is sexuality, what Lacan calls 'the impossible knowledge of sexuality'. Sex, Freud says, is infinitely forgettable. Indeed, we talk about it so much *because we have forgotten about it*. The forbidden is not something you can chat about. If, in its provenance, our sexuality is incestuous – if the object of desire is by definition a forbidden object – no one is going to be easygoing. Everyone is going to be anxious all the time. If what we seek is what we must not find, our sense of purpose is askew; wholeheartedness, passion, authenticity, integrity all begin to look rather different if we are so radically averse to what we so radically desire. Irony is the religion of the incestuously minded.

Freud – and he was not alone in this – thought that sexuality had become especially traumatic for modern people; not just that some people had been sexually traumatized as children, which many of his patients had been; but that there was something intrinsically traumatic about sexuality. Decadence is when the forbidden becomes the impossible; and it was the impossibility of a satisfying erotic life that Freud was hearing about in the form of symptoms (the patient's symptoms are his sexual life, as Freud remarked). A normal sexual life was a disturbing sexual life. This was Freud's paradoxical conclusion (and this, as I shall come back to, is the opening Freud offers us). It is not, in Ford's language, easy to pigeon-hole and padlock what we think of as our sexual inclinations. There are nasty turns at every turn of our erotic life. A reputation for sanity is always going to be a mixed blessing.

The continual discrediting of Freud, and the endlessly announced death, disproof and fraudulence of psychoanalysis, is not merely the sport of bigots. When psychoanalysis is being wholeheartedly valued it is not being taken seriously; because the understanding of psychoanalysis involves a continual resistance to it. To accept psychoanalysis, to believe in psychoanalysis, is to miss the point. Indeed psychoanalysis makes us wonder what we might do with ideas, propositions, sentences, if we don't have to believe or disbelieve them. A French psychoanalyst once said to me that Judaism is the only religion in which you are not allowed to believe in God. In the same way, you cannot believe in the unconscious, you cannot believe in sexuality, as Freud describes them. Believing in incest is not like believing in God.

Your resistance is the only form your acknowledgement could possibly take (there's no such thing as a free love). And even this isn't quite right because the whole notion of resistance implies that there could be acceptance; and psychoanalysis is, among other things, a redescription of the question: what would it be to accept ourselves and others? It is Freud's view that we are ineluctably averse to ourselves (and others) because our desire is fundamentally transgressive. If what we want is what we must not have we are going to be, to put it as mildly as possible, divided against ourselves. If what we once wanted was to live a good life, or to be redeemed by God's grace, what we now want — or what we actually want — in Freud's view, is an object that is by definition forbidden. And this is going to make our relationship to our so-called selves at best ironic and at worst horrified. People, of course, are only ever ironic about the things that they don't feel ironic about. So what then would be a good life for incestuous animals like ourselves? What would be the values, what would be the moral aspirations of a creature whose desire, whose life-force is utterly transgressive, for whom the taboos are in place as a continual reminder of his most intractable needs?

Freud, let us say by way of a beginning, had a genius for describing the impossibility of our lives. He master-minded a story about how and why we are not the masters of what we have been taught to call our minds. By privileging the obstacle over the way forward, what can't be done over what is to be done; by seeing the drama in the interruption, the attention released in the lapse of attention, Freud was encouraging us to prize our incompetence; to be amazed and not merely dismayed by the persistent error of our ways. Freud wants to tell us the success story of failure. So Freud's genius was to describe to us just how and why it is a good and necessary thing — a good thing because a necessary thing — for us to live in conflict with ourselves and others (there is no peace for the Freudian); and, of course, if we are so minded, to live in conflict with Freud. If psychoanalysis is the kind of common sense that common sense doesn't want to hear about; if it addresses the recognitions involved in refusal, Freud is someone with whom we will feel uneasy. Enthusiasm is a wonderful thing, but one should be wary of the enthusiasts of psychoanalysis. Admiring Freud is not part of the solution to the problem he poses, it is part of the problem. And the problem is: since we are ineluctably unacceptable to ourselves, what kind of relationship is it possible for us to have with the unacceptable?

Adorno once famously remarked that in psychoanalysis only the exaggerations are true. It is also true that Freud was interested in the uses of exaggeration; in the ways in which a culture that forces people to downplay certain of their feelings makes them play up – both the feelings and the people. A Freudian slip exaggerates the difference between an intention and its result. In 'a good many cases' of these slips, Freud writes in *The Psychopathology of Everyday Life*,

> the disruptive ideas can be shown to originate in suppressed emotions in mental life. In normal people selfish, jealous and hostile feelings and impulses, upon which the pressure of moral teaching weighs very heavily, quite often make use of slips in order to find some way of expressing their forces, forces that are undeniably present but are not recognized by the higher authorities in our minds. Permitting these slips and fortuitous actions to occur reflects, to a considerable extent, a useful toleration of amorality. Sexual currents of many kinds figure prominently among these suppressed emotions.

It is worth noting, as I mentioned earlier, that in Freud's view we are, however unwittingly, the active makers of our slips. Reputedly normal people quite often 'make use' of slips, Freud writes, in order to find some way of expressing these unacceptable feelings, 'these amoral forces'. As though a slip were an opportunity or a genre, like the sonnet or a linguistic medium; as though we have to be the artists of our amorality – the artists, but also the pragmatists. We make use of slips as though they were one of our tools to get us from A to B, to realize one of our projects, to get us something we want. In replication of the external world Freud suggests that the internal world too has its higher, forbidding authorities – the mind too is a society – who, he says, won't recognize certain feelings. But if we can make use of these secret messages called slips then there can be what Freud calls, pragmatically, a 'useful toleration of amorality'. And these moments of linguistic carnival perform this amorality, they don't merely tolerate it (when I say 'it was just a mistake' I'm hoping for tolerance). What might once have been called bad manners, a lack of self-discipline or, indeed, a mistake, is now being referred to by Freud as both a 'useful' tool and a moment of artfulness, a way of 'expressing' powerful feeling. How does the modern individual deal with unacceptable sexual feelings, with 'selfish, jealous and hostile feelings'? He makes what he needs to call mistakes, Freud says, so the 'disruptive ideas', the amoral, find the expression they are seeking (in talking about slips in this way, Freud makes us wonder, what does saying what you want feel like you are doing?). So to answer my earlier questions – what would be a good life for incestuous animals like ourselves? What would be the moral aspirations of a creature whose desire was utterly transgressive? – to answer these essentially Freudian questions: a good life would be one in which mistakes were continually sought by someone equipped with a rhetoric to discredit their significance. We are the kind of animal that can say, 'I was only joking.'

But Freud, it should be noted, is not exactly satirizing our hypocrisy. This would hardly be news; or evidence of a master-mind at work. He is encouraging us to be connoisseurs of the cover story. For Freud our lives literally depend upon the aesthetics of duplicity. If we are not the artists of our own pleasure there will be no pleasure (and no art). Where once there was the moral authority of satire, the moral high ground of mockery, there can now be a more straightforward, apparently scientific, account of the necessities of pleasure-seeking, and of the necessary difficulties, the ruses, of pleasure-seeking. After Freud people can be accused of being consistent.

But why, in Freud's view, does the amoral seek, indeed require, expression? Why has Freud replaced the language of willpower and self-control with the language of pragmatic artistry? Why can't we behave ourselves instead of expressing ourselves, or behave ourselves *by* expressing ourselves? And Freud's answer is that we are the animals who live in a continual state of temptation. Even though we love safety and self-preservation it is as though something in us likes something else more (the most interesting art is never about safety but about what threatens safety). Darwin virtually says we want to preserve ourselves in order to reproduce our genes; Freud says there is something, which he wants to call sexuality, that is always threatening to destroy us. Our sexuality endangers us – endangers our sense of ourselves, our ego – because it is transgressive. We are, in Freud's view, a continual risk to ourselves. So when he writes to his absent collaborator Fliess in 1897 (in *The Origins of Psychoanalysis*) of his 'surge of guesses' – that he is 'about to discover the source of morality' – it is because interest in the forbidden, in the unacceptable, is by definition guess-work. 'Only one idea of general value has occurred to me,' he writes:

> I have found love of the mother and jealousy of the father in my own case, too, and now believe it to be a general phenomenon of early childhood . . . If that is the case, the gripping power of Oedipus Rex, in spite of all the rational objections to the inexorable fate that the story presupposes, becomes intelligible . . . the Greek myth seizes on a compulsion which everyone recognizes because he has felt traces of it in himself. Every member of the audience was once a budding Oedipus in fantasy, and this dream-fulfilment played out in reality causes everyone to recoil in horror, with the full measure of repression which separates his infantile from his present state.

This is not the place to try to establish the truth or otherwise of the Oedipus complex, its apparent universality or its possible significance. It has to be conceded though that the incest issue doesn't tend to leave people feeling indifferent. What is noteworthy is Freud wanting to account for people's horror of sexuality. Leo Bersani remarked in his great essay 'Is the Rectum a Grave?' that the big secret about sex was that most people don't like it. The big secret about sex isn't quite that most people don't like it, it's that most people don't like it because they are with people they are either not excited by or are too excited by. And if they are with people they are not sufficiently excited by, Freud would say, it is because they are terrified by their own desire. As budding Oedipuses their desire is either incestuous or it is nothing. Real desire is always a reminder of something at once overwhelming and forbidden. When it comes to the choice of sexual partner, better safe than sorry: from the ego's point of view, it's always better not to get too excited. When it comes to sexuality it is what Freud refers to as 'the recoil of horror' that is the sign of desire. This, one might say, goes against the grain of our common-sense assumptions about pleasure-seeking. Isn't pleasure supposed to be at least a pleasure as well? If sex is that Darwinian project why is it so much trouble for us? Freud shows us how if we are not in trouble we are not having sex.

Freud links so-called normal sexuality with a recoil of horror. And we may remember the blander instance of this as the Freudian slip in which we and/or our audience can recoil in surprise at what has been said inadvertently. Whatever this is – call it 'love of the mother and jealousy of the father'; call it 'selfish, jealous and hostile feelings . . . Sexual currents of many kinds' – Freud is describing himself, his patients, among others, as suffering from it. It puts us at odds with ourselves, but in secular terms. It is still a world of forbidden desires, but it is an Enlightenment world in which it is acknowledged that the higher authorities that are doing the forbidding are human and not divine in origin.

For Freud, as he works out his own mythology – and his

works should be read, I think, as Harold Bloom intimates, as more akin to William Blake's 'Prophetic Books' than to William James's *Principles of Psychology* – the question becomes: what are the higher authorities higher than in a secular society? Or, rather, what is there to be higher than, what is it that requires this kind of distance in order to be believed, and what is it deemed to be distant from? And Freud's answer is, perhaps unsurprisingly, that it is the parents, and particularly the father, who are the higher authorities for the child. But, perhaps more surprisingly, what there is to be higher than, what there is to distance oneself from and create the illusion of mastery over, is what Freud calls 'infantile sexuality', and that is alive in the adult as unconscious desire. The unconscious, which is Freud's word for the desire of childhood, and the history of its formations – a desire so enduring, so prodigal in its ingenuity, and so extravagant in its claims – is the stumbling-block that is Freud's most wonderful invention. The act alone of describing that which is at once irresistible and that one most resists – whether or not 'it' exists – is a great folly, an act of linguistic heroism. But it is in Freud's desire to describe how what he calls the unconscious works – both its provenance and its wayward logic – that his special claim on us makes itself felt. Our desire, Freud suggests, is always a work in progress, unfinishing and unfinished; and so is Freud's lifelong account of the unconscious. And if you want a picture of the kind of thing the unconscious does – the kind of thing it makes, and makes known – think of a dream, Freud says, or a joke or a slip; or of something you more patently suffer from, like a phobia or an inhibition or an intrusive thought (like the one Tietjens suffered from suddenly in the middle of a perfectly sensible conversation). It is an unusual, perhaps unprecedented, category Freud has created; a category that links, that connects up, the dream, the joke, the slip, the symptom. It is a category of unconsciously inspired performance, in which the identity of the performer is obscure. And in which the performance is deemed to be a communication, however enigmatic, to the interested parties. This communication, which is in some sense baffling to both the performer of it and its recipients, is an allusion, a referring back, to the desires of childhood. For Freud, childhood is the forbidden, and memory is always at best a guilty pleasure. There is nothing more transgressive than talking about one's childhood. Except, that is, like a budding Oedipus, to re-create it in adult life. It isn't, in other words, that Freud destroyed the innocence of childhood; it is that Freud showed us that the idea of innocence was invented to destroy the truth of childhood. Our childhood, he wants us to believe, is most akin to a Greek tragedy. We call Oedipus a tragic hero because he is the most ordinary man in the world.

Oedipus, of course, had never seen the play. Just like ourselves as children, he is going through it all for the first time. By the time we get to see or read or even hear about the play, it is far too late. We are already confounded by our fate. Psychoanalysis – and this is another paradox at the heart of Freud's work – is always after the event. It doesn't cure people so much as show them what it is about themselves that is incurable. Or, rather, it shows them the areas of their lives in which 'cure' would be the wrong word; in which we have to come up with something else to do other than get better. And one thing we can do, Freud – irrepressible as ever – suggests, is track the unconsciousness of our lives. We can, he occasionally intimates, learn to enjoy just how unwitting we are. There is nothing more entertaining – nothing more daunting and amusing and horrifying – than the ways in which our intentions and attentions misfire. There is nothing more poignant and absurd than our forlorn and sincere attempts not to wreak havoc. So when Auden writes in his great poem 'In Memory of Sigmund Freud' that Freud 'would have us remember most of all / to be enthusiastic over the night' he was also reminding us that for Freud it was night all day as well. And that enthusiasm, too, is something that has to be remembered. Children are nothing if not enthusiastic given half a chance and an object of desire. But enthusiasm is always going to be counter-phobic, the rushing of a resistance. Freud offers us a way of noticing the ways in which we don't notice; he wants us to reconsider whatever it is about ourselves that we are so tempted to ignore. He invites us to be unselectively attentive. And then to see what happens. Because the problem modern people have is that things keep occurring to them that they don't know what to do with. Without a sense of sin, they don't know what to make of what they are so troubled by.

There is a nasty, perhaps Freudian, moment in Dostoevsky's novel of 1868, *The Idiot*, in which something suddenly occurs to the hero, Prince Myshkin, as he wanders the streets of Moscow:

> Occasionally he would start peering at passers-by with great curiosity; but most often he did not notice either the passers-by or precisely where he was going. He was tormentingly tense and uneasy, and at the same time felt an extraordinary need for solitude. He wanted to be alone and to give himself over to all this suffering tension completely passively, without looking for the least way out. He was loath to resolve the questions that overflowed his soul and heart. 'What, then, am I to blame for it all?' he murmured to himself, almost unaware of his words.

The prince oscillates between a state of vigilance and a state of inner preoccupation; at once holding on to external reality – peering at passers-by – and being quite elsewhere, not knowing where he is going, and surrendering to his thoughts and feelings (to try to 'resolve the questions that overflowed his soul and heart' would have been to wrench himself out of those very questions). And suddenly he finds himself as good as talking to himself: ' "What, then, am I to blame for it all?" he murmured to himself, almost unaware of his words.' On the one hand the 'all' for which he feels, momentarily, responsible is the fate of Rogozhin and Nastasya Filippovna; but it is also everything else, all the suffering and confusion in the world that Prince Myshkin confoundingly believes, as he says it to himself, is his fault. This is clearly an extraordinary thing to find oneself suddenly saying to oneself; though, of course, it is not rare for people to suffer revelations of chronic over-responsibility for the terribleness of things. And it is consoling to believe that someone is to blame, that somewhere there is a responsible agent. But Prince Myshkin murmurs this to himself, 'almost unaware of his words'. One can be aware of one's words, the narrator implies; but what is it to be aware of one's words?

To be almost unaware of one's words is as good a description as any of telling one's dream. All the words one uses probably have known referents, and yet what one is actually recounting makes no sense. We are describing something that we have seen, though not with our eyes. But to speak and to be almost unaware of one's words sounds more like a trance state, a being possessed by the words; as though at that moment the prince, rather like the dreamer, is the medium rather than the instigator of what he has to say. He is struck, as we say, because he doesn't quite recognize himself in his sentence. 'Something,' the narrator writes, 'was certainly pursuing him.' This, in Freud's sense, is the individual unconsciously at work; the self as a discrepancy. The self as real – or at its most real – in its unfamiliarity with itself. The unconscious is the fictive source of news, in Freud's mythology; it is where the surprises come from, the surprises whose moral status is always ambiguous. It is the home of trauma and desire, and of the trauma that is desire. The individual never quite knows what to think of what he has thought. Thoughts and feelings that come from the unconscious part of the self have indeterminate consequences. They are the stuff of dreams, not of routines.

But why did Dostoevsky describe the prince as murmuring this sentence to himself, rather than describing it as simply a thought that crossed his mind? And why did Ford describe Tietjen's sudden thought as one in which 'He had been as good as talking to himself'? What both instances are drawing our attention to – and the reason I describe them both as perhaps Freudian moments – is the difference between something occurring to someone, someone having a shocking thought, and this thought being spoken, if only to oneself. Freud's invention of psychoanalysis as a therapy – or as a new kind of conversation – turns, after all, on this difference. Freud invited his patients to 'as good as talk to themselves', but aloud, in his presence; to be almost unaware of their words, that is to free-associate, to speak without censorious vigilance whatever happened to, in both senses, cross their minds. There is nothing more defensive, Freud implies, than understanding what one is saying. Psychoanalysis, in short, is based on the idea that talking is different to thinking; and also that surprising or shocking oneself in the presence of another person is of value. Indeed, the point is that such nourishing surprise, such productive shock, may be possible only, is made possible only, by the very presence of the other person. The project of the unacceptable in oneself is to make itself known. The forbidden, the transgressive, is always an annunciation. It is a demand made on at least one other person. Freud invented a therapeutic setting, called psychoanalysis, in which this self could be overheard. The experiment, of course, was what followed from that overhearing. Unlike confession, psychoanalysis offers a person, at best, an essentially unpredictable redescription – an unpredictable consequence – of what they have said.

The psychoanalyst – the new figure that Freud invented; the other protagonist in his epic poem, his never-ending story called *The Unconscious* – is a person with an unusual conversational manner. He responds to what his so-called patients say to him not quite like anyone else. And this is because he has two aims, which are actually more at odds with each other than Freud was ever prepared to acknowledge, or perhaps even to mention. On the one hand he aims to cure, to relieve suffering, to help to make a life more worth living. But on the other hand he aims for what is technically called 'maximal symbolization'. He wants, that is to say, to respond only in ways which will facilitate the expression of unconscious desire. He wants to 'let the unconscious speak'; to modify the person's defences against what he has to say, and what he has to hear himself saying. The question is – and it is, of course, a political question – does freer speech, does the frankest possible articulation of wants, give people a life they prefer, or make a better world? By inventing psychoanalysis, Freud invented what he might have called a laboratory for the evaluation of the effects of free speech and free listening. And, perhaps unsurprisingly, not everyone liked, or likes, the sound of it. People want to speak freely only about what they must not speak about.

In Freud's view the question the modern individual seems to be asking herself is whether she can make her wanting compatible with her (psychic) survival. For Freud, to speak is to articulate one's wants, to make known to oneself what is absent, what of significance is lacking in one's life. And the performance of wanting – in mood, in language, in action – puts one's life in danger. There is the danger of punishment for desiring the forbidden, which Freud infamously (and accurately) referred to as castration; and there is the danger of acknowledged dependence, and the potential for loss. One cannot live, one could not have survived, without wanting; and without having achieved some success at it. But the wanting that is our lifeline throws us into interminable conflict: it involves us ineluctably with others and ourselves. 'Originally,' Freud writes in *Civilisation and Its Discontents*, 'renunciation of instinct was the result of fear of an external authority: one renounced one's satisfactions in order not to lose its love.' There is the urgency, the emergency of instinctual desire, and there is the fear of loss of love as a ruling passion. A person begins, Freud tells us, in fear of losing his parents' love; and then, having internalized their authority, he ends up fearing (and courting) losing his love for himself. And this self-hatred, that can be so obscene in its voraciousness, is called guilt. We cannot help but be harmed by what we cannot help but want. We have morality that we may not perish from the truth. We are the animals that need to be protected from themselves.

Good, now, means safe and satisfied, or satisfied safely enough; bad means deprived beyond measure of one's need. Good means, as it always has done, desirable; but desirable now also means forbidden. What is good is against the law. Bad now means traumatic, but traumatic is not simply or solely the things that happen to oneself; or, rather, one's desire can feel like something that happens to oneself, like having an attack of one's own nature. So 'trauma' becomes another word for living a life. For Freud, in other words, we are in shock; in shock, but wishing our way through. It is as though there is a design flaw in the human animal; our childhood is more than our development can cope with. We are all in recovery from having been children.

As Freud tracked, in his clinical work, the ways in which the old-fashioned solutions of childhood became the repetitions of adulthood; and how repetition was a refusal to remember, and how memory was full of hiding-places, he was struck by a peculiar fact: that suffering can sometimes be transformed by applying words to wounds, by being seen as meaningful. In the nonsense that we talk there is the spectacle of happiness; in and of itself the appeal to another person to listen and reply is fraught with hope. Freud shows us just how extravagant it is to speak. The task of the modern person, as Freud sees her, is to find the new ways of wanting that keep wanting alive; but in the full knowledge that wanting is a species of risk. What became known, after Freud, as psychoanalytic theory is nothing but an encyclopaedia of modern risks. And desire is usually the contemporary word for the risk not taken, for the missed opportunity; the unlived life that seems the only life worth living.

So Freud, I want to suggest, leaves us with one overriding

question: what is a good life for incestuously minded people like ourselves, people who must not have what they really want? People whose fraught, doomed love for their parents has made love a hopeless passion; and who fear the loss of love they know to be their birthright and their fate? It is always going to be difficult for us, Freud says, to be excited and kind, to be fair and satisfied. Because, in reality, we can never be or have the object of our desire, we are always the left-out ones. And because the object of our desire is forbidden, it is imperative for our (psychic) survival that we *are* left out. Oedipus was the man who couldn't bear being left out.

Freud, then, has given us a lot to be going on with. We must start, he seems to be saying, by ironizing the masteries of the mind. We must not hide ourselves away for safe-keeping, because safety only keeps us safe. We must learn to desire with guile and without hope; to love in conflict, rather than betraying our desire in fantasies of harmony. We must, in short, take our pleasures where we may. And speak as well as we can of what we want. People have not been keen to recognize that the reality principle was Freud's most exciting idea.

For the Family

If this is a lesson in love, well what's it for?

John Hiatt, 'Cry Love'

Ideally, families are groups of people of more than one generation who have a passion for living together. No child growing up in a family, of course, has anything to compare it with for some time; nor is the child in a position to leave. To begin with, whatever the actual arrangements, the family from the child's point of view is just the way the world is. The child in the family is, in this sense, like Sartre's rebel, the person who keeps the world the same so he can go on rebelling against it; he is not the revolutionary who wants to change the world. However discontented we are at the beginning of our lives we are not, for many years, critics of the family. And when we first become critics of the family we are critics of our own families, not of what we might later call *the family*. It is worth wondering what has to happen to someone, or what someone has to make of what happens to them, to make them begin to wonder not what was wrong with *their* family but what might be wrong with *the* family as a way of doing things. Families being primarily now ways of bringing up children and regulating sexual relations.

If the family, at its very best, inspires and is inspired by a passion for living together, this passion, like all so-called passions, involves frustration. Because the thing the family exposes, perhaps more intensely than any of our other social arrangements, is each individual member's capacity to bear frustration. What is revealed in every family is the way each person deals with frustration, their attitude to it; their 'relationship' to not getting what they want. However good the family is it is the place where we learn not to get what we want, and how to do this. Before you have children, the novelist Fay Weldon once said, you can believe you are a nice person; after you have children you understand how wars start. All critiques of *the family* that are not simply or solely grievances against one's own are grand narratives about possibilities for satisfaction. At their best they are stories about new ways of bearing frustration, at their worst – at their least promising and most utopian – they are about abolishing at least some of our frustrations. If, as Wittgenstein proposed, the way to solve the problem you see in life is to live in a way that makes the problem disappear, then the family would seem to be the place to start.

And yet, in so far as people want to have children and regulate their sexual desire, it has been very difficult to live in a way that makes the problem, and the problems, of the family disappear. Modern critics of the family have been unable to provide compelling or even plausible alternatives to it; alternatives that have caught on. And psychoanalysis, which has tended to be a great consolidator of the family by being a critic of it, has never found ways of saying that there is far more to our lives than our relationship to our parents. Of course, families come in more configurations, more unprecedented varieties now than ever before. But they are all variations on a theme; and the theme seems to be the link between having children and the organizing of desire. The question is: what, if anything, does the raising of children require us to be faithful to? In our erotic lives we abandon our children, and in our familial lives we abandon our desire. It is not that couples with children don't desire each other, even though the having of children radically refigures desire in the couple; it's that their erotic connection, in the moments of enacted desire, excludes the children. In the family, of whatever configuration, what cannot be hidden is the fact that two people's pleasure in each other is always someone else's exclusion. That in our pleasure, whatever else we are doing, we are frustrating someone; and this is one of the things that makes our pleasure-seeking so difficult, so guilty, so confounding. Couples, of whatever kind, can be partners in crime. Once they have children they are the criminals.

Most people feel far worse about betraying their children than about betraying their partner. And children can be used far more effectively for the policing of desire than partners; at its most extreme it is as though the thing we can't do to our children is live our desire outside the family. Given that we can't always live our desire that intensely inside the family, it might seem sometimes as though a strange sacrifice is being made. In so far as we have become the animals who have to choose between having children or having sex we have made a terrible pact that must be to everyone's detriment, particularly the children's. It casts them as both the objects and the saboteurs of their parents' desire. This could make someone at once both a critic of the family and unable to conceive of anything better.

The Dream Horizon

I

I don't like to dream (or to recall that I've dreamed); if it was a
bad dream it darkens my awakening; if it was sweet it tears me
to pieces when it stops: I could never imagine a sleep utopia
filled with dreams, with sweet dreams.

Roland Barthes, *The Neutral*

If no one had ever dreamed, if dreaming was something that
nobody had either ever done or ever remembered, the way we
describe prophecy, reality, scepticism, memory, desire, identity,
irrationality and hope – to take the more obvious examples –
would be quite different. And to imagine what kind of difference
the absence or non-existence of the dream would make to our
lives – what effect it might have had, for example, on the invention of photography, or on the sense we made of sleeping – seems
baffling. So much seems to depend, so to speak, on the fact of
our dreaming; or, rather, on our capacity to remember and represent our dreams. The dream as example, the dream as analogy,
the dream as material for interpretation, the dream as vitalizing
enigma, the dream as key to something or other, as clue to something essential about ourselves and our fate; the sheer usefulness
of the dream as an object in the cultural field, and of dreaming
and the telling of dreams as a cultural activity, is striking. How
dreaming fits into so-called waking life, what the dream has got
to do with the rest of a person's activities, what if any significance should be ascribed; these are issues, it seems, that most if

not all cultures have something to say about; and usually something quite forceful. When people speak about dreaming they tend to be speaking about something that somehow matters to them. Dreams, in other words – to adapt Lévi-Strauss's formulation – are good to think with. I want to consider in this essay what talking about dreams is an opportunity to talk about. Or, perhaps more exactly (and exactingly), how talking and writing about dreams gets people talking and writing. If, for example, the figure traditionally referred to as the Dreamer was a character in a novel, what can the novelist, the dream-theorist, use him to do; to give voice to? The Dreamer as hero – the heroism of dreaming – is like a permission or an invitation or even an incitement to say certain things that are otherwise difficult to articulate. The fact that we dream is an opportunity to describe someone we call the Dreamer. The Dreamer, we might say, at its most minimal is a character subject to alternative constraints. In our dreams we can do things and things are done that we can't do and can't be done. It is a familiar elsewhereness, but it is elsewhere nonetheless.

So, to ask the pragmatic question: what do we want to talk about when we talk about dreams? What do dreams help us describe? In the modern period they help us describe our uncertainties, our not knowing who or what to believe or, indeed, what kind of experience believing is. They show us radical disorientation, they make us spectators of the unintelligible. 'Wee owe unto dreames,' Sir Thomas Browne writes in 'On Dreames',

> that Galen was a physitian, Dion an historian, and that the world hath seene some notable peeces of Cardan, yet hee that should order his affayres by dreames, or make the night a rule unto the day, might bee ridiculously deluded.

Dreams, Browne tells us, force us to speak in contradictions and about contradictions; they make us sound paradoxical to ourselves. Galen, Dion and the Italian physician and mathematician found their true vocations, made their original discoveries, in their dreams; and yet if we were to order our affairs or use the dream as blueprint or guideline for our waking life we might be ridiculously deluded. It's not clear, of course, how we would do this even if we wanted to. But what Browne is intimating – and this is a common intimation in modern writings about dream – is that we may be ridiculously deluded creatures; and that part of our deludedness – or the conundrum of our delusion – is that there is no available reality compared with which we can see ourselves as deluded. Dreams tell us the truth about ourselves, and they could not be more misleading. One of the things we are implicitly seeking reassurance about is that there are two distinct realms, night and day, sleeping and waking, dreaming and . . . what? There is a danger in not seeing the difference. It is as if for some reason we see or want to see that there are two realms – even if they are somehow interwoven – but we are not quite sure how to prove that there are. When Browne asserts that to order our affairs by dreams, to make the rule of the night the rule of the day, might be to ridiculously delude ourselves he is suggesting that Dion, Galen and Cardan might therefore be ridiculously deluded and we doubly so to be impressed by them. If we might be ridiculously deluded we might not be. And why would it matter even if we were ridiculously deluded? Who is ridiculing us? Presumably the figure who is in touch with the reality that makes delusion discernible. This, one could say, is the territory you get into; these are the kinds of sentences that come up when you write and read about dreams. What do dreams provide? What do we owe to them? Are there two orders, two sets of rules: a self by day and a self by night?

It is notable that Browne assumes that the night, the dream life, is rule-governed, is organized, although quite differently to the waking life. What do dreams reveal to us? Or what are we tempted to make of them? Two quite different questions. Browne says that one thing we could make of dreams is a model for waking life. And this, again, becomes a familiar and enigmatic question asked by modern writers: how would we live if we were to live according to our dreams (a question implied, if not asked, by Freud)? What would our lives be like if we lived them as though they were dreams? Why is it better to live undeluded, and hence with the distinction, uppermost in our minds, as it were, between truth and reality? Is it better for us to become creatures who seek out and are impressed by people who can tell us the difference between truth and delusion? There is something, maybe several things, that dreamers are not good at; and other things that we are not good at when we are wide awake. If we didn't dream we would have no Galen, and we would have no picture, in Browne's view, of what it might be to be ridiculously deluded. 'That some have never dreamed is as improbable as that some have never laughed,' Browne writes in a conjunction that looks forward to Freud. We are amused, we dream, we can be deluded and subject to ridicule for our delusions. Dreaming is integral to who we are – we can't imagine ourselves without it; it is one of the ingredients with which we essentialize ourselves, even if dreaming is the very thing, according to one view, that undoes our essentializing of ourselves – and it spells, or we spell it out as, a dangerous and/or a benign dividedness. There isn't, Browne leads us to believe, a third realm; the fact that we dream – whether or not dreams are divine or daemonic – doubles us. The fact of the dream invites us to speak of ourselves as divided with and against ourselves; as subject to division, but to uncertain purposes. If the dream represents here our paradoxical obscurity to ourselves, it also exposes something our sentences want to get to grips with, something fascinating that we do, or that is done to us, at night. Something that makes us wonder about the provenance of our images and what they have to do with us; what being interested in dreams is being interested in. One thing being interested in dreams is a way of being interested in is wondering what we see when we are not looking. And what it is – what kind of experience it is – to recognize what we see when we are not looking.

The thing that is most striking to Browne – as I would guess it is to many other dream writers – is the disparity, the incongruity, the gap between what happens, what we see, in dreams and what happens, and what we see and feel, when we are not dreaming. In other words, an alternative to dreaming is being proposed – another scene – and it is the kind of life we have after waking. It is worth noting that the dream experience is often described as a kind of journey, as though dream-telling was a species of travel writing. We live in two worlds, waking and sleeping, and they must be linked because we ourselves are the link; we do both, even though it is as if one is done in our presence and one in our absence (or with our absence). We want to tell stories, for some reason, about these two worlds and the links between them; we are both the makers of these links, in our various cultures, and we are the ones who believe there are links; that there must be senses in which the two worlds are one world. We can reverse our perspective and imagine, for example, a culture for whom dreaming was the norm, so to speak, and waking life was the enigma, the thing we wanted to know more about, the source of endless bafflement. If dreaming was the norm we might not assume, say, that looking was something we did with our eyes, or that language rather than images was second nature, or indeed that more or less intelligible verbal communication was expectable. We would have a quite different sense of what it was to hear things or smell them; and we probably wouldn't describe time as cyclical, or as a medium that connected events together, and so on. All this serves to illustrate is that we tend to describe the dream-world as a world of recognizable but not obviously assimilable differences; as an elsewhere to which we are ineluctably joined, but where we are not, in the ordinary sense, at home. 'The idea that we are all strangers to each other,' Adrian Poole writes in a review of A. C. Bradley's *Shakespearean Tragedy*, 'is no more or less of a fiction than the idea that we can reach fair understandings' (*Essays in Criticism*). And, one can say, the idea that we are strangers to ourselves in dreams is no more or less of a fiction than the idea that we can reach fair understandings of ourselves in dreams. Or, to put it slightly differently, in much of the Western writing about dreams – which would include, of course, the writings of Western anthropologists – the supreme fiction tends to be that our dreams are strange; or that in our dreams we, or our more usual life, have been made strange. Dreams, in other words, seem to encourage us to describe waking life as fairly understandable or at least more intelligible than something else: this is the reassurance offered by dreams; we can wake up from them. We may live in two realms but one, supposedly, is more intelligible; or one requires less, or maybe different forms of, interpretation. But dreams show us – which means in my version that we can use them to say – that there is somewhere else, somewhere beyond our sovereignty though, which each individual is nevertheless the sovereign reporter of; and that this somewhere else, this alternative place, which we come to or which comes to us unbidden, is the holder of clues or secrets that can help us live the lives we prefer; if only we can find the right take or the right method or the right person dreams will provide unique access to otherwise unavailable resources. The dream is an opportunity to talk about obscure resources; apparently unheard-of desires, or versions of ourselves, or predictions of the future, or messages about our physiology or our destiny, or our wishes. Paradoxically, for the dream valuers, for the keepers of dreams, in our dreams we are at once most obscurely and most essentially ourselves. Dreams, that is to say, are frequently recruited – and, indeed, are suitably recruitable for – what is now called essentialist discourse. Dreams tend to be described – and Browne intimates this in his reference to his great geniuses Galen, Dion and Cardan – as being closer to, or revealing of, something more true or more real or more necessary than so-called ordinary consciousness is aware of. It is perhaps one of the most interesting things about dreams that when they are valued they are always highly valued. They are taken to be and presented as something or other that matters very much. And it is, of course, assumed that there is some connection between obscurity and value, or that cultures that associate mystery with value are more likely to rate dreaming; that we have to go the distance, that there will be obstacles in our quest for the best resources (as though we use the dream to ask ourselves, what good is strangeness? Or, what do we need or use strangeness for?). Dreaming is always the prime suspect when the conversation is about the dividedness of the individual, as though dreams are used as reminders that we don't know what's going on inside us, as if we needed reminding of this. The stress, the imaginative energy, tends to fall on telling us how different sleeping is from waking, dreaming from consciousness, consciousness from unconsciousness. In these familiar binaries it is the differences, not the similarities, that we are prone to spell out and insist upon. It can often sound as though it isn't so much that our dreams are so different, so bizarre, so wayward, but rather that we want them to be; as though, whatever else is going on, we crave this radical otherness in ourselves that dreams are our favourite picture of.

II

. . . for the unconscious is an orphan.

Gilles Deleuze and Felix Guattari, *Anti-Oedipus*

'When we are awake,' the psychoanalyst W. R. Bion said in a seminar at the Tavistock Clinic,

> I don't think we really know much about the state of mind in which we are when asleep. As a psychoanalyst I have been taught a good deal about the interpretation of dreams. The only thing I am not quite clear about is, what was the dream? Because when I am told that the patient has had a dream, it is told me by a

person who is in an 'awake' state of mind. I sometimes ask patients, 'Where were you last night? What did you see? Where did you go?' I don't accept the answer that they didn't go anywhere, they simply went to bed and went to sleep. But I still think they went somewhere and saw something. It is possible that if the patient says he had a dream, it is a sort of vestige that is sufficiently robust still to be apparently available when he is awake.

Bion is quite clear – that is, quite insistent – that sleeping is not of a piece with waking, at least epistemologically: 'When we are awake I don't think we really know much about the state of mind in which we are when asleep.' Not much, but perhaps something. The question 'Where were you last night?' alerts us, with its echoes of the jealous partner or the anxious parent of an adolescent, that something must have been going on last night, whether admitted to or not. The intractable assumption is that the patient has been away overnight and, indeed, has seen something. But perhaps the most interesting moment in Bion's account – apart from the tone of indomitable certainty about such definitionally uncertain territory – is his use of the word 'vestige': 'It is possible that if the patient says he had a dream, it is a sort of vestige that is sufficiently robust still to be apparently available when he is awake.' A 'vestige' is something that has survived, though no longer used (the *OED* has 'a surviving memorial or trace . . . serving as an indication of its former existence', though I suspect Bion was using it in its more biological sense as 'a surviving trace of some part formerly existing in the species; a vestigial organ or structure'). If a remembered dream is akin to a vestige, then, despite Bion's presumably unintended implication that the remembered dream is merely a survival of something redundant, he is wanting to say that the dream has to be extremely resilient, 'robust', to survive for so long, to have come such a long way from sleep to waking. The sleeper went a great distance that night, and only if the dream is a robust vestige will it be what Bion calls 'apparently available' on waking.

'Apparently available' makes a compact point; the dream is only apparently available – that is, it's not entirely clear whether it is or it isn't; and it is not clear what this robust vestige is available for (what it avails). There is intimated here the heroism of dreaming, the dreamer has been on a mysterious journey and he has brought back ambiguous treasure; the status, the nature of the dream as an object, is not self-evident. We make dreams, or in Bion's picture we go and see them and bring them back as memories of experience; and then dreams are what we make of them. We experience them whether we want to or not; at night I have no choice but to be in the audience. But how they are described – the genre of dream-telling – and what is done with them, the nature of the redescriptions to which they are subject, are, as we say, culturally constructed. Dreams may be unusual and uncanny but the images in which they proliferate and the languages in which they are told and interpreted come from nowhere but the culture of the dreamer. They are, let us say, an intriguing example of the way culture goes all the way down; it goes all the way down into our unintelligibility to ourselves. Dreams are sometimes apparently available and we have to make what is apparent to us available. Which is to do no more and no less than to see what occurs to us in the hearing of the dream; the told dream, whatever else it is, is a singularly evocative object. The listened-to, the listened-for dream – associated to by the dreamer and the listener – takes us off in expected directions. And this is because, for want of another way of putting it, something in us responds to something in the dream. In the cultural field we have learned that dreams are worth our attention. The dreamer has, in Bion's picture, gone somewhere and seen something, and it may stay with her; and she knows that, for some reason, seeing certain things, and remembering them, matters. If dreams are democratic artefacts – if everyone has access to them irrespective of wealth or status – their value, once we assume they require interpretation of whatever sort, is something we have to make up. Dreams don't speak for themselves; we make them give voice. In this sense dreams – dreams as told stories – are what we might call literary; not simply because they exist in the shared world in language (even if you paint your dream you have to say something, if only, this is my dream), but that they observe conventions (a dream sequence in a film works only if it dawns on us that this is a dream sequence). Culture goes all the way down into our dreams in ways that we can't give an account of, or can give only competing accounts of.

So when the art historian Michael Baxandall says in his book *Patterns of Intention: On the Historical Explanation of Pictures* that 'We do not explain pictures: we explain remarks about pictures – or, rather, we explain pictures only in so far as we have considered them under some verbal description or specification,' this could also be said of dreams. We cannot explain our dreams, we can explain only our descriptions (or explanations) of dreams. We only ever interpret or associate to the story of the dream. And when Baxandall goes on to describe the history of art criticism he touches something peculiarly pertinent to the dream, something that the psychoanalyst Bion is getting at: 'The history of art criticism in the last five hundred years,' Baxandall writes,

> has seen an accelerating shift from discourse designed to work with the object unavailable, to discourse assuming at least a reproduced presence of the object. In the sixteenth century Vasari assumes no more than a generic acquaintance with most of the pictures he deals with; in particular his celebrated and strange descriptions are often calculated to evoke the character of works not known to the reader . . . in the nineteenth century [art] books were increasingly illustrated with engravings and eventually half-tones . . . We now assume the presence or availability [through reproduction] of the object, and this has great consequence for the workings of our language.

In talking or writing about dreams there can never be this shift Baxandall describes from 'discourse designed to work with the object unavailable, to discourse assuming at least a reproduced presence of the object'. When it comes to dreams we are all Vasarians whose strange descriptions are always calculated to evoke the character of works not known to the listener. All we can compare our descriptions and explanations of our dreams to are other people's descriptions and explanations. The object of description and explanation will never become available, it will never be reproduced, there will be no progress. We will only ever have words for dreams, the description, never the thing itself. Our dreams will only ever be apparently available in language. This is one of the many reasons why the attempt to give what one might call an accurate account of one's dream is such an interesting experience; by the time you are providing your account the dream is no longer there, and the listener is never in a position to compare the account with its object. This is true, of course, of any recounted memory; the questions are what, if anything, is the teller being true to? And what is this truthfulness deemed to be in the service of? Freud believes the dreamer has to tell himself what is not there in the dream, through the process of free association. The Freudian dreamer is a Vasarian in the sense that he has to provide strange descriptions to evoke the character of a work not known by the listener; but he also has to provide a different kind of strange description, called his freeish associations, to evoke the character of a work not known by the dreamer himself. It is as though he is describing a work that is not as yet there, except in its apparent form. He is a historian of pentimento rather than of a work of seeable art. If the Freudian dreamer was an agent we would say he was an agent that did not want to disclose his work; he, the dream agent, so to speak, wants to pass off a satisfying fake in order to smuggle through the Old Master underneath the surface. In this sense the Freudian dreamer is akin to the listener of his dream in that neither of them has seen the dream; the dreamer has seen what Freud calls a 'façade', and it is only in words, in his view, that we can get behind or get through the scenes (of unacceptable desire). Without associations, the dreamer's associations mostly, both the dreamer and the analyst or listener are outside the dream. Like Vasari, the dreamer has to describe what he has seen; but after that it is as though a new sense, a sixth sense, is brought into play. Language becomes the lure and the lead. The dreamer neither goes on describing his dream nor does he try to explain it; he just notices and reports the words that occur to him from the verbal descriptions he has already given. When the Lacanian analyst does what she calls 'returning the signifier' she is simply repeating back to the dreamer a word or a phrase from his account of his dream to see what other words it prompts in him. For the Freudian dreamer, like the art critic Vasari, the visual becomes the pretext for the linguistic. The visual object is soon left behind as an opportunity for description, a source of clues and angles and sentences. It is there to stir us into words, to call up language, an appetite to speak; to take the direction of our desire.

III

. . . the text of the last hours of the night is, theoretically speaking, the text the furthest removed from the day that is about to dawn.

Louis Althusser, *For Marx*

For Freud, in a sense it is simple; on the one hand we are Darwinian creatures bent on survival, and on making survival as pleasurable as is possible. We are essentially desiring animals, appetite being the medium through which we survive and, if we are able, reproduce. But we are also in Freud's view possibly the only desiring animals whose desire is forbidden. Desire in the Freud–Lacan account is that without which our lives feel futile, and yet desire is that which puts us in mortal danger. Dreaming is simply one of the ways we manage this conundrum of our being. When Freud famously wrote that dreams were the 'royal road to the unconscious' (and we know that 'royal roads' according to *Chambers English Dictionary* are 'a short and easy way of circumventing difficulties'), then we know that Freud is telling us that dreams – or, rather, dreams under his description of their workings – are the most direct way of getting at our desire. Which in turn is the most direct way of getting at the constitutive conflicts that make us who we are. The unconscious is, in his words, 'the other scene' because it is where our forbidden desire formulates itself, and our forbidden desire is other to, is outside of, what we prefer to think of ourselves as wanting. Freudian people would rather not know what they want – indeed, are likely to devote their lives to this not-knowing, seeking out substitute satisfactions at all cost; and dreams as 'disguised fulfilments of childhood wishes' are ways of more or less successfully keeping this secret of our desire from ourselves. Freud, that is to say, agrees with Sir Thomas Browne that 'hee that should order his affayres by dreames, or make the night a rule unto the day, might bee ridiculously deluded'. In the infantile part of the mind that in Freud's view is of a piece with the dreaming mind, a desire always prompts a picture of its satisfaction, and we always believe the picture. Our desiring selves are indeed ridiculously deluded, that is, excessively wishful. Desire is always in excess of any object's capacity to satisfy it, in the Freudian universe, and this is what we get to hear about if we can bear it, through the interpretation of our dreams. Whether we would prefer to or not we do order our affairs by dreams – or, rather, dreams show us how our affairs are ordered – we do make the night the rule of the day and we are therefore essentially ridiculously deluded. Freudian dreams expose that we prefer wishes to reality, that we instinctively replace a negative hallucination with a positive hallucination – that is, we have tricks for hiding our essential frustrations from ourselves – and that in order to survive psychically we believe that above all we must not know ourselves. Dreams tell us that our delusions and illusions are our preferred truths, and that truth means to us just whatever gives us enough pleasure to bear our lives. Perception is distorted by wish and this is what we are seeing night after night in our dreams. According to Freud, Charles Rycroft writes in his sober *A Critical Dictionary of Psychoanalysis*, 'the function of dreams is to preserve sleep by representing wishes as fulfilled which would otherwise awaken the dreamer' and that they are 'normal processes, with which everyone is familiar, but which none the less exemplify the processes at work in the formation of neurotic symptoms'. But the implication is that the dream, described like this, is a literalization, a stark picture of a permanent state. Awake or asleep we do not want to be awakened to, or by, our wishes, the wishes that represent our unconscious forbidden desire. Dreams just help us to stay asleep when we are asleep. Though Freud never, to my knowledge, says, as Jung does, that we are dreaming all the time, I think Freud uses dreaming as a way of wondering what it might be to be awake. If the dream's function is the preservation of sleep, this makes the dream something that stops us from waking up. If it is a sleeping device we might wonder whether there is a comparable waking device; we know we are asleep if we are dreaming, but what is the complementary sentence? We know we are awake when we are . . . what? Thinking, perceiving, feeling, remembering, daydreaming?

What wakes us up, what causes the dreaming process to break down into nightmare, is, in Freud's view, the failure of the dream-work to make a sufficiently satisfying, a sufficiently settling, dream out of the memory and desire that are its medium. The project is not to be woken up, not to be overly disturbed by memory and desire, and by the memory that, Freud believes, is of desire. But waking up becomes another way, the next way, of not being overwhelmed by these experiences. It is as if the first, preferred container is the dream; the next one, if the dream-work fails, is waking up; and the final one is psychosis. This makes a spectrum or a repertoire out of the series: dreaming, waking, neurosis/psychosis; they all become artefacts for bearing memory and desire. And they could all be described as different forms of sleep, or ways of not being too starkly awakened. And one implication of this might be that the dream is one of the best ways we have of remembering and desiring because in it nothing happens to the dreamer except the experience of the dream. There is no exchange, no one else is present, ideally nothing else happens but the dream. In dreams we desire by ourselves so nothing can happen to us.

'All we know of dreams,' Freud writes in *The Interpretation of Dreams*, 'is derived from consciousness'; so it's not quite true to say that dreams are the royal road to the unconscious, because consciousness is the royal road to the unconscious, even if dreams are particularly good to think with or to speak of in this regard. Dreams thus become emblematic, in the Freudian descriptions, of the fact that all experience is mediated. The unconscious, as far as we can know, is something in this sense derived from consciousness, which could mean, inferred by consciousness, constructed or made by consciousness, of a piece with consciousness. In other words, Freud intimates here (and not only here), we may have thought that there were two discreet, antagonistic realms called the unconscious and consciousness, but one is a derivation of the other. There are continuities, shared projects, even if they are obscure ones; the so-called divided subject might be a convenience for the sake of a certain kind of description. We may be the animals who want to escape from their desire, but this very escape is in the service of preserving the life of this desiring creature. We are divided against ourselves in order to sustain our dividedness. And the dream becomes Freud's best way of talking about this absurd modern predicament; the modern desiring subject desires most successfully when he is immobilized in sleep. His safest satisfactions – and in this sense his most viable satisfactions – are the ones he gives himself when he isn't there.

Dreams, for Freud, are above all functional; they guarantee, when they work, that the individual is not disturbed by his desire. Desiring, he seems to suggest, is something we do best in our sleep. 'When once we have recognized,' he writes in *The Interpretation of Dreams*,

> that the content of a dream is the representation of a fulfilled wish and that its obscurity is due to alterations in repressed material made by the censorship, we shall no longer have any difficulty in discovering the function of dreams. It is commonly said that sleep is disturbed by dreams; strangely enough, we are led to the contrary view and must regard dreams as the guardians of sleep.

We must not, Freud implies, be awakened to, be awakened by, our desire; without dreams doing their work we wouldn't be able to sleep. It is, in actuality, a very strange picture. We have a physiological need to sleep, akin to hunger in the sense that without sleep we cannot survive; and yet our desire, our wishes from childhood, are such that without the artistry of dream-work – which is essentially an artistry of disguise and distraction – we would not be able to sleep. Our (childhood) wishes would kill us. Sleep requires its guardians because it is vulnerable to attack, to disturbance. In the dream, to all intents and purposes, we sleep off our desire; we represent it in an acceptable form – that is, in a form acceptable to the censor – and we represent its fulfilment, its satisfaction. A great and essential drama has taken place overnight inside us, but there again nothing has actually happened, nothing has been done in the so-called shared world with anyone else. We have pleased ourselves without including anyone else. We have reversed the dependency of infancy and childhood – gathered it, in psychoanalytic language, within the range of our own omnipotence – and made the fulfilment of wishes a matter of self-contained fantasy.

Now it is self-evident that a meal we dream of eating may be satisfying but it will never be nourishing. We cannot live by dreams alone, even if, as Freud suggests, we want to, and indeed try to each night. At some point, in some way, if we are to survive psychically, desire has to be brought to bear on a real object. At whatever cost, and Freud believes that it is at considerable if not actually unbearable cost, we have to bring our wishes into some kind of exchange with external reality. And a lot of psychoanalytic writing after Freud is precisely about this, about adding to the repertoire of descriptions of what our wishing does to reality and vice versa. But it is clear that for Freud, at least – if not always for his followers and critics – the dream has a special place in his thinking about our relations with reality.

In one version of his account he has what might be called a logical, almost commonsensical, view of the process by which the developing individual gets to reality with its inevitable frustrations, but very real satisfactions. And it is a view that has been taken up, certainly by Winnicott and Bion in the British tradition, and become part of mainstream psychoanalytic thinking. Freud says, in his 'Formulations on the Two Principles of Psychic Functioning' of 1911, that he 'developed' these thoughts in *The Interpretation of Dreams* but is now reiterating them because they are no less than the definitive account of something momentous. 'The state of equilibrium in the psyche,' he writes,

> was originally disrupted by the urgent demands of inner needs. At this stage, whatever was thought of (wished for) was simply hallucinated, as still happens every night with our dream thoughts. It was due only to the failure of the anticipated satisfaction, the disillusionment as it were, that this attempt at satisfaction by means of hallucination was abandoned. Instead, the psychic apparatus had to resolve to form an idea of the real circumstances in the outside world and to endeavour actually to change them. With this, a new principle of psychic activity was initiated; now ideas were formed no longer of what was pleasant but of what was real, even if this happened to be unpleasant. This inception of the *reality principle* proved to be a momentous step.

We have an inner need, a desire; we hallucinate, we fantasize its satisfaction; that is, we fast-forward the wish to its fulfilment, and this is pleasant for a bit. But then we notice we are still in need, and that the only way we are going to be properly satisfied is by finding what we want in the external world, or by changing the external world so it gives up to us what we want. Reality is our second choice but our best option; we feel it is our worst option because once we move out of self-satisfying states we are prey to a proliferating range of feelings and conflict. We had tried for an efficient narrow-mindedness in relation to our wishing, but we have to open things up; we have to, as we say, get involved with other people; other people who, of course, are engaged in a similar project but from different histories and genetic endowments.

And yet, Freud also says, the dream works because we don't do this; and not only that, but when Freud starts writing exclusively about the dream he begins to wonder what it would be to wake up, and whether in fact it is possible. The story in the 'Formulations on the Two Principles' is really rather reassuring in one, limited sense: it says that there is a reality principle, a reality we can get to; that we can 'abandon' attempts at satisfaction through hallucination; that, in short, it is possible to wake up. That, in Sir Thomas Browne's words, there is a genuine alternative available to us, we don't need to order our affairs by dreams, or 'make the night a rule unto the day'. The dream when we are asleep works because it is the guardian of sleep; the hallucination in waking life doesn't work, indeed must not work if we are to survive. The hallucination in waking life must be abandoned; the dream when we are asleep must not be. But the dream works because we are not in a position to abandon it. There is a difference between containing desire and satisfying it. Freud, we might say, is wondering whether the best container of desire is the one that leads to its real, rather than its fantasized, satisfaction. Freud is considering, through speaking of the dream, whether desire, as it is for modern human animals, isn't often or mostly best satisfied in fantasy, when the individual is effectively immobilized. Hallucination and dream may not ultimately work for hunger – or, indeed, for the need to sleep – but they may work for the desires that are sexual. After all, if unconscious desire is forbidden, is incestuous, where can it better be conducted than in fantasy? Transgression when we are asleep wreaks less havoc than it does when we are awake. Fantasies are, of course, actions, and therefore we can feel guilty about them; but, Freud intimates, the guilt of fantasy may be more bearable than the guilt of action. In dreams responsibilities end.

So, on the one hand, Freud is saying: the safest time and place to desire is at night in your sleep, when you are at your most solitary. And this is not an especially new thought; sex is for daydream, for art, for sublimation; is best done by not doing it. What D. H. Lawrence called disdainfully 'sex in the head' is the best place for it. This acknowledges that for all sorts of reasons sex disturbs us and we will go to great lengths not to engage in it; indeed, one of our best ways of not engaging in it *is* engaging in it, getting rid of sex through sex, as Winnicott called it. But then, on the other hand, there is the more interesting thought that Freud needs dreaming in order to articulate; and this is that it may be impossible for us to wake up to our desire, to fully acknowledge it; that our project is not exactly, as Lacan said, to escape from our desire, but to maintain the guardians of our sleep. It's not that we can't bear reality, it's that we can't bear our desire; and this means, in part, that we can't bear what it leads us into, the labyrinthine entanglements of conflicting feeling. Dreams are simple, intelligible and innocent in their virtuality; reality is complicated, bewildering, and we are never innocent in our dealings with it. No one likes the ways they lose things, so finding is preferred. Dreams are the way we talk about the unintelligibility of reality, and about the ways in which we acknowledge this. Desire, that is to say, makes sense only in dreams. And that is why, Freud seems to suggest, there is no waking up for us.

The Uses of Desire

Religious moderates are, in large part, responsible for the
religious conflicts in our world, because their beliefs provide
the context in which scriptural literalism and religious
violence can never be adequately opposed.

Sam Harris, *The End of Faith*

I

'If we consider just the verbal expression of intention,' Elizabeth Anscombe writes in her book *Intention*,

> we arrive only at its being a – queer – species of prediction; and
> if we try to look for what it is an expression of, we are likely to
> find ourselves in one or other of several dead ends, e.g.: psychological jargon about 'drives' and 'sets'; reduction of intention to
> a species of desire, i.e., a kind of emotion; or irreducible intuition of the meaning of 'I intend'.

It is, indeed, true that in psychoanalytic writing – which is more
often than not 'psychological jargon about "drives" and "sets"' –
desire often sounds like a strange, rather glamorized form of
intentionality. An intentionality with no identifiable agent, and
with no discernible end. It seems to describe some kind of emergency about purpose. It seems to be making some kind of
mockery of intention as traditionally conceived and discussed.
Or it is another way of talking about something akin to intention that the language of intention can't deal with. In
psychoanalytic writing the word is used either as utterly and
undistractedly ordinary – as an obvious synonym for strong

wanting or biologically based need – or as distractingly privileged. That we desire, that we have desires, is not news; the *OED* has the noun and the verb in Middle English. That there may be something – call it a force or a drift or an energy or a shifty line-up of words – at work inside us or between us despite our best intentions, that has not a mind of its own but ways of its own; that we may be neither masters nor servants in our own houses but something else apparently unheard of; this is, depending on one's inclinations, or perhaps affiliations, either startling or merely mystifying. For some psychoanalysts, using this word keeps them psychoanalytic; and for others, not using it, or using it as though one wasn't particularly using it, has become a statement of intent. And what is at stake here, I think, is something about intelligibility and its uses; and something about that form of intelligibility called prediction. Desire as a keyword – as a term of affiliation, as an attempt to legitimate psychoanalysis as a science of the uncanny – is indeed a queer species of prediction; predicting, as it does at its most glib, unpredictability, and, at its most ironic, predicting hope. In talking about desire, at least from a psychoanalytic point of view, we are talking about the genealogy, the provenance, of hope; even when that hope is a hoping for death. We are talking about the unpredictability of aliveness in the human subject; and the forms of death-in-life, the modern forms of death-in-life, that psychoanalysis sets itself the task of addressing. Psychoanalysis describes what happens when we live as if our wishes can come true; and what happens when we live as if they can't.

In Laplanche and Pontalis's formative dictionary, *The Language of Psychoanalysis*, there is no entry for 'desire'; but there is an entry which reads: 'Wish (desire)'. A translator's note tells us that 'French psychoanalysis uses *désir* for all these words' – that is, lust, desire, wish – but that desire as an English term is best used to talk about wishing. But then there are two concluding paragraphs of the entry about Lacan's 'attempt to reorientate Freud's doctrine around the notion of desire, and to replace this notion in the forefront of analytic theory' (the translator's 'reorientate' for the 'recentre' of the original slightly lowers the temperature of what is being said and done). In making their brief case for Lacan's *désir* Laplanche and Pontalis are characteristically and pointedly lucid. 'This perspective,' they write,

> has led Lacan to distinguish desire from concepts with which it is often confused, such as need and demand. Need is directed towards a specific object and is satisfied by it. Demands are formulated and addressed to others; where they are still aimed at an object, this is not essential to them, since the articulated demand is essentially a demand for love.
>
> Desire appears in the rift which separates need and demand; it cannot be reduced to need since, by definition, it is not a relation to a real object independent of the subject but a relation to fantasy; nor can it be reduced to demand, in that it seeks to impose itself without taking the language or the unconscious of the other into account, and insists upon absolute recognition from him.

What is the problem, then, that Lacan is wanting to solve or to elaborate with the notion of desire? What does he want desire to do for him here? At its most minimal, the problem for Lacan is that there is a misleading straightforwardness, a bewitching empiricism, about need and demand. It is as though both concepts take for granted exactly what psychoanalysis, in Lacan's version, puts into question. Need and demand are such sensible transactions, such pragmatic exchanges, that they are more like contracts, or agreements; more like the kinds of thing people without unconscious desire (or thought) would arrange for themselves. The notions of need and demand are rife with assumptions; the performers of such needs and demands are relatively transparent to themselves and to the people (or objects) they recruit for their quasi-biological rituals. Need has a definite and definitive object, and is satisfiable. Demand – which is essentially and intelligibly a demand for love – is unambiguously formulable – is heard as such by its addressee. The notion of desire is brought in by Lacan to expose, as it were, the unreality of human wanting. The object of desire is a fantasy; wanting goes on in a virtually closed system of wishing; we want something, though we don't know what it is, from someone who doesn't exist. And our needs, as demands, can never be in the form of orders – demanding can never be a straightforward instrumental operation – because language is the language of the unconscious. To speak is to want – and to be heard to be wanting – otherwise than one intends. Indeed, the whole notion of an intention, from this point of view, is a defensive trimming of the way language ranges. With the concept of desire Lacan is showing us the ways in which our wanting cannot be an object of knowledge. He is wanting us to see how psychoanalysis, his version of psychoanalysis, ironizes our favourite idea of knowing what we want. Desire asks us to mind the gap between our wanting and our knowing. When I claim to know what I want – and I would claim this with inflexible rigour in what psychoanalysis would call a perverse state of mind; my so-called perversion is a knowing exactly what I want and need; when I claim to know what I want I have already constituted an 'I' that I recognize by its predictive talents, and by its already familiar and looked-forward-to states of satisfaction; this 'I' has a repertoire of relatively formulable wants, formulable in a medium deemed to be an effective tool for want-gratification. In this picture, whether I am satisfied, whether I get what I want, is to do with my competence, my relative efficiency as a wanter; there is nothing about the nature of wanting itself that is a problem. The machine works if one can find a skilled operator. After all, our survival as one of Darwin's species has meant that something about our wanting has worked, even if Darwin hasn't quite plucked out the heart of the mystery.

Lacan's critique of the 'adaptationism' of American ego-psychology is, therefore, from his own point of view, only a continuation of what Freud started with psychoanalysis: providing certain kinds of description of the unfit between modern people and their internal and external environments. It was only through certain forms of suffering – through the adaptations of suffering – that modern life was bearable. What Lacan's notion of desire adds to our modern picture of our unease is that when we attend to the medium of wanting, language – both our agency and the way our wanting actually works – is put into question. It was clear that Freud knew that language was what psychoanalysis was about; but what he didn't have was the modern science of linguistics. So desire refers, as it were, to the non-instrumental unreason of our wanting. But it also refers to something of Freud's that Lacan took with unusual and insistent seriousness and wit; and this is the incest taboo. The fact that the object of desire is a forbidden object; that what we most passionately want is what we most certainly mustn't have. The medium of desire is enigmatic; and the object of desire is aversive. How we want is baffling, and what we want is impossible. When Lacan says, as a kind of advertising slogan – as an advertisement of the modern – 'man's desire is desire of the Other', he is saying that we desire what others desire (we desire by identification), and that our desire is other to what we think of ourselves as desiring. But this means that our desire is nothing to do with us; that there is desire, but not for us. 'It' comes from a wholly other outside and/or a wholly other inside; the so-called I is a middle man in no man's land. Lacan's psychoanalytic sentences serve to estrange us from what seems most intimate, most immediate about ourselves; it makes our wanting integral by being alien. The concept of desire, one might say, is part of Lacan's estrangement technique; his psychoanalytic attempt to avert the domestication of the drives through ethology and bourgeois morality (and the bourgeois morality that is ethology). Desire, as a concept, keeps something alive in psychoanalysis.

What it keeps alive, I think, is the hope involved in not knowing what we want. Desire, I want to suggest – whether or not

Lacan suggests this – refers to the fact that the fantasy of knowing what one wants is a form of despair. And that what the incest taboo compels us to do is to give up both the knowledge of what we want, and to give up on knowing what we want. Because what we know we want is impossible – our psychic life depends upon our not, as it were, getting it – we have to find what it is about our wanting that is possible. We are fully alive only when our wants surprise us. The Oedipus complex says to us: when it comes to wanting you must not be essentialists; you thought hope springs from knowing what you want, but actually it comes from abjuring the magic that that knowledge is. Desire is the queer form our unpredictability takes. Where intentions were, there accidents of pleasure shall be. Desire, as I am using it, takes our pleasures to be happy accidents, and accidents will happen.

II

I want to suggest that the antonym of desire is what psychoanalysts call perversion, which I would rather call an anxious narrowing of the mind when it comes to pleasure. An intent knowingness – a determined and determining knowing what one wants – characterizes so-called sexual perversions. The person in a perverse state of mind has no conscious doubt about what will excite and satisfy him. He is sceptical, if he is sceptical at all, only about the critics of his object of desire. And he becomes concerned about his unappeasable self-knowledge only when it makes him suffer too much. Scepticism becomes a defeat (for the ego), a fall into too much unhappiness. But, above all, in a perverse state of mind, pleasures can be calculated, satisfactions can be arranged for the self, often by the self. It's a set-up. What psychoanalysts in the past have tended to call perversions – or, rather more circumspectly, perverse states of mind – could also be described as a given individual's self-cure for the problem Lacan articulates in his useful distinction (despite the problems of translation) between need, demand and desire. The individual is deemed to have biological needs, covered by the traditional concept of instinct; but the beginning individual has to make his need known in the form of a demand. And this is where the complications occur; because the infant is not self-satisfying, he recruits, through vocalization, another in order to live. There is, Lacan suggests, a split between need and demand; the finite need to be fed contains within it an infinite demand for love. The mother can satisfy the child's need but she can never fulfil the demand for love. In this meeting of need, and this unmeeting of demand, something insatiable persists; and this Lacan calls desire. In his view there is no such thing as pure need; all hungers are informed by, contaminated by, the pressure of desire. To ask for anything is to ask for everything. Need is the fall guy of desire. 'And just as the symbolic function of the object as a proof of love overshadows its real function,' Dylan Evans writes in *An Introductory Dictionary of Lacanian Psychoanalysis*, 'as that which satisfies a need, so too the symbolic dimension of demand (as a demand for love) eclipses its real function (as an articulation of need).' The question Lacan is asking, is using the concept of desire to ask, is what is the demand for love a demand for? What happens, as in so-called perversions, when the demand for love is pre-empted by or located in an apparently recognizable object? If, say, the demand for love is a demand for hope, what kind of hope is there in a shoe? It's all about keeping ourselves hungry and unharmed.

Lacan is stringent – indeed, at his most starkly insistent – about just how misleading is our desire to recognize the objects of our desire. As though all our talents for representation were to reassure us that representation works. That we can know what we want; and, at least in principle, at least logically, get it. That our terror inspires us to try to reduce all desire to need, and all demand to instrumental reason. That we can know what we want, and because we can know it we could have it. I want to wonder in this essay what the terror is that might make us want to abolish desire in favour of biological need and unambiguous demand. Why, in other words, should we dream of a language that is unbluffing, and of a love that is fathomable?

In Lacan's view, the answer in shorthand is that we are phobic about lack; that the experience of lack is a kind of psychic devastation, a destitution that makes us want to believe that lack is like a question which has an answer. It makes us simple-minded, literal-minded in our picturing; if something is empty it can be filled. If something is empty it is empty of something. We become mathematical and think of proportions and equations; of measuring what's missing; of making a felt absence intelligible, as in two halves in search of each other. Or we think in terms of completion or perfection or closure; whatever it is that would make my life what it could and should be. Man's project is to escape from his desire, Lacan famously said, because on the daydream horizon there is the absence of conflict and the abolition of lack. In Lacan's – and, indeed, Freud's – anti-utopia there is only the (ironic) permanence of the wanting Lacan calls desire; the only reliable object – the only object one can depend upon – is what one is lacking. And what this lack itself, by definition, lacks is accurate representation. The perversion version of ourselves seems to know, seems to register, exactly what turns us on; what absorbs and possesses us; what makes us dreamy. And yet, Lacan suggests, this is itself a cover story; this is how we ablate our terror, this is how we assuage the enigma of our desiring. Lacan urges us – against the blandishments of American ego-psychology and British object-relations; against the utilitarian lures of behaviourism – to face the unknowingness of desiring. And for Lacan the unknowingness of desiring is not merely or simply or solely a problem; it is a psychic necessity. All the so-called pathologies of modern desiring are states of virtual conviction – conscious conviction – about the object of desire. Either a person seems to know what they want or, with equal certainty, not know what they want. The knowing is apparently intact. For Lacan, at least in his Seminar II, it is precisely such unassailable recognitions that Freud has challenged. 'The domain of the Freudian experience,' Lacan writes,

> is established within a very different register of relations. Desire is a relation of being to lack. This lack is the lack of being properly speaking. It isn't the lack of this or that, but lack of being whereby the being exists. This lack is beyond anything which can represent it . . .
>
> We necessarily believe that, at the centre, things are really there, solid, established, waiting to be recognized, and that the conflict is marginal. But what does the Freudian experience teach us? If not that what happens in the domain of so-called consciousness, that is on the level of the recognition of objects, is equally misleading in relation to what the being is looking for? In so far as the libido creates the different stages of the object, the objects are never it . . .
>
> Desire, a function central to all human experience, is the desire for nothing nameable. And at the same time this desire lies at the origin of every variety of animation. If being were only what it is, there wouldn't even be room to talk about it. Being comes into existence as an exact function of this lack, in the experience of desire . . .
>
> The self-conscious being, transparent to itself, which classical theory places at the centre of human experience . . . says – I'm the one who knows that I am. Unfortunately, if it does perhaps know that it is, it knows nothing at all about what it is. That is what is lacking in every being.

The metaphysical incantation of lack and being can be wearying; though the rhythms of Lacan's baroque liturgy seem somehow integral to the void he pursues and is clearly so enchanted by. But I am less interested in the persuasiveness or otherwise of Lacan's quasi-Freudian assertions than I am in whatever it is he is trying to work with; and how he cannot do without the notion of desire. His dual and complementary insistences here – that lack makes being, self-conscious being, possible; and that the object of desire is unnameable, essentially beyond representation – say: if you can name it, it isn't what you want. Desiring is privileged over satisfaction; and desiring depends upon not knowing what one wants. It is perhaps not surprising that for some people this has seemed rather more theological than traditionally psychoanalytic in its affiliations. Once again, one might say, it pits idolatory against true desiring; and even though the desiring being spoken of is irredeemably carnal, it sounds intractably metaphysical. Lacan is ironic but not earthy; he is witty, but like all psychoanalysts he is not bawdy.

Lacan insists that what he calls 'the self-conscious being, transparent to itself' knows nothing at all about what it is. This may overstate the case – and the self-conscious being transparent to itself has surely never quite existed, except as an apt caricature of scientistic, mercantile man – but it may also be a psychoanalytic way of stressing that knowing and wanting go uneasily together. So Lacan is a useful springboard to say something simple that perhaps could not have been said before psychoanalysis, or could not have been said in the same way; that knowing what one wants is a form of terror, and therefore a form of terrorism (of oneself and of others). And so to talk about desire might be to talk about the beneficence of this form of unknowing. We are familiar with what Laplanche in *Life and Death in Psychoanalysis* has called 'the attack of the drives on the ego'; with a human subject constituted by his aversion to his own nature, or thrown by his relation to the forbidden. But there is also a paradoxical kind of freedom in not needing to know what one wants, while knowing that one wants. What Lacan calls desire is the impossibility of such knowing; and yet this is the knowing that we seem to be doing, and wanting to do, much of the time. We have to imagine a wanting not in the form of a knowing.

What psychoanalysts tend to call perversions describe a state of frantic certainty; a knowledge of what is needed for excitement, a fear of its unavailability or of its unavailingness (that is, it's not working); and an often repressed doubt (or question) about its moral worth. Perversion could be construed as the antonym of desire; as the individual's self-cure for desiring. A pre-emptive strike against the differentness of another person – of their unknownness to themselves and to oneself – the perverse act requires accomplices rather than collaborators. As a calculated staging it aims to minimize surprise or shock; as though what is being acknowledged is just how distractable one is when it comes to excitement. It is as though sexuality is only viable, is doable, so to speak, only when the preconditions for sustaining excitement, for sustaining interest, are known beforehand. A perverse act, one could say, is one in which nothing must be discovered. In this sense perversion might just mean whatever is the enemy of the new, whatever is horrified by the future (the past may be knowable, unlike the future). The hope in a perverse act is that the future will be just like the past. Desire, one can see, has a quite different sense of what hope is: for the desiring subject the future is an object of desire, but the future in all its indescribable promise (the future is not a retirement home for achieved and therefore discarded projects). It would be like hoping for whatever actually happens.

It would be worth wondering, in order to get some sense of what desiring might be, what the preconditions are, from a psychoanalytic point of view, for perversion. What is the terror that informs the need to know what one wants; or that would make a person translate the demand for love into the demand for nameable excitement?

III

In the contemporary non-Lacanian psychoanalytic writing about so-called perversion there is, if not a virtual consensus, at least an overlapping of preoccupations about the provenance of perverse solutions; and, indeed, a shared sense that what are called, diagnostically, perversions are solutions to developmental conflicts. And these perverse solutions are described in terms of revenge, mastery and repair. The emphasis in these accounts is on the mother/infant, mother/child relationship; and they circle around the (relative) helplessness of the child vis-à-vis maternal care, and the hostility mobilized by this helplessness.

'Perversion, the erotic form of hatred,' Robert Stoller writes in *Perversion*,

> is a fantasy, usually acted out but occasionally restricted to a daydream (either self-produced or packaged by others – that is, pornography). It is a habitual, preferred aberration necessary for one's full satisfaction, primarily motivated by hostility. By hostility I mean a state in which one wishes to harm an object . . . The hostility in perversion takes form in a fantasy of revenge hidden in the actions that make up the perversion and serves to convert childhood trauma to adult triumph.

'There are those that fuck from desire,' Masud Khan writes more starkly in *Alienation in Perversion*, 'and those that fuck from intent. The latter are the perverts. Because intent, by definition, implies the exercise of will and power to achieve its ends, whereas desire entails mutuality and reciprocity for its gratification.' 'The pervert,' Khan says, 'puts an impersonal object between his desire and his accomplice: this object can be a stereotype fantasy, a gadget or a pornographic image. All three alienate the pervert from himself as, alas, from the object of his desire.' Without intent, without this impersonal object, the person, we must assume, feels radically endangered. For Stoller perversion is sex as hatred; for Khan it is – unlike what he calls desire – it is sex as erotic engineering. In both cases the object wanted is experienced primarily as threat. In other words, the so-called pervert acts as though he knows what to expect; because he knows what other people are like – he knows, that is, what they want to do with him – he has learned how to manage them for his own excitement. It is the immediacy of the other, wanted person that has to be mediated, either by hatred and/or the impersonal object. The satisfactions all seem to be in the direction of distancing and controlling the person who is, apparently, wanted. But it is rather as though the other person is wanted as a kind of excitement experiment; what is being tested is whether one can get excited in the presence of another person and psychically survive. Desire – which in Khan's language involves mutuality and reciprocity – as the alternative to perversion would seem to entail something like wanting the very unknownness of the other person; as though what one desired was their sentient presence. There would, in other words, be two differently desiring subjects in the room; both of whom are unconscious of their desire.

Dehumanization tends to be the term of choice when it comes to perversion, though this, of course, puts the cart before the horse; that is to say, it claims a privileged knowledge of the human in order to do its talking, when it is the human, as Lacan insisted, that is always at stake. But then, by the same token, it is in writing about dehumanization that people can formulate their versions of the human. For Arnold Cooper 'dehumanization is the ultimate strategy' in perversion; and 'the attempt to dehumanize', he writes in an instructive synthesis of Khan and Stoller, 'The Unconscious Core of Perversions', 'is carried out through the use of three specific fantasies':

> the perversion is always a result of mixtures of three key unconscious fantasies constructed in the perverse defence against fears of passivity when confronted with maternal malevolence. These fantasies are all efforts to deny the experience of being the helpless, needy baby at the mercy of a frustrating, cruel mother. First fantasy: 'I need not be frightened because my mother is really non-existent; that is, she is dead or mechanical, and I am in complete control.' Second fantasy: 'I need not be frightened because I am beyond being controlled by my malicious mother because I am myself non-human – that is, dead and unable to

feel pain – or less than human, a slave who can only be acted upon rather than act.' And third: 'I triumph and am in total control because no matter what cruelty my squashing, castrating, gigantic monster mother creature visits upon me, I can extract pleasure from it, and therefore she (it) is doing my bidding.' . . . these three unconscious fantasies . . . erase passivity by denying human maternal control of oneself as human, by defensively converting active to passive, and by extracting pleasure out of being controlled. These three fantasies deny that the mother has hurt or can hurt the child. In effect the infant says, '(1) She doesn't exist, (2) I don't exist, (3) I force her – now a non-human "it" – to give me pleasure.'

The project in this sexualized process is self-protection and restoration; it is essentially a turning of the tables, a getting even for the victimizations of childhood. And what is most striking in these three descriptions is that the so-called pervert acts as if he knows so much about the person he wants; and so much work, so much psychic work, goes into acting on this supposed knowledge. As if to say: you know the other person, and yourself in relation to the other person, in order to take revenge on them. Knowing oneself and others is in the service of self-protection. Desire, by contrast, could be described as non-vengeful wanting. Its aim is not restoration, but a making new.

The vengeful wanting that is perversion is a return to a scene, to a drama already suffered; the non-vengeful wanting that I want to call desiring has nothing and no one to return to. Vengeful wanting, one could say, is productive of the illusion of invulnerability. Where once I was the object-victim of another's psychic need – another whose need I needed in order to survive – now I can, in Stoller's words, 'convert childhood trauma to adult triumph'. Like someone who cracks codes in order to be able to use them himself, I have become, in a certain sense, knowledgeable about my past. Even if I inflict on others a version of what was inflicted on me, I can now, at least, work the system. Indeed – and this is my greatest triumph perhaps – where once I suffered now I can enjoy. Because I can now, in Cooper's terms, 'extract pleasure' from my mother's domination, it is as though she is 'doing my bidding' (and the pun may be instructive here; a bid is at once an offer, a command and a calling). It is like learning a skill or, perhaps more exactly, it is like acquiring the tricks of a trade. There are, above all, two tricks, two quasi-redemptive magical acts: first, where suffering and confusion were once inflicted and endured, now, by a kind of psychic alchemy, pleasures are made available (now, I am saying, secretly or otherwise, you think you are hurting me, but actually I am gleefully happy, I am delirious with success). And second, where once I was the target, object and instrument of the other person's need, I am now the one in charge; I have made the drama my own; my subjectivity, my sense of myself, is made, is fabricated, out of the materials I have endured. I have, as it were, made it my vocation to convert childhood traumas into adult triumphs; to devise impersonal objects – stereotype fantasies, gadgets, pornographic images, prejudices, hobbies and hobby-horses – to hold myself together as a pleasure-seeker. Of course, excitement itself can become one of these impersonal objects. Above all, in my (excited) dealings with other people I will decide the nature of the exchange that will take place. I will administer the occasion, I will be doing the pleasure deal. And in my dealings, wittingly or unwittingly, I will always have recourse to the past. I will be resorting to the check-points of childhood traumas; I will be driven to go on rescuing myself from situations and exchanges of which I am largely unconscious. My pleasure will be that once again I have survived my history; the confounding rigours of my past, far from undoing me, have glued me together again.

This is why Stoller's term 'conversion' – the converting of childhood trauma into adult triumph – is so apt. Trauma is loss of confidence; the shattering of belief; the traumatized individual (all of us) has to somehow convert himself – usually through converting others – into some kind of triumphalist. What we call perversion is our secular, sexualized, ersatz form of redemption. The so-called pervert – the perverse part of ourselves – lives in an empty afterlife of having survived sexual excitement. Sex is used to get rid of sex, to ditch excitement. Because it was the impinging excitements of childhood – the rages and frustrations and gratifications and confoundments – that couldn't be borne. Those were the experiences of childhood that couldn't be transformed; they could only be stored, like secret weapons, in order eventually to be expelled. Perversion, it would be more exact, and exacting, to say, bears witness to whatever is irredeemable in experience. Revenge is nostalgia.

IV

Perversion, then, is a sacrifice of sorts; it sacrifices surprise, it sacrifices mutuality, it sacrifices the resonance of the other person and oneself. It sacrifices, in other words, the future in the name of the past. By getting even, by attempting to restore an impossible invulnerability, by willing an anti-romance of efficient excitement, perverse acts are characterized, at least in psychoanalytic writing, by their determination, by their ambition. They are like the hauntings that make people mechanical, the pieces of the past that make us feel programmed, or even robotic. It is the redress of the past that makes the past seem ineluctable. It reiterates, through unconscious memory, the trauma it seeks to undo.

I want to suggest – prompted by Lacan, but quite at odds with his account – that desire can be a way of talking about an alternative to what psychoanalysts (and others) have described, albeit unfortunately, as perversion. In my version desire is not so much in opposition to perversion as at odds with it. As a story about un- or non-vengeful wanting it depends upon our being surprised by our pleasures; pleasure ceases to be, as it were, part of our calculations; and is more like luck than justice. In this account we do not suffer from not knowing what we want, because knowing what we want is something we cannot do. Indeed, the phrase 'knowing what we want' is like Anscombe's queer species of prediction. Knowing what one wanted would be like knowing what the future holds; wishing is what we do about the future and this, as Freud went to great lengths to show us, is different from knowing (knowing the future, knowing my future satisfactions, is perverse in the sense that it makes me seem more powerful, more omniscient, than I really am). Desire, in short, is the wanting that comes from the part of ourselves that is without grievance. And if such a part of oneself seems unimaginable it is because perverse wanting is, by definition, such a stark tyranny. When our grudges are suffocating we really know we are omniscient. So my tag would be, not: where id was there ego should be; but: where perversion is, there desire should be. Perversion would be described, would be analysed, as: all the ways I have of keeping myself in the know. Desire would be described as all the ways we can find of replacing knowledge with hope. Falling in love is when what I am calling desire begins (again) to contend with perversion, to stake a claim. Indeed, any experience that would have been described in old-fashioned language as a passion I would describe as a clash and a collaboration between perverse intent and hopeful desiring. For the desiring self it will always be the surprises sprung rather than the programmes entailed that will be the real draw. For the desiring self ideology all too often sounds like more of the same.

By way of conclusion – or perhaps by way of elaboration – I want to suggest that if the term 'desire' should be reserved for the unpreordained, then the two forms of sexuality, the two forms of wanting that I am describing, might be akin to two ways of writing history. Perversion is like a revisionism that keeps failing; it is the 'true' story of a subject people seeking justice and redress. But their zeal is born of terror, so they terrorize. They can't afford their doubts about themselves – about the stories they tell themselves about themselves – because they equate doubt with injustice and intimidation. Perverse history is triumphalist; self-protective and self-justifying. Perverse history is excessively patriotic; it is nationalist propaganda. What other kinds of history could there be, except the history that keeps returning to the scene of the crime, to the trauma that forged the sense of nationality?

Desire, by (my) definition, is unprepared; it has not been equipped or instructed or even inspired by the past. It has nothing substantive to recollect or recycle. It could never be, like perverse history, the history of the future; or a story about how history will reward our intentions. It is not a form of prospecting or divination; nor is it a form of wishing as a conventionally transitive act. You can't exactly wish to be surprised because this would mitigate against the experience of being surprised. The past is carried in our expectations, which make our shocks and surprises possible. But the new is anything that by definition modifies such expectations as we have. And Lacan's notion of lack implies a subject already too knowing – too consciously or unconsciously sensible – of himself as a set; too mindful of himself as a plenitude depleted. From the point of view of desire, in my sense of it, we are not lacking what we find; the notion of lack is our retrospective rationalization, our coherent narrative, about finding as recovering. There can be addition where nothing was previously missing. I would notice, in other words, that what I might call my expectations and assumptions, far from being exclusively baggage from the past, are also forms of omniscience. The perverse version of the self is replete with expectations.

So the history of my desiring self would also be a history of pleasurable experiences unwarranted by expectation. It would not, therefore, be a history of my achieved intentions; nor could it be a success story in terms of obligations met and ambitions secured (it would have no truck with the self as predictor or reader of omens and portents). It would be a story that would disfigure my wish (or my talent) for coherent narrative. It would be a story about how my stories were interrupted or broke down or didn't hang together. It would, to all intents and purposes, be a history of accidents and anomalies; all convincingly pleasurable but of uncertain consequence. Not a history of intentions realigned by circumstance, but a story of lucky coincidences, for which no credit could be taken by anyone (or anything), and from which no resentment could ensue.

Need makes perfect biological sense. The demand for love – however exorbitant, however unconscious its sources, and however ironic its consequences – is a consoling and exhilarating and sensible intention for people like us who have heard and overheard so much about love. Need and the demand for love are indeed the queer species of prediction we are born into. But desire is wanting as a species of luck.

Talking Nonsense and Knowing When to Stop

Tyrants always want language and literature that is
easily understood.

Theodor Hacker, *Notes*

I want to start with two propositions and entangle them with a view to saying something about the vexed question of endings in psychoanalysis, and about what, if anything, the issue of endings in psychoanalysis has to tell us about endings elsewhere. The first proposition is that it is impossible to know the consequences of one's words – the spoken, the heard and the overheard. The analyst can never predict the effect that his words will have on the so-called patient, and vice versa. So, for example, whatever psychoanalytic training is, it can never train people to know what to say when, if knowing what to say means knowing what one's words can do for the patient. By the same token, one can be taught what to listen out for, but, by definition, one could never be prepared for the surprising, for whatever it is about someone else's words that is peculiarly evocative. Lacan was referring to this when he said that if the analyst has been properly analysed, he is more not less likely to fall in love with the patient. However well educated one is about one's unprotectedness, the words used are unpredictable in their effect. Language is to the speaker and listener what the dream-day is to the dreamer, idiosyncratically enlivening. Learning to speak, learning to interpret, is never merely learning what to say. Learning to listen can only be learning – if that is the right word – to bear what listening calls up in you. It would have been better if Freud had said: speaking and listening is like dreaming in language. What is called interpretation is the dream evoked by a dream. It is impossible to know the consequences of one's words, the spoken, the heard and the overheard.

The second proposition is – to adapt Valéry's famous remark about completing a poem – that an analysis is never finished, it is only abandoned. And in this, despite suggestions to the contrary, the so-called analytic relationship is like, or at least similar to, every other so-called relationship. The language of completion is unsuitable for what goes on between people. It is possible to know that one no longer sees someone, no longer has sex with someone; it is less possible to know whether one no longer thinks of someone. Indeed, one of the things psychoanalysis reveals is just how haunted we are, in spite of ourselves, by other selves, by bits and pieces of others. It is impossible, though, to know when or whether a relationship has ended. Or what it is for a relationship to end, rather than change. And yet the idea that a psychoanalysis must end – or, indeed, that one of the things that makes it so-called real analysis is that it is undertaken with a view to its ending by consent or decision rather than death – is more or less taken for granted (though perhaps in different ways) by both the practitioners and the recipients of the psychoanalytic opportunity. The opportunity of the psychoanalytic relationship is, for some people, precisely the opportunity of working through, as they would say, the ending of a relationship – something that rarely happens, and never happens in this special way, in ordinary life. 'Cure' is the psychoanalytic word for the happy ending.

The assumption that a psychoanalysis must end – and, ideally, that it must end in a particular way that can be described and taught to the aspiring practitioner – is itself an assumption worth analysing and is something that both Freud and Winnicott were exercised by. If, say, there is a sense in which what we call relationships never end, then there is a sense in which what we call mourning may be, for want of a better word, unrealistic.

(If it was a how-to book, it would be called *How to Go On Having a Relationship with Someone Who Isn't There*.) If, as Freud suggests, pleasure-seeking or unconscious desire is unceasing, if the unconscious is timeless and without contradiction, then a capacity to bear frustration settles nothing. It is not about something ending but about something stopping. That wanting is endless, and that we have to have a sense of an ending; that desire is transgressive; that we fear loss of love, loss of the object and castration — these are the preoccupations at the heart of psychoanalysis. Endings in the plural — endings as experiences that go on happening — are what psychoanalysis is about: frustration and taboo, murderousness and the limits of one's life encompassed by the word 'death'. Endings are to psychoanalysis what full stops are to punctuation: they refer to, they arrange, a transition. Whether they are formal periods of hesitation — a resistance to going on that looks like a satisfactory place to end — always remains to be seen. One of the best things Winnicott did for psychoanalysis was to add the word 'transition' to its vocabulary. And this is because of what it does to the idea of endings, to the strange notion of knowing when to stop. An analysis is never finished, it is only abandoned.

I want to suggest that what are loosely called endings in analysis should often be called something else, but that a capacity for abandon, and the abandon that is abandonment, could be one of the things we might hope to get from a psychoanalysis. Giving up, or giving up on, is better than finishing because it acknowledges limitation in a way that the sense of a good ending never can. Endings are not there to be engineered by us; they (and we) are not that kind of thing. If a good ending is other than a great piece of luck, it can only be a contrived (that is, defensive) calculation. Endings, like so-called beginnings, are risks; there is nothing to tide us over except what happens next. If an analyst was described as being good at endings, we might wonder exactly what it was that he or she was so good at.

It may be useful to think of at least some endings in psychoanalysis in terms of knowing when to stop. And, to be more specific, knowing when to stop talking and knowing when to stop turning up. But what, from a psychoanalytic point of view, does knowing when to stop mean? If knowing and acting upon one's so-called knowledge are often so at odds with each other; if psychoanalysis makes us wonder, to put it mildly, who the knowing subject is; if the human subject is constituted by something unstoppable called, variously, unconscious desire, instinctual drives, lack – then how is the stopping going to happen? And even if we don't take psychoanalysis on its own terms, or at its word, the knowing-when-to-stop question turns up as one among many telling critiques of the psychoanalytic method. Is the analyst, for example, trained to know when to stop the patient associating, when to interrupt, given that association is both unpredictable in its rhythm and pace and uncircumscribable in its reach? Wittgenstein was famously struck by this in his discussion of Freud's method of dream interpretation. Freud, Wittgenstein is reported to have said in *Lectures and Conversations on Aesthetics, Psychology and Religious Belief*,

> wants to say that whatever happens in a dream will be found to be connected with some wish which analysis can bring to light. But this procedure of free association and so on is queer, because Freud never shows how we know where to stop – where is the right solution. Sometimes he says that the right solution, or the right analysis, is the one which satisfies the patient. Sometimes he says that the doctor knows what the right solution or analysis of the dream is, whereas the patient doesn't: the doctor can say that the patient is wrong. The reason why he calls one sort of analysis the right one does not seem to be a matter of evidence.

What Wittgenstein calls, wittily, Freud's 'procedure of free association and so on' is, of course, a matter of putting a stop to the 'and so on' of the patient's associations. How many associations are enough, and how could the analyst or the patient know whether the more telling, decisive associations lay up ahead, after the intervention that interrupted them? Clearly the phrase 'an associative chain' itself jumps to conclusions about pertinence. It is likely, after all, that knowing where to stop – at least from the patient's point of view – means knowing how to keep at bay the forgotten, the forbidden, the altogether unsettling material. Knowing and stopping can too easily be redescribed in psychoanalytic language as resisting. Knowing when to stop the flow (or otherwise) of associations can be, for both the analyst and the so-called patient, a mechanism of defence. A mechanism because it can have an automatic, seemingly inevitable quality; it feels right at that moment.

The queer things that Wittgenstein is picking up on are the puzzles and paradoxes associated with free association, and the resistances to it, as a procedure of truth-telling, of finding the right solution. 'Freud never shows how we know where to stop,' Wittgenstein says. But how could such a thing ever be shown? Where to stop cannot be known; it can only be tried out. And it will have been right not because the analyst could predict the effect of his intervention – that is, predict what the patient might say next – but because more valuable words will accrue from it. Knowing when to stop the associating makes no more sense than knowing when to stop dreaming, or knowing when to stop making slips.

The idea of knowing when to stop implies, perhaps, more coherence, more narrative structure, than is always available. We say that novels and pieces of music and films end, but not paintings; the painter finishes her painting, but that is not what the viewer does. The viewer walks away, abandons the picture, and may return to it. Winnicott suggests in *Playing and Reality* that for some people, sometimes, 'free association that reveals a coherent theme is already affected by anxiety, and the cohesion of ideas is a defence organization'. The patient's presenting or revealing a coherent theme, and, presumably the analyst interpreting a coherent theme in the associations, is a defence. The analyst's need to find, to articulate, a coherent theme, Winnicott intimates, may also be a defence organization. Psychoanalytic theory, we should remember, is always the presentation of a coherent theme. Knowing when to stop, in this context, means not allowing the nonsense to happen.

> Perhaps it is to be accepted that there are patients who at times need the therapist to note the nonsense that belongs to the mental state of the individual at rest without the need even for the patient to communicate this nonsense, that is to say, without the need for the patient to organize nonsense. Organized nonsense is already a defence, just as organized chaos is a denial of chaos. The therapist who cannot take this communication becomes engaged in a futile attempt to find some organization in the nonsense, as a result of which the patient leaves the nonsense area because of hopelessness about communicating nonsense. An opportunity for rest has been missed because of the therapist's need to find sense where nonsense is.

'An opportunity for rest has been missed,' Winnicott says; and it is rest from the vigilant self-holding that coherence involves. It should not be missed that in this passage (and elsewhere), Winnicott is describing a new need of the individual, the need to speak the nonsense that he is, the need for his incoherence to be accepted as such by another person; with the implication that, sometimes at least, our coherence is a front (and an affront to ourselves), including, of course, theories of psychoanalysis, such as Winnicott's. He is also describing a new kind of person. Winnicott is always careful on these writing occasions to stress that he is talking about a certain kind of patient or a patient at a certain kind of time in the treatment.

For him, it is the environmental deprivation that necessitates the vigilant self-holding of coherent narrative. The patient, let us say, as a child had recurring experiences of having to know when to stop forgetting himself; he was absorbed in whatever he was doing, and this was interrupted, periodically, by a bout of need, either his own need (the need for the object) or the object's need for him. The problem of need, the problem of demand, for Winnicott is that in his view it over-organizes the individual. There is the chaos born of need that misfires because the object is unable to respond adequately. Ideally, in what Winnicott calls 'the full course of the experience', the appetite experience has a more or less coherent narrative. There is dawning appetite, the breast is hallucinated, the hallucination fails to work and the baby cries, at which point a good-enough mother turns up, hungry to be eaten. For Winnicott, it is not about knowing when to stop, because, if all goes well, the process, as he calls it, has an inbuilt conclusion. Knowing when to stop in this picture could only equal inhibition about damaging the mother through appetite, or using the mind to control the process. Here, the individual has to make himself coherent against the problem of appetite; appetite is only chaotic, is only made chaotic, in Winnicott's view, by the object's insufficiency. Appetite will be a good story for you if you are lucky enough to have the right mother.

But what Winnicott is most interestingly attentive to is the ways in which the demand of the object over-organizes the individual by organizing at all. Winnicott is, I think, the first analyst who wanted to let the nonsense speak, as opposed to letting unconscious desire speak through free association. There are, Winnicott seems to be saying, very good psychoanalytic stories – Oedipal and pre-Oedipal – about the hazards of desire, and the consequent necessities of conflict, defence and symptomatology. There is clearly, he acknowledges, a desiring subject as described by Freud and Klein. But there is also an incoherent, chaotic, nonsensical, eccentric subject, described by no one in psychoanalysis but suggested by the idea, the method, of free association, but free association listened to in a certain way. This is the person Winnicott wants to introduce us to. The chaotic person who needs, however temporarily, to speak nothing but his own nonsense. Winnicott finds it extremely difficult to marry, or even link, the nonsensical person with the desiring person. (His useful distinction between disintegration and unintegration is an attempt at this.) The desiring person, as he develops, is always involved, one way or another, in having to know when to stop. But knowing when to stop is the enemy of chaos, or it is the omnipotent delusion that chaos can be under control. Perhaps, Winnicott intimates, what we most need to defend ourselves against, what we most believe needs to be stopped, is not the appetite – or only the appetite – but the nonsense. And nonsense can only be stopped by making sense. Why, he asks us to wonder – but in a psychoanalytic context and language – can't we let the nonsense be? Why couldn't an aim of analysis be to enable the patient to speak and hear, and even enjoy, his nonsense? And, indeed, to be able to hear the nonsense of others?

Winnicott, it should be noted, refers very infrequently to free association. He quotes with approval, indeed italicizes, in his 'Child Analysis in the Latency Period', Berta Bornstein's comment in her 1951 paper 'On Latency': '*Free association is experienced by the child as a particular threat to his ego organization.*' Indeed, it seems as if for Winnicott 'play' is the word for the kind of free association that need not be a threat to ego organization. And play, of course, is not exclusively verbal. In a paper dated 1954 (but not published until 1989), 'Play in the Analytic Situation', Winnicott reports on a supervision:

> After the interpretation given by the student the patient leaned over and rearranged the mat and gave associations to this bit of play. In the circumstances it is understandable that the student neglected to continue on the subject of play and became bogged down in the material of the free associations which indeed were important on their own account.

Clearly, getting 'bogged down in the material of the free associations' is to be doing psychoanalysis as traditionally taught, but for Winnicott, in this example, that is to miss the point, which is the play. So there is free association, which, in latency, and not only in latency, is a threat to ego organization, and there is play, which for Winnicott is famously the aim, the means and the definition of psychotherapy:

> Psychotherapy takes place in the overlap of two areas of playing, that of the patient and that of the therapist. Psychotherapy has to do with two people playing together. The corollary of this is that where playing is not possible then the work done by the therapist is directed towards bringing the patient from a state of not being able to play into a state of being able to play.

Winnicott here, in 'Playing, a Theoretical Statement', has re-described the so-called golden rule of free association in terms of play, thereby de-emphasizing, in practice and through analogy, Freud's privileging of the verbal and the necessity of teasing out the unconscious desire being kept at bay. And somewhere between free association and play there is nonsense, which is verbal, but not exactly to be played with so much as to be accepted as such. If free association is supposed to reveal the unconscious logic of desire, playing, for Winnicott, is something quite different. 'Bodily excitement in erotogenic zones,' he writes, 'constantly threatens playing, and therefore threatens the child's sense of existing as a person. The instincts are the main threat to play as to the ego.' The instincts, in Winnicott's counter-Freudian story, are a threat, a word used three times in the sentence; and what they threaten is the child's 'sense of existing as a person'. Once again it is about sense, and once again Winnicott's phrasing might make us wonder what, if the child no longer exists as a person, he will have a sense of existing as. This takes us straight to the nonsense question and to whether, or in what sense, talking nonsense threatens a person's sense of existing as a person.

Instinct, in Winnicott's view, puts a stop to playing – and so, presumably, to psychotherapy, which is supposed to be a form of playing. Free association, in Freud's view, can lead to the wording of desire. Do we want to be able to play or to seek sexual satisfaction or to talk nonsense? Of course, we don't necessarily have to choose; but if we want to play or be free to talk nonsense, our psychotherapy need never end. If we are seeking sexual satisfaction, the analyst's couch won't, beyond a certain point, do the trick.

If you look up 'free association' in the Index of Marion Milner's book *The Suppressed Madness of Sane Men* you find: 'free association – *see* absent-mindedness in art.' This is, I think, instructive. Free associating, playing, nonsense and states of sexual desire are all, at their best, states of absent-mindedness, of self-forgetting, of abandon. The psychoanalytic question becomes – and this is bound up, as we shall see, with the notion of knowing when to stop – what might make someone stop something as potentially pleasurable as two people playing together? If you end up getting on, and the conversation is good, why stop? This is a question any child would be radically puzzled by. (Freud, in his correspondence with Binswanger, refers to 'one of my closest women friends, formerly a patient'.) Winnicott, it should be noted, does not say that psychotherapy is two people playing together: he says that it 'has to do with two people playing together', and that the psychotherapy, as such, cannot begin until the patient is able to play. If psychoanalysis, in the Winnicott way, is somehow like playing – has, at least, something to do with playing – then what makes playing stop? What must be acknowledged, as Winnicott does, is the difference between a set game – which has a defined beginning, middle and end – and open-ended play. Open-ended play is open-ended play or a defence against open-endedness. This chapter is about whether the phrase 'open-ended' could possibly mean anything, and in particular could mean anything in a psychoanalytic context.

Winnicott is quite explicit that it is 'bodily excitement in erotogenic zones' that 'constantly threatens' play, and 'therefore threatens the child's sense of existing as a person'. In other words, it is play that gives the child a sense of existing as a person, whereas it is instinct, which constantly threatens play, that gives the child a sense of existing as something other than a person, or as not existing at all. So it is time to drop the idea that in some sense Winnicott wasn't interested in sex, or has nothing to tell us about what Freud wanted to tell us about. Winnicott is acutely mindful of 'bodily excitement in erotogenic zones' as that which is disruptive. It is defined by him as that which interrupts, that which waylays and disfigures play. Sex, to put it as crudely, as Winnicottianly as possible, is what threatens play, what constantly threatens to put a stop to it – and, of course, to put a stop to the playing that is psychotherapy. If you want to know what sexuality is, see what you are up against when you start playing. Or, indeed, notice what stops you playing. Play is sexuality in abeyance. At a certain point, one might say, the artist loses her absorption and finds herself all too mindful that she needs something, needs someone else, something the activity of painting cannot supply. And by the same token, as it were, the point of analysis, the making and breaking point, is that the analyst and the so-called patient do not have sex with each other. The analyst, in the traditional story, is the one who is supposed to know when to stop.

Just as the Freudian analyst traditionally analyses the resistances to free association, the Winnicottian analyst, in his project of enabling the patient to play, is going to analyse the obstacles to such playing as is possible; and the obstacles are 'bodily excitement in erotogenic zones'. But is the aim a capacity for such excitement, or a capacity for play? How is the excited, desiring self linked, if at all, to the self that plays? And what of the version of the self that needs the 'rest', as Winnicott calls it, of talking nonsense? It is essential to the whole idea of playing, Winnicott intimates, to acknowledge what playing cannot do for the self. You can't eat art. When appetite starts, playing stops. 'The pleasurable element in playing carries with it,' he writes in 'Playing, a Theoretical Statement', 'the implication that the instinctual arousal is not excessive . . . Playing is inherently exciting and precarious. This characteristic derives *not* from instinctual arousal . . .' There is a hint of equivocation here, but it is at the moments when Winnicott's language is at odds with Freud's that the text can wake us up. Playing is pleasurable because instinctual arousal is not excessive; but – or and – the pleasure in playing is that it does not derive from instinctual arousal. The threat for Winnicott is the instinctual arousal that waylays development by over-disturbing the individual's ego organization. Playing, for him, either has no instinctual pressure, or just the right amount. In one reading of Freud, that is precisely what instinctual arousal is: the threatening of ego organization, what Laplanche refers to as 'the attack of the drives on the ego'. For Winnicott, where instinctual arousal was, there play should be. Or, to put it another way, the best form our instinctual life can take is in play.

And yet what playing, in Winnicott's version, cannot contain – excessive arousal – might be more exactly what psychoanalysis is about. Knowing when to stop playing might be as important as knowing what stops playing. It is, perhaps, the transitions that count: how the child moves from and through playing towards appetite and satisfaction; how the adult goes from absorption to arousal and gratification (from the vertical to the horizontal). The transition, I want to suggest, involves – is through – incoherence. One kind of chaos occurs when absorption, or preoccupation, begins turning into appetite and the hope of satisfaction. The no-nonsense self cannot make that move. Wanting comes out of an incredible muddle. Life's nonsense pierces us with strange relation.

'When we scrutinize the personalities who, by self-selection, became the first generation of psychoanalysts,' Anna Freud wrote in 1968, in her Freud Anniversary Lecture 'Difficulties in the Path of Psychoanalysis', we are left in no doubt about their characteristics. They were the unconventional ones, the doubters, those who were dissatisfied with the limitations imposed on knowledge; also among them were the odd ones, the dreamers, and those who knew neurotic suffering from their own experience. This type of intake has altered decisively since psychoanalytic training has become institutionalized and appeals in this stricter form to a different type of personality. Moreover, self-selection has given way to the careful scrutiny of applicants, resulting in the exclusion of the mentally endangered, the eccentrics, the self-made, those with excessive flights of imagination, and favouring the acceptance of the sober, well-prepared ones, who are hard-working enough to wish to better their professional efficiency.

There is a poignant nostalgia in these words, delivered in New York in that fateful year, 1968. It is, as it were, a plea for the incoherent, for the self-contradictory, for the nonsensical; for what the critic Naomi Lebowitz calls 'styles that slum in an avid adoption of *amateurism*'. We are now fairly and squarely in the age of the sober professionalized ones, the people who know all too well when to stop. Psychoanalysis as the art and science of the indeterminate is what Winnicott and what Anna Freud, in her quite different way here, are speaking up for. The unconscious and professional efficiency are uneasy bedfellows. Which brings me back to my initial propositions: the coherence and incoherence of my theme, the connection between knowing when to stop and talking nonsense. Something about which Anna Freud's wonderful repertory company of the unconventional – the doubters, the dissatisfied, the odd ones, the dreamers, the neurotics, the mentally endangered, the eccentrics, the self-made – would know a lot about.

My two propositions were that it is impossible to know the consequences of one's words – the spoken, the heard and the overheard – and that an analysis is never finished, it is only abandoned. Both formulations are sceptical in Stanley Cavell's sense: 'Our relation to the world as a whole, or to others in general, is not one of knowing, where knowing construes itself as being certain.' 'Scepticism,' he continues in *Must We Mean What We Say?*, 'is a function of our now illimitable desire.' In other words, there would be a kind of madness, a kind of omniscience, in believing that it was possible to know the consequences of one's words, or to finish – in the sense of complete with any kind of certainty – an analysis. Our illimitable desire, Cavell intimates, can be displaced into an illimitable desire for certainty.

But how are we then to define, to publicize, the professional competence of the psychoanalyst – especially in the present technologically driven economic climate – if we can never be quite sure what to say or what we are saying, and if we can't know when and whether a psychoanalysis should end? How, to take up Anna Freud's late challenge, are psychoanalysts going to be selected, let alone trained? If hard work and bettering one's professional efficiency, to use her terms, are not going to be the ambition or even the aim of the aspiring psychoanalyst; if self-selecting dreamers, eccentrics and the mentally endangered are the preferred candidates for a psychoanalytic training – what is this training going to be like? To be acceptable to such a group of people, the training would have to be unusual, as indeed the trainings of the first analysts inevitably were. More of a circus school, or a singing school.

When Winnicott is speaking up for nonsense – 'organized nonsense is already a defence' – and Anna Freud is promoting the 'mentally endangered, the eccentrics, the self-made', they are both, in different ways and in quite different contexts, telling us that there is something valuable, from a psychoanalytic point of view, in not being impressively coherent, something about not being wholly plausible, or, in a conventional sense, intelligible, that psychoanalysis might ignore to its cost. It is as though they are asking us to wonder what we are doing when we are making sense; when, for example, we are being, or wanting to be, strong theorists or persuasive interpreters – as though we might be at our most defensive when we are at our most plausible.

Of course, the idea that we should be suspicious of intelligibility is itself paradoxical. As an aesthetic principle, it is perhaps best captured in the poet John Ashbery's remark that 'the worse your art is the easier it is to talk about'. This might translate as: 'The more defensive you are the more plausible you will seem to yourself (and other people).' This, of course, has implications for the practice and theorizing of psychoanalysis. Making the case for nonsense, like making the case against 'the sober, well-prepared ones', at least in a psychoanalytic context, allows us our dismay about making sense, while making us wonder where in psychoanalysis we can find now the intoxicated and the unprepared. It would be silly to take this too literally, but it would be sillier to ignore what was at stake for both Winnicott and Anna Freud in taking the positions that they did. They bear witness to the fact that, after Freud, we are awkward about our reasonableness. And our reasonableness seems to depend on our talking sense, and knowing when to stop.

If psychoanalysis has made us reconsider our beginnings – indeed, the whole notion of our origins as human subjects and objects – it has also revised our sense of endings. When I suggested at the beginning of this chapter that an analysis is never finished, it is only abandoned, I wanted to draw attention to relationships as by definition incomplete, and uncompletable. Another way of saying this would be that the ways we talk about finishing things, or about things coming to an end in other areas of our lives, are peculiarly unsuited to the ways we talk about so-called relationships ending. As readers we know where the poem on the page ends, and we know when the ironing is finished, when we have done our homework, when the football stops at the final whistle. Of course, the poem may linger in our minds after we have read it; we may find ourselves thinking or talking about the football afterwards. But there has been an official, an agreed-upon end that is recognizable. I think the formal ending of relationships bears only a superficial resemblance to these examples. A psychoanalysis ends, officially, when either the analyst or the patient decides, for whatever reason, to stop, or when the two parties agree to stop. But the question is, what is knowing when to stop knowing about? Knowing when to stop a football match means knowing about the rules of football; knowing when to stop reading a poem means knowing about the conventions of poetry; knowing when you've finished the ironing means seeing what's in front of your eyes.

There are no comparable conventions or perceptions available in knowing when to stop a relationship, unless, of course, you have prepared criteria for what it is for a relationship to end. And yet, relationships do end, in the sense that people stop doing certain things together. In professional relationships at their most pragmatic, the relationship ends when the problem is solved. And this is clearly one reason why the concept of cure has been so important, and so contentious, in psychoanalysis. It makes perfect sense, using a quasi-medical analogy, that the patient and the analyst stop seeing each other when the patient is cured. Knowing when to stop means feeling cured; knowing about people in a cured state, so to speak. But what of the afterlife of relationships, which is as real in its own way as is the life of relationships? And yet, as everyone knows who likes the sound of psychoanalysis, it is not solely or simply a problem-solving exercise. For some people, the relationship can end when the presenting problem has been solved. It is a kind of common sense that if you go to a psychoanalyst with claustrophobia, your involvement with the analyst will finish either when you are no longer claustrophobic or when you have finally given up hope of ever being changed by this kind of therapy. But you may also find, given a psychoanalytic opportunity, that whether or not you get symptom relief, you may want to go on; you may even come to believe that symptom relief may not be the be-all and end-all of the process. Not suffering matters, but not living as well as you can may matter more, and that is likely to involve suffering. Indeed, when Freud was offering us the prospect of transforming hysterical misery into ordinary human unhappiness, he was offering us a better life in terms of a better form of suffering. In other words, knowing when to stop should mean knowing what's good for you; and so, by the same token, the analyst knowing when the patient should stop means that the analyst knows what's best for the patient. My knowing what's good for me, and someone else's knowing what's good for me, can be the difference that makes all the difference.

Everything we do in psychoanalysis is a version of knowing what's good for someone; agreeing to begin the therapy, intervening (or not) in the patient's associative flow, not giving advice or giving it, and, of course, finishing the analysis. There are the generalizations of theory – in Winnicott's view, say, being able to play is good for people; in Freud and Ferenczi's view, being able to free-associate is good for people – and there is the singularity of the individual analyst and the individual patient. And, as everyone knows, singularity and theory are uneasy bedfellows. There is, as it were, the order, the coherence, the no-nonsense of theory, and the uniqueness, the idiosyncratic singularity of the individual. 'Only a true theory,' the Lacanian analyst Serge Leclaire writes in *Psychoanalysing*, 'can advance a formalization that maintains, without reducing it, the domain of singularity; the always recurring difficulty of psychoanalysis, which no institution will ever be able to resolve, derives from the fact that it is vulnerable on the one hand to the degradation of a closed systematization and, on the other, to the anarchy of intuitive processes.' What Leclaire is drawing our attention to is the senses in which theory, systematization, is supposed to protect us from what he calls the 'anarchy of intuitive processes'. But the countervailing risk is that singularity, the individual in his personal delirium, is abandoned. In the 'degradation of a closed systematization', there is no place for the individual's nonsense; and it may be, as Winnicott only intimates, that his singularity resides in his nonsense. I think we should consider the possibility that Winnicott also believed that a person is at his most compliant when he is at his most coherent, that making sense, the wish to make sense, can be a species of conformism. In promoting the potential value of incoherence Winnicott is part of an honourable and perhaps fading tradition in psychoanalysis. There have always been nonsense and no-nonsense schools of psychoanalysis.

Singularity begins where a person's intelligibility to him/herself and others breaks down. This would be one possibility. Or, we might say, a person's singularity is his or her own idiosyncratic way of being coherent. Of course, how it has come about that singularity matters to people like us is a larger question with a contentious history. But psychoanalysis, if it is to be anything other than indoctrination, has to pay attention to the connections, and otherwise, between the ambitions of theory and the (unconscious) projects of singularity. This chapter wants to offer up, as case studies for this particular issue, the related and unrelated notions of talking nonsense and knowing when to stop in psychoanalysis. In what sense can there be a psychoanalytic theory about knowing when to stop – that is, knowing when to stop the patient's associations to interpret, or clarify, or comment, and knowing when to stop the treatment? Could there be, for example, exemplary instances of these things, vignettes that illustrate a general point? Are there individual examples that could serve as general guidelines? If there were, could they be anything other than a consensual agreement among a group of people about what constitutes an excellent finish? We could, for example, formulate a list of the aims of psychoanalysis and see whether or not they have been achieved; we could look at all the sentences in the professional literature about interpretation, and about endings, and see what, if anything, they have in common. We could do some research into outcomes – but where would it end? How would we know, other than by agreement, when to stop our inquiries? Some things finish; some things are brought to an end; and some things finish or are brought to an end, but are discovered to be neither finished nor to have ended. Having the last word is never going to be the last word. What makes the last line of a nonsense poem the last line could never make sense. It is part of the ambition of theory to be coherent, plausible and persuasive; knowing when to stop the associations, the analysis, the nonsense, is more like what the religious would call a ' species of prophecy' and the secular might call 'guess-work'. In psychoanalysis there is, then, the dream-work, the death-work and the guess-work.

Knowing when to stop, whatever else it is, is always guess-work. Psychoanalytic theory about clinical technique, whatever else it is, is a more or less coherent, plausible and persuasive account of guess-work; of why the guess-work worked, when it seemed to, and why it didn't when it didn't seem to. Whatever the analyst's decisions are informed by, whatever their prehistory, their preconditions, whatever their training, to speak or not to speak, to end the analysis or not to end the analysis, is a guessing game. Indeed, these moments of decision may be anybody's guess; they are certainly, judging by the controversy that surrounds these issues, undecided and undecidable. Psychoanalysis, at its best, tells the individual that he or she does not need a consensus in order to speak and that that sometimes involves talking nonsense and not knowing when to stop. 'Life's nonsense,' Wallace Stevens wrote, 'pierces us with strange relation.'

Arbus's Freaks

. . . but we have the right to be seduced.

Dave Hickey, *The Invisible Dragon*

If it is too often said about Diane Arbus that she photographs freaks it does at least suggest, at its most minimal, that we know what normal people are like, what people look like when they are not odd. It is reassuring to be reminded not only that we are not all freaks, but also that we know a freak when we see one. There are, of course, points of view, angles from which we can all look like freaks to ourselves; and Arbus, as we shall see, is unusually eloquent about this and about how the camera is, as it were, good at picking up the unwanted perspective. But the enthusiastic unease that Arbus's work generates, and the pleasure we take from her work, must have something to do with our wondering what it must be to be people like that; and, by the same token, what it must be to be people like us, who are not freaks like that but for some reason – and Arbus was herself exercised by this – are fascinated by freaks like that. Indeed, we want pictures and exhibitions of them; and we want something from representations of them that we mostly don't want from them in person. Pictures of these people – or, rather, Arbus's unique way of not turning a blind eye – satisfy something in us. She has not, it should be noted, created a fashion for her subject matter, but for her photographs. Arbus's photographs, whatever else they do, create a kind of vicarious sociability with people we suspect we mostly wouldn't be able to get on with.

One of the many interesting things about photography as a

relatively new art form is that photographers talking and writing about their work is also a relatively new genre. And Arbus, it seems to me, was unusually eloquent as well as unusually keen and willing to articulate something about what she thought she was doing, mindful as people usually are that words for pictures is a peculiar form of exchange. When Arbus speaks of her work she often enough talks of photography as a form of sociability: 'some pictures are tentative forays without your even knowing it'. The camera, of course, gives the photographer something to do with other people, and the camera is like a safe lead, a 'licence', as she calls it, into the unpredictable. Who you can and can't be with, for Arbus, is bound up with what you can and can't know about people. As a certain kind of modern artist she thinks of intentions as passwords that get you what you never expected; and she locates the mystery that matters most to her, her preferred mystery, in the unfamiliar (the family being the place where unfamiliarity begins). 'I remember one summer,' she writes:

I worked a lot in Washington Square Park. It must have been about 1966. The park was divided. It has these walks, sort of like a sunburst, and there were these territories staked out. There were young hippie-junkies down one row. There were lesbians down another, really tough, amazingly hard-core lesbians. And in the middle were winos . . . They were like the first echelon, and the girls who came from the Bronx to become hippies would have to sleep with the winos to get to sit on the other part with the junkie-hippies. It was really remarkable.

And I found it very scary. I mean, I could become a nudist, I could become a million things. But I could never become that, whatever all those people were. There were days I just couldn't work there, and then there were days I could. And then, having done it a little, I could do it more. I got to know a few of them. I hung around a lot. They were a lot like sculptures in a funny way. I was very keen to get close to them, so I had to ask to photograph them. You can't get that close to somebody and not say a word, although I have done that.

I take this to be a kind of parable of Arbus as a photographer. There is well-known biographical material that would seem to make a certain sense of this, to do with Arbus's recollected sense of being secluded, segregated in the affluent Jewish family she grew up in. 'One of the things I suffered from as a kid,' she said, 'was I never felt adversity. I felt confirmed in a sense of unreality which I could feel as unreality, and the sense of being immune was, ludicrous as it seems, a painful one . . . the world seemed to belong to the world. I could learn things but they never seemed to be my own experience.' The gist of the recollection is her strong sense that there was somewhere else she needed to get to, some other kind of experience, some necessary illness that she was immune to. It is unlikely that she never felt adversity as a child, but likely that she might have felt in retrospect that she didn't get the adversity she wanted. In Washington Square Park in 1966 the world seems to belong to the world again, she doesn't belong to it. And what she's interested in in the groups she observes is how people who are so separated can get together: 'the girls who came from the Bronx to become hippies would have to sleep with the winos to get to sit on the other part with the junkie-hippies'. And Arbus is quite clear that here she has reached her limit, the horizon of her ambition: 'I could become a million things. But I could never become that, whatever all those people were.' But what you can't become you can photograph; you can get close to. And the way to get close to them is to ask them for something: 'I was very keen to get close to them, so I had to ask to photograph them. You can't get that close to somebody and not say a word, although I have done that.' If you ask someone for a photograph of themselves you are asking them to give you one, not to let you take one. Arbus — for some reason she doesn't need to articulate — wants to get close to these people 'whatever all those people were', and the way is to ask to photograph them: words for pictures. But in this process – and I think the parable is calculated, wittingly or unwittingly, to make us wonder about this – what does that make the photograph? If her work, if the camera, is an ice-breaker – a way of having something to do with these people who she could never become – what is the picture a picture of? If we take Arbus at her word, the pictures are of an impossible aspiration: 'I could never become that, whatever all those people were.' They are records, or reminders, so to speak, of a thwarted closeness; of where sociability stops. You can't be with these people; and this is where the photography, the work, comes in.

Sometimes Arbus starts from the diametrically opposed position, with no affinity, no longing, as though alienation from, or the irrelevance of, the subject matter was the precondition of the work. 'The Chinese have a theory,' she writes, 'that you pass through boredom into fascination, and I think it's true. I would never choose a subject for what it means to me or what I think about it. You've just got to choose a subject, and what you feel about it, what it means, begins to unfold if you just plain choose a subject and do it enough.' In Washington Square Park she starts with the fascination; here she ends up with the fascination through apparently arbitrary choice and dogged persistence. But in this latter formulation the photograph is far more, and far more obviously, significant; it is the revelation of feeling and meaning. The photograph gets you closer not to the object, but to the photographer's unfolding apprehension of the object. As ever with Arbus, closeness is the issue; and it is presumably not insignificant that so many of her photographs are so close up, and quite often of people one mostly wouldn't want to be that close to; at least in so-called real life.

'Nothing is ever the same as they said it was,' Arbus says. 'It's what I've never seen before that I recognize.' What other people say distances you; if it's 'what I've never seen before that I recognize' we have to assume that this is because 'they' prevented her with their words from seeing the thing that mattered to her. '[T]hey' have kept her away, immune, unreal, and her project, the

New — 'what I've never seen before' — becomes the desired; it represents, it becomes symbolically equated with, the necessary thing from which she has been somehow excluded. Her question, I think, or rather her dilemma, is, how much does she want to know, how close does she want to get to whatever it is she believes she has been excluded from? Arbus starts from a position of exclusion; the people in Washington Square Park, like the arbitrarily chosen subject, are nothing to do with her. Arbus is never sure whether she is interested in the experience of exclusion — and her so-called freaks are, by definition, the excluded that she is including — or whether she is interested in finding out exactly what it might be that she is excluded from, which is what her so-called freaks make us think about. Becoming obsessed with exclusion can become a way, perhaps *the* way, of not thinking about what it might be that one is excluded from. So when Arbus (a bit too famously) says, 'A photograph is a secret about a secret. The more it tells you the less you know,' she is both making a distinction between showing and telling which photographs draw to our attention, and also giving us her potted theory of secrecy. What a photograph apparently tells you is what you don't need to know; that in photography the explicit is always misleading; and that photography, at least in Arbus's version, is a peculiarly intent form of secrecy. A 'secret about a secret' means that what is being kept a secret is that there is a secret. Photographs, unlike photographers, can't actually speak; and a 'secret about a secret' is as good a definition of the unconscious as one is likely to get. But a 'secret about a secret' is two degrees of separation. Arbus is not saying that she knows what the secret is; she is just saying she knows that what is being kept secret in the photograph is that there is a secret.

The photograph, or, rather, Arbus's words about the photograph, has something to show us, if not tell us, not about odd people, but about how odd we are about closeness and exclusion. Many of her photographs have a baroque longing in them. And many of her remarkable statements about her work have something to say about the dread and the draw of being left out. 'Lately I've been struck', she says, 'with how I really love what you can't see in a photograph. An actual physical darkness. And it's very thrilling for me to see darkness again.' To see darkness is to see what you can't see, and what you can't see through. In Arbus's photographs the thrill of being left out contends with the dread. It would be terrible to believe that there is nothing to be left out of. What, we are invited to think about Arbus's photographs, are the so-called freaks in her pictures left out of, and what is it about this that is at once so poignant and so horrifying for us? Or, to put it a little more glibly, who is left out of what? If we so much want to look at Arbus's pictures of freaks, what are we feeling excluded from?

The story Arbus wants to tell us explicitly about freaks – that is to say, in words rather than in photographs – is that she is envious of them. 'Freaks was a thing I photographed a lot,' she says, not wary of using either word:

> It was one of the first things I photographed and it had a terrific kind of excitement for me. I just used to adore them. I still do adore some of them. I don't quite mean they're my best friends but they made me feel a mixture of shame and awe. There's a quality of legend about freaks. Like a person in a fairy tale who stops you and demands that you answer a riddle. Most people go through life dreading they'll have a traumatic experience. Freaks were born with their trauma. They've already passed their test in life. They're aristocrats.

This is characteristically shrewd and unsettling, both in its blitheness and in its gravity. Like some of her best photographs it's somewhere between a comedy routine – 'I just used to adore them. I still do adore some of them. I don't quite mean they're my best friends' – and an existential fable. They are at once both unreal – things, legends, people in fairy tales, aristocrats – and very intensely real: they've got their trauma in first, they've 'passed their test in life', they are aristocrats. They are, one could say, from a slightly different angle, or 'corner', to use Arbus's word; a bit like Jews, born members of the aristocracy of trauma. And what is striking about Arbus's account is just how explicit she is about the erotics, the fantasies, in being a fan. There is a terrific kind of excitement, adoration, shame, awe. And the lives of her freaks, in her version, are constituted by what they are excluded from. Because they are born with their trauma they are born with the very thing that will separate them out from others. That's where they start from, not what they have to go in search of, as Arbus did in Washington Square Park. It is as though their test in life, *the* test in life, for Arbus, is what you make of your exclusion, or of the thing that excludes you. The camera, one can see in Arbus's Washington Square Park parable, is the object that at once includes you and excludes you. But Arbus, quite rightly, is keen to remind us always that the photograph is not in any simple sense its subject; it is its so-called subject represented, recognized in a quite different medium. And clearly to talk about photography is to talk about this difference in new ways because photography appears to be so effortlessly mimetic. 'What I'm trying to describe,' she says, 'is that it's impossible to get out of your skin into somebody else's. And that's what all this is a little bit about. That somebody else's tragedy is not the same as your own.' Perhaps the thing one is most left out of is other people's traumas, other people's tragedies. You don't need a photograph of a freak, or indeed to photograph a freak, to tell you that you are not a freak yourself. So what, to ask the pragmatic question, are Arbus's photographs of freaks for? Why photograph them, and why photograph them like that? 'Freaks was a thing I photographed a lot. It was one of the first things I photographed and it had a terrific kind of excitement for me.' One of the first things, that is, after the fashion models she and her husband photographed in the 1940s. There is possibly a suggestion here that freaks were Arbus's way into her own kind of photography. So it is worth wondering, by way of conclusion, what that was a way into.

Arbus describes becoming fascinated in the 1960s by a blind street performer who, she says, 'lives in an atmosphere as dense and separate as an island with its own sea'. An 'island with its own sea' is indeed a very separate island. If Arbus was drawn to the impossibilities of closeness then it is tempting to suggest that her photographs at once both record this impossibility and try to break it down. Eudora Welty remarked that Arbus's work 'totally violates human privacy, and by intention', as though Arbus couldn't bear or, more interestingly, didn't trust the privacy of others. As though privacy was some kind of mystification; as though the opaqueness of ourselves and others was becoming sacralized. Welty was overstressing something – violation tends to be total, no one talks of feeling 'a bit violated' – that is important about Arbus's work. If anything, though, I think it may be truer to say that Arbus's work is more often showing us just how inviolable modern human privacy actually is; however close or close up you get, you never get that close. And that there is something about modern life that generates fantasies of closeness, of intimacy, that are way in excess of human possibility. Secrets can be found out, but privacy cannot be violated because once it is violated it is no longer privacy. The idea of secrecy is the last refuge of romance. It may not be that we have secrets, but that each person sees us differently. It may not be that we are at our most revelatory in our intimacies, but at our most anonymous. These, at least, are the areas that Arbus leads us into when she talks and writes about photography. 'Our whole guise,' she writes, 'is like giving a sign to the world to think of us in a certain way but there's a point between what you want people to know about you and what you can't help people knowing about you.' Other people see us in ways that we cannot anticipate; we cannot know ourselves because we cannot be everyone else in relation to ourselves; and so on.

It is clear from all this just how psychologically minded Arbus is when she talks and writes about photography. And like all good psychological writing it sounds compelling and pertinent;

and it is not surprising that Arbus, growing up and working when and where she did, found this kind of language to hand. But this way of talking can take us a long way from the photographs as photographs, especially when someone is as eloquent and canny as Arbus obviously was. The worse your art is, the American poet John Ashbery once remarked, the easier it is to talk about. What I think is truly odd about Arbus's work is not her subject matter, but how difficult it is to resist speaking psychologically about it; or, to put it another way, how difficult it is to conceive of not talking about it in psychological terms. And I don't mean as an alternative to this talking technically. To look at Arbus's photographs without trying to imagine what might be going on inside her subjects; as if, in fact, you couldn't. A person who is as dense and separate as an island with its own sea may not be available for that, and so may be available for something else. For being photographed.

My Happiness Right or Wrong

I

. . . because people in the West are not threatened by concentration camps and are free to say and write what they want, the more the fight for human rights gains in popularity the more it loses any concrete content, becoming a kind of universal stance of everyone towards everything, a kind of energy that turns all human desires into rights. The world has become man's right and everything in it has become a right: the desire for love the right to love, the desire for friendship the right to friendship, the desire to exceed the speed limit the right to exceed the speed limit, the desire for happiness the right to happiness . . .

Milan Kundera, 'The Gesture of Protest against a
Violation of Human Rights'

'He was not to be described as a happy person,' Diana Trilling wrote in *The Beginning of the Journey*, a memoir about her husband the critic Lionel Trilling. 'Indeed, he thought poorly of happiness and of people who claimed to be happy or desired happiness above other gratifications in life . . . seriousness was the desirable condition of man . . .' It is easy to make all sorts of assumptions about why an unhappy person would not value happiness; and indeed why seriousness might be seen as an alternative, as the alternative to happiness; or just to say that it was seriousness that made Trilling happy. Indeed one of the ways in which happiness is made to seem like an inclusive ideal, one of the ways it charms us, is by our asserting that by definition the things that matter most to us must make us happy, that that is how we know they are good; as though one word could do the work of the moral imagination. Clearly if happiness is what we want, is what we are after, the field is narrowed. If happiness is one's aspiration, is one's preferred condition, then learning about the history of the slave trade, say, or watching the news, or indeed growing up, are all to be avoided. And yet, of course, learning about the terrible things people can do to each other, and the history of the terrible things people do do to each other, is important – we can't imagine a life without it – and gives some people a great deal of pleasure; pleasure, as psychoanalysts might say, of various kinds. Anyone who has or knows children, or remembers being a child, will know how happy tormenting their siblings can make them. And so if we value happiness we can't help but wonder what morality it entails, what kind of morality it might involve us in. If we desire happiness, what kind of good do we have to be? It is not surprising, in other words, that happiness has always had rather a mixed reception. No one in their right minds, we might think, especially now, would be promoting unhappiness; and yet the promotion, the preferring of happiness – the assumption of a right to happiness – brings with it a lot of things we may not like. And the desire for happiness may reveal things about ourselves that we like even less. 'A people who conceive life to be the pursuit of happiness must be chronically unhappy,' the anthropologist Marshall Sahlins wrote. How do we experience ourselves, what do we find ourselves to be, if happiness is supposedly what we want? And what are we going to have to do, what are we going to have to become, what are we going to have to renounce or ignore, if we want to be happy? Or if we are to propose happiness, or its pursuit, as some kind of right? We tend to make rights of things we assume to be in short supply, things perpetually under threat. Wherever there is scarcity now human rights are asserted; and the assertion of rights is reactive to a sense of scarcity deemed to be needless. Or, to put it slightly differently, calling something a right can be a way of rhetorically enforcing an important wish, a way of making a wish sound important. We legitimate wishes by calling them rights. We give them a dignity and a force they might not otherwise have, and give ourselves something similar by doing this. 'Individuals and groups . . . feel empowered,' Andrew Clapham writes in *Human Rights: A Very Short Introduction*, 'by the language of human rights and by the framework that has grown up to develop solidarity in ensuring respect for these rights.'

I want to start with three fairly obvious propositions that are also, in a sense, misgivings about the right to happiness or its pursuit, with a view to asserting that the right to frustration may be more useful and interesting – more enlivening – than the right to happiness. To waylay, that is to say, the common idea, the all too plausible idea, that the solution to frustration is satisfaction, or that happiness is the answer to unhappiness. I want to say in this essay that happiness and the right to pursue it are sometimes wildly unrealistic as ideals; and, because wildly unrealistic, they are also unconsciously self-destructive. And that because happiness, when we do want it, cannot always be pursued, is not always the kind of thing that can be pursued, we should view it, more often than not, as a lucky side effect but not a calculable or calculated end; making it such an end all too easily brings out the worst in us. If this is a version, to rewrite John Lennon's famous line, of 'Happiness is what happens to you when you are doing something else', it also wants to hold on to a view of happiness as something that includes the acknowledgement that scarcity is integral to a sense of reality; that we should be thinking of what Philip Larkin called in 'Born Yesterday' 'a skilled, / Vigilant, flexible, / Unemphasised, enthralled / Catching of happiness' rather than of the engineering of it. The right to pursue happiness may itself be a resistance to, or a doubt about, the thing it pursues, knowing as we do that expecting happiness is perilous; as is believing that we always know beforehand what will make us happy. Believing in happiness makes us too knowing, too omniscient, too prophetic. Indeed our relation to happiness – the kind of thing we take it to be – often betrays an unconscious desire for disillusionment. The wanting of it and the having of it can seem like two quite different things. And this is what makes wishing so interesting; because wishing is always too knowing. When we wish, we are too convinced of our pleasures, too certain of our bliss. The belief that we can arrange our happiness, that we can, in some sense, organize it – as though happiness were akin to justice, which we can work towards – may be, at least sometimes, to misrecognize the very thing that concerns us. If this were true it would be, to use Trilling's (and Arnold's) word, 'serious'. Because we so often know the preconditions for unhappiness it is easy to assume that we know what makes us happy. The right to the pursuit of happiness tends to mean the right to remove the obstacles to our happiness; once you take the bully out of the classroom the children are once again left with themselves. All scapegoating can ever do is remove the scapegoat.

So my three fairly obvious propositions are, firstly, in Freud's formulation from, perhaps appropriately, *Civilisation and Its Discontents*, 'Happiness is something essentially subjective'; subjective, I take it, in the sense of being not only personal but also idiosyncratic. We can be surprised by what makes us happy, and it will not necessarily be something that makes other people happy. This has significant consequences not least in the area of our lives that is sometimes conducive to happiness, sexuality. And this makes happiness as a social or communal pursuit complicated. We have only to imagine what it would be for someone to propose that we had a right to sexual satisfaction to imagine both how we might contrive this, and what terrible things might be done in its name. Secondly, bad things can make us happy; and by bad things I mean simply things consensually agreed to be unacceptable. It clearly makes some people happy to live in a world without Jews, or homosexuals, or immigrants, and so on. There are what we might call genuinely bad things, such as the serious harming of people and other animals that gives some people the pleasure they most crave. I remember a very unhappy boy of ten telling me in a psychotherapy session that he was happy only when he was cutting the feet off rats that he had caught; he said it made him feel 'really awake', it was like 'turning on the light in your favourite room in the world'. Cruelty and humiliation make some people happy, and perhaps lots of people happy some of the time; and this issue is not dealt with by merely saying that they are not really happy, or that they are in some way perverse or indeed sick. We tend to diagnose or pathologize the forms of happiness we cannot bear. If we have a right to happiness or its pursuit – two different things – we are then having to acknowledge the full range of things that make people happy; and that the word 'happiness' covers, as it were, a multitude of sins. This means not merely interpreting what people say about their happiness, but also taking them at their word. People take drugs because they are frightened of other people; people don't take drugs because they are frightened of themselves. Both taking drugs and not taking drugs make people happy. Which kind of happiness do we prefer – that is, want to justify and promote – and why? Cruelty can make people happy, fear can make people happy. And we might then want to think about what problem, or, rather, problems, happiness is deemed to be the solution to. What in us happiness is a self-cure for. It is not, for example, incidental to our predicament that so many of our pleasures are, or are felt to be, forbidden. That the good that we desire can be forbidden (this is what Freud's account of the Oedipus complex is a way of thinking about). So put briefly – as every child and therefore every adult knows – being bad can make you happy; not only happy, but also happy. This makes the right to pursue happiness the right to break the rules. There is, we might say, the happiness that comes from being good – from abiding by the rules, from being safe from punishment, protected by the authorities having earned their love through virtuousness; and there is the happiness that comes from being bad, from transgression – from breaking the rules, from feeling guilty, from defying or triumphing over the authorities. Happiness is subjective, it takes many forms, and one of its forms is immorality. And last, but not least – though the least exciting – is the third point: some people like being unhappy. Indeed for some people their lives can be construed as the pursuit of unhappiness. What is happiness if it can be dreaded or feared; it is astounding the lengths some people will go to to be unhappy, to contrive their own misery; as though happiness itself were a phobic object, and held terrors. And we don't talk of the right to be unhappy, when we should. Unhappiness, after all, among many other things, can be the registration of injustice or loss. At its best a culture committed to the pursuit of happiness might be committed, say, to the diminishing of injustice; but at its worst a whole range of feeling and perception are proscribed by the culture of happiness. We have only to think of the moral guidance provided by advertisements; the promise of shopping. The losses in any life cannot be offset. It is perhaps not surprising that cultures organized around the idea of redemption might then be organized around the idea of happiness (and indeed around the idea of human rights). But it is not clear what might come after happiness.

II

Not every public has a common or public good.

Raymond Geuss, *Public Goods, Private Goods*

It is sometimes said now that psychoanalysis is one of the last places in the culture where people are allowed to be unhappy, and to be seen to be. And clearly, psychoanalysis, as a form of treatment, protects, if it does not actually foster, a person's right to be unhappy; and all the things I have been referring to, psychoanalysis, among many other disciplines, has something to say about. And I will be saying some of these things later. The subjectivity of happiness, what it is that the individual really loves and gets pleasure from; the immorality of pleasures and the lure of transgression; happiness as a perversion; the fear of pleasure and the masochistic solution; this is all the material of psychoanalysis, and not only of psychoanalysis. And yet, of course, historically, psychoanalysis is the inheritor of a set of political propositions that it would seem to be at odds with; or at least at a very odd angle to. If Freud and happiness doesn't sound like a very promising subject, Freud and the rights of man seems even less so. There is, in fact, only one reference to the rights of man in the *Standard Edition* of Freud's work, and it is, perhaps unsurprisingly, a strange one. Rights, like class, have never really been the thing for psychoanalysis; omissions, one would think, of some significance. Under the guise of talking about something Freud calls 'the condition of melancholia' and which sounds rather more like the human condition, Freud refers to the rights of man as a kind of brief holiday, a temporary respite from the more normal state of affairs which is one of the severest self-criticism. 'The most striking feature of this illness,' Freud writes in the *New Introductory Lectures on Psychoanalysis* of 1932,

is the way in which the super-ego – 'conscience' you might call it, quietly – treats the ego. While a melancholic can, like other people, show a greater or lesser degree of severity to himself in his healthy periods, during a melancholic attack his super-ego becomes over-severe, abuses the poor ego, humiliates it and ill treats it, threatens it with the direst punishment, reproaches it for actions in the remotest past which had been lightly taken at the time – as though it had spent the whole interval in collecting accusations and had only been waiting for its present access of strength in order to bring them up and make a condemnatory judgement on their basis. The super-ego applies the strictest moral standard to the helpless ego which is at its mercy; in general it represents the claims of morality. And we realise all at once that our normal sense of guilt is the expression of the tension between the ego and the super-ego. It is a most remarkable experience to see morality, which is supposed to have been given us by God and thus deeply implanted in us, functioning as a periodic phenomenon. For after a certain number of months the whole moral fuss is over, the criticism of the super-ego is silent, the ego is rehabilitated and again enjoys all the rights of man till the next attack.

What is striking about the passage is how much irony this dire predicament calls up in Freud about God, about morality and about the rights of man. There is only one thing stronger than all these things, he seems to be saying, and that is the super-ego at its worst (what Lacan refers to as the 'obscene super-ego'). Here, 'moral fuss' and the rights of man are in opposition, when the rights of man we might think of as moral fuss at its very best. The ego 'enjoys all the rights of man' only when the super-ego recedes, as though it might be on day-release; as though the rights of man were a liveable, a bearable, a liberating form of morality. And from the super-ego's point of view morality is the opposite; it is merciless, abusive and humiliating. Like the referee in football, the super-ego is always right, whether he is right or wrong. In this picture the rights of man are as nothing compared with the severity of the super-ego, which every so often, as a presiding dictatorial presence, dissolves these rights. Don't have much confidence in the so-called rights of man, Freud seems to be saying; they are no match for the ferocity of inner morality. The whole business of rights turns up only when the individual, the melancholic individual, is briefly released from his internal regime. Morality, at least in these patients, is periodic, as are the rights of man, the gift, as it were, of a higher power; God-given rights of man. '[O]ur normal sense of guilt,' Freud writes, 'is the expression of the tension between the ego and the super-ego'; this translates as: our happiness depends upon the distance between who we are and who we should be; who we should be according to the dictates of our internalized morality. We are mostly unhappy because we are rarely as we should be. Who we should be according to the rights of man is tenuous and largely unconvincing as a picture. When the internal authorities are so implacable and sadistic – over-severe, abusive, humiliating, as Freud writes – what are the possibilities for happiness? And what is the status, at least from a psychoanalytic point of view, of the so-called rights of man, which in Freud's account here sound rather more like God's grace than any form of right or entitlement; or, rather, more like luck than judgement; more of a holiday from real life. The right to happiness, or to its pursuit, would, in this picture mean the right to a generous super-ego, the right to a super-ego that was on the side of one's pleasure. As it is, given the scale of our guilt, it seems as though it is the right to be punished that we are fighting for. It will be one of Freud's more horrifying ironies that the pursuit of pleasure incites, calls up, the super-ego. And, of course, when and if pleasure is forbidden it requires punishment. There is no such thing as a free lunch. Virtue has to be its own reward. To pursue pleasure is to be pursued by punishment. There is no one more moralistic, more coercive, than a hedonist. The right to pursue happiness is the right to court punishment.

As the right to happiness or its pursuit is my subject, and I am by training a child psychotherapist, all this is by way of a lengthy preamble to eventually putting together the famous sentence from Thomas Jefferson's founding declaration with something from the paediatrician and psychoanalyst D. W. Winnicott's story about child development. And in the context of what has already been said, or briefly noted, I want to ask what, if anything, the right to happiness or its pursuit has to do with the child's development; whether the Declaration of Independence, a sentence from it, has anything to do with the declaration of independence that is the child's personal development, in Winnicott's declarations. And where, if at all, a right to happiness, or its pursuit, might figure. The famous sentence from Jefferson's

Declaration of Independence formulates something essential about what most modern liberals believe about both human nature and about government; about the preconditions not merely for survival but for human flourishing. 'We hold these truths to be self-evident, that all men are created equal, that they are endowed by their Creator with certain unalienable Rights, that among these are Life, Liberty and the pursuit of Happiness.' Some of us might not believe in the Creator part now, and some of us might find more and more difficult the idea that people are born equal, when the conditions in which they are born, for example, are manifestly so unequal, though we might want to keep hold of a sense in which we are all born equal, equally vulnerable, say; and we would assume now that by 'men' Jefferson has to mean both men and women of whatever creed and colour. And we also know what people are capable of doing to protect the right to life, liberty and the pursuit of happiness. And yet, as many people have noted, among these unalienable rights, not all of which are articulated, the pursuit of happiness – something not mentioned, for example, in the French Declaration of the Rights of Man and of the Citizen, nor in the Universal Declaration of Human Rights – seems peculiarly salient; it is the only one of the things listed that is a pursuit (it is perhaps not incidental to note that in the eighteenth century a pursuit was, in the words of the *OED*, 'persecution, annoyance . . . the action of pursuing a fleeing object, as a hunted animal or an enemy . . . a profession, business, recreation, etc.'). We pursue things that are either necessary, hostile or frivolous; and happiness, as we have seen, can be all or any of these things. But what exactly might it mean to have an 'unalienable right to the pursuit of happiness', given, as I have said, that it is fairly obvious that the pursuit of happiness is so morally equivocal; could be, among other things, a threat to the society that promoted it? But at first sight it seems to be a pretty good idea; no one, as I have said, would, presumably, promote the pursuit of unhappiness, though a case could be made for the value of unhappiness (it would be odd to be happy, or only happy, when someone you love dies, or indeed after watching the news). If we are convinced of anything now we are convinced that we are pleasure-seeking creatures, who want to minimize the pain and frustration of our lives. Or at least a 'we' could be consolidated around these beliefs. We are the creatures who, possibly unlike any other animal, pursue happiness. But the pursuit of happiness, like the pursuit of liberty – the utopian political projects of the twentieth century – has legitimated some of the worst crimes of contemporary history across the political spectrum. 'Like the utopian projects of the far left and right,' the political philosopher John Gray writes in *Gray's Anatomy*, 'the liberal ideal of a world of self-governing democracies has spilt blood on a colossal scale.' At least from the point of view of their critics these utopian projects look like the pursuit of unhappiness under the guise of the pursuit of happiness. They certainly evidence a carelessness of, if not a relish for, human suffering on a startling scale. It is one of the unalienable consequences of rights that they sanction unpredictable consequences. They are never quite what the philosopher Elizabeth Anscombe called a queer species of prediction. If you make something a right you are ineluctably involved in a queer species of legitimation. And what you are legitimating is something taken to be essential to human nature as it is or should be.

The Declaration of Independence was made because it was not a description of America as it was; it was a picture of America as it should be, a preferred America. And what makes it exhilarating is precisely the boldness of its claims. 'There is no existential quibbling,' the art critic Dave Hickey writes in his commentary on the Declaration, *The Invisible Dragon*,

> Equality is posited whether it exists or not. Life is guaranteed under the rubric of Safety. Happiness (whether *it* exists or not) is not assured, but its pursuit is protected. This final permission to pursue happiness with no promise of getting it has always

been the most beguiling to me. By distinguishing safety from the pursuit of happiness and promising both, the language of the Declaration introduces dynamic instability into the philosophy of public governance. Liberty is defined both positively and negatively: the government will act to ensure our safety, and it will stand back as we act on our own behalf in the 'pursuit of happiness'. When that pursuit putatively threatens our safety, however, the government invariably steps in. Safety trumps happiness, the government always wins . . . we are each free to pursue our own happiness [so] the relative value of all [our] 'goods' – beans, true love, biscuits, or paintings – may be, and should be, determined independent of governmental edict, regardless of scientific proof, and, whenever necessary, contrary to religious or metaphysical certainty . . . It is hardly imaginable, in fact, that citizens of a society like this, for whom the pursuit of happiness is a primal mandate, would *not* produce grails to embody the apotheosis of their quest. It is inconceivable that icons of happiness and desire would *not* proliferate in the tides and currents of this fluid central weather system.

Beginning his list of 'goods' with 'beans', probably an allusion to Thoreau's bean-field – 'beans, true love, biscuits, or paintings' – is a sign both of what is at stake in this primal mandate, and the extraordinary variety of proliferating icons of happiness and desire such principles of government might produce. In one sense what Hickey is referring to is what I quoted Freud as saying earlier: 'Happiness is something essentially subjective'; and what happens, Hickey says, when a government effectively both affirms and promotes this is what might look like, or perhaps is, a virtual anarchy of icons of happiness and desire. But what I want to take out of, or read into, Hickey's account, for the purposes of this talk, is the way he is also describing, through the prism of what we have learned to call liberalism, a certain kind of parenting; 'Happiness . . . is not assured, but its pursuit is protected . . . the government will act to ensure our safety, and it will stand back as we act on our own behalf in the "pursuit of happiness". When that pursuit putatively threatens our safety, however, the government invariably steps in. Safety trumps happiness, the government always wins . . .' It is not too much of a stretch here to see, in this account, the government as the parents, and the citizens as adolescent children; the governmental parent protects the pursuit of happiness, but prioritizes safety; the adolescent happiness-seekers go on producing grails 'independent of governmental edict', as Hickey writes, 'regardless of scientific proof, and, whenever necessary, contrary to religious or metaphysical certainty'. In this picture everything depends on the definitions of safety; on, as it were, the criteria of sufficient danger, or harm. We are allowed a multiplicity of aims, of objects of desire, of what Hickey calls 'grails'; indeed we are encouraged to make them, but with one proviso, the safety of others (and, at least for the adolescent, the safety of herself). What this acknowledges is that our happiness can endanger others and ourselves, and if we don't want to mandate danger we need government. There is, in other words, an acute apprehension about what the pursuit of happiness might entail, and what making this a right might cost. This, of course, was formulated succinctly by John Stuart Mill in *Auguste Comte and Positivism*:

> Why is it necessary that all human life should point but to one object, and be cultivated into a system of means to a single end? May it not be the fact that mankind, who after all are made up of single human beings, obtain a greater sum of happiness when each pursues his own, under the rules and conditions required by the good of the rest.

The single end is happiness even if all happinesses are different; differences are diminished by being promoted. But again, taking this out of context, it is clearly applicable as a description of the growing child in the family; the greater sum of happiness obtained by each person in the family pursuing their own ends, their own grails, under the rules and conditions required by the good of the rest can be redescribed as – the developing child pursues his own happiness under the rules and conditions provided by the adults. Children cannot bring themselves up, and children cannot bring up children (in *Lord of the Flies* the question 'Are there any adults?' recurs). So one naturalistic description of the child growing up in the family is of somebody with more or less of a primal mandate to pursue her happiness, to discover her objects of desire, what and who it is that she loves. While at the same time the culture, via the parents, will be showing her and telling her both what it is appropriate to love, and what the appropriate ways of loving are, what Mill calls 'the rules and conditions required by the good of the rest'. All parents, all families, all governments have their own more or less articulated, more or less unconscious, sense of what the rules and conditions are, and what the good of the rest includes. But at its most minimal, if there is a right to the pursuit of happiness – or whether this is what the child pursues naturally, so to speak – there is the necessity, the inevitability, of limits being set to it. The right to the pursuit of happiness always necessitates the right to set limits to the pursuit of happiness. The government, Hickey says, invariably steps in. And again, from a more naturalistic point of view, as the child soon discovers, if someone can satisfy her, then that same person can frustrate her. That we love the people we need because they give us what we need, and we hate the people we need because they can withhold it. So we must hate the people we love, indeed those are the people we hate; no one else is worth hating. There may be what adults, some adults, call a right to the pursuit of happiness, but this has built into it the ineluctability of unhappiness. Psychoanalysis just follows on from this fact.

So if it is said, or written, that we have a right to be happy or to pursue happiness it is assumed that happiness is something we are capable of, something that is available, if certain obstacles are removed. If liberty is there when tyranny is taken away, happiness is there when whatever makes us unhappy is removed. From a pragmatic point of view the art of a good life involves removing the obstacles to happiness; the picture, if we visualize it, is of something looked for, something looked forward to, and of there being something in the way. And this something in the way could be called: an unavailable mother, a prohibitive father, a competing sibling, not having enough brains or beauty, or charm, or money, or education, or luck. We would get closer to our happiness were these things removed or acquired; and a reality sense would be something to do with acknowledging which of these things cannot be acquired. It is all about, in short, our relation to obstacles; our distinguishing the intractable from the changeable; what we have to acknowledge from what we can influence; whether our desire is forbidden or not – whether we want a cream cake or another man's wife – it is, in pragmatic terms, about knowing what is possible. And everybody, it seems, is shadowed by an imaginary other person, a lucky counterpart, who gets all the happiness going. Lacan writes in the 'Ethics Seminar' (from *The Ethics of Psychoanalysis*) of 'the jealousy born in a subject in his relation to an other, in so far as this other is held to enjoy a certain form of jouissance or superabundant vitality, that the subject perceives as something that he cannot apprehend by means of even the most elementary of affective movements'. This other person, presumably, enjoys his happiness, his 'superabundant vitality' with no conflict, with no thought of safety, with no consideration of the rules and conditions required by the good of the rest. A right to the pursuit of happiness must be a right to remove the obstacles to happiness. This, at least, is the logic of the case. The man called 'the happiness tsar', Lord Layard, says we now know what makes children happy. What, then, are the obstacles to the child's happiness, and why can't we set about trying to remove them? And, of course, some of them we can remove. But what if the so-called obstacles to happiness are, or sometimes are, among the things that matter most to us? If, say, we love both luxury and justice? What if two mutually exclusive things make us happy, and one has to be abrogated? And, what if some obstacles are immoveable, untransformable into anything other than obstacles? There is something about the sexual drive, Freud suggested, that makes it intrinsically unsatisfiable. There are not infinite resources of food, of energy, of medicine. It is, for example, true, as every mother knows, that the mother cannot give the child everything that he wants, and that if she could it wouldn't be what he wanted. That everyone feels left out of something. It is misleading to think that one's parents have been the obstacle to one's happiness, even if they have radically thwarted it. Indeed, we might end up thinking that a right to irresolvable conflict might be the most realistic right we could come up with. That the attempt to resolve at least some conflicts was a distraction from finding better ways of living with them; that the right to pursue happiness has seduced us into pursuing happiness when we could have been doing something better. And that if we have a right to pursue happiness we have to acknowledge that unhappiness is not merely integral to the pursuit but to the right itself. It is not simply that we want happiness because we are unhappy, though this must be true, that unhappiness is the precondition for the pursuit of happiness. It is that, in a too logical way, we have been bewitched by the idea that if we are unhappy it must be happiness that we want. It may be a bit like thinking that if we are dissatisfied it is food we want; if we are feeling obscurely lacking, or at a loss, it is a drink we need. In other words, happiness may be – or can be used as – something more like an addiction than a desire; and the right to pursue it might be a way, as all addictions are, of being fobbed off, of being distracted. Alcoholics often believe that everyone should drink. How could anyone say now that they didn't want to be happy? Why should this be such a compelling good, such a compulsory 'single end', to use Mill's phrase? And, of course, it doesn't look like a single end because it takes so many forms; it is, as Freud reminds us, 'subjective'; in Dave Hickey's terms it produces so many 'grails', such a proliferation of 'icons of happiness and desire'. If the alternative to happiness is not, in the binary way, unhappiness; and if happiness has become so insidious, so hypnotic a single end for the good life, convincing us that happiness as an aim pays tribute to our variousness, our singularity, while reducing us, at the same time, to one single goal, why have we wanted this strange narrowing of our intent? What have we lost, or forgotten, or ignored, or payed insufficient attention to, or protected ourselves from, by wanting happiness? Happiness, it would seem, is the most plausible of our aims in life. But what psychoanalysis can chip in with here is that we are at our most defensive when we are at our most plausible.

I want to say that one of the other things we most want is to be able to feel frustrated, and that frustration issues in many things, only one of which is happiness; and that happiness can be, at its worst, a pre-emptive strike against frustration, a refuge from it rather than any kind of productive, unpredictable transformation of it (in the language of the psychoanalyst W. R. Bion, it is as though we can either evacuate frustration or attempt to modify it, and a great deal depends upon that distinction). So if we want to talk of a right to pursue happiness there needs to be a prior right, as it were, to feel frustration; to be able to bear and to bear with – with a view to future action – an experience, a sense of what is lacking in one's life. And not simply because frustration makes satisfaction possible in the way that hunger can make a meal delicious. But because frustration and satisfaction do not only or always have a logical, a causal, a pragmatic, relationship with each other. Or, to put it rather more obviously, what we are lacking when we are unhappy is not always happiness, any more than what the alcoholic is lacking is a drink. And proposing a right to the pursuit of happiness may seduce us, by a kind of word-magic, into thinking that happiness is just the thing. An addiction is an unarticulated frustration. What the alcoholic is suffering from is sobriety; and what that means is that he is suffering from the sobriety in which he might be able to feel and to get a more approximate sense of what it might be that he does need (and which is unlikely to be one thing). Alcohol as a self-cure has become the sole representation, for the alcoholic, of what is missing that matters. It cannot, as they say, be unpacked. It leads to nothing but itself.

So it is of interest that when the paediatrician and psychoanalyst D. W. Winnicott writes about deprivation in children he too talks about rights. 'Let us consider the meaning of the anti-social act,' he writes in a paper called 'The Deprived Child' (from *The Family and Individual Development*),

> for instance, stealing. When a child steals what is sought (by the total child, i.e. the unconscious included) is not the object stolen; what is sought is the person, the mother from whom the child has the right to steal because she is the mother. In fact every infant at the start can truly claim the right to steal from the mother because the infant invented the mother, thought her up, created her out of an innate capacity to love. By being there the mother gave her infant, gradually, bit by bit, the person of herself as material for the infant to create into, so that in the end his subjective self-created mother was quite a lot like the mother we can agree about. In the same way the child who wets the bed is looking for the mother's lap that is meet to be wetted in the early stages of the infant's existence.

There is here a whole theory of so-called creativity – of how the child makes the mother he needs and gradually through disillusionment and hatred disentangles her, to some extent, from the mother she happens to be. But for the purposes of this paper it is 'the mother from whom the child has the right to steal because she is the mother' that I want to consider. Winnicott is saying that the infant begins life in a commonwealth, the mother/infant unit; when he feels deprived of the mother he locates, he oversimplifies, this deprivation into the need for a particular object, which he steals. We have to imagine a hidden process, a secret narrative here, secret to the child, and therefore unconscious: the child feels a range of proliferating non-specified needs for the mother that are then gathered up as, narrowed down into, the specific object, which, we must note, has to be stolen, can't be asked for. So this is a peculiar right; the right to steal something, and the right to steal something that is felt to belong to oneself; indeed without which one cannot really live; or without which one lives radically deprived. (One is, in this sense, entitled only to what already belongs to oneself.) But because the thing stolen is not quite or even nearly the thing wanted – which is not a thing, but a mother – it can never satisfy. It is a picture of the right to pursue happiness getting stuck, something that I think it is prone to do; as though there is something about the pursuit of happiness that sponsors and endorses addiction. The theft requires communicable translation; it requires, as it were, someone to be able to say, or otherwise communicate, what it is that is really being pursued. Why is it stolen? Because it has not been given or cannot be taken. And because this is the only way, the only form, in which the deprivation can as yet be represented. The child, of course, will have to go on stealing unless or until this is understood and met in a way that works for the child. In Winnicott's declaration the child has a right to the pursuit of a mother to get what he needs for his development. He is entitled to a mother; she belongs to him in the sense that his own development belongs to him. As though Winnicott believes that we are entitled to our own development, something, one would have thought, that might require analysis also in terms of class. From a psychoanalytic point of view – or, rather, from one of the many psychoanalytic views – the child has a right to parents, or to people who care for his needs, and all subsequent rights follow on from there. But then we enter the world of competing accounts of what a good life is. Because, of course, in this picture, if you have a good-enough mother – a sufficiently responsive, a sufficiently generous, a sufficiently attentive mother, you are OK. The only problem with this is that it isn't true. Not everyone has one, and people who have had one have all kinds of lives. Lives are not the kinds of thing that can be guaranteed, even by mothers. It is unquestionably better to have had a so-called good-enough mother but it is not necessarily sufficient (all parents too quickly discover both how much and how little they can protect their children from). And people who have had, by their own accounts, bad experiences of mothering can have good and good-enough lives. A good-enough mother or parents might, say, give you the wherewithal for your pursuit of happiness; they may have backed your desire; helped you to believe in and not only be fearful of your pleasures. But it is more complicated than this. And this is where the idea of a right to pursue one's own happiness – which means, presumably, acquiring a sense of what makes one happy, and might make one happy – becomes more interesting. Do children want to be happy? And if they don't want to be happy what else might they want to be? This would seem to be of some importance because they are growing up in a world in which their parents mostly want them to be happy, or at least don't like them being unhappy, admittedly for a variety of different reasons. And by a 'world' I mean the particular cultures for whom happiness has become the preferred object, or the preferred fetish. Other questions might follow on from these, such as: what would a child have to have experienced to grow up into an adult who invents or endorses a belief that adults have a right to pursue their happiness? But now I just want to acknowledge that happiness, like all words, is a word the child inherits as being in some way applicable to her experience; and, as everyone knows, this is something parents often demand of their children; we, as we say, want our children to be happy; we were once children whose parents wanted us to be happy. And that means the whole spectrum, from not being a worry to them, not making their lives more difficult, being curative of their woes; to the pleasure our parents could take in our pleasure and our well-being. Whether or not children want to be happy, their parents tend to want them to be. We, if there is a we, are more dependent on our children than they are on us; and we are dependent, in brief, on their happiness. What makes the child happy is not going to be unlinked to what makes the parents happy. So it is worth holding in mind the possible connections between childhood experience and the desire for rights. Clearly if a parent lives as if their child has a right to happiness, or a right to its pursuit, and that they are the guardians of this right, they are going to have a difficult, an even more difficult, task on their hands. Lovers often feel that they should be making each other happy when they are in fact making themselves a problem to each other, which may make them happy. So by way of conclusion I want to suggest that a right to the pursuit of happiness is asserted when a capacity for absorption has been sabotaged. Happiness becomes important when the possibility for absorption is under threat. That the child does not want to be happy – or perhaps, more exactly, the child doesn't want only to be happy – the child wants first to be safe, and then to be absorbed. Indeed, of the three things that matter most – kindness, sexuality, and forgetting oneself – it is the forgetting of oneself – the capacity to be absorbed in something or someone else, that is the main casualty of our contemporary will-to-happiness. Nothing makes us more self-conscious than wanting to be happy.

There is an interesting moment in *Lord of the Flies* when Henry, one of the 'littluns', wanders away from the main group of children. 'He went down the beach and busied himself at the water's edge . . .', William Golding writes,

> . . . There were creatures that lived in this last fling of the sea, tiny transparencies that came questing in with the water over the hot, dry sand. With impalpable organs of sense they examined this new field. Perhaps food had appeared where the last incursion there had been none . . . This was fascinating to Henry. He poked about with a bit of stick, that itself was wave-worn and whitened and a vagrant, and tried to control the motions of the scavengers . . . He became absorbed beyond mere happiness as he felt himself exercising control over living things.

The adult narrator can see Henry as in some way identified with these rudimentary scavengers; and the narrator intimates that without adults the children feel how much is out of control or under-controlled. And then there is the remarkable sentence: 'He became absorbed beyond mere happiness as he felt himself exercising control over living things.' He feels himself exercising control, but he is not, and his absorption is beyond, in excess of, mere happiness. Something else is wanted more than happiness by Henry, and it seems to be the exercise of control over living things, one of which is himself. It would be easy, and partly true, to say that what Henry is absorbed by here, what is beyond mere happiness, is power, control over living things. But Golding is clear about two things: it is an illusion of power – Golding refers to Henry having 'the illusion of mastery' – and it is also the absorption itself that is beyond mere happiness. 'He became absorbed beyond mere happiness.' It is an illusion that absorbs him beyond happiness; in other words, he is playing. Absorption is not in and of itself a moral good, of course; in the novel the tyrannical, sadistic Jack absorbs the attention of a lot of the children who do his bidding. But in proposing, in the context of the novel, that there is a beyond to mere happiness, something else or further that is wanted; and that indeed happiness may be a poor substitute for something else – that happiness may be something that can get in the way of whatever is beyond it; by proposing this, Golding is saying something about what can override the pursuit of happiness, and what may be lost in its pursuit. For better and for worse, being able to feel our frustration is the precondition for becoming absorbed; when this is impossible the pursuit of happiness tends to take over. The right to pursue happiness may be, at its worst, the right not to feel frustrated. And if frustration is not allowed to take its course, to take its time, there is no absorption, only refuges from unhappiness. The right to the pursuit of happiness can be a cover story for the wish to hide.

Judas for Now

TO BETRAY. 2. To discover that which has been
entrusted to secrecy.

Samuel Johnson, *The Dictionary*

I want to start with a modern, and for some people iconic,
return of Judas, a moment in relatively recent cultural history in
which Judas was, as it were, resurrected. In 1965/6 the erstwhile
folk singer Bob Dylan released a great trilogy of albums, *Bringing It All Back Home*, *Highway 61 Revisited* and *Blonde on Blonde*,
and set off on a world tour that would change popular music. At
a now famous concert at the Manchester Free Trade Hall, in
which Dylan was playing his new electric and electrifying
music, a disaffected folkie shouted 'Judas!' from the audience,
and Dylan responded with an instruction to the band to 'play
fucking loud' what turned out to be an extraordinary performance of 'Like a Rolling Stone', a song about someone having to
change; a song about someone disillusioned by who they had
become. Some people had been wanting Dylan to be one thing
when he turned out to be another, and they felt betrayed. By
doing something new, by doing something unexpected, Dylan
was Judas. In this context the betrayer is someone who wanted
something to change; in retrospect we can see that what sounded
like a betrayal was innovation. Something was betrayed – the
folk-music tradition – to make something else possible. This
Judas was bringing a new vision, a new sound. And it is worth
noticing Dylan's response; as though being called Judas incited
him, released him more completely, or perhaps more excessively,
into being the person he had become. He played the loud music

even louder. He took on the role, and it freed him, for the moment. Dylan, like Judas, now had, in the words of the song, 'no direction home'. You can do a lot of things with betrayal, but you can't undo it. It feels irredeemable. And that can be the point that masquerades as the problem; to betray is to create a situation that there is no going back from. After betrayal there is no direction home. What begins as new can end up being real.

In the 1940s Wittgenstein wrote, 'I think one of the things Christianity says is that sound doctrines are useless. That you have to change your life.' Clearly our lives are changed by our being betrayed; but do we change our lives through betrayal? Is this one of the ways, or even the way, in which we, as we say, make a change? How do people, in Wittgenstein's words, change their lives? Well, sometimes, at least, by betraying and being betrayed. So perhaps we should talk not only of the fear of being betrayed, but also of the wish, the willingness, to be betrayed, and indeed to betray. And then we would be talking, at least from a psychoanalytic point of view, of, for example, consciously or unconsciously, engineering our own betrayal, and looking for people (or traditions) we can betray. We would be talking of betrayal as an often unconsciously sought transformational act; we might even talk of betrayal as an object of desire – or as what the psychoanalyst Christopher Bollas calls a 'transformational object' – and start noticing how we seek it. And also, by the same token, notice all the opportunities to betray and be betrayed that we have missed, risks that for various reasons we have avoided, or that misfired. Many of our uncompleted actions are uncompleted because they are forms of betrayal. Failures of nerve that we have redescribed to ourselves as commitment, or loyalty, or integrity, or kindness. Just as betrayal is born of frustration, we are often loyal when we fear disillusionment. Talking about Judas is an opportunity to say that a betrayer is someone who enacts, who voices, a frustration; and psychoanalysis wants us to ask, what happens to frustration when it isn't voiced? Or, to put it another way, what could Judas have been wanting, other than money or punishment, from betraying Jesus? This question tends to go begging because what Jesus so crucially wants from being betrayed dominates the story. Judas, we should note, was not a man who invented his own religion. This should give us pause.

And yet to talk in this way, to promote betrayal – to make the case for it – is also morally reprehensible; indeed it reveals just how starkly our sense of ourselves as moral creatures is organized around the question of betrayal, and whatever we take to be its opposite, or take to be the alternatives to it. What would the social bond look like – and, indeed, the bonds between individual people – if we thought of the capacity to betray and be betrayed as a virtue; or at least, as in some sense, integral to the moral life; as something, say, to be taught in schools? Or, alternatively, what would be the consequences for a person's life if they were unable to betray or bear betrayal? What would this stop them doing, or feeling, or desiring? In what sense, for example, would they be able to leave home; to begin to live as if there were no direction home? In what ways would they be able to change, and what kinds of change would be precluded?

I want to ask these questions because we live in a culture in which there is a short story about our lives called psychoanalysis that puts betrayal, or something akin to betrayal, at the centre of human development. And in which there is another larger and longer story about our lives – not merely or simply a story to believers – called Christianity in which betrayal, in the person of Judas, is both integral and alien to the fundamental story of Christ's life and death and resurrection. In psychoanalysis, betrayal is called, variously, weaning, the birth of a sibling, the Oedipus complex, and puberty. At each of these developmental stages, in the psychoanalytic story, the child suffers what feels like a breach of trust, a loss of entitlement, a diminished specialness. As in the sexual infidelities of adulthood, something that was taken for granted and taken to be exclusive has had to be shared. But of course these cumulative betrayals – not intended as such by the parents, but felt as such by the child – are in the service of development of more and new life. And the child, at least initially, feels betrayed by the new life he is precipitated into; he is like the man in Dylan's audience shouting 'Judas!', but at his parents. How do we know something is new, that something is changing? We feel somehow betrayed.

When we talk about morality, about what it is to lead a good life according to our various cultural standards, we have to talk about betrayal. Indeed without betrayal none of the stories would make any sense. And this, I think, is worth noting. What is morality, if we can't talk about it without talking about betrayal? And what is betrayal if we can't talk about it without talking about morality? And these are versions of the question, who is Jesus (or God) if we can't talk about him without talking about Judas? We need only think of the child's inevitable disillusionment with the parents, the adolescent's astonishment at adult morality and immorality, and the adult's agony of sexual jealousy and dismay at ageing to see how much work the idea of betrayal, and the talismanic figure of Judas, are doing for us. It is what Dylan was singing about in 'With God on Our Side': 'In many a dark hour / I've been thinking about this / that Jesus Christ / was betrayed by a kiss / But I can't think for you / you'll have to decide / whether Judas Iscariot / had God on his side.'

The question becomes – if we can get over the straightforward demonization of Judas that has been a strong arm of the demonization of the Jews – can we also make a virtue of betrayal? And if not, what, if anything, can we also make of it? Both psychoanalysis and certain interpreters of the New Testament want us to believe that it is a terrible and necessary thing. No betrayal, no real life; or no real afterlife. If Judas had God on his side, what kind of God is he? Perhaps one who can see the boon of betrayal. We don't kiss everybody. And we don't betray everybody. Indeed you know someone matters to you if they can betray you, or be betrayed by you. Once there is the possibility of betrayal a great deal has already happened (there can be betrayal only if there is a history, some real relationship or affinity). Betrayal is possible, in other words, only when there is something to betray; and that something takes time, and is of paramount importance. You know there is something of value when there is the potential for betrayal. Sexual jealousy is not just one of the things that happens when you become attached to someone; it is the sign of attachment. It is how you know that someone matters to you.

If there was no such thing as betrayal in the world how would anything matter to us, or how would we know that it did? Judas, for better and for worse, helps us make a lot of sense. So the answers to the question, why is there such a thing in the world as betrayal? – what are we doing by betraying and being betrayed? – take us to the heart of what used to be called the moral life. There is a reason – several reasons – why we can't imagine a world without betrayal in it; and Judas – as both a character in the New Testament, and in the more recently discovered and deciphered Gospel of Judas – is, among many other things, a way of thinking about this. Betrayal is something that we shouldn't do, but that has significant consequences – Christ's crucifixion, say, and his subsequent resurrection; and inevitable consequences – it causes a great deal of suffering. And when it is not providential it is predictable and unpredictable in its effect. And it often presents itself as a temptation: that is, it promises pleasure.

So, perhaps unsurprisingly, there have always been at least two questions about Judas – what was he doing, and why was he doing it? And in answering these questions – which means interpreting the story and the figure of Judas – we have to bear something simple but significant in mind: that in betraying someone (or something) one is protecting someone (or something) else. And that someone or something else may be – in fact is likely to be – of real value; and may be startlingly new (betrayal might be another word for revision, or renewal). When E. M. Forster said that he hoped he would have the courage to betray his country rather than his friend, he was drawing our attention to this fact that adds a necessary complication to the act of betrayal. So we have to bear in mind what Judas might have been protecting – what values he could have been serving, or promoting, or trying to articulate, other, that is, than Satan's – in his betrayal of Jesus. And, of course, whether it was a betrayal. And if it was not a betrayal, then we have a quite different kind of conversation on our hands.

Unless, of course, as in the Gospel of Judas, it is a good betrayal; indeed one of the reasons that the story in this gospel is so illuminating is that it makes Judas's betrayal of Jesus a virtuous act. It 'seems to end in disaster', Elaine Pagels writes in *Reading Judas* (co-author Karen King), 'Jesus is betrayed; Judas will be stoned to death by his fellow disciples. But . . . both have already achieved salvation. Jesus's sacrifice signals the end of death itself by acknowledging our fundamental spiritual nature. Gazing upward and entering into the luminous cloud Judas is but the first fruits of those who follow Jesus.' So there is the case made for Judas – as the one who truly recognizes Jesus. 'I know who you are and which place you come from,' he says to Jesus in this gospel, the only one of the disciples that Jesus then initiates into the divine mystery; and the case made for betrayal. The Gospel of Judas could be taken to be saying: only someone who truly recognizes someone can betray them, and so-called betrayal can be the best thing they can do. The Gospel of Judas, that is to say, encourages us to believe that we have misunderstood the nature of betrayal; we have not been able to see how it is linked to recognition and transformation. It has been tempting to exonerate Judas – to portray him as one of the misunderstood – and so to avoid or disqualify the betrayal issue from the start. The Gospel of Judas says fairly and squarely that Judas did betray Jesus, and it was a good thing too.

When it comes to Judas one obvious interpretative option, then, setting aside the newly discovered and non-canonical Gospel of Judas that only really came to light in the 1970s, has been to mitigate or even disavow the whole notion that he was betraying Jesus – by suggesting that since he was, say, fulfilling a necessary role in God's master-plot, Judas is a functionary rather than a fully paid-up evil person; or, as William Klassen argued in his appropriately entitled *Judas: Betrayer or Friend of Jesus?*, that there may have been some kind of agreement between Jesus and Judas to introduce Jesus in a more conciliatory way to the authorities, and that it all went terribly wrong. 'He may have thought,' Klassen writes, 'that, by meeting Temple authorities, Jesus could become better disposed toward the traditional way in which changes were made in the Temple.' Klassen's title, we should note, makes us choose between Judas as betrayer and Judas as friend when we need, I think, to see that he might have been, or must have been, both. But Klassen's argument is clear: Judas may not have been a betrayer, and, by implication, Jesus did not need a betrayer. And when Judas is not being excused, freed from his traditional role, it is proposed, with enough textual evidence, that Judas, as the typically money-crazed, servile Jew of anti-Semitic provenance, sold Jesus to the powers that be for thirty silver coins. Judas, in other words, either straightforwardly betrayed Jesus in the most nefarious way, or was rather cruelly dictated to by God to play an essential role in betraying him in this way; or was trying to help Jesus, and it misfired. What is rarely said – though intimated in the Gospel of Judas – is that Judas was harming and helping Jesus by betraying him; and perhaps not merely, or not only, in the providential sense that Jesus required a Judas to fulfil his mission, which makes Judas essential to the story but perhaps less complex as a figure (it gives him a function but not a very subtle project). We can imagine Othello having had his life without Iago, but not Jesus having had his life without Judas. We need to wonder why in this story the betrayer is so less interesting than the betrayed; even though for obvious reasons the story doesn't want us to think like this. In Matthew, for example, Judas is given a peculiarly unenviable role, intimate but cursed: Jesus 'answered and said, "He that dippeth his hand with me in the dish, the same shall betray me. The Son of man goeth as it is written of him: but woe unto that man by whom the Son of man is betrayed: it had been good for that man if he had not been born" (26:23–5). This is having it both ways in the most terrible way; it is written that this will happen – that someone will have to do this particular piece of dirty work – but, paradoxically, it would have been better if this person had not been born. Better for him, but not, it seems, better for Jesus, or indeed for the fate of the world, given Judas's crucial role in the story. 'I think one of the things Christianity says,' Wittgenstein wrote, 'is that sound doctrines are useless. That you have to change your life.' Perhaps Jesus had plenty of sound doctrines – but he needed to change his life.

The Judas of the New Testament – which we know now to be four gospels among many – is not an impressive figure; though he is an enigmatic one, partly because we are told so little about him, which invites modern readers to ascribe motives, and partly because he is such a decisive presence in the story. But we do need to bear in mind that he is one of the disciples, and this in itself would seem to give him some kind of privileged position. It also invites us to ask what Judas was that the other disciples were not such that he was the chosen one; the only one of the disciples that Jesus could use, so to speak, to transform himself, or to be transformed by in this way. 'The betrayer,' Elaine Pagels writes, 'always intrigues us more than the disciples who remain loyal'; and it is worth wondering why this is so. Pagels is intimating, perhaps, that we get a certain kind of pleasure from stories about betrayal that we can't get from stories about loyalty; more pleasure, or a different kind of pleasure. As though, to put it as crudely as possible, disloyalty offers us something that loyalty cannot. As though, for some good reason, we are intrigued by the part of ourselves that can betray people, particularly people we love and admire. As though there may be some forbidden vitality in this part of ourselves, something morally equivocal and alluring.

We are encouraged by the gospel narratives not simply to not identify with Judas, but actually to disidentify from him. As if to say, no one would want to be Jesus's betrayer, no one could possibly aspire or desire to betray their master, someone they really believed in and loved. But why not? It is, after all, one of our modern myths about development, about independence, that the adolescent betrays his parents, the student betrays his teacher; that without betrayal the disciple remains always and only a disciple. Indeed in the romantic myth of unbounded independence of spirit, being an eternal disciple, a bit like being an eternal student, can be a form of arrested development. There is, we might say, a kind of modern cultural double-message, or double-bind, here – betrayal is a terrible thing, but without betrayal there can be no development. We must grow up and become the people who we are, but without betraying the people we believe in. Or we must betray people and call it something else, such as eccentricity, or idiosyncrasy, or independent-mindedness.

But in the story of Judas in the New Testament, Judas's betrayal is his gift to Jesus; in a strange reversal of the modern myth, it is being betrayed – having the capacity, the wherewithal to be betrayed – that is transformative, at least for Jesus. In the New Testament version Judas gains nothing; in Matthew, Judas, 'cast down the pieces of silver in the temple, and departed, and went and hanged himself' (27:5); and in Acts – in another version of an unfortunate fall – with the money he had gained, Judas, in Marvin Meyer's lurid translation, 'bought a piece of land, and there he fell face first, and his body burst open and all his intestines spilled out' (Acts 1:18). Both Judas and Jesus are transformed by the betrayal, but only Jesus and the world benefits; only Jesus dies into new life. In the New Testament account – and this, oddly, is where it joins up with part of the psychoanalytic story – everything depends upon what the individual can make of being betrayed. And in order to be betrayed you need – you might have to find, to recruit, to seduce – a betrayer. After the ordinary, inevitable, catastrophic betrayals of childhood, betrayal signifies the movement of life. Betrayers matter so much because being betrayed makes us who we are. It is probably easier for modern people to want to sympathize with Judas as envious, or even glamorize Judas as transgressive. But we needn't be trying to make Judas somehow better than he is – as the Gospel of Judas does so winningly – we just need to see what Jesus and Judas are doing together. And seeing here means reading, interpreting, redescribing this extraordinary and ordinary relationship. And this might even mean, in Johnson's *Dictionary* definition of 'to betray', which I used as my epigraph, to 'discover that which has been entrusted to secrecy'. One thing that has been entrusted to secrecy in the story of Judas's betrayal of Jesus, is that betrayal is one of the forms revelation takes.

After the discovery of the Gospel of Judas – apparently written in the middle part of the second century, a few decades after the New Testament gospels, and discovered in the 1970s in Middle Egypt but not coming properly to light, after much shady dealing, until 2001 – there was more textual evidence, as it were, for further reconsideration of the figure of Judas. 'After the Gospel of Judas and the re-examination of New Testament and other early Christian sources,' the biblical scholar Marvin Meyer writes, 'it may be difficult to maintain that Judas was simply the evil betrayer of Jesus. Rather, in these accounts, a more attractive and inspiring Judas comes forward, within the story of Jesus's life and death, as a model of what it means to be a disciple of the Master.' I am not sure it is possible to be 'simply the evil betrayer of Jesus'. But what Meyer is alluding to – and what even brief reference to the Gospel of Judas shows – is that betrayal is an uncanny form of intimacy. That we can be betrayed by people only if they know us well; and that the wish to be known can be, among many other things, the wish to be betrayed. That somewhere in ourselves we associate being loved with being betrayed, and being betrayed with growing. And we do a lot of work trying not to know this when it is, in fact, something worth acknowledging; something the unpleasant figure of Judas helps us to notice.

Punishing Parents

I

Every Man being . . . naturally free and nothing being able
to put him into subjection to any Earthly Power, but his own
Consent; it is to be considered what shall be understood to be a
sufficient Declaration of a Man's Consent.

John Locke, *Second Treatise on Government*

'Original sin' is the phrase some people use for the fact that scarcity
tends to bring out the worst in us. And scarcity is where we start
from. Just like our 'first parent', our parents are never enough for us,
and our parents themselves are living in a world of finite resources
that are unequally distributed. All the ways we have, as children, of
voicing our protest and our frustration, threaten to estrange us
from the very people we need and depend upon. We cannot avoid
hating the people we love, because they never seem to love us
enough, or love us in quite the right way; the right way being the
way in which we would never have to feel frustrated. And this
hatred is a continual threat to these relationships we need. Something or someone has to manage this incredible insufficiency we
are born into, and the ambivalence, the love and the hate it evokes.
'Authority' is the word we use for all the ways we have of managing the consequences of scarcity (and indeed of ambivalence).

'At the beginning,' Freud writes in *Civilisation and Its Discontents*, 'what is bad is whatever causes one to be threatened with
loss of love'; if the child 'loses the love of another person upon
whom he is dependent, he also ceases to be protected from a

variety of dangers. Above all, he is exposed to the danger that this stronger person will show his superiority in the form of punishment.' This, one might say, is an important clue about the so-called nature of authority; and about the kind of authority, the kind of power, parents have over their children. Power and authority, in the first instance – that is, from the child's point of view – are the freedom to withhold love, and the protection they bring. A parent is someone who has the power to expose a child to danger. We are subject to authority because we are dependent creatures. It is something we crave and dread. Because authority is a problem, many people have a problem with authority. We begin in a state of intimidation; and then the worst thing we ever do is intimidate other people.

When Freud is talking about loss of love he is talking about the origins of authority, and the problems of parenting; two things that for him are inextricable. Authority, though, like parenting, is not really a problem because it cannot be solved; it is, rather, Freud intimates, something we must endlessly long for and ineluctably suffer; something our essential neediness traps us into needing. We were all once children, dependent on the protection of others, who were free to punish us. This, in its Darwinian (and Hobbesian) common sense, is what binds us to each other. In this stark vision, this sociable realism, all love is conditional love – even mothers are ambivalent about their children, really want them and really want to be rid of them (Oedipus, after all, is a story about a mother's – as well as a father's – wish to kill her son); and all love is a kind of deal, even if in its political form it is called a social contract: consent or submit and you will be protected, fail to comply and you will be punished. In this story authority is good because the alternative is worse; power is good because powerlessness is (supposedly) unendurable. We should remember, though, perhaps especially when we talk again about authority, that the absence of something can be a way of not questioning whether it ever really existed.

A lot of people now don't believe in the existence of adults.

They believe, consciously or unconsciously, that grown-ups are people – presumably children – playing at being grown up. And this version has been an endless source of ironic amusement and revelation about the so-called adult world. But this view also has its drawbacks; and it comes to a crisis when people who don't really believe there is such a thing as an adult have children. Like the children in William Golding's *Lord of the Flies* they may keep asking, implicitly or explicitly, where are the adults, are there any adults here? – that is, they buy books about child-rearing – keeping their spirits up by sustaining their belief that if there are children there must be people around who know how to look after them (the real problem of being a child is that children can't bring themselves up). Or they may live in what is effectively a family of siblings – which is always somewhere a family in a panic – and do what they can. And probably they will do a bit of both. Though the historical explanations for this must be complex – and they are indeed many and varied, but adulthood, like God, and the author, has clearly been a long time dying, and to no avail – the loss of confidence in adulthood declares itself most tellingly in the dilemmas and perplexities of child-rearing. And there are these perplexities and dilemmas partly because, to return to Freud, parents, of course, were once children who themselves feared loss of love, as were their parents' parents, and so on and on. There is more to it than this, but this is something, in William James's words, to be going on from. Where there is love there is fear of loss of love; where there is hatred there is fear of its perpetuity (after an argument you have to wait and see whether the other person becomes loveable to you again; our love, that is to say, is not within our gift). Parents have to be able to bear being hated by their children; and being hated always rings alarm bells from the past. In family life it's important not to take things personally. An adult is someone who is capable of not taking things personally.

So when, for example, parents fear the loss of their children's love – or indeed the loss of their love for their children – chaos is come again. Or that is what it can feel like. Love becomes the magic potion in the fairy tale of family life. Before you have children, the novelist Fay Weldon once remarked, you can believe you are a nice person; after you have children you understand how wars start. Family life, in other words, is the great love test. And a great war. Once people have children they begin to wonder what love is, and what it can do; and when, or whether, it's stronger than hate. Because even though the family is the first place you get what you want it is always, by the same token, the place where you first find out about frustration, about the nothing that can come from not being all; and about the mixed blessing of specialness being that it can be lost. If we add to Fay Weldon's useful point the psychoanalyst Neville Symington's suggestion that having a baby is like dropping a bomb on a family, we have, broadly speaking, got if not the picture then an essential part of it. It is not, it seems, that in the so-called modern era family life has become difficult – given its members it could never be anything else – but that, at least from the end of the nineteenth century, it has become so distressing as to make people wonder what the alternatives to it might be. When the death of the family – another wished-for death – was being predicted in the 1960s – *The Death of the Family* being the title of a slightly crazed and shrewd book by the anti-psychiatrist David Cooper – it was because the life of the family was increasingly unbearable for too many people. Psychoanalysis, among many other things, was invented partly to address this, to treat the casualties of modern family life. The family was a problem because parents were once children. And childhood was being described by the modern mind-doctors as a 'cumulative trauma', not as an idyll. Every couple, every family, is a rendezvous with a transgenerational history that they are unconscious of and haunted by (it takes three generations, the French psychoanalyst Françoise Dolto remarked, to make a psychotic). And every child grows up in the climate of his parents' mostly unconscious history, which is the medium in which he tries out his always risky development. The difficulties of modern parenting, one might say, are grossly underrated. It is not, in other words, that there is no such thing as a happy childhood, but that no childhood can be only happy. It would be better to replace the idea of the happy childhood with the idea of the real childhood (and to realize that childhood informs everything in one's life and predicts nothing). We make childhood sound alluring because we fear adulthood may not be. It is strange to have become the animals who are so ambivalent about growing up.

Indeed the problem for many modern parents – and this is partly the legacy of psychoanalysis, which is part of the legacy of romanticism – is that they are continually being reminded that because they were once children they are really children; and that a child is the most authentic thing one can be. And this, as we shall see, cuts both ways. At its best it breaks down what we have been encouraged to think of as the Victorian divide between adults and children, making parents more sympathetically imaginative about their children's needs (though by privileging the child's point of view the adult's point of view is easily lost, or made to sound too knowing, or too self-important). But at its worst it produces adults who are complicit with their children, and so merely enacting a child's view of what it is to be an adult (adults as super-heroes, super-hedonists, super-moralists: adults as people without limit or limitation, people who can do whatever they want). Which is why so many adults seem to be, consciously or unconsciously, a parody, a caricature, of adulthood, exposing it by performing it at its most ridiculous (for the most riveting exposé of adulthood in these terms one should read Oscar Wilde and Samuel Beckett). Like a transvestite, the adult impersonator, the child dressed as an adult, performs a precocious cartoon of what they have been subjected to (pompous potency, sentimental moralism masquerading as morality, and so on). As though the adult as seen by the child, and the adult as seen by the adolescent – and think how much successful modern fiction is written from these points of view – has usurped the adult's view of the adult. Adulthood, that is, as a version of camp; not just growing up absurd, in Paul Goodman's sharp title, but growing up kitsch.

There have been many benefits of this blurring of generational differences, even though we hear so much in the right- and left-wing media mostly about the losses involved and the damage done. In exactly the way that democracy can be described, in the words of the political philosopher Pierre Rosanvallon, as 'institutionalizing mistrust', adulthood is only as good as its response to its critics. And no one is usually more critical of their parenting than the parents themselves, followed of course by their children. But just as it seems strange to us now to imagine a world in which children and adolescents have, as they say, no voice, it may be equally strange to live in a world in which adults have no voice, or no voice that can be reliably recognized; a world in which the adult's voice is valued for its inclusion of childhood freshness and ingenuousness and adolescent mockery and idealism, but not for its distinctiveness. After romanticism we have the voice of the child, after two world wars we have the voice of the adolescent; we have always had the voice of the adult, but the voice of the adult changes once we start believing, once we start living as if, the child is mother and father to the man. Once you take childhood seriously, how do you take yourself seriously as an adult? And do you even want to? Adulthood can all too easily seem like the long hangover after childhood. Or merely childhood without its supposed innocence. Childhood ironized.

Being a parent must always be, to some extent, performing being a parent; first we identify with the parents and then we become them, as the traditional story goes, though imitation is clearly not the only form that inspiration or education takes. But as in the theatre, the quality and the truthfulness of the performance make all the difference. The question is not merely, are there any good roles now? Or, which are the best lines? The question is, what's realistically possible, in the light of our transgenerational histories, most of which we cannot know about, and the knowledge we claim to have about ourselves, most of which can't be put into practice? We have to wonder, that is to say, not only (and pragmatically) which are the versions of adulthood and of parenting that will bring us the lives that we want, assuming we have the wherewithal to perform them, and assuming that we know what we want (and that it won't change); but also how we can diminish the humiliations of childhood. The only real question about child-rearing is, how, if at all, can we make childhood less humiliating? And how much is this a pragmatic question – what is to be done? How can we change our practices – and how much do we have to acknowledge limits set by our histories and the unconsciousness of our desire? Real limits, as every child knows, are both found and made by experiment, by testing them out. They are not limits until they are tested. The overprotected child begins to believe there must be something truly terrifying out there, or that he must be terrifyingly weak, if so much protection is required. It is the vulnerability of children that makes parents at once overprotective and sadistic, the two things not always being quite so different as they may seem. And yet to be a parent is to face how little you can protect your child from. And powerlessness, given what we are educated to believe about it, doesn't tend to bring out the best in people.

II

Too much of a good thing can be a good thing.

Mae West

If children can make parents feel powerless, what kind of power do parents really have? Or, rather, what kind of power, or authority, do they want to have, or assume they should have, given how inadequate they are now prone to feel doing that most ordinary thing called living in families and bringing up children (if powerlessness wasn't stigmatized a lot of things would be easier)? Now that there is a consensus – shared, surprisingly, by many politicians and psychoanalysts – that parents' failure to discipline their children is the source of all our, and their, woes, it is worth wondering what the cultural fantasies – or the fantasies in different cultures – might be about what discipline is and how it works. Not to mention the larger question of how and in what ways we want to be able to influence other people, especially those most influenceable people, the young. Discipline, when it is not the learning of a skill, is an enraged impatience about people's salutary unwillingness to comply.

What the critic Harold Bloom called the anxiety of influence among post-romantic poets – the wish to kill off, or revise, the precursor poets that inspired them – is as nothing compared to the widespread anxiety, the anxiety of ineffectiveness, among parents, the fear that they have little influence, or little influence worth having, over their children; while often believing, paradoxically, that it is their own parents' fault that they are like this. We may, in a certain sense, learn to parent from our own parents, but what do we do if what we learned from our parents was what we considered to be bad parenting; that, say, our parents' parenting was not a passion and a pleasure, but a burden and a duty, that they were not committed to our flourishing but to their own narcissism; that, in different ways, they were very ambivalent about our presence, that they were people and not failing gods, and so on (as the modern complaint does tend to go on)?

It is worth starting, I think, with a simple proposition – no one ever recovers from the sado-masochism of their childhood. We may not want to think of the relations between parents and children as power relations – indeed it might sound like a perversion of parenting to do so; and, of course, we don't want to think of parents and children being in any sense sexually gratified by their status in relation to each other, nor indeed of parent–child relations fixing the terms for adult sexual engagement. But to get a sense of this – of what it might mean to describe child-rearing as, among many other things, a sado-masochistic set-up – we have to see the ways in which, to put it as cutely as possible, feeling big can depend upon someone else being made to feel small. When your child zooms round the house saying he is a super-hero you can tell him, one way or another, that actually he's a little boy, or you can say something about why this may be an incredible thing to be. When your child falls over you can get cross with her for not looking where she's going, or you can comfort her in a heart-felt way. These are not pictures of the bad and good parent so much as responses, states of mind, every parent is capable of. In identifying with the child, which involves imagining his strengths and his vulnerability, we join him in something; in disidentify-ing we separate him out. We take a spurious distance; if you feel for your child when she falls over, you feel it in your body; if you scold her you are exempt. One is a sado-masochistic solution – the pleasure, the excitement, is in the correcting of the child – the other is not. One assumes a sameness, an of-a-pieceness with the child, the other asserts a difference, an inner superiority; one is in solidarity, the other is punishing. It is the difference between wanting to win an argument and wanting to enlarge one's experi-ence, the difference between wanting to be right and wanting to be kind (and so of the same kind). It is, in short, the difference between two kinds of authority. One is in essence humiliating, and breeds resentment, the other is reassuring and makes a com-monwealth. So the solution would seem to be to find ways of stopping people wanting to humiliate each other.

And yet we know that some people's psychic survival – every-body's psychic survival some of the time – depends upon their capacity to humiliate others; to turn the tables, to make others experience what they have suffered, to reassure themselves that they are the humiliators rather than the humiliated (as though that was the repertoire, and it is of some significance how often this does feel like the repertoire); to, in the psychoanalyst

Robert Stoller's terms, 'convert trauma into triumph', the trauma of helpless, vulnerable neediness transformed into the triumph of omnipotent control, the trauma of being a child into the false triumph of being an adult (as though adulthood had been conceived to be the solution to childhood, rather than its realization, or even its fulfilment). The child as abject supplicant becomes the adult as arrogant sadist (ritualized, consensual sado-masochism is the staging, the theatricalization, of this scenario: and abjection, of course, can be intimidation by other means). We have to start from the position, in other words, that the wish to humiliate is part of everyone's survival kit. It is our (often preferred) self-cure for the inevitable frustrations of childhood.

Because we also know, that is to say – the two facts being obviously connected – that there is something intrinsically, and unavoidably, humiliating about being a child (and this is aside from the other fact that a good or good-enough childhood makes all the difference and guarantees nothing). Every child has felt humiliated by his dependence on his parents – by his relative powerlessness in relation to the people he needs – and everyone has been left feeling vengeful by this ineluctable diminishment (it is our madness, as adults, to believe that there is something humiliating about not being self-sufficient). The question is always how much the parents – wittingly or unwittingly – have exploited the child's inevitable dependence upon them; whether they have made the child's dependence feel humiliating (how much they have used the child's smallness to make themselves feel big). And in so far as they do this – and all parents do it some of the time – it is not simply that they are bad people, but more often than not because they are re-enacting unremembered (and sometimes remembered) experiences from their own childhood. To punish child abusers is to punish them for the abuse they have suffered as children.

So there are two salient facts about childhood that are worth reiterating because they are everywhere assumed and insufficiently noticed; and because, although they predict nothing, they inform everything about an adult's life. And they are both to do with what is often called discipline, or a lack of it, in the family. Firstly, that the child is absolutely dependent, in the initial instance, on a person (or people) whom he cannot control ('The mother is everything to the child,' the psychoanalyst Enid Balint once famously remarked, 'but the child is not everything to the mother'); and this, unsurprisingly, can make the child enraged, both cruel and punitive. And secondly, that the child has to do something to transform – to make bearable – the unavoidable suffering that this involves.

One of the things the parent has to do is frustrate the child and help her bear this frustration. And the child, and the adult she will become, has to find ways of surviving the frustration and the helplessness that is integral to the neediness of childhood. Sado-masochism is the solution to this problem; the adult turns the anguish of having to frustrate his child into a pleasure in order to make it bearable, and the child turns his frustration into a pleasure in a similar way. The adult becomes sadistic, the child becomes masochistic. It is a kind of psychic alchemy – whenever something is unbearable we are inspired to make it into something as pleasurable as possible; or at least to find a way to get pleasure out of it. No pleasure, no point. So prevalent is the sado-masochistic solution, the double-act of the superior and the abject, that it seems like merely the way of the world. Think, for example, of the recondite writer and the inadequate reader, the artist as genius and the audience as baffled. And think of how much pleasure – of bafflement, of puzzlement, of the desire to be left out and the desire not to be – that this predicament generates. The pleasure – and it is clearly, as we say, a gift and a curse – is in the conversion of pain into pleasure. It is in childhood that we learn how to master our arts.

When the American family therapist Carl Whitaker was asked what the definition of a good parent was he replied, 'someone who enjoys being hated by his children'. It might be sadistic (and masochistic) to enjoy being hated by one's children; but it may be tolerable only if one can get some pleasure from it. Whitaker's remark, though, acknowledges just how much depends upon the parents being able to stand, without undue retaliation, the hatred of their children; and just how difficult this is for many parents to do without taking refuge in punishment, bitterness, or dispiriting stories about human nature. Children always hate their parents, however much they love them, because it is the parents who, from their point of view, are the source of their frustration. Children, that is to say, don't know about Freud's useful suggestion that desire is by its nature insatiable ('desire', Freud wrote, in his celebration of insufficiency, 'is always in excess of the object's capacity to satisfy'). Anyone who tries to fully satisfy anyone else – and this is particularly true of adults in relation to children – is, as it were, fighting a losing battle, playing the game that can only be lost. The promise of total satisfaction is a promise of catastrophic disillusionment; and so an incitement to violence. Every child feels punished by being frustrated, and is then sometimes really punished for his response to being frustrated. At its best, parental authority contains, instead of creates, this fateful escalation.

We soon learn, as children – even though we are prone to forget it – that we can't have what we want when we want it; and we can't always have it at all. And even if the defeats of appetite can be turned into the triumphs of will, we have to do something with, and about, our frustration. In the basic picture, in the founding double-act of our lives, one person is helplessly in need, and the other person can take or leave this needing. That is to say, everyone begins their life at a loss, dependent on someone infinitely more powerful and resourceful than themselves. And every parent begins as sublimely promising to their child (this, and the memories re-evoked of one's own childhood, are what makes parenting so daunting). So we can only assume, as children, that if someone doesn't meet our need who could, it is because they don't want to. And in this sense – in what we might call this subjective sense – all the frustrations of our childhood are caused by a sadist. Our parents mostly didn't and couldn't enjoy frustrating us – or so we might hope – but whether they did or not, we took it for granted, as unredeemed pleasure-seekers ourselves, that they must have got some kind of pleasure from depriving us; why else would they have done such an obscene and unnecessary thing? And we, in turn, helpless as we were in that predicament, had to make a virtue of necessity, a thrill out of privation. We found ways of getting, as they say, pleasure from our pain. Once one has been victimized, becoming a so-called victim is always a temptation.

Every child unconsciously believes that whatever else his parents are they are sadists; and every child, as a way of managing this unpalatable fact – and of sustaining his vital and vitalizing connection to the parents – has had to become, among many other things, a talented masochist. If we can't get pleasure from our pain our lives cease to be worth living; when we are unable to perform this psychic alchemy we are filled with our own futility (and in this sense art is always the enemy of despair, and especially when it is at its most despairing). Masochism becomes our guarantor of survival, the best trick in the book (we have to learn, in Beckett's so successful words, to 'fail better'); and whatever else masochism does – and we should not underestimate just how useful a tool it is to help us get by – it also addicts us to punishment. Unconsciously we believe, because we were once children – 'no adulthood without childhood' should be our motto here – that anyone who punishes us loves us, however secretly. But, more importantly, once we start getting pleasure from pain – and we start, I think, very early – pain is sought out for the pleasure we can render from it. We want to test our talent. We need to endlessly reassure ourselves that it still works; that we will always survive, or more than survive, our future privation.

What we call, quaintly, a challenge, or, rather more bracingly, the pleasure of what is difficult, or the uses of adversity, is the proving and the pressing of our talent for masochism. What can't we get pleasure from? becomes the question, the question that prompts the most Faustian of ambitions (and pacts); and it prompts a strange and abiding belief – indeed it becomes an article of faith – that the greatest pleasures are from sufferings transformed. Not from ease, not from the conveniences of luxury, but from torments survived; this is the source of our profoundest pleasure, as though pleasure itself has to be ennobled in order to be taken seriously, or to be taken at all. When someone does something we call punishing – all heroic endeavours, all religious and spiritual ordeals – it is always to their credit. Punishment, that is to say, is one of our most easily available pleasures. So it is not entirely surprising that it is so keenly courted (nor does it seem astounding that all criminality – as psychoanalysis tells us, often so glibly – whatever else it is, is the wish to be caught). Punishment starts at home, and it is called frustration; frustration is taken to be punishing, and is the form punishment always takes. 'The masochist,' the psychoanalyst Sheldon Bach writes in *On Sado-Masochistic Object Relations*, 'says: "Do anything you want to me but don't leave me", and the "anything you want" feels pleasurable because it means that his partner is still with him . . . [but] if the masochist says, "Do anything you want to me but don't leave me", the sadist proclaims, "I can do anything I want to you, and you'll still always be there!" ' For 'masochist' read 'child', and for 'sadist' read 'parent'. To stave off the ever-present terrors of abandonment devastating sacrifices are made. And then the sacrifices themselves are transformed into pleasurable triumphs. We have been very adept, it should be noted, at using our sexuality more for our psychic survival than for our other pleasures. It is worth wondering what our erotic lives would be like if they were not recruited merely for our survival.

We learn from childhood, in other words, the link between intimidation and scarcity. That to need is always to be at a loss. It is not simply that we can't control the resources that we need (though we can't), but that our desire is exorbitant and the resources are not. Sado-masochism is our self-cure for the fact that we are not self-satisfying creatures (that is what it is to be an organism, to be in need of exchange); it is our (excited and exciting) solution to the problem of needing as a form of diminishment. By definition no one can afford to lose what they need, and no one can ensure that they won't (in order for a god to be omnipotent he must be without need). Punishment, which is the prerogative of the powerful and the revenge of the powerless, more often than not diminishes people. It cuts them down to size. Punishers – like parents, though there is, as we know, rather more to parenting than punishing – are people who know what size people should be. All punishment is humiliating, and we can't imagine a world without punishment.

So if we ask the question, what kind of authority do parents have? – at least with the very young child – we can say, the parents have the power to satisfy and frustrate the child. If someone can satisfy the child they can frustrate the child. We know someone matters to us because they can frustrate us. The parents' authority is an authority to provide; this means both knowing something about the child's need, and having the wherewithal to respond to it, or not. Not all needs can be met but all needs can be acknowledged. What might be called primitive authority is the power (if not the freedom) both to more or less satisfy needs and also, by way of punishment, to recognize needs with a view to frustrating them. Punishment is the infliction of frustration.

But punishment, we should note, and the authority that legitimates it, is based on a prior knowledge about needs – you can frustrate someone only if you know what they need. You can harm or discipline someone only if you know what gives them pleasure. Parents are the ones who are supposed to know; and what they are supposed to know about, essentially, is what a child needs. And they get this knowledge from their culture, mediated by their own parents. Our most fundamental knowledge – the knowledge on which all other knowledge is based – is about what children need (and this means that culture becomes, in the psychoanalyst D. W. Winnicott's words from a different context, 'the imaginative elaboration of physical function'). And so it is of some interest, to put it mildly, to live in a culture in which there are so many competing stories about what it is that children do actually need; about what it might be, now, to be a good parent. If what is good for children is so contentious, if there is so little consensus about what it is best for parents to do for their children; if, in short, there is such a hunger for authorities on children and child-rearing, what does this say about the parenting of the parents who are in this predicament? Authority may be always something that is in crisis, or may itself be a crisis – a solution to an insoluble problem – but there are no authorities who can tell us what is authoritative, what we should believe about parenting. But once no one knows in any absolute sense what children need, room is made to find out what else they might need; and, not incidentally, within certain psycho-biological constraints, what it is that adults need children to need, and why.

In the much-spoken-of detraditionalizing of modern cultures, child-rearing practices (and the care of the elderly) are, as it were, the first casualties. It seems as though we must choose how to bring up our children now that our parental instincts, that is, traditions, are fading. People will always have parents, but they may not have parents who know what they are doing. And even though we still have nostalgic and reactionary (that is, militant) longings for people who know what they are doing when it comes to human relationships – experts on child-rearing, experts on education, experts on mental health – we should be encouraged, and not only dismayed, by the radical uncertainty of contemporary parents ('I will show you fear in a handful of specialists,' John Ashbery wrote in his great poem 'Flow Chart'). Despair about authority is the precondition for its redescription, for a change of heart; just as our singularity often resides in the particular way we have of not understanding things, not understanding things that certain people seem to have understood all too well.

In a larger view of this we would need to put two things together: a historical story that we are more or less familiar with about the cumulative loss of confidence in traditional forms of authority (the Reformation, the Enlightenment, the French Revolution, the scientific revolution, the rise of capitalism, etc.); and the overconfidence in authority that goes with it (the rise of fascism, communism, fundamentalism, etc.). And the fundamental fact of scarcity, both the actual scarcity of resources in the world, and their unequal distribution, which in terms of individual development means the ineluctable, and therefore necessary, frustration that begins at the very beginning, in childhood; and which psychoanalysis can tell us a useful and interesting story about (it is indicated by saying that there is only one mother who is mortal and has to be shared, and an infinite desire for her, which becomes incestuous and has to be forbidden, mostly by the father; all of the participants being also mostly unconscious of what they want and what they do). Authority, after all, is what we use to manage our frustration; and all our frustration – whatever our forms of political organization and child-rearing – will never go away. It can be significantly modified, which is the source of our political hope; but it cannot be abolished, which should be the source of our psycho-biological realism. The question is not, how can we get rid of it (it is not a question of apocalypse or redemption, or even, perhaps, of revolution), but what can we do with it, what can we transform it into? Whether there are other solutions apart from the sado-masochistic ones, which we are presently bewitched by, of the exploiter and the exploited.

If authority is a solution to frustration – a way of managing it, a way of bearing it, a way of stopping it turning into murder or suicide or torture; and at best a way of preventing it becoming humiliating – what kinds of authority are more suited to the frustrations of childhood? Or, to put it rather less abstractly, what is the best thing to do when a child has a tantrum – the primal scene of frustration, and not only for children – and what makes it the best thing to do? Once again, broadly speaking, there are two approaches to this ordinary demonic event of family life with small children and adolescents (not to mention parents). The child can be punished – through isolation, through violence, through the imposition of penalties; or the parent can stay with the child with a view to containing him – stopping him harming himself, stopping him doing too much damage, but not trying to stop him having the tantrum. This involves, of course, a belief that the tantrum will end.

The child has the tantrum often over some apparently trivial thing, though the thing represents a catalogue of pent-up frustrations. It is the magical act of a desperate person; if I get enraged enough I will get what I want, or I will destroy myself and the world in which I have to suffer such torments. The child needs to know, or rather to experience, at this moment that there is someone stronger than his rage that can hold him and his world together. The child's terror is of being too powerful, of being able to destroy his world; the child needs the adult above all to show him that there are brakes on his fantasy life, in which all violence is murder and all appetite voracious. The parent who punishes the child for his tantrum – punishment being always a kind of tantrum, a despair about the rules rather than their enforcement – says to the child: my tantrum is more powerful than yours, but tantrums are all we have got. The child is made to suffer for his suffering; as if to say, suffering inspires suffering, rage and frustration create nothing but rage and frustration. From a psychoanalytic point of view – and not only from a psychoanalytic point of view – a person's development depends upon the dosing of frustration. The child who is punished for his frustration learns that frustration is contagious, and unbearable; it has to be evacuated as rage. Frustration is not a raw material to be transformed, but a foreign body to be expelled. The child in a tantrum is given what we have learned to call a double-message by the punitive parent; the child is being told that he should not be enraged by his frustration by someone who is enraged by their frustration.

People usually punish other people when they don't know what else to do with them. And it is, indeed, striking that no alternative to punishment has yet been dreamed up. But it is clear from this example that, once again, there are two versions, two stories, here about authority; and it would be worth being able to tell the difference because it takes us to the heart, or to one of the hearts, of at least the contemporary perplexities about parenting. Consumer capitalism has conspired to persuade us that we are phobic of frustration, that frustration is the last thing we want. All the difficulties of modern parenting are to do with how and why and whether and of what children need to be frustrated. And, unsurprisingly perhaps, the way adults deal with these issues is bound up with the history of their own relationship, if that is the right word, to frustration.

For many people the whole experience of frustration is made bearable only through the sado-masochistic solution of making the frustration and the frustrating not simply pleasurable but at best even sexually exciting (by making it sexually exciting it is as though one is getting as much pleasure out of it as possible). But by becoming what the psychoanalysts Gear, Hill and Liendo call either frustrated satisfiers (masochists) or satisfied frustraters (sadists) we get muddled. And these fateful and terrible muddles – this loss of a reality sense, the real being, in Henry James's words, that which it is impossible not to know – are often the consequence of making pain pleasurable. Of never knowing the difference, if there is one, between mastering pain and enjoying pleasure (or 'suffering pleasure', as the psychoanalyst Bion puts it more pointedly). It is not that we should be exclusively – that is, in a superior, sadistic way – disparaging the sado-masochistic settlement, because it can also be described as one of our most brilliant cultural inventions. A possible solution to an impossible problem. And between adults potentially the source of a great deal of sexual excitement, even if it is not always the excitement most wanted. We should just be dismayed that sado-masochism has bewitched us into thinking that it is the only game in town; so compelling is it, so much second nature, that it addicts us into thinking that there is nothing else we can do.

It is, in other words, like all successful solutions, like all compelling self-cures, a way of forgetting what the original problem was that it solved. And of forgetting that the original problem might be redescribed. The problem might not be, for example, how can we, as parents, avoid frustrating our children, but how can we make frustration more bearable for them (and for us)? Why can't we experiment when we are inclined to judge, or acknowledge that every judgement is a refused experiment? If frustration – like the conflict it always entails – is not taken to be a problem, we might be able to do something other than try to solve or resolve it. The problem might not be only how should I punish my children, but also what else can I do other than punish them? And what are we assuming to be the meaning or the intention of the child's act if punishment is deemed to be the answer? The day-to-day muddling through that is family life – in whatever form it takes – is about creating the conditions, as far as it is realistically possible, for people to be able to have a passion for living together. The sado-masochism in child-rearing, both its inevitability and its exploitation, is, as it were, a natural element. Nature as the unavoidable; culture as what we, by nature, do about it.

So we might say realistically that the problem of parenting now is how not to be too sado-masochistic, or sado-masochistic only with one's children; and what the alternatives might be, what else might be possible? And that means imagining how we might live our, and their, frustration differently. Our frustration and the fear that accompanies it. First frustration, then fear – the terror of resourcelessness that is called, rather optimistically, the fear of abandonment – then rage, then some satisfaction; or, instead and as well, pleasure forged from pain and, if not, extinction. This is the process, the basic narrative, the underlying story that the parent is both guardian of for his child, and the bearer of for himself. And that never goes away.

When I believe I really am who I think myself to be, I am not merely, in Freud's all too familiar language, in denial, but deluded. What psychoanalysis adds to the conversation about parenting – which is also a conversation about authority – is that the parents, the authorities, are always at their most dangerous when they believe too militantly that they know what they are doing. Kafka, whose father was, apparently, overbearingly sure of himself, wrote, 'you can hold yourself back from all the suffering in the world and that is the one suffering you could have avoided'. The one suffering no one can avoid, and everyone needs to be able to suffer, though they can try to hold themselves back from it, is frustration.

All the problems parents have with their children are about what to do about frustration; their own and their children's. And frustration is, by definition, something we can't just leave as it is. Frustration makes us work – it gets us to work and it gives us work to do – but we are not always sure which is the work that is worth doing. And many of our so-called satisfactions do not appease, or even touch, the frustration we feel. It is something we can neither ignore, nor be indifferent to. Because frustration is something that, in desperation, we are always tempted to make pleasurable or to punish. Where once the frustrations of adulthood might lead to political solutions, now they are more likely to lead to the private refuge of sado-masochism; to be turned against the family. Can we imagine so-called forms of authority that do neither, or that can do something else as well? And if not why not?

On Compromise

> . . . you will have to decide whose view of you is
> most valuable to you.

> Stanley Cavell, *Cities of Words*

It would be reassuring to believe that it all depends on the issues, that we can compromise when we have to. That, in a sense, the issues decide for us. That compromising is something we can do when and if we want to. We may not be able to compromise, say, on abortion, but we can compromise on gay marriage; we can't compromise on paedophilia, but we can compromise on taxing the rich; we can't compromise on rape, but we can (apparently) compromise on torture; we can't compromise on the killing of children, but we have compromised on this in all modern warfare. Wherever, in liberal democracies, there is conflict now, compromise is always proposed, as the only realistic solution; even if it is all too often a sign of conflict resolved by being avoided, or deferred. Because our histories, not to mention our personal relationships, are littered now with temporary truces that are called 'peace treaties' – with the havoc of appeasement, and the resentment born of excessive sacrifice – it is worth wondering how we imagine conflict, how we picture it, if compromise is what is required. Are we assuming, for example, that a fight to the death can be averted only by both sides sacrificing something of value, as though we believe that compromise is the cure for violence? It would be reassuring to believe that there might be a cure for violence, though it seems unlikely. 'Compromise' has become the magic word, perhaps because it has the word 'promise' in it; like all magic words it promises more than it clarifies.

The idea of compromise turns up only when important things are at stake. Indeed we know something really matters to us when compromise seems out of the question, but when the question of compromise is nevertheless raised. It's not clear, in other words, what being good at compromising is being good at. So it is still worth wondering why the capacity, the ability, the talent – it is difficult to know which is the right word – for compromise is so essential to whatever we think of as our morality. Indeed we can't imagine morality, or political life, without it. At its simplest, making compromises means acknowledging that people have competing needs; and that politics, like family life, involves trying to reconcile rival claims. We are forever being told now that relationships involve making compromises, but without being told what making all these compromises might compromise in ourselves. What do we think relationships are for if compromise is essential to them? What is it about the way we think of relationships that makes compromise seem so key? Perhaps compromise has become so important to us because we have got the wrong picture of what relationships should be, as though compromise has become the solution to a problem we still can't quite formulate. As though our motto has become: when all else fails, sacrifice something or punish someone. It is as though, making a virtue of necessity, we have turned the fact that losses have to be borne, punishment endured and sacrifices made, into a reassuring story about the ultimate value of compromise. But this apparently coming to terms can be a terrible (masochistic) distraction, an analogy that endangers us. Once mourning becomes our religion we start thinking things like, ageing is the loss of youth, or that life is disappointing, when it is only our expectations that are wrong. We love mourning because it kills wanting.

So, compromise could, say, be the issue because we want

more than we can have, and because what we want is often enough not available. So it looks as though children need to learn to compromise because there is no real alternative. And yet we can't help but notice that children go on believing for a very long time – throughout their lives, in fact – that there may be an alternative. And this is not because they are intractable hedonists – though they are, fortunately, also that – but because they have what might be called a moral intuition, which adults are so troubled by they often have to punish it. And this moral intuition is that compromising our desire can be the cruellest thing we can do to ourselves, and to other people. It isn't always – we do have to be able to compromise – but it can be. What Emerson called 'self-reliance' was the need not to be too agreeable; as though the worst thing we can do to other people is to betray ourselves. Another way of saying this is: tell me how an adult responds to a child's tantrum and I will tell you everything about the adult's character.

Children know in some way that if and when they compromise – or, rather, when they make certain compromises, or when they compromise before they are ready and able – they betray their own desire; and by doing that, by agreeing, they also agree to turn the adults who demand these compromises into people they can only resent. If the child could ask it, his question would be: how do you have pleasurable exchanges with adults – exchanges of food, of affection, of thoughts and feelings, of love and hate – without losing faith in exchange? Which translates as, how do you grow up to be an adult who believes sex and conversation are worth having?

All the best new thinking about sex, perhaps unsurprisingly, has not been about how we can get round the agony of sexual jealousy, which no one will ever do, but about whether it is possible to have uncompromising sex without bullying; whether it is the compromises in sex – the accommodation to the other person – that are the point or the problem. It is unavoidably true that compromises of the wrong kind – too much compromise, compromise as paramount – poisons pleasure and passion. People who believe too much in compromise believe too much in not getting what they want. And this makes them somewhere enraged, and ashamed of just how enraged they are. When self-betrayal doesn't make people depressed it makes them murderous. Education should be there to teach us – to give us a language to find out – which self-sacrifices are forms of self-betrayal, and which are all to the good. So, given compromising is the best and the worst thing that we do, we need to know what we think we are doing when we do it. And what we think we are not doing. We don't want to find ourselves in compromising positions, and we don't want to be compromised. As though there is something shameful about compromise, that it exposes something about us that we would rather conceal. At its most minimal our addiction to the idea of compromise reveals the paucity of our moral imagination; it reveals just how inhibited we are in our imagining of sociability. As though when it comes to our morality we never get a second wind. A person who has, as we say, never learned to compromise is either a monster or a genius (or both). But a person who has learned too well will be a danger to herself, and so a danger to other people.

We are encouraged to admire people who are uncompromising about the right things; but that doesn't solve the problem of how we decide what the right things are. It is as though compromise is something we should be able to do when it is appropriate; and yet we define the things we value most as those things we won't compromise about. And this can make compromising the thing we do when we don't care enough, or when we feel intimidated (the morality born of intimidation will always be secretly hated). Or when we care about something else more (if you hate conflict and the disapproval of the well-wishers you might as well smoke less). Should we be fundamentalists about the things that matter most to us – democracy, truth, free speech, making money, religion? And if we are not – if we are willing to compromise over the fundamental things – how will we know that these things really matter to us, that they really are fundamental? We compromise because we value something, but we can't always be sure what it is. Sometimes it might be because we want the love and approval of those who value compromise. We have to imagine what it would be like to live in a world in which we valued compromise more than any of the things we were willing to compromise over.

We have education, Robert Frost once said, so that we can listen to other people without losing our temper. There is a real sense in which education begins as education in compromise. We have tantrums and we have compromises. Children have to learn to wait, and learn to share, and learn to bear frustration, which means they have to learn to compromise. It comes naturally to them, but it doesn't come easily. And the reason it doesn't come easily is because every child has to find a way of being sociable without betraying themselves. Other people are only a problem for us if we have to give up on too much of ourselves in order to be with them (what is worth protecting is our pleasure in each other's company). So compromising always confronts us with the possibility of self-betrayal; and anyone promoting compromise in any given situation is asking us to give something up in order to get something supposedly better. When someone knows what's best for us we have to wonder how they know. And what they know. Growing up, presumably, might mean being able to do this uncompromisingly.

Psychoanalysis; or, Is It Worth It?

'Don't look just at what they say, think, believe, but at what they actually do and what actually happens as a result.'

Raymond Geuss, *Philosophy and Real Politics*

After reading Darwin it is easy to see people as doing nothing else really but trying to survive, but not quite so easy to see everyone as trying to reproduce. What Freud, as a committed evolutionary biologist, added to the Darwinian story was that there was a death instinct – that one of our two profoundest desires was to die, the 'organism', as he put it, with a telling qualification, 'wants to die in its own way' – and that human sexuality was also quite often unrelated to procreation. Freud showed us that we have a vocation for survival only because we have a vocation for pleasure; and that even if pleasure was a 'bribe', as he put it, the desire for pleasure could be stronger than – could override and displace – the wish to survive and reproduce. Not only, as Freud was keen to point out, did people risk their lives and their dignity for sexual satisfaction, but, worse than this – or better, depending on one's point of view – it was satisfaction that people desired and not necessarily other people. 'The object,' Freud wrote, giving the impersonality of the whole project its due, 'is soldered on to the instinct.' Desire is implacable, but objects of desire are merely accessories; and sexuality is fuelled and informed by aggressive and predatory drives. And to add insult (and guilt and shame) to injury, we have found a way of making harming ourselves and others into one of our greatest (sexualized) pleasures; sadism and masochism, as Freud described them, were psychic devices, cultural artefacts, that helped us survive by making our suffering all too pleasurable whether or not it was meaningful. We are so ingenious at making things bearable because there is always so much we cannot bear.

One of the ways we survive, Freud suggested, was by not wanting to survive or reproduce. Man, as Freud called modern people for reasons that have become clearer and clearer, is the ambivalent animal: he is ambivalent about himself and his desires, he is ambivalent about love, he is ambivalent about science, he is ambivalent about ambivalence, he hates it and he loves it (he doesn't have mixed feelings, he has opposing feelings). But beneath it all, he is ambivalent about survival and reproduction. Making pain pleasurable doesn't make it any less painful.

So when Freud said to the poet H. D. in her extraordinary *Tribute to Freud*, 'My discoveries are not primarily a heal-all. My discoveries are a basis for a very grave philosophy. There are very few who understand this, there are very few who are capable of understanding this,' he knew what he was talking about. He spoke English to H. D. so he presumably knew, if only from reading *Hamlet*, what 'grave' meant (not to mention the word 'basis'). Freud's discoveries – if that's what they are: they could happily be called descriptions or acknowledgements, or even inventions – could never be 'primarily a heal-all' because Freud was preoccupied, above all, by the unpredictable rather than the predictable effect people have on each other, and that people have on themselves. This was incompatible, unsurprisingly, with traditional concepts of cure, and put psychoanalysis, as it has always been despite denials to the contrary, at odds with medicine.

We can see in retrospect that Freud was using psychoanalysis, among other things, to clarify what cannot be healed ('healing', for example, is the wrong word if there is no original wholeness or health to be restored). Freud said on several occasions he had never really wanted to be a doctor; and this was partly because he was always interested in what medicine couldn't do. Psychoanalysis was there to do what religion, and science as it then was, couldn't do for people's suffering. Freud was interested in how you could describe pleasure and pain, sexuality and violence, language and dreams, if you didn't describe them in the language of religion, and if you didn't describe them exclusively in the language of contemporary science. And this is what psychoanalysts – psychoanalysts unintimidated or unimpressed by neuroscience and pharmacology, or the marketplace – are still now wanting to do. They are interested, in other words – or at least they should be – not in cures but in new ways of living. No one associates psychoanalysis with new ways of living any more, and this is an oversight.

When Freud described what he called the unconscious he invited people to live as if what he described were true; and particularly, of course, for psychoanalysts to do this. If you believe in the unconscious you can't promise to make people feel better, but if you are a scientific pragmatist you need to be able to make promises. If you believe in the unconscious your word can never be your bond in the sense that a medical doctor's word should be his bond. If you believe in the unconscious you begin to see language as taking us even more seriously than we take ourselves; or, rather, you begin to see how we can use language to do this. If you believe in the unconscious you believe sex gets everywhere, and especially in the places it shouldn't. If you believe in the unconscious words like 'trust', 'curiosity', 'integrity', 'honesty', 'kindness' and 'good intentions' are both more and less useful than they once seemed. If you believe in the unconscious you can only in a very limited sense claim to know what you are doing (and this limited sense includes never being able to exactly specify the limits). These were the contradictions and confoundings that Freud found himself in, and that the psychoanalysts he invented have had to deal with. In so far as they have tried to resolve these complications rather than live with them, they have got into a terrible muddle. Freud, that is to say, very soon realized something that psychoanalysts are only just beginning to come to terms with: that no one in their right minds – that is, no one who grew up in cultures that live by the principles of scientific verification, consumer confidence and religious faith, and who want to abide by these principles – would want to undergo psychoanalytic treatment. Freud knew in his heart of hearts that any psychoanalyst that is worth her salt must start from Hamm's principle in Beckett's *Endgame*, 'You're on earth, there's no cure for that.' But in the full knowledge that there may be something better to get than better, though you can't know beforehand what this is. That when psychoanalysis is not a Schopenhaurian project it can be an Emersonian one (living with an unconscious means never knowing what's possible). The psychoanalyst has to be a double agent; on the side of the (so-called) patient's adaptation – there isn't another world for him to live in other than the one he is in; and on the side of his need for revision – his desire to make a world more suited to his desire. But the only thing the analyst can't afford to do – and this sets him apart from other professionals – is to have too much of a sense that he knows what he is doing. It is not surprising, in a way, that psychoanalysts have found it so difficult to give a good account of themselves; and it may be to their credit.

Psychoanalysis – after its brief honeymoon period in the 1950s and 1960s as cultural heal-all – should never have fallen for trying to fight dogma with dogma. Psychoanalysis has only ever been for people who find it moving, illuminating, revealing, amusing, exciting, useful and comforting; not for people who find it misleading, untruthful, fraudulent, exploitative and diminishing. It is certainly not clever or funny now to assume that people who disparage psychoanalysis are resisting it, even if sometimes they are (so what if they are?). Nor is it worth asking any longer why people would want to devote so much of their time to discrediting psychoanalysis (though it is worth asking which therapies, if any, they recommend to their friends and loved ones, and why). No one any longer should be trying to persuade other people of the value of psychoanalysis; people who like it should just recommend the curious and the desperate to try it, or to read some of the best psychoanalytic writing, and see what they think. And if it does capture their imagination, if it does become for them something, in William James's words, 'to be going on from', psychoanalysis may also enable them to see why this is, and whether it's a good thing.

Coda: Up to a Point

I

Professions create traditions that exceed their own histories.

Louis Menand, *The Marketplace of Ideas*

Psychoanalysts don't usually write essays; they tend to write lectures or papers or chapters, or what are called, perhaps optimistically, contributions. Melanie Klein, according to her editors, wrote works, and Lacan, from a quite different tradition, wrote *écrits*. And when their writings are selected or collected, though the word may be used by way of introduction, essays are not what these writings are entitled. Nor indeed what they are often entitled to be called. When Ernest Jones, for example, the founder of the British Psychoanalytical Society, published a collection of his writings in 1912, it was called *Papers on Psychoanalysis*; when the International Psychoanalytical Library published a selection of what the editors called John Rickman's 'papers' in 1957, the book was entitled *Selected Contributions to Psychoanalysis*; it being assumed, I think, that there was something to contribute to called, say, the progress of psychoanalysis. As late as 1999, when Julia Borossa edited a selection of Sándor Ferenczi's writings for Penguin, it was entitled *Selected Writings*. There is no collected or selected essays of Klein, Anna Freud, D. W. Winnicott, Marion Milner, R. D. Laing or Masud Khan.

So it is striking when the psychoanalyst Charles Rycroft refers in the Introduction to his 1991 book, *Viewpoints*, to it being his 'third volume of essays' (and indeed quotes in this Introduction Maynard Keynes's *Essays in Biography*). And having announced, in the first sentence of his Introduction, that it is essays he has written, he goes on immediately to tell the reader of his 'withdrawal' from the British Psychoanalytical Society – 'because of its resistance to any unorthodox views' – and of his beginning to write for the *Observer*, *New Society*, *New Statesman*, *TLS* and the *New York Review of Books* on what he calls 'matters psychoanalytical'. For Rycroft, as a psychoanalyst in the British Society, calling his book a volume of essays – and by implication his previous books – is like a declaration of independence. He has withdrawn from the ruling institution and has written for a wider audience. Writing essays, and the literary essay as a form – at least in this psychoanalytic context – is a resistance, a protest, a refusal to meet certain criteria. It is a disengagement from something in order to be able to engage with something else.

The avoidance of the essay as a term of art in psychoanalysis – Rycroft being the exception that proves what is a kind of rule – is not simply or solely the consequence of psychoanalysis's forlorn attempt to keep itself fairly and squarely within the realm, and the cultural prestige, of science. It is, as it were, a considered refusal. Because everything in psychoanalysis endorses Marianne Moore's famous epigraph to what she pointedly called her *Complete Poems*: 'Omissions are not accidents'; there being a link, as she intimates, between completion and omission. Psychoanalysis, which has been so illuminating about omission and about fantasies of completeness – about the paradoxical idea that something becomes complete through omission – has, for reasons that may be of interest, discarded the essay as a useful term and a useable form. It is a strange omission, and not an accidental one.

Because of the uncertainty of its status – as an art or a science, as psychology or metaphysics, as religion or therapy, and so on – psychoanalysis has often had to define itself by saying what it is not. And one of the ways psychoanalysts have done this is by determinedly not writing essays. So psychoanalytic writing may have something to tell us about the essay – what it represents, what distinguishes it, what it forecloses – through its refusal of the genre; through its preference for writing writings and papers and lectures and contributions and works. What is there about the essay, or about the writers of essays, that one might want to disassociate oneself from? What are psychoanalysts writing that makes the essay form unsuitable? What does an essay involve you in that you might not want to be associated with? What, in short, are essays, or indeed essayists, assumed to be like if psychoanalysts want to disidentify from them? Geoffrey Hartman perhaps offers us a clue when he writes in the Preface to his book *The Third Pillar*, 'My contributions are, on the whole, neither erudite nor highly specialized, but rather essays'; psychoanalysis has always feared not being a specialism, and has wanted to sound erudite while never quite knowing what it should be erudite about. There are, of course, lots of forms that psychoanalysts don't use, or claim to use, in their writing, and yet the essay, given Hartman's definition of the genre, might seem to be rather more germane to the so-called discipline of psychoanalysis than most. Not much harm would be done, seemingly, if a psychoanalyst said he was writing an essay; or included the word in his professional vocabulary. It is sometimes more interesting when the least unacceptable thing is omitted. What, we might wonder, could the psychoanalyst fear, from both within and outside his profession, if he claimed, as Rycroft did, to be writing essays? It seems like a ludicrous question, and it also is one.

When Judith Butler said in an interview that 'crafting a sexual position . . . always involves becoming haunted by what's excluded. And the more rigid the position, the greater the ghost, and the more threatening it is in some way', she could also be taken to be saying, in a rather psychoanalytic way, that any genre is haunted and defined by the genres it excludes. And indeed that how you exclude something informs both its return and the form its haunting takes. It would be melodramatic to say that psychoanalytic writing is haunted by the essay form; or to intimate that the choosing and using of a literary genre is necessarily akin to the crafting of a sexual position. And yet, from a psychoanalytic point of view, the exclusion could be taken to be, in both senses, overdetermined. Freud was famously struck in his *Studies in Hysteria* when, as he put it, his case histories 'read like short stories'; he had wanted them to have what he calls 'the serious stamp of science'; they were 'intended to be judged' like 'psychiatric' case histories. If they read like short stories they smacked of the literary. And for psychoanalysts, by the same token, to write essays, or to write psychoanalytic essays, might also smack of the literary (Rycroft, in his Introduction referring to his essays, quotes George Eliot, T. S. Eliot and Iris Murdoch as well as Keynes on Goldsworthy Lowes Dickinson). The question, obviously, is what does the literary smack of such that the literary would be something that the psychoanalyst fights shy of in her writing? As though there is something that needs to be excluded from psychoanalytic writing, something that haunts it which is called the literary, or in this case the literary essay; and despite the fact that 'great' works of literature are routinely quoted and praised to the skies by psychoanalysts; though often, of course, as evidence of the truth of psychoanalysis (and the essay, unlike poetry, the novel and the play, is the genre least often referred to, I suspect, in psychoanalytic writing; certainly in the British tradition of psychoanalysis there are few if any references to Addison or Steele, or Johnson, or Lamb or Hazlitt, or Pater, or Chesterton, or Eliot or Woolf, to mention the most obvious candidates; and Freud, perhaps surprisingly, never quotes Montaigne). It makes a certain kind of sense that psychoanalysts wouldn't want to think of themselves as writing fiction or indeed poetry or drama; but the essay seems somehow more inviting, less of a threat, to use Judith Butler's word, to the psychoanalytic project.

II

Poetry was a communal voice for us – it spoke as
we would not speak for ourselves.

Robert Duncan, *The H. D. Book*

It would be silly to make a drama out of something that is hardly a crisis; but in a psychoanalytic context even Virginia Woolf's vague, struggling definition of the essay in her review article 'The Modern Essay' of 1921 almost begins to make sense. 'A novel has a story,' she writes,

> a poem rhyme; but what art can the essayist use in these short lengths of prose to sting us wide awake and fix us in a trance which is not sleep but rather an intensification of life – a basking, with every faculty alert, in the sun of pleasure?

And her answer is that the essayist 'must know – that is the first essential – how to write'. We know what she might mean, in a collusive sort of way, even though novelists and poets must also know how to write, whatever that might mean. But perhaps psychoanalysts, when they write their papers, lectures and contributions, don't think of themselves as writing, or don't want to think of themselves doing that, or of writing in the traditions of the literary essay. In its by now traditional form the psychoanalytic paper begins with what is appropriately called an 'abstract'; then it begins again with a proposal or a suggestion, sometimes called a 'hypothesis', based on observations made in the clinical situation; preceded or followed by a review of the so-called literature and some clinical vignettes that are supposed to validate the hypothesis. There is then a conclusion in which there is often a modest disclaimer about how Freud, Klein, Bion, Winnicott or Lacan have already said this or something similar;

and sometimes we are left with a challenging question or a set of possible implications. It is clear, in short, what and who the psychoanalytic writer is aligning himself or herself with; what the interpretative community is that is being addressed. It is certainly not a version of the albeit rather romanticized eighteenth-century coffee-house culture, nor the avid Victorian reading public; nor, indeed, the so-called common reader. Because psychoanalysts now tend to write for each other, and for a scientific community whose recognition (and cultural legitimacy) they crave. Whether or not the essay as a genre circulates in a way the often rather elitist and embattled profession of psychoanalysis might fear or be wary of, or whether it smacks of amateurism – despite the patent absurdity of being professional about the unconscious and sexuality – the essay has not been the chosen genre of the psychoanalysts. It would be portentous, as I have said, to suggest that in the psychoanalytic literature, as it is in fact called, the essay is repressed. It is, though, certainly not included.

In what is called *The Complete Psychological Works of Sigmund Freud* – which is neither complete nor self-evidently psychological though it goes under the unfortunate name of the *Standard Edition* – there are, it is worth noting, only two of Freud's works that are entitled, at least in their English translation, essays: *Three Essays on the Theory of Sexuality* (1905) and *Moses and Monotheism: Three Essays* (1939) (the word 'essay', incidentally, is not in the Index of the *Standard Edition*). Both controversial, and both, in their different ways, about origins, neither of these remarkable books of three essays – three being the privileged number in psychoanalysis – is more obviously essays, or essayistic, than a lot of Freud's other writings (Freud refers to what he calls, or what his translators call, the 'essays' in *Totem and Taboo* (1918) and *The Future of an Illusion* (1927), but the books are not called books of essays; and he refers to his 'essay' of 1901 'On Dreams', but he titles it simply as 'On Dreams'). It would be pointless to attempt a generic definition of the essay, let alone speculate about how Freud might define the genre; and even though there are family resemblances between these two works they are not particularly salient. But there is one thing, I think, worth considering; and this is that the *Three Essays on the Theory of Sexuality* were, in the words of James Strachey, Freud's translator and editor, 'submitted by their author, in the course of a succession of editions over a period of twenty years, to more modifications and editions than any other of his writings, with the exception of, perhaps, *The Interpretation of Dreams* itself'. *Moses and Monotheism*, being among the very last things Freud wrote, was not subject to revision or emendation. The *Three Essays on the Theory of Sexuality* kept announcing, as it were, its incompleteness.

There is, of course, no way of knowing whether Freud, had he lived longer, would have added or omitted anything from *Moses and Monotheism*; but the *Three Essays* kept on being, in Freud's view – that is, retrospectively – full of omissions and in need of elaboration and qualification. No one has had, as yet, the last word on anything; but there was something not about sexuality but about the theory of sexuality that for Freud went on being unfinished. The so-called essays on the theory of sexuality were then exactly essays as defined by the *OED*: 'The action or process of trying or testing; an assay . . . An attempt, endeavour . . . A first attempt in learning or practice . . . a first draft . . . A short composition on any particular subject; originally "an irregular, undigested piece", but now said of a finished treatise.' An 'essayist' the *OED* defines as 'one who makes trials or experiments'. For Freud, not incidentally, sexuality – not to mention its theorizing – was a trying and a testing, a trial and an experiment; as was psychoanalysis itself. Each psychoanalytic session itself being, in the words of the *OED*, a 'short composition' that is also something of a trial and an experiment; and can, of course, be trying and testing for both participants.

Gillian Beer has written very interestingly in her Introduction to the New Penguin Freud *The Wolfman and Other Cases* about how, as she puts it, 'the techniques of production in nineteenth-century fiction, particularly serialization, also help to shape Freud's account of his working method, and perhaps the method itself with its series of encounters'. If the serialized nineteenth-century novel is akin to the serialized sessions of a psychoanalysis – and from which the fiction called a 'case history' can be written – then so too could the nineteenth- (and eighteenth-) century essay be usefully linked to the once new form of treatment called 'psychoanalysis'; in which something is tried out in words with no aspiration to the complete or the definitive; in which enlarging one's experience can take priority over winning an argument, proving a point, or coming to conclusions (Johnson's *Dictionary* definition of the essay as 'a loose sally of the mind . . . not a regular and orderly composition' is a useful definition of a psychoanalytic session). And in which the sessions, like the essays of any given writer, develop an idiom, and a disparate continuity (which is partly the continuity of incompletion); psychoanalysis asks, what can two people say to each other if neither of them needs to be right? The concluding words of Freud's *Three Essays* tell us, after over a hundred pages of fascinating speculation, that no theory of sexuality is, as yet, either possible or plausible. 'The unsatisfactory conclusion, however, that emerges from these investigations of the disturbances of sexual life,' Freud writes, 'is that we know far too little of the biological processes constituting the essence of sexuality to be able to construct from our fragmentary information a theory adequate to the understanding alike of normal and pathological conditions.' The essay, as a genre, thrives on the conclusion that conclusions are unsatisfactory. That it's all in the trying, and the trying it out. An essay, like a psychoanalysis, is an experiment without a proof. It is experimental writing – again, rather like psychoanalytic writing – but without its avant-garde associations. The essay, it should be noted, though an experiment, a trying of something, is a stable form, not subject to much innovation.

'In the realm of thought,' Theodor Adorno wrote grandly in 'The Essay as Form', 'it is virtually the essay alone that has successfully raised doubts about the absolute privilege of method'. Certainly when it came to sexuality and its theories Freud found – as his *Three Essays* and their prolific footnotes extended themselves through six editions of the text – that privileging the method of psychoanalysis raised doubts about method, about psychoanalysis, about sexuality, about theorizing and about the absolute privileging of anything (or anyone). It is difficult to know quite what to make of Adorno's assertion about the essay form – and the phrase 'virtually the essay alone' suggests that he had his doubts – but it does draw attention to the essay as a sceptical form; and it can make us wonder, in relation to Freud's *Three Essays*, whether psychoanalysis is a method – whether it ever was a method, and whether and why it became one – and what method might have to do with the unconscious, or with sexuality, and the theorizing about it. And, of course, why Freud called his formative book on sexuality a book of essays. When Harold Bloom in *The Anatomy of Influence* writes, 'Freud's theory of the mind or soul, after a century or so, is alive and valuable while his scientism is quite dead. I urge us to regard him as the Montaigne or Emerson of the twentieth century', he is urging us to regard Freud as he did not, mostly, regard himself; that is, as an essayist, with all that that entails, which in Bloom's terms means being a theorist without being a scientist. The essayist is the writer who extricates theory from science, who can write without method about method, who can write truthfully without needing to know what the truth is.

And Freud's *Three Essays* were not, it should be noted, on sexuality but on the 'Theory' of sexuality (in Shaun Whiteside's New Penguin Freud translation it is called *Three Essays on Sexual Theory*; the *Standard Edition* equivocates, calling it, on the cover of Volume VII, *Three Essays on Sexuality*, while giving it its real title on the Contents page). Essays are often 'on' something or other but there is clearly a difference between an essay on sexuality and an essay on a theory of sexuality; or this, at least, Freud's essays might make one wonder about. Is there sexuality or are there only theories of sexuality? might be a good question to try out in an essay. As would the question, what is a theory of sexuality a theory of?

Freud warns us – and this is where what Freud calls in his Preface his 'field of scientific work' joins up with the essay's aesthetic of the unfinished (and the unfinishable) – that his *Three Essays* could never 'be extended into a "complete theory of sexuality"'. And we only need these essays, he writes in the Preface to the fourth edition, because we can't see what is in front of us. 'If mankind had been able to learn from a direct observation of children, these three essays could have remained unwritten.' Freud had to write these essays because our perception is distorted by our wishes; because we wanted to see children as innocent, we couldn't see them as they are; and because we couldn't see children as they are, we couldn't see our sexuality for what it is. It is interesting, and unusual, to have the essayist telling us what would have had to have happened to make the writing of his essays unnecessary (and it may be an interesting question – the sort of thing that can be thrown off in passing in an essay – to ask of any piece of writing, what could have happened that would have made the author not need to write it?). For Freud, his *Three Essays* are a corrective for the failures, the avoidances, of empirical inquiry; what direct observation shied away from, the essays had to investigate. What science had turned a blind eye to, the essayist could be curious about; the essay itself – like sexuality – being perhaps the form that keeps making links between curiosity and sociability. The implication being that one of the preconditions for sociability is shared curiosity.

His essays, Freud intimates, seek to reveal something that has been concealed. 'The progressive concealment of the body which goes along with civilization keeps sexual curiosity awake,' he writes in the *Three Essays*. 'The curiosity seeks to complete the sexual object by revealing its hidden parts.' Our curiosity can go to sleep – we want to sleep off our desire – so we need concealment to keep it awake; and our curiosity is the way we try to complete something – call it the object of desire – that cannot be completed (we can never have total knowledge, total access, total possession). Essays, which are nothing if not curious, seek to go on trying to complete something that cannot be completed. 'It is out of the question,' Freud writes, that his *Three Essays* 'could ever be extended into a "complete theory of sexuality".' It is, we can surmise, the impossibility of completion that frees the essayist to write, that frees our sexual curiosity to be somehow endless. So a Freudian question here might be, how are we imagining the object of desire when we believe that the essay might be the best way to approach it? Not, simply, what is the essayist wanting, but what is the essay a good way of wanting? And what is it about the essay form that makes it this good way of wanting? These are among the questions prompted by Freud calling his great book about sexuality a book of essays.

Freud's *Three Essays*, that is to say, draws our attention to the way the essay as a genre investigates our sense of an ending, our sense of what completion might be; both what we might be wanting by wanting it, and what we imagine it might do for us. We can ask of any piece of writing, what makes this the end? And in what sense, if at all, has it turned out to be the promised end? But in an essay – like a lyric poem or a short story, unlike a novel or a play, or indeed an epic poem – we know the end is always near; essays tending to be, like lyric poems, as A. R. Ammons intimates in a phrase from his poem 'Essay on Poetics', 'brief completions'. Freud ends his *Three Essays* by saying that he has reached an 'unsatisfactory conclusion', and that he has barely begun to have an 'adequate' theory of sexuality. Freud offers us the (ironic) satisfaction of being unsatisfied. The essays, like the sexual satisfactions Freud describes in these essays, are nowhere near complete. The desire for completion is all there is to desire, at least in Freud's account. The desire for completion is the nearest we are ever going to get to completion.

If we go back to Freud's words, to Freud's misgivings in the *Studies in Hysteria*, there was what he called 'the serious stamp of science', and then there was the short story, possibly less serious than science, but certainly less scientific. And not quite what Freud wanted his writing to sound like. But somewhere in between the serious stamp of science – the psychiatric case history, the scientific treatise or paper – and the fictional short story, there is, we might say, the essay. The essay that can incorporate both – the empiricism of the scientist and the fabulation of the writer of fiction, 'direct observation' and fantasy – without excluding either. Or can take from both without having to declare an exclusive allegiance. The essay tends to allow for, if not to actually encourage, digression – like psychoanalytic treatment there is no rule about keeping to the point; but it has points to make. It is susceptible to throwaway lines and what Charles Lamb called 'half-baked notions'. And even though essays can be written by, and for, so-called specialists or experts, it doesn't tend to be a recondite or esoteric form; at least in the British and American traditions of the literary essay. The essay has been good at genial scepticism, hospitable curiosity, the sociability of knowledge; and, of course, at inspired dogmatism. So – at least in its Enlightenment versions – the essay can be, to put it psychoanalytically, the genre in which we are free of the tyrannical parents. And so it lets us imagine what it would be like to live (and write) as if there were no tyrannical parents. This, paradoxically, is not something the ethos of psychoanalysis has always encouraged. Psychoanalysis just helps us notice what we find ourselves listening out for in all the sounds and voices that we hear. The essay is all too easily part of that project.

What Freud's *Three Essays*, and the subsequent disavowal of the essay in psychoanalysis after Freud, reveals, I think, is that the writing of psychoanalysis – if not its clinical practice – has been tyrannized by the wish to get something right at the cost of saying something interesting and useful. Another way of saying this would be to say that psychoanalytic writing has not allowed itself to be Emersonian; or pragmatic in the Jamesian way (more interested in possibilities than principles, more taken with consequences than causes). In his book *Byron and Romanticism*, comparing his own essays on Byron with his editing of Byron the critic and scholar, Jerome McGann had this to say:

> Under the horizon of a literary practice that has idealized the standard critical edition, however, critical commentary itself reflects that aspiration to – that apparition of – finishedness . . . Even writing in the essay form we have wanted to get things right, to say something definitive (the supreme quality, we used to imagine, of the critical edition). And while we can achieve this under certain limitations and conditions, we can never know that we have done it. (Alas, we often imagine that we do know such things.)

'Even writing in the essay form we have wanted to get things right, to say something definitive'; as if, even in the essay, we haven't been let off the hook, that the essay could or should be the form in which we can get things other than right, say something that need not be definitive. As if there is no refuge from this distraction of what McGann calls 'finishedness', and I have been calling 'completeness'. But then there is McGann's wonderfully definitive point: 'while we can achieve this under certain limitations and conditions' – this rightness, this definitiveness – 'we can never know that we have done it'. It is possible to be right, but not for us. What the literary essay offers the psychoanalyst, and that the psychoanalyst has refused, is the opportunity to be neither definitive nor right, but in a psychoanalytic way. It exposes the senses in which the desire for truth can also be a desire for something we can do nothing about, for something ineluctably confining: for something that will simplify ourselves. The psychoanalyst, in other words, could do in his writing what he should be doing in his clinical work (trying things out in a more or less informed way). But to do this he might need to start writing essays, to let the essay form inform what he does. And then we will be able to see what, if anything, the psychoanalyst can contribute to the essay.

Acknowledgements

The pieces in this collection have been selected mostly from my earlier books; only one chapter, 'Arbus's Freaks', has been taken from my latest book of essays, *On Balance*. Quite different versions of the new writings 'Judas for Now', 'Punishing Parents', 'Psychoanalysis; or, Is It Worth It?' and 'Coda: Up to a Point' were first published in the *London Review of Books*, *Threepenny Review* and *Salmagundi*; the editors of these journals know by now, I hope, the difference they have made. Of the other new writing in this selection, 'My Happiness Right or Wrong' was originally an Amnesty lecture given at Oxford and published in *Self-Evident Truths? Human Rights and the Enlightenment*, edited by Kate E. Tunstall. 'On Compromise' was commissioned by *The New York Times*. Simon Prosser has been a consistently inspiring and engaged editor; having him in mind has been essential to my writing for longer than I can remember now. Sarah Coward I have relied on as a remarkable copy-editor of my books, all of which have been immeasurably improved by her attentiveness. My agent and friend Felicity Rubinstein has done more, possibly, than she realizes for how the writing in this collection, and indeed in all my other books, has turned out. Mia Rose made an enormous practical difference at the last moment.

This book is dedicated to my children, and so, in a sense, to Judith Clark also.